Invisible Men

Invisible Men

Fatherhood
in Victorian
Periodicals,
1850–1910

Claudia Nelson

The University of Georgia Press

Athens & London

© 1995 by the University of Georgia Press
Athens, Georgia 30602
All rights reserved
Designed by Erin Kirk New
Set in 10/14 Bodoni Book
by Tseng Information Systems, Inc.
Printed and bound by Thomson-Shore, Inc.

The paper in this book meets the guidelines for permanence and
durability of the Committee on Production Guidelines for Book
Longevity of the Council on Library Resources.

Printed in the United States of America

99   98   97   96   95   C   5   4   3   2   1

Library of Congress Cataloging in Publication Data

Nelson, Claudia.
Invisible men : fatherhood in Victorian periodicals, 1850–1910 /
Claudia Nelson.
       p.   cm.
Includes bibliographical references (p.   ) and index.
ISBN 0-8203-1699-7 (alk. paper)
1. English periodicals—History—19th century.   2. Fatherhood in
the press—Great Britain.   3. Journalism—Social aspects—Great
Britain.   I. Title.
PN5124.P4N45   1995
306.874′2—dc20   94-18033

British Library Cataloging in Publication Data available

Contents

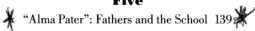

Contents

Acknowledgments

I am glad to have the opportunity to note here my indebtedness to the many people who helped to make the publication of this work possible. For their encouragement and support when I first began thinking about this project, I thank Mary Burgan, Alfred David, and Donald Gray, all of Indiana University; Cynthia E. Patton of Mesa State College; and Gillian Adams of Austin, Texas. The holdings and the periodicals librarians of the University of North Carolina at Chapel Hill, the University of Michigan, and the Cincinnati Public Library provided invaluable resources and assistance. The National Endowment for the Humanities made it possible for me to spend a summer discussing with a helpful and supportive group of colleagues some of the ideas developed during the course of writing this volume; I thank my fellow participants in the NEH-sponsored summer seminar at the University of Michigan, and especially the seminar's leader, Martha Vicinus, for their comments on, contributions to, and interest in my work. My new colleagues at Southwest Texas State University have likewise offered a supportive atmosphere in which to complete this project. Ann Sumner Holmes, Lynne Vallone, and an assortment of Nelsons have read and commented on portions of the work; I am grateful for their feedback and for that of Nancy Grayson Holmes, Karen Orchard, Elizabeth Johns, and the two anonymous scholars who refereed the manuscript (with painstaking care and impressive erudition) for the University of Georgia Press. Many of the improvements introduced into the work in its later stages are due to this group of readers, while the mistakes, of course, remain my own. David Nelson and Caleb Nelson provided sterling examples of fatherhood today. Finally, I must express my deep gratitude to Anne Morey, who not only offered detailed criticism on every chapter and assisted materially in the gathering of sources, but also provided unflagging and enthusiastic encouragement over the several years this book has been in progress. It is difficult to imagine having completed this work without her help and companionship.

Invisible Men

Introduction

Born into an era of political and social ferment, the generations that flourished between 1850 and 1910 inherited a nation still shaken by the upheavals of an earlier age: the French menace, the Industrial Revolution, the reforms of 1832. And the aftershocks continued, from the Continental turmoil of 1848 to the internal crumblings that followed the preachments of Charles Darwin—or, for that matter, of Annie Besant or John Henry Newman. For all the complacency some of their heirs have described as the archetypal Victorian middle-class sin, the bourgeoisie as a whole knew itself to be suspended over an abyss. As social class, religious faith, and other props and stays of the national order came increasingly under attack, there seemed ever less solid ground on which to stand. It is against this backdrop of uncertainty and change that we must consider the Victorian and Edwardian fixation on the family, which at once promised respite from doubt and acted as the cradle in which all doubts were formed.

This study will concern itself primarily with the father, whose position vis-à-vis the Victorian family was increasingly ambivalent and even antagonistic, and who, not coincidentally, has received comparatively little attention from present-day social historians. But to understand some of the pressures that assailed the British paterfamilias over the Victorian and Edwardian eras, we must consider also the period's exaltation of motherhood. Partly (one supposes) in response to the feminine rulership of Queen Victoria herself, partly due to a complex network of social and political and intellectual circumstances (some of which I will explore in more detail later in this volume), the Mother as Icon served simultaneously as ultimate panacea and ultimate horror, prospective solution to the national unrest and potential cause of a future upheaval next to which Napoleon would seem trivial.

For most Victorians women were defined by maternity, actual or potential, to a far greater extent than paternity defined men. In an era in which changes in the structure and importance of families were not the least of the alterations to the social fabric, motherhood was variously seen as patriotism, reform, science, and religion; it formed the basis for arguments both pro and con about woman's suffrage, education, employment, and prospective legal status. This spotlighting of maternity has had, of course, vast ramifications, which are by no means limited to the Victorian and Edwardian periods. Predictably, motherhood has received considerable attention from literary scholars and social historians over the past two decades. The feminist emphasis on understanding women's experience (whether within or beyond the family) has enormously advanced our exploration of questions about the mother's role in theory and in practice; one thinks of the disparate work of such researchers as Françoise Basch, Carol Dyhouse, Peter Gay, and J. A. Banks and Olive Banks, to name only a very few.

But there is still a tendency to assume that the Victorian male existed only in his "proper" place, the public sphere—that he had no meaningful role, and certainly no problematic role, to play at home. Although for every Victorian daughter, wife, or mother there was also a son, husband, or father, the former have drawn a heavily disproportionate amount of scholarly interest, while studies of the latter figures almost invariably place them against an all-male and antifamily backdrop of school or workplace.[1] Such an emphasis, I would argue, continues the same process of erasure that disturbed many Victorian writers on the home. Today's scholars need to examine men's domestic invisibility, its manifestations and its ramifications. I offer the present study as a preliminary step, and by no means a definitive one, in that direction. This work will concern itself with the shifting attitudes toward paternity in the sixty years between 1850 and 1910, identifying some of the ways in which, as motherhood came under scrutiny, fatherhood lost more and more of its symbolic power while always, perhaps, appearing as a cause for anxiety.

The year 1850, as it happens, is the endpoint of Leonore David-off and Catherine Hall's important work on the pre-Victorian middle classes at home, *Family Fortunes*. The world they describe is one in which domesticity and masculinity existed in harmony. There men engaged in "intense involvement" with their offspring,[2] supported in this effort by an evangelical revival that stressed the importance of child-rearing while still celebrating the primacy of the male. Fathers oversaw discipline, led the family in prayer, determined the nature of their children's educations and marriages and careers; nor did contemporaneous commentators significantly challenge their authority.

This idyll, however, was about to come to an end. Families were changing: men were increasingly identified with their occupations rather than with their households; women's symbolic value as moral influences was outstripping their practical value as, say, keepers of their husbands' accounts. Even childhood was coming to serve a new emotional purpose for adults as children came to be seen not as *tabulae rasae*, not as small sinners to be snatched from perdition by watchful adults, but as icons of innocence, harbingers of a better world to which adult males could hardly hope to aspire. Evangelicalism left in its wake anxiety about selfishness, greed, and the gratification of the ego; thus, to many Victorians of both genders, the commerce in which the middle-class man was daily engaged seemed as tainted as it did necessary. In short, although the division is somewhat arbitrary, the year 1850 may stand to mark the full flowering of the development of the Victorian doctrine of separate spheres. On the one side was the pre-Victorian hierarchical construction in which the privileged adult male and his concerns were central. On the other, and developing both from women's demands for recognition and from public life's new significance in eighteenth-century Britain,[3] stood the concept of domesticity as a space apart, one increasingly controlled by women and increasingly—at least as far as rhetoric went—more important emotionally and morally. The complacency or bluster of the Victorian paterfamilias of popular myth was beginning to mask profound ideological tensions.

By 1910, of course, observers knew that the principle of separate spheres was in jeopardy. Middle-class women frequently worked outside the home, at least before marriage;[4] the vote was imminent; and the approaching world war would wreak unimaginable changes upon English life. Women had already made considerable incursions into the public sphere by the simple expedient of defining it as an extension of the private, a strategem I will examine in more detail later in this study. For all the changes in the scope of their influence and even the pattern of their daily lives, however, ideas of motherhood changed little before the war. There was good reason for the static quality of the maternal image: women's power in the Victorian years chiefly depended upon their ability to present themselves as icons. Motherhood, actual or potential, was their stock in trade, and to divest themselves of the secular mariolatry that surrounded them during the high Victorian period would have been to destroy the fulcrum by means of which they expected to move the world.

All this is not to say that female domesticity during these sixty years was never problematic. Certainly individual women found the life constraining rather than empowering, and certainly critics often charged that women were failing to live up to the maternal ideal. But the ideal itself promised power and remained more or less stable throughout the period; moreover, it was constantly reinforced in such media as novels, sermons, and housekeeping manuals. The monumental quality thus inhering in Victorian maternity was the primary influence on the conceptualizing of paternity during the same era. It was motherhood that defined fatherhood; and because commentators were so sure they understood the role of the good mother, they were correspondingly doubtful about what might characterize the good father. The paternal ideal was weak, ambiguous, and fraught with conflict, producing discussions of fatherhood that varied in quantity (building to a peak in the last twenty years of the century) far more than they varied in content.

Hence the discussion of fatherhood involved fewer voices, and consequently more timid ones, in 1850 than it did in 1880, say; but the paternal images both men and women invoked remained strikingly similar, just as the broad outlines of the maternal ideal remained static as well. It was the relocation of virtue from father to mother that fueled the debate. Whereas eighteenth- and early-nineteenth-century writers could be sure that the father was the center of the family, the seat of power within it just as God was Father in heaven, later writers had no such certainty. Faced with the suspicion that, as essayist Anne Mozley put it in a reversal of Pope's dictum, "the proper study of mankind is *woman*,"[5] Victorian commentators found it more and more difficult to study man, at least in the role of paterfamilias. If motherhood was as significant for good or evil as conventional wisdom claimed, there could only be doubt about the importance of fatherhood. Moreover, the possible positions on paternal influence seemed limited by the maternal ideal, and here again they remained static while "mother-worship" remained in place.

Deprived of the intimacy consequent upon having been one flesh with their offspring over nine months of pregnancy, assigned by society and perhaps (writers theorized) by nature itself to the part of provider rather than caregiver, fathers seemed inevitably distanced from their children, onlookers at a primal scene that for many Victorians consisted not of union via sex but of union via breast-feeding. Writers thus saw a limited number of options in their depictions of male parentage. They could treat fathers as lesser mothers attempting with indifferent success to give the child what he or she was already receiving from another source; they could claim fathers as the obverse of mothers, brutes or martinets yoked to angels in human form; they could argue that fathers served a function complementing rather than duplicating that of mothers; they could discuss fathers metaphorically, explicating the parental role as it related to such surrogates as headmasters, judges, or even state programs. But each strategy forced an acknowledgment of mothers' superior influence and fathers' dwindling role within the family; as women became more visible socially and theoretically in the culture's constructions of itself, men lost power accordingly.

One essential forum for the depiction of parenting during this period is that of periodicals, which, at once immediate and reflective, unified and varied, serve as a magnificent digest of opinion on almost any topic. (Of course, it is necessary to remember that what a culture writes about its family life describes its expectations rather than actual practice.) The nineteenth-century explosion of newspapers, journals, and reviews represented an astonishing increase in both generalist and specialist publications, whether dailies, weeklies, monthlies, or quarterlies. Given the era's interest in defining femininity, a high proportion of this mountain of material discusses women, particularly as mothers; simultaneously, and in opposition to the complex image of maternity thus built up, there emerges an equally complex but more shadowy portrait of fatherhood.

To focus on visions of parenting presented by the periodical press is necessarily to eliminate much valuable material, from household advice manuals to novels—not to mention such glimpses of actual "family practice" as we can get from contemporary letters, journals, autobiographies, and so on. It is the ideal, not the real, that will principally concern us. And because London was the center of the magazine industry throughout the period (followed by Edinburgh and, a distant third, Dublin), the ideal examined here will be disproportionately English and urban. Although contributors and consumers alike might have lived anywhere in Britain or beyond it, it is as well to bear in mind that most of this unwieldy "camel" of prose passed through the geographical "needle's eye" of downtown London, and through the hands of editors and publishers attuned to London sensibilities. Accordingly, the model of Victorian fatherhood we may have built up from individual histories or other examinations of real life, in the provinces or indeed in London itself, will perhaps be strangely at odds with the picture these periodicals present; the explanation may lie in the difference between realistic representation and stereotype, in authorial intent, in anomalies of geography or class, or in any number of equally elusive factors.

Moreover, the bulk of my study will examine evidence from general-interest magazines (albeit of varying circulations and influence; see the Note on Sources for a more detailed discussion of principal texts). We will step aside only occasionally to remark on articles in professional journals or periodicals devoted to child rearing. I regretfully exclude such material, in part because ours is an age of specialization (it would take a Victorian to read, let alone write, the work that would result from a consideration of *all* comment on parenting during the period at hand)

and in part because what I seek is the picture of fatherhood that would have been assimilated by the Victorian and Edwardian generalist, the middle-class "common reader" with a practical rather than a theoretical interest in parenting.

The specification "middle-class"—shading toward "upper-middle-class" or even "aristocratic"—is necessary. While my sources include a few radical and feminist journals (*Shafts*, the *Englishwoman's Review*, the *Victoria Magazine*) aiming at a multiclass audience interested in the specialized area of women's rights, the monthly and quarterly journals I will be examining in this study catered by and large to the educated reader of intellectual pretensions and comfortable means, to an audience who expected periodicals to comment on a wide range of topical and philosophical subjects rather than to offer advice on keeping house on fifty pounds a year or to provide sensational reading for newsboys. Articles in such mainstream publications as the *Westminster Review*, the *Nineteenth Century*, and the *National Review* typically ranged from public-school reminiscences to analyses of foreign affairs to reports on parliamentary proceedings; contributors included anyone from the daughter of an impoverished country clergyman to foreign royalty. In this Establishment setting there was little room for comment by members of the working classes, and while, as we shall see, the families of the respectable and not-so-respectable poor were a frequent topic for discussion, it was a discussion by outsiders, illuminating the opinions of the affluent more reliably than those of the underclass. Nor, plainly, is it possible to isolate even middle-class ideology as either stable or monolithic. Attitudes toward parenthood were inevitably colored by attitudes toward other issues, among them politics, feminism, eugenics, education, and social welfare; at best we can hope that the chorused or conflicting voices of these periodicals may indicate which areas, at which times, were particularly contested and which seemed temporarily secure.

Chronology, too, may appear in this study to be more a whirlpool than a progression. One of the striking features of the body of material to be examined here is often its uniformity over time, the tendency of a mid-Victorian writer to recapitulate the Edgeworths, Jean-Jacques

Rousseau, or John Locke, or the tendency of an Edwardian writer to reprise the mid-Victorians. (Nor is this circumstance a thing of the past; pick up any of today's newspapers or magazines, find an article relevant in some way to child rearing, and the same concerns appear all over again.) To be sure, social theory undergoes its changes: ideas about prison management or human evolution or school discipline vary as new voices become dominant, even though the old voices are often still to be heard at the back of the chorus. But even as the terms of the discussion shift to accommodate the issues and ideas of a particular year or group of years, there remains underneath the up-to-date façade the same structure of anxious debate about fatherhood that is apparent from the beginning of the period this study covers.

Thus we cannot confine our examination of the troubles besetting the paternal image to a consideration of what is obviously domestic. The Victorians and Edwardians themselves invoked parenthood in a wide range of circumstances, seeking not only to understand paternity in terms of child rearing or science but also to understand public issues in terms of paternity, maternity, or home life in general. Nor was this fascination with domesticity a particularly feminine trait; male writers were at least as likely as female to cast their discussions of various issues in such terms, although their stances were not always identical. This book, then, will examine an assortment of arenas in which paternity as image or paternity as metaphor loomed large, even while it was often subsumed under a still more powerful image of (male or female) motherhood. The first two chapters will contrast domestic writers' views of mothers and fathers at home. Chapter 3 explores scientific constructions of fatherhood, from the biological to the anthropological and finally to the image of the scientist within the nursery; chapters 4, 5, and 6 deal respectively with legal, educational, and social welfare issues.

All this leaves many gaps, of course. Some of these omissions result from the scope of this inquiry: general-interest periodicals are not the best sources of material on theological questions, for instance. (A book remains to be written on the gendering of God in Victorian sermons.) Others, inevitably, signal a failure of imagination or understanding on my part. But as we shall see, neither maternity nor paternity in the period under discussion lends itself to the clear and unproblematic synthesis that might suggest that a single book on these topics could be definitive. Perhaps every generation finds it necessary to redefine gender ideals and reinvent the family. But of course such tasks are never simple. The Victorians, who so often stand for our own day as the epitome of placid domesticity and "family values," may have gained this reputation from their very anxiety about what so many of the commentators quoted here saw as their inability to conform to these standards.

1

The Fascination with the Maternal

Maternal love is a mystery which
human reason can never fathom.
It is altogether above reason;
it is a holy passion, in which all
others are absorbed and lost.
It is a sacred flame on the altar
of the heart, which is never
quenched. . . . The mother is the
mainspring of all nature, the fountain
of all pure love—the first likeness
on earth of God himself.

In terming one of their major preoccupations the "Woman Question," Victorian pundits risked vagueness; while it is true that the Woman Question included inquiries into the education of girls or the employment of spinsters, it ultimately took its urgency from the sense that as a potential mother, any woman, married or single, seemed connected to a source of energy forever inaccessible to men. To the Victorians, the real concern was the Mother Question. The danger of the superfluous woman, the fallen woman, and the New Woman, who might be cut off from matrimony by population imbalance, sexual mores, or even choice, was less their numbers than their possession of a natural power that, lacking its proper outlet of bearing and rearing children, might break through the social structure at any point. Conversely, within the mother (or even the potential mother) lay the ability to cure the malaise not only of an individual home but even of a nation, as she applied her maternal genius to its natural object, the question of making happy the human family.

The personal, the domestic, and the maternal had not always enjoyed the cultural status some Victorians ascribed to them. Many historians of private life argue, with Philippe Ariès, that the late eighteenth century "witnessed not only an industrial revolution but an emotional revolution as well," in which feelings previously directed outward became concentrated instead on the immediate family circle.[1] As ideals of marriage came increasingly to emphasize companionship, equality, and romantic love, the family—now separate from the workplace—became a walled garden for tenderness, a space presumed to be separate from the noises and resentments of business obligations. This sentimental domesticity

depended in part on a new respect for the individual, which undermined traditional hierarchies and replaced authoritarianism with gentle
influence. The effect of this shift was in general to reduce the perceived
power of the father within the middle-class family, to elevate the moral
status of the mother, and to bring the child into sudden prominence as
an object of major concern both in the home and in society as a whole.

The increased importance of childhood in the nineteenth century is
evident in many areas: the virtual invention of entertaining children's
literature, for instance, or the flood of legislation affecting children,
the sudden sharp attention given to the education of both sexes and
all classes, the new interest in childhood as an appropriate field for
scientific study. I shall refer to the latter phenomena in greater detail
later in this study; for now let it suffice to note in a domestic context
that the goal of marriage was becoming not simply "the procreation of
children" but their maintenance in health and happiness. The resulting
shift from a family model based on duty and respect to one grounded
in warm emotion emphasized nurture over the merely biological fact of
birth.[2] Correspondingly, the father's erstwhile role as family lawgiver
was minimized by the Victorian domestic ideal, which privileged em-
pathic understanding over hierarchical control. As the notion of separate
public and private spheres gained in importance, so did the mother's
perceived value at home.

Thus in Victorian opinion, while it takes two to make a baby, one
(ideally the mother) may be enough to rear it. Although legally women
lost control of their children at birth, socially they were achieving new
power because, as Julia Wedgwood wrote in 1867, they "do not only
constitute one-half the human race, they supply much more than half
the influences by which it is moulded."[3] The recipe for bringing up the
perfect child changed from the eighteenth-century belief in discipline
to a new emphasis on emotion. To the Reverend T. V. Moore, analyzing
"The Family as Government" in the *British Mother's Magazine* in May
1856, "The great agent in executing family law is love. . . . The parent
whose cold and repulsive manner represses all confiding familiarity in
the child, is building a wall of ice between himself and his offspring."[4]

By the 1850s, in other words, an authoritarian approach was coming to seem detrimental to raising a happy and moral child. This trend was to gain ground over the next fifty-odd years. Although childish obedience and self-control were certainly still valued, the number of theorists who advocated breaking the child's will was dwindling. And the father, once the principal authority figure within the family, was put in a peculiar position by this changing model of the family, in which the central issue was no longer deportment but feeling, and in which the central actor was likely to be the parent who had more time to spend with the children. This caregiving parent was typically the mother, who was now cast not simply as breeder but also as the gentle moral influence molding her children's characters in an almost imperceptible fashion. Thus, for instance, in their content analysis of American magazines between 1850 and 1865, Herman Lantz, Martin Schultz, and Mary O'Hara note a sharp rise in the amount of overt moral and domestic power these periodicals arrogate to women.[5] The observation is valid for the English middle classes as well. Looking back at the century just ended, an anonymous writer in a 1902 *Quarterly Review* singled out for comment the nineteenth century's "quickened sense and recognition of the paramount importance of the home."[6] Hand in hand with the domestic values that may be said to have reached critical mass in the late 1850s went a changed understanding of who should dominate at home.

While one of the raisons d'être of the domestic Eden was to give the adult male "rest and spiritual reparation" after "the din of the battle" in the marketplace,[7] Richard Sennett points out in an American context that precisely this attempt to benefit the father may have helped to undermine his authority at home by presenting him as a "weakling," a moral invalid for whom the expectations of the world had proved too much. Whatever a man's dominance in public life, Victorian convention (to be sure, a convention individual families often challenged) increasingly decreed that his role at home was less significant than that of his wife.

Nor was woman's part as materfamilias seen as a sinecure. "Punch's Almanack for 1853," for instance, contended that "if we are to compare these two spheres, the woman's—while the narrower—is, in many respects, the nobler of the two, and her part in the battle of life not infrequently the more important and dangerous one."[8] Antisuffrage writers continued on this note throughout the century, as in political historian Goldwin Smith's 1888 assertion, "The home is in reality at least as high a sphere as the State"; positivist Frederic Harrison's claim in 1891 that "for all moral purposes the Family is more vital, more beautiful, more universal than the State"; or the Queen of Romania's 1905 advice, "Women should never forget that they stand on a superior level, and when they place themselves on an equality with man, they do but descend from those heights."[9] While such rhetoric may fail as an argument against extending equal rights to women, it does suggest the age's widespread sense that at least with regard to ethics, the ideal home was not a patriarchy (as the prevailing stereotype has it) but a matriarchy.

In such a context, one may take issue with Miriam Lewin's contention that the ideology that gave men power over the public sphere and women power over the private exacerbated male worries about becoming female: "By emphasizing . . . women's general inferiority, the dire nature of the man's potential fall into femininity was increased."[10] To most periodical writers, assertions about women's "inferiority" seemed unfounded. Even those loudest in claiming men's greater intelligence (and they were by no means an overwhelming majority) were eager to acknowledge women's greater sensitivity, morality, and capacity for emotion; the qualities that seemed central to motherliness also proved women more competent than men at ruling the home. And although the home was separate, it was not to be deemed unequal. There is no evidence to suggest that Victorian society's overall attitude toward domesticity was contemptuous, as concern about a "fall into femininity" might suggest. If anything, it was the male-dominated public sphere that was disdained; the fear that most animated nineteenth-century commentators was not that men would become feminized but that women—mothers—would become masculine.[11]

Exploiting this terror built a career for the antifeminist Eliza Lynn Linton, a frequent contributor not only to the waspish *Saturday Review*[12] but also to a wide range of journals including Charles Dickens's *Household Words* and *All the Year Round*, the *Athenaeum*, the *Cornhill Magazine*, the *National Review*, and the *Nineteenth Century*. That her

commentary appealed to both liberal and conservative markets suggests
the fluidity of nineteenth-century thinking about women; the image of
good woman as the Angel in the House and the image of bad woman
as somehow male proved equally productive for reactionaries, centrists,
and radicals. Linton's notorious early satire in the *Saturday Review* of
14 March 1868, "The Girl of the Period," linked fashionable maidens
at once to sexual immorality and to masculinity of mind, an argument
that Linton was to reiterate over the next thirty years. Thus her "Wild
Women" series in 1891 inveighed against the feminists' "curious inversion of sex, which does not necessarily appear in the body, but is evident
enough in the mind," arguing that a woman who refuses maternity and
dominion over the private sphere demonstrates the spiritual equivalent
of "the bearded chin, the bass voice, flat chest, and lean hips of a
woman who has physically failed in her rightful development."[13] Only
three years before her death in 1898, she was still complaining about
"the Middle-Sex," those women who either prove themselves "unloving
to children, impatient of home and all that this includes" or demand
sexual license, preferring "the roses and raptures to the lilies and lan-
guour."[14] As ever in Linton's writings, motherliness is the sole antidote
to immorality and masculinity in women.

Others echoed Linton's fears. H. B. Marriott-Watson, for instance,
criticized the American woman of 1904 on the grounds that her asser-
tiveness and restlessness had "driven her to abdicate those functions
which alone excuse, or explain, her existence. . . . The doctrine of the
superiority of women . . . has resulted in a breach of the laws of maternity. Evasion of child-birth follows . . . the higher feminism."[15] The
argument was an old one in antisuffrage debate; Emily Faithfull's feminist *Victoria Magazine* had in 1867 reprinted a similar piece from the
Chronicle warning that "history shows that the dissolution of family life
leads to the decline and fall of the State. . . . To enfranchise women is to
induce them to quit the family circle, and to make them unwomanly."[16]

It is not my purpose here to trace the history of Victorian and Edwardian feminism and its opponents, but merely to observe that for both
sides, motherhood was the major ground on which the battle was fought.
The question of mothers' legal rights over their children, touched off

by Caroline Norton, resounded through the nineteenth century, as we shall see in chapter 4. Similarly, debate over women's education never strayed far from the concern on the one hand that girls' minds should be sufficiently cultivated to maximize their eventual influence for good over their children, and on the other, as respected physicians such as Henry Maudsley and the American Edward Clarke warned, that girls who study too hard risk diverting essential menstrual blood to their brains and destroying their maternal capacity.[17] Over and over, feminists such as Millicent Garrett Fawcett (proud mother of the first woman to score above the male prizewinners in the Cambridge mathematical tripos) held that it is precisely "women's special experience as women, their special knowledge of the home and home wants, of child life and the conditions conducive to the formation of character," that qualifies them for equal rights.[18] And as often, their opponents responded that women's duties as mothers are so all-consuming as to preclude involvement in public affairs.[19]

Even for many feminists, then, women's reproductive system was their most essential characteristic. In an era in which class was losing some of its rigidity, biology provided an increasingly useful standard for defining the virtuous and the alien. But while men's sexual drive existed to be controlled (recall the Victorian crusades against prostitution, male homosexuality, masturbation, and excessive marital sex), women's capacity for motherhood, which eclipsed their experience or nonexperience of desire, existed to control them. "Indeed," commented L. Vansittart de Fabeck in 1896, "only by virtue of their potential motherhood are they women."[20]

Maternity thus served a dual function, both raising women above the purely physical plane and paradoxically bringing them back to it. If the womb somehow bestowed moral superiority, it also governed women's bodily inferiority and rendered them objects rather than subjects in Victorian medical science. As an anonymous writer for the *Quarterly Review of Science* observed in 1878, "The female is more exclusively constructed for, and more totally absorbed in, the task of reproduction than the male. The share of the latter in this function is, strictly speaking, momentary."[21] So bound up was women's health in their ability to conceive that if they did not become pregnant, ophthalmic surgeon

Dr. Charles Taylor warned in 1882, they risked organic damage: "Accumulated force must find an outlet, or disturbance first and weakness ultimately results."[22] The controversy over using chloroform to alleviate pain during childbirth, which Queen Victoria's endorsement of the drug helped to settle, surely resulted in part from a sense that if giving birth was indeed what a woman was "exclusively constructed for," she ought to be awake for it. And psychiatry's fascination with hysteria—literally, "suffering in the womb"—and flirtation with ovariotomy as a cure for neurosis (or simply for sexuality) suggest the difficulty Victorian doctors found in separating the female person from the mother.

Psychologically as well as medically, the woman *was* the womb. Feeding on the theories of Darwin, Theodor Bischoff (who in 1843 provided the model of spontaneous ovulation), Herbert Spencer, and others, the mid-Victorians and their heirs learned to view the maternal instinct as inherent in every normal woman, the link that made the Colonel's lady and Judy O'Grady "sisters under their skins" while the Colonel and Sergeant O'Grady were eternally estranged. To the prominent physiologist and expert in mental evolution George J. Romanes (writing in the *Nineteenth Century* in 1887), maternity was both innate and environmental, bred in the bone by natural selection and reinforced by emotional intimacy with one's children:

> Alike in expanding all the tender emotions, in calling up from the deepest
> fountains of feeling the flow of purest affection, in imposing the duties of
> rigid self-denial, in arousing under its strongest form the consciousness
> of protecting the utterly weak and helpless consigned by nature to her
> charge, the maternal instincts are to woman perhaps the strongest of all
> influences in the determination of character.[23]

To writers such as Romanes, who voiced dominant anthropological and evolutionary opinion, women's positive and negative qualities alike were products of instincts programed over millennia, and no legislative or social change could alter them.

Respect for the maternal instinct was particularly strong in men, an identity of attitude that transcended politics. In her study of the radical Men and Women's Club (which met between 1885 and 1889 to discuss sexuality, procreation, eugenics, and socialism), Lucy Bland

observes that the group's men were more convinced than its women that
parturition was women's finest hour. Its founder, eugenist Karl Pearson, spun arguments centering on the maternal instinct to suggest that
evolution might demand women's permanent subordination. His stance
irked feminists Henrietta Müller and Emma Brooke, who denied that all
women share the talent for motherhood.[24] Likewise, James Macgrigor
Allan told an audience of anthropologists in 1867 that "Nature has declared, in language which cannot deceive, that woman's chief mission
is maternity. Woman craves to be a mother, knowing that she is an im-
perfect undeveloped being, until she has borne a child." In contrast, a
feminist writer scoffed three years later that the idea "that every female
is, by nature, endowed with a genius for . . . the care of children . . . [is]
about as reasonable as would be the notion that all men had, by right of
sex, an inherent taste for the practice of military tactics or the conduct
of commercial speculations."[25]

Even among women, however, to deny an overweening maternal instinct—and the doubters included Harriet Taylor and her husband John
Stuart Mill[26]—was to embrace a minority stance. Most conceded instead that, as Mary Jeune put it, "deep down in every woman's heart, if
we care to analyze it, lies the strong, intense longing for motherhood"
and argued that this passion is the root of feminine superiority: "The
strong instinct of maternity which is an essential part of women's character has helped to keep the lives of women pure and clean."[27] A typical
exposition of the centrality of maternalism is Julia Wedgwood's essay
in the *Contemporary Review* in 1889. Wedgwood drew on Darwinism,
anthropology, history, literature, and comparative religion to explain,
"Woman inherits a longer tradition of moral relation than man does: she,
in the very dawn of her existence, finds herself dowered with a heritage
of instincts unknown to him; he passes through a long stage of his education before he knows himself to be a father, but she is, from the first,
consciously a mother." Not only is mother worship humankind's central
religious impulse (even Christ, she commented, is really a type of the
feminine), but maternity brings woman closer than man to the divine,
bestowing upon her a greater sense of justice, self-denial, love, and
community.[28]

In positioning the mother as eternal and preternaturally virtuous, Wedgwood formed part of a chorus proving that whatever might be the tendency toward mother worship latent in humanity as a whole, in the Victorians and Edwardians it ran strong. The mystical feminism of Frances Swiney, for instance, could find a forum in the mainstream *Westminster Review* for the statement that "Nature and Femininity are one. Motherhood is the basic principle of creation. . . . Feminine energy is the initial force in the world working for development, and . . . making men human." Swiney called for the (re)institution of matriarchy, for the acknowledgment that women are more highly evolved than men, and (in a subsequent article) for the understanding that "the ultimate victory of the Feminine Principle was . . . foreshadowed in the birth of Christ, who, as a male organism, was yet free from any male element and was the outcome of the pure Feminine spirit and of the pure Feminine substance." [29] Adapting the work of researchers such as the biologists Patrick Geddes and J. Arthur Thomson and the sociologist Lester F. Ward to their needs, Swiney and others—theosophists, feminists, and moderates alike—invoked a religion of motherhood based on the principle that Woman, as the superior sex, "the Saviour, the up-raiser, the true life-giver of the world. . . . the highest manifested form of life on this planet," is the key to the perfecting of mankind. [30]

That the Victorian and Edwardian passion for social reform coexisted with a deep pessimism about legislation's effectiveness helps to explain the attractiveness of the vision of the mother as divine instrument. If the public sphere was as corrupt and corrupting as the socially concerned knew it to be, it could never cleanse itself through its own institutions. The remedy lay in the home, natural opposite of the outside world and already ministering to beleaguered businessmen on an individual and daily basis. Appropriately directed, maternal power could do wholesale in a generation or two what legislation was attempting piecemeal. In the words of late-century feminist Margaret Shurmer Sibthorp, mothers could bring about world peace and purity:

They will take them [sons] before they have left the cradle, and gently, powerfully, with the almost divine authority and influence of every true

mother, potential or actual, they will train their thoughts and actions. . . .
Watch the boys, mothers, sisters, teachers, watch the boys! They need
wings of eagles to rise up, up to the glory of day; but when you have made
the average boy as pure in thought and as peaceful in purpose, as the
average girl now *is*, you will have done a great work for the world.[31]

The altruism inseparable from maternal instinct, the mother's expertise
in instilling morality, suggested that if only the nation's mothers could
be unified they would accomplish what Agnes Grove referred to (with no
sense of hyperbole) as woman's new "conscious mission: the perfecting
of the human race."[32]

The question was not one of feasibility but one of method; should
women work their miracles in the small compass of their own homes
or confront the contaminating world directly by becoming, in historian Carroll Smith-Rosenberg's phrase, "public mothers"?[33] The public mother—she who fulfilled her maternal function by serving as a
Poor Law Guardian empowered to extract child-support payments from
delinquent parents, a member of a board of education, a child-welfare
lobbyist, and so forth—not only could combine nurturance with celibacy (thus solving the eternal Victorian problem of middle-class gender
imbalance) but also might hope to accomplish still more than the private
mother, since her actions would affect more people than a single family
contained.

Even relatively early in the period, favorable images of the public
woman abounded. Suggesting that under existing conditions celibacy
is preferable to wedlock, feminist and animal-rights activist Frances
Power Cobbe commented in *Fraser's Magazine* in 1862 on the nobility
possible to the free spinster, whose philanthropic existence "may be as
rich, as blessed, as that of the proudest of mothers with her crown of
clustering babes. . . . devoting her *whole* time and energies to some benevolent task, she is enabled to effect perhaps some greater good than
would otherwise have been possible."[34] Likewise, Mill's stepdaughter,
Helen Taylor, urged woman suffrage on the ground of the increasingly
"quasi-domestic character" of legislation—the growing governmental
interest in sanitation, education, child labor, housing, and other mat-

ters within the expertise of the mother. She argued that it could only benefit both parties for "women to extend their interest to the comfort and happiness of other homes besides their own."[35] Moreover, while women dominated this area of discussion, men often concurred with their assumptions. For example, the metaphor of legislative domesticity still rang true for an unnamed American clergyman who contended in 1906 "not that the home is in danger because loving and intelligent motherhood radiates its influence in society, but that society is in danger when it withholds from motherhood a voice in our municipal and national housekeeping."[36] Such rhetoric suggests the extent to which motherhood had become sanctified; even men opposed to female activism took on a wistful tone when contemplating the maternal capacity in which they could never share. As we shall see throughout this study, the male inability to compete in the motherhood stakes left many men agreeing that their wives belonged to a higher order of being than they themselves did.

Thus, in England as in the United States, women's claims to political power often fed on assumptions about their superior talent for child rearing.[37] Over time, the feminist movement widened its focus to include not only "feminine" issues such as social purity and the treatment of disadvantaged children but also any public question that might affect women, and almost all did. If the maternal instinct was innate, adherents argued, then the appropriate sphere for women's moral influence was the whole world, which not only could but should be made to resemble the home. Masculine law, the American Elizabeth Willard charged in 1867, "is the law of division and antagonism, the law of discord, combat and destruction"; editorialists in both countries suspected, in Joe L. Dubbert's words, that "the moral superiority of women must be allowed to triumph or men would corrupt everything—including women—and chaos would result."[38] Or as the feminist *Englishwoman's Review* (whose editors and contributors included Dr. Elizabeth Garrett Anderson, Barbara Bodichon, Jessie Boucherett, Emily Davies, and other distinguished Victorian and Edwardian activists) put it, what the public sphere needed was "the vitalizing warmth of woman's work, and still more of woman's control—the *mother* influence."[39]

While they acknowledged the mother's wider reforming power, other commentators held that it is most effective in its natural setting, that of the home. In exalting maternal influence, early-Victorian domestic writers such as Sarah Ellis and Sarah Lewis (respectively the authors of the *Women of England* series and *Woman's Mission*, popular household tracts of the 1830s and 1840s) had envisaged its regenerative powers as indirect, working through moral sons in public and moral daughters in private. Particularly in the early years of our period, subsequent contributors to periodicals often continued to recommend this pattern. In an 1851 excursion into prose, for instance, the poet Coventry Patmore hailed the woman who stays at home as absolute monarch of her domain, free from all supervision (her husband apparently making only a financial and conjugal contribution to family life) and correspondingly bound to use her influence responsibly by maintaining her sway even over her grown children. "More is done for national virtue and prosperity by such women, than by the best of kings and legislators," Patmore rhapsodized; nevertheless, he nowhere suggested that these powerful figures would be capable of surmounting the "servile drudgery and indignity" meted out to men employed in the outside world. Their influence must perennially be refracted.[40] Similarly, the historian and polymath Henry Thomas Buckle noted in 1858 the inexorable progress of women in reforming education, literature, public mores, even science and law—not by direct lobbying but by inculcating in their sons feminine qualities of imagination, mind, and love.[41] What would later worry Linton was not women's influence as such but its exercise outside the home.

Women's power—which was based on their superior morality, sensitivity, altruism, and feeling, all the hallmarks of ideal motherhood—was qualitatively different from men's power, which to the Victorians and Edwardians was ultimately grounded in physical strength. To conservative commentators, woman's influence seemed dependent on precisely her inability to defend herself against brute force, which force often included the workings of government. Thus a Reverend Adams explained in the *Westminster Review* in 1850 that women, whose "*genius* is *influence. . . .* have fed on nectar, and their spirit has become that of Gods' [*sic*]." This ethereal and subtle power is best exemplified in child rearing: "What the mother *is* will emanate from her, be most likely *in* her child. . . . her own spiritual standard will be the average one of those around her." (The children around her, in fact, include her husband, as "Man, save here and there one, has no standard of his own by which to regulate his conduct to woman, but uses hers.") Given the vast, if invisible, extent of her sphere, woman is bound to redress the acknowledged wrongs of her legal situation not by combat or complaint but by influence, since any direct action diminishes womanliness; the less she moves, the more she gains.[42]

The model of influence expressed by Adams and his ilk continued throughout the period, being taken up by such "advanced" thinkers as sexologist Havelock Ellis in the 1890s.[43] Based as it is on a concept of the child as both accomplishment and champion and of the mother as the child's environment, it resembles a Victorian model of pregnancy. Here the child's health depends upon the mother's quietude, her agreement not to strain her passions or her limbs, her readiness to think of herself as a medium for her offspring's growth; communication between herself and the child takes place not vocally but biologically, as her unspoken thoughts travel toward her family with the speed of nerve impulses. In this highly charged environment, the mother's every action risks being too forceful. The novelist and physician Arabella Kenealy, for instance, contrasted the moronic baby of her New Woman patient Mrs. Graham with the superb baby produced by the delicate Mrs. Eden and concluded that women owe it to their children not to cultivate their own talents, but to stockpile this nervous energy for reproductive use: "Mrs. Graham had artificially forced into activity, and for her own use, the latent power of her son."[44] In this construction, in which children and even husbands never entirely leave the womb, it is no wonder that influence is normally gendered female.

But the influence/action dichotomy merely symbolized rather than constituted the problem. As much as the question of what woman are, the extent to which men and women differ and the implications of that difference for the behavioral patterns of the sexes were contested territory for the Victorians as for ourselves; the debate spanned education, employment, psychology, and politics as well as child rearing. Those who argued for innate and inevitable difference included Montagu Burrows. He criticized the 1868 report of the 1867–68 Schools Inquiry Commission (which investigated, separately, both boys' and girls' educations and noted the inadequacy of the latter) for failing to "take into account the real difference between boys and girls" that would have allowed them to understand why women's education ought to be inferior to men's: besides study's tendency to imperil women's reproductive capacity, "The learned woman does not make the best educator of children."[45] Likewise, the upholders of difference included conservative novelist Margaret Oliphant, who countered Mill with a plea for separate but "complementary" lives: "The two [sexes] are not made to contend and compete and run races for the same prize," she explained, as maternity makes outside employment impossible.[46] They included Maudsley, whose 1874 article "Sex in Mind and Education" touched off a flurry of responses over the next decade, generally (like Romanes) dismissing "the absurd theory that the mental faculties of the two sexes are identical, though [Romanes] by no means denies that they may be equal."[47] And again, they included feminists such as the Swede Ellen Key and her German cohorts (the Teutonic women's movement, according to Havelock Ellis, "so far from making as its ideal the imitation of men, bases itself on that which most essentially marks the woman as unlike the man") or I. D. Pearce, who remarked in 1907 that "equality does not necessarily imply similarity."[48]

But as in the debate over maternal instinct, others—again including Mill, for example in his 1869 essay "The Subjection of Women"—saw the differences between men and women as socially constructed. This argument could run both ways; antifeminists, such as an anonymous writer on "Female Labour" in 1860, worried that to expose women to "the strife, the coarseness, the violent and the ignoble passions" of the outside world would cause them to lose "much of the truest charms of womanhood." The "mental cultivation" to which women should be subject must be used to counteract the "fierce competition for gold," not to join it.[49] To this school it was immaterial whether women's intellect equaled men's, since the major difference between the sexes was one of temperament, and temperament, it seemed, was a product of environment.

Discussions of relative intellect, however, had their place, and it became an antifeminist cliché to comment that women had produced no
Shakespeare (until exasperated women retorted that even men had produced only one!). But many believed that even intelligence was made,
not born—an argument that implied that family environment (and especially, perhaps, the maternal influence governing it) was all-important
to society. Mill and Harriet Taylor, writing in 1851, applauded the good
sense of Sydney Smith for having noted forty years earlier, "If you catch
up one-half of these creatures [children], and train them to a particular
set of actions and opinions, and the other half to a perfectly opposite set,
of course their understandings will differ."[50] So too Lydia Becker, activist editor of the *Women's Suffrage Journal*, held "that any broad marks
of distinction that may exist at the present time between the minds of
men and women collectively, are fairly traceable to the different circumstances under which they pass their lives."[51] And novelist and clergyman Charles Kingsley (whose support of woman suffrage was at Mill's
behest) commented in *Macmillan's*, "The only important [intellectual]
difference, I think, is, that men are generally duller and more conceited
than women"—again, a product of childhood mismanagement.[52] This
idea of the fluidity of the psyche persisted, operating in such influential
essays as Mona Caird's 1890 "The Morality of Marriage," which contended that with sexual equality, "we shall have a totally different kind
of people to deal with from the men and women of to-day."[53]

Especially toward the end of the Victorian era (as will be demonstrated later in this study), the scientific establishment protested against
this emphasis on environment. Humanists, however, were equally opposed to science's stress on a biological version of original sin, preferring to believe that there is no such thing as a child who cannot be
redeemed by good treatment. If the family thus seemed the natural locus
for social reform, and the mother—as noted earlier—reform's chief dis-
seminator, it became important to establish that the influence of the
mother did indeed dominate over that of the father. Some commentators
made this point through metaphor, as in Patmore's and Sarah Grand's
recastings of the marriage tie into the mother-son bond: compare the
conservative Patmore's 1851 comment that "not only does the mother
mould the mind and disposition of her children, but she exercises over

the mind of her husband an almost equal power" with the progressive Grand's 1894 explanation, "It is the woman's place and pride and pleasure to teach the child, and man morally is in his infancy. . . . now woman holds out a strong hand to the child-man, and insists, but with infinite tenderness and pity, upon helping him up."[54] Influence is clearly impossible for a father who cannot even be considered an adult.

Others invoked science to explain why the maternal voice should be stronger than the paternal. Feminists of the 1890s drew on anthropological discussion of the "Mutterrecht" (literally, "mother-power" or "mother-rule") to shrink the father's role into that of "pollinator."[55] Biology also proved useful; addressing the National Congress of [American] Mothers in 1905, the child-study pioneer G. Stanley Hall contended that woman's soul "is larger and more typical, more generic . . . than that of man, is nearer the child and shares more of its divinity than does the far more highly specialized and narrowed organism of the man."[56] Here it is the woman who is depicted as the more childlike and primitive. (Most scientists contended that specialization signals biological superiority, although they did not always link this view with the equally prevalent opinion that women are wholly geared toward reproduction while men serve a variety of functions.) At the same time, however, the traditional family hierarchy has been inverted to place the "generic" but divine child at the top, the mother in the middle, and the father at the bottom, farthest from God, a typical pattern in Victorian sentimental fiction as well.

Politically, motherhood was used not only to show why women should or should not be enfranchised but also to show that women were effectively enfranchised already. Taylor and Mill expressed concern about the possibility that women, confined to private life by maternity, might misuse their influence as wives to get their husbands to vote against the public good; subsequent writers worried also about women's influence as mothers, judging like an anonymous writer for the *Saturday Review* that women are "more powerful than men to disturb the deeper foundations of order, as they have probably been more powerful to insinuate custom and to mould the first impressions of the young."[57] On a more positive note, T. Cave-North argued in 1908 that it is fully within women's power to produce sons "of such a type that they would go into parliament, on to the various boards on which they act, into all the manifold paths of life, and carry out the ideals with which their mothers sent them into the world"; women do not need the vote because "the mother's influence should be in the main the formative one." [58] Cave-North's contemporary Ben Elmy (feminist husband of the suffrage leader Elizabeth Wolstenholme Elmy) took a similar tack in supporting women's emancipation on the grounds that because "by the plan of Nature woman has the inestimably greater share in the physical and mental formation and nurture" of children, "her own intellectual and physical development is of supreme and vital importance." [59]

In short, the maternal capacity typically appeared to be the overriding factor in determining the extent of women's right to public involvement. No such arguments were constructed around men's ability to sire children, which in turn implies that the mother-child bond is more significant for both participants than that between child and father. Feminists and nonfeminists alike agreed with this enduring belief; witness Maudsley's comment in 1874 that "Men are manifestly not so fitted mentally as women to be the educators of children during the early years of their infancy and childhood" and the 1895 remark of Thomas Case (the Wayn-flete professor of moral and metaphysical philosophy at Oxford), "A wife is much more the mother of a child, both before and after its birth, than the husband is the father." [60] The question was merely how this truth should be used in the political arena.

At the same time, however, if there was a possibility that motherhood was itself a product of environment, and if sons were supposed to be largely the creatures of maternal influence, then the creation of a race of androgynous men who in adulthood would behave more like mothers than like fathers seemed to some both possible and desirable. In part because the ideal mother—unworldly, self-sacrificing, loving, and pure—was identical to the ideal Christian, acceptance of an androgynous manliness reached its zenith around the middle of the century, just before both faith and masculinity came under new pressures. [61] In terms of the mother-son bond, this development required that the son give what Smith-Rosenberg calls "absolute and unquestioned obedience to his mother's will," [62] not because parental authority symbolized divine command, as was earlier the case between son and father, but to reflect society's endorsement of domesticity. Similarly, Carol Zisowitz Stearns and Peter N. Stearns observe (focusing, like Smith-Rosenberg, on America) that at mid-century the domestic ideal demanded that within the home, both sexes should rigidly control anger—and one might add other manifestations of the self, such as desire and ambition. Theorists hoped that mothers, who because they "were" the home were sometimes assumed to be incapable of feeling anger in the first place, might pass this incapacity along to their sons, so that "sons and daughters alike were to be modeled on mother." [63]

While mainstream (male) society became increasingly doubtful about feminized boys as sexologists began constructing new definitions of gender and of sexual "normalcy"—a trend I have discussed in *Boys Will Be Girls*—women's advocates continued throughout the century to argue that the mother was the best behavioral model for all children, girls and boys alike. Thus a writer signing herself "Espérance" commented in *Shafts* in 1893 that ideally for "our social improvement," all teachers of boys should be women: "It would be almost impossible for them to follow a bad father's bad example when they become men." (Still more radically, the editor's addendum to another *Shafts* article suggested, "Why not train the boys to do all household work equally with the girls?" [64])

Especially at issue, for *Shafts* contributors as for other feminists, was social purity. That moral reform and child rearing were indissolubly linked during the latter nineteenth century meant that boys were frequently urged to follow a model of sexual continence defined as female. Whether this took the form of the stock advice "Never do anything you would be ashamed of confessing to your mother and sisters" or of putting the sex education even of sons under maternal control (as periodicals of all stripes recommended in the late nineteenth century), both sexual silence and sexual discussion were often organized along the mother-son axis, necessarily marginalizing the father and encouraging an androgynous model of child rearing. Far from jeopardizing her purity, a woman's motherhood was usually seen as putting it beyond doubt (in novels such as Elizabeth Gaskell's *Ruth* [1853], maternity could cleanse even the fallen). But this trope applied only rarely to men and fatherhood. It was therefore necessary that maternal influence create not only a beneficial environment for child rearing but also children stamped in the mother's own image.

Androgyny, while among the more interesting currents in familial ideals during this period, was not the most dominant. A stronger model still for motherhood was that of the scientist, the domestic polymath fully as professional as her husband; having its roots in the early Victorian era, this model continued to prosper without significant interruption long past Edwardian days and indeed is still with us (albeit muted) today. Its first major expression may be said to have been the flood of housekeeping manuals and magazines that roared out of nineteenth-century presses, a phenomenon that both assured women of the inevitability of married motherhood and presented domesticity as a many-faceted and challenging skill.[65] Reporting on Dr. Benjamin Richardson's lecture on "Woman as a Sanitary Reformer" in 1880, for instance, the *Englishwoman's Review* noted the need for women to receive training in housekeeping and cooking as sciences and to be well grounded in chemistry, biology, and medicine; in 1889 an anonymous contributor commented also on the challenge posed by motherhood, described as "The extremely difficult and complicated task of educating a young child's faculties."[66] Antifeminists such as Linton concurred, complaining, "We give less thought (not less love), less study, less scientific method, to the management of our own young than to the training of future racehorses or the development of the prize heifer on the farm."[67]

Reformers sought to professionalize motherhood throughout the period by recommending the payment of salaries (feminists wanted the money to come from husbands, eugenists from the state), the establishment of the "lady help" as a career for would-be auxiliary mothers and wives, the creation of cooperative housekeeping endeavors so that mothers could concentrate on their families rather than on overseeing servants or dinners, and the offering of college-level courses in "domestic science." The latter, particularly important at the end of our period, emphasized food chemistry, hygiene, economics, ethics, bacteriology, and, above all, educational philosophy and child psychology. Practice and theory were inseparable; the Froebelian institute Sesame House, for instance, included among its facilities three babies (whose parents paid five shillings a week for their care), whom the students were told to treat on a strict scientific basis and were not allowed to cuddle.[68]

As is evident from these examples, the need for scientific motherhood extended into the dominant classes. But at least to middle-class eyes, working-class mothers seemed still more in need of training; rising rates of infant mortality embarrassed and horrified fin-de-siècle Britain, which associated the trend with working women. Likewise, when the Boer War revealed that a shockingly high proportion of recruits could not meet the army's physical standards—only two in five volunteers, Major-General Frederick Maurice warned, were healthy enough to make effective soldiers—the nation knew the fault to lie with working-class women. Not only the present crop of mothers but their own mothers, invading the factory instead of staying home to teach motherly skills, were to blame. (Maurice approvingly quoted the Kaiser's dictum "Küche, Kirche, Kinder."[69]) The problem, according to such social reformers as Helen Dendy Bosanquet, was not poverty but mismanagement, "the ignorance and carelessness of parents who do not lack the means to do better"; the solution was home visiting by middle-class volunteers whose own mothers, presumably, had been more knowledgeable about proper infant feeding and the prevention of malnutrition and diarrhea.[70]

As Patmore had warned as far back as 1851, "The maternal instinct alone will be found . . . insufficient to form a mother."[71] The lower working classes, then, served as a convenient repository for middle-class concerns about British family life in general, because these more marginal members of society could be depicted as notoriously improvident, unchaste, ill-disciplined, and tied to the marketplace—in other words, as masculine rather than feminine. (Middle-class writers on domestic violence among the poor depicted women either as exaggeratedly frail or as exaggeratedly brawny; at neither extreme was it to be expected that the women could function as true homemakers.) If the maternal instinct seemed especially lacking or inadequate within such a group, readers were excused from drawing uncomfortable parallels to the "real" (middle-class) home.

The parallels, of course, were there for those who sought them. Poor Law workers such as A. D. Edwards, working within a system that tended to equate poverty and criminality, might confine their censure to the proletariat when discussing the evils of working women; Edwards charged that these women's children starve whatever the quantity and quality of the food the mother's employment provides, due to the "lack of mother-care. A woman cannot work in a factory and still undertake her parental responsibility." [72] Other writers had less reticence. Edwards's contemporary Clara Jackson, for instance, extended the accusation of national flabbiness upward, observing that well-to-do boys are just as likely as their less privileged counterparts to have poor eyes, narrow chests, and other evidences of maternal neglect. The remedy she proposed was of course maternal education, but an education drawing on the skills of Victorian grandmothers rather than on the precepts of Edwardian scientists. The way to Jackson's utopia was backward, via old accomplishments and a feudal system in which aristocratic women would behave as the mothers of their grateful, childlike servants: the answer to class ill-feeling was to "establish a relationship between them and us," a relationship essentially maternal. [73]

Jackson's delinquent mothers, whose own mothers have neglected to train them properly and who live only for their artistic and athletic pastimes, are plainly the daughters of Linton's "girls of the period," whose addiction to fashion precludes true womanliness. (For that matter, they are also prefigured in the writings of Alexander Pope and Jean-Jacques Rousseau; the Victorians were certainly not the first to experience anxiety about motherhood. [74]) The concern in each case is that for all the vaunted strength of the maternal instinct, women are easily distracted from giving in to it. Seduced by other gratifications, they may ignore the call to give birth; worse, they may consent to have children but refuse to give the maternal care essential to family-centered reform. In another jeremiad against fashionable society, Linton warned in 1868 that the social straitjacket was making children at once prohibitively expensive, unrewarding, and passé, as remote mothers turned their offspring over to the care of nurses, indifferent to the infants' moral and physical corruption at the hands of dissolute or ignorant servants:

"There never was a time when children were made of so much individual [financial] importance in the family, yet in so little direct relation to the mother." [75] Forty years later Reginald Brabazon, twelfth earl of Meath, expressed the same concern in similar terms, opining that "women are showing the white feather" by refusing to bear children and that even among those who do become mothers, "the children are more and more being left to the care of governesses and nurses. The desire for pleasure and for personal ease seems to have taken firm hold of the minds of many well-to-do women, and to have driven out the maternal instincts." [76]

Certainly the Victorian period underwent a marked diminution in the amount of labor the middle-class woman was expected to spend on housework. The famous rise in nineteenth-century standards of living was tied to the explosion of servants into bourgeois homes; however much commentators might insist upon the wife's expertise in chemistry, bookkeeping, and up-to-date sanitation theory, everyone knew that her primary function was emotional rather than active and that even the most professional homemaker was a manager rather than a worker. Writers less pessimistic than Linton and Brabazon, however, held that families could only benefit from the increased amount of leisure time at the disposal of a woman who had neither to cook nor to clean. As "L. M. S." explained in the April 1855 issue of the *British Mother's Magazine*, a mother owes it to her family to ignore routine tasks of housekeeping so that she can concentrate on the "moral development of her family." [77] Linton and her supporters were correct in supposing that the routine household tasks neglected by the Victorian mother included chores having to do with children; to quote historian Joan N. Burstyn, "the higher the status of the family, the less a mother had to do with the hourly activities of childcare." [78] But if the affluent mother merely oversaw rather than executed details of her children's bathing, dressing, feeding, bedtime, and so on, her abdication in these matters only magnified her influence.

As Christina Hardyment notes, from the mid-Victorian era on, "Who looked after the baby was no longer decided by whether they could efficiently cope with it physically—it was a matter of soul nourishment." [79] For most writers in this period, motherhood was a state of mind. The symbiotic relationship established in the womb between mother and child continued after birth, with the mother's instinctive and perhaps unconscious nurturance creating a beneficial environment for all who came within her orbit: she did not act so much as she acted *upon*. As we have seen, this model of ideal maternity could extend from the nursery into the workhouses, the slums, the voting booths—or indeed Windsor, given that the most influential example of the "public mother" was certainly the Queen. Alternatively, the mother who allowed her energies to be diverted by matters having nothing to do with the emotional sustaining of her family or pseudo-family (whether these matters were defined as frivolity or as attempts to rival men) risked ruining her children and eradicating her own femininity.

It is too easy to dismiss the model of mother as Angel in the House as merely a way for Victorian Britain to control the restlessness of middle-class women who suddenly found themselves marooned on an island of inactivity by demographic currents that had reassigned bourgeois women's traditional work elsewhere. We must also recognize that the sanctification of motherhood over this period, a process furthered at least as often by women as by men, gave women a means of channeling their restlessness to achieve power even within male-dominated spheres. That this maternal ideal would have encouraged many women to resign themselves to idleness (while their servants did the housework and their children were raised by nursery governesses and public schoolmasters) is undeniable, as Joan Perkin notes; as Perkin also observes, however, the ideal simultaneously permitted other women to establish a virtual matriarchy at home and even beyond.[80] Presumably individual temperament would have been the deciding factor. Thus Neil Smelser's ascription of middle-class Victorian feminism to "the social fact that women's roles were becoming generally more empty, unrewarded and unrewarding"[81] seems debatable: while some women's *lives* were certainly being drained of meaning, women's roles as social icons (which particular women might not have been able to take advantage of) were so fraught with contrasting and portentous meanings as to permit a wider range of possibilities than had ever before been available.

In their reflection of the activities possible to women during the period we are examining, periodicals show that women were to be primarily defined not as individuals, not as daughters or wives (although all of these categories are in evidence), but as mothers—a classification that rather increased than declined in strength toward the turn of the century. For all the social upheaval that separates 1850 from 1910, the terms of the debate over maternity remained remarkably constant, changes in emphasis only throwing into relief the essential continuity of thought on (even across) all sides of the question. To be sure, the late Victorians seem to have devoted more column inches to motherhood than did their predecessors of 1850, while simultaneously their rhetorical flights grew more extreme: women of the 1890s were probably likelier to be described as queens and goddesses than women at any other moment in British history, before or since. But what reached its full growth at the turn of the century was embryonic, not nonexistent, fifty years earlier.

Despite the Victorian and Edwardian interest in defining and redefining manliness, there was no such unanimity on the subject of male roles. It is difficult to argue for any kind of consensus about what characterized the ideal father, in part because so few Victorians seem to have imagined that ideal fatherhood was possible. Significantly, an informal survey of periodical literature will suggest that men were no more likely to be described as fathers than as sons, husbands, or free-standing individuals; the most common criterion for their categorization was probably economic, that of social class. Men, in fact, were not icons.

This lack of a strong symbolization of the man within the Victorian and Edwardian family, something that might correspond to the overwhelmingly forceful image of woman as materfamilias, has had its effect on subsequent scholarship: in contrast to the large bibliography of excellent works written over the past twenty years or so on English women as family members, there are still very few studies of middle-class English men at home.[82] Furthermore, the inability or unwillingness of nineteenth-century commentators to provide their readers with an image of father Adam to match the image of mother Eve seems both cause and effect of an uncertainty about the family man that still plagues us today. While individual men have always managed to construct satisfying answers within their own daily lives, our culture in general works to separate men from the personal and from their children. Thus, for instance, conventional melodramas seem radical if they focus on the nurturing father (as in *Kramer vs. Kramer*); glamorous careers at once promise enormous financial rewards and exclude leisure (family) time, in an exaggeration of Victorian dichotomies; much of psychoanalytic theory depends on the assumption that children undergoing the oedipal crisis will perceive their fathers as unloving; and so on through a seemingly infinite range of cultural details.

The nineteenth century did much to establish this paradigm of negative fathering, and it did so in large part through the fascination with ideal motherhood that this chapter has outlined. The remaining portion of this study will explore the construction of fatherhood that emerges in opposition to that of motherhood, expressed in the contexts of family life, science, law, education, state involvement in child rearing, and sentimental fiction and memoirs. As is the case with the commentary on motherhood, while emphases may change in response to topical concerns, chronology has in general a minimal influence over the expression of images of fatherhood during this period; to a surprising extent the arguments of 1850 are the arguments of 1910. And, perhaps, of 1950 and 2010 as well.

2

The Father in the Family

Is not a father condemning his
children to frivolity by never bringing
to bear on their pursuits the influence
of a manly mind? . . . to work so as
to obtain a father's approbation is
surely the best object that an ordinary
child can look to. Is it not because
their fathers have merely played with,
instead of training them, that our
young ladies so often trench on
the verge, at least, of the rules
of decorum?

I suggested in chapter 1 that the Victorian separation of daily life into public and private spheres did not merely establish two discrete but similar realms. Rather, the values of the private world reversed those of the public. While the marketplace stressed aggression, "self-help," firmness, and materiality, the home emphasized altruism, purity, feeling, and spirituality. The former demanded hierarchy; the latter claimed that true power is located in the meek and unassertive. Women who accepted these ideals, as we have seen, thus found themselves in an advantageous position psychologically, since they could look forward to the day when the domestic ideology would dominate not just in private life but in public life as well. Such a shift represented a longed-for reform, one promised both by Christianity and by "advanced" thinkers of a more secular stripe. Moreover, when women did leave the home for the outside world, they were encouraged to bring the values of domesticity with them. Popular conceptions of female reformers—Florence Nightingale, Elizabeth Fry, Josephine Butler—showed them battling selflessly to transplant the principles of moral good housekeeping into a wilderness of male error.

In contrast, no right-thinking man could claim to look forward to the day when the home would recapitulate the marketplace. Furthermore, men, unlike most women, could expect to shuttle between public and private spheres; the result was often a sort of institutionalized schizophrenia, in which the rules that held in the daytime would be turned inside out for evening and Sunday use. In this context fatherhood played a confusing part because it tied the adult male to the private sphere (which he was supposed to have escaped) without restoring the domestic authority he had enjoyed in earlier centuries.[1] Moreover, for most middle-class Victorian men the home was the only environment in which they had any significant contact with women; their role as husbands and, particularly, as fathers thus forced them to see simultaneously their difference from and their similarity to the "opposite" sex. Both perspectives could be terrifying.

Throughout this period, then, many explications of ideal fatherhood by both men and women attempted at once to link it to and to differentiate it from the stronger ideal it was perforce defined against, that of motherhood. The differentiation could be accomplished in a variety of ways. As we shall see, some writers denied that fatherhood exists in any significant sense; they portrayed men as ghosts within the home, for whom real life could only occur in a nondomestic setting. Others held, with novelist Effie Johnson Richmond, that biological distinctions are so profound as to permit men and women to perform "the *identical tasks*" without risking the erasure of that bodily "difference between them which nothing eradicates, modifies, or alters"; fathers could mirror mothers without endangering their own gender. And a third group stressed that fatherhood and motherhood operate in separate territories of location or authority, complementing each other without overlapping.[2]

Once one has identified these various and conflicting ideals of fatherhood, one seeks in vain for a reliable pattern to pin them to. It is unfortunately not possible, for instance, to determine that high-church Anglicans were likely to see fathers' and mothers' tasks as identical, or to link conservative politics with the "complementary" ideal, or even to say that one ideal dominated early in the period and another at the turn of the century. Certainly individual cases may suggest ideological or chronological matches, but each such case has its counterexample. What seems worthy of notice is rather the breadth of appeal of each of these often contradictory views, so that a conservative male journalist of the 1860s may well be operating from the same basic assumptions as a radical feminist of 1905, while both in turn will disagree with a colleague of their own political stripe writing in the same issue of the same periodical.

Sometimes chronology and politics are indeed important factors, of course, and I will note their influence on those occasions when a pattern does become evident. But in general, the focus in this chapter will be on the longevity and scope of various ideas about fatherhood in this sixty-year span, on the echoes and mirrorings that make themselves apparent, often from unexpected sources. I will argue that the stresses placed on the father's role by maternal domestic primacy, by changing work patterns, by suspicion of masculine biology and masculine preoccupations, and by a host of other interrelated factors, resulted in a fragmentation of voices about the male role within the home. These may in turn be traced in Victorian doubts about the male ability to operate successfully within the nursery, to serve as a moral influence over children to the extent that was possible for women, to discipline the young effectively, or even to perform specifically "male" tasks within the family. If self-control was one of the values most frequently enjoined upon Victorian boys (it was also desirable for girls, of course, but boys often seemed less likely to acquire it), control over the family sometimes seemed to be slipping inexorably from the father's grasp.

Such powerlessness represented a significant shift within the Victorian home. In the preindustrial and especially the evangelical family, in which the father stood "in the place of God" to his wife and children,[3] child rearing and other issues of domestic management were ultimately matters for male concern. Not that fathers busied themselves with toilet training and nursery diet; rather they were the divinely appointed shapers and arbiters of family life, and contravening their will was a pocket version of both lèse-majesté and sacrilege. As the ultimate family authority and moral voice, the father was the presumed audience for child-rearing manuals, which until the eighteenth century typically addressed him rather than the mother.[4] But with the advent of industrialization and the consequent separation of adult males from the household, the hierarchical family lost cultural support. As masculinity came to seem less domestic, it took on what John Demos calls "a certain odor of contamination," lessening the father's perceived right (or even ability) to be the king of the family castle.[5] At the same time, as Leonore Davidoff and Catherine Hall note of the period they examine (1780–1850), godliness came increasingly to be associated with women, who were more likely to attend church and were considered to be "more susceptible to religion"; by the 1850s, the home was often viewed as the site of *woman's* religious mission to the family, not man's.[6]

Thus while the pre-Victorian father took for granted that he would serve as his children's teacher, externalized conscience, and counselor, the model of fatherhood operating between 1850 and 1910 was at once less structured and more narrow. As the ideal mother's prestige and authority increased—and again, to discuss the ideal is not to argue that individual parents invariably conformed to it—the father's traditional areas of power diminished, leaving periodical writers unsure about the nature and extent of the paternal role. The core of this role had long been guidance, authority, and financial support; over the course of this period, however, commentators redefined various aspects of at least the first two components (among them influence, instruction, and discipline) to stress what they considered predominantly feminine characteristics. The more confident such essayists became about maternal primacy and maternal virtue, the less sure they seemed about whether fathers existed to mirror, to complement, to subsidize, or to undercut their partners.

While such doubts resulted in the proposal of a wide variety of roles for the paterfamilias, none of them became culturally dominant. Thus some saw the male parent as disciplinarian, others as playmate; some sought to define his activities in the public sphere in the same terms as his wife's in the private, others to delineate a discrete set of paternal responsibilities; some insisted that he remained the primary instrument of family and social reform, while others viewed him as the primary reason such reform was necessary. And while evangelists of motherhood arose on every side (as the preceding chapter describes) to portray maternity as the salvation of women and even humankind, fatherhood could count itself lucky to find even the occasional apologist. Again and again, critics discussed paternity in terms of absence and lack: for many Victorian periodical writers, the father is simply not there.

Take, for instance, "influence," the Victorian mother's most important if perhaps most nebulous function. Seventeenth-century commentators took for granted the father's primacy of influence over the family; their Victorian and Edwardian heirs had no such certainty. One major difference, of course, was that while the paternal influence of earlier generations had been a matter of discipline and control exerted within a predictable hierarchy, the influence of the Victorian mother was primarily that quality that permitted her to critique the male's domestic performance. As potentially powerful as the commands of the Puritan father, it directed its force toward a subversion of the old order, seeking to control those instincts society defined as masculine: sexuality, competitiveness, egocentrism. Women could also wield influence outside the home; a noteworthy example is their share of the very journalism this study discusses, which gave its authors yet another chance to attempt to mold men's behavior within the private sphere. That men could, and did, reciprocate would not always have compensated for the uncomfortable sensation of being scrutinized.

Men's absence from the home offered writers of the day their first pretext for analyzing the extent of male authority and influence within it via discussions of marriage and parenthood.[7] Early nineteenth-century American advice manuals, Nancy F. Cott notes, depicted fathers as "neglecting their paternal duties in favor of business pursuits" and, like Timothy Dwight's *The Father's Book* (1835), sought "to encourage every father to 'be careful not to underrate his own duties or influence' " within the family,[8] an instruction that earlier ages would have found superfluous. The same pattern is apparent in the periodical literature of mid-nineteenth-century England. An anonymous contributor to the *Cornhill Magazine* in 1869, for instance, linked children's misbehavior to their workaholic fathers' failure to exercise real influence over the home:

> Men toil early and late for their wives and children, and think that they have done well. The man who said that he had never seen his children by daylight except on Sundays, expressed with only a very little exaggeration what is a common state of things. And I say that such fathers do well in their generation as "bread-finders"; but might they not do better, if they lived less in the counting-house and a little more in the nursery and the school-room?[9]

A generation later Mona Caird reprised this idea, voicing concern about the effect on the nation "when men grow absorbed in the business of money-making, and have no time or ability to assist in the development of a higher type of manhood."[10] Men's ideal role here mirrors without equaling that of the mother (they "assist"); their actual role is so separate as to be utterly without effect.

Conversely, the conservative novelist Charlotte M. Yonge hearkened back to a model of evangelical parenting "where the father's loving, yet sometimes grave and stern authority, can really form the child's thought of his heavenly Father" and where " 'Papa' is not only the supreme authority, but the model of all that is good, wise, or noble." At the same time, however, she acknowledged that the working father is unlikely to play more than a symbolic part for his children: "If he be a man of leisure, he ought to do far more for them [than inspire them to do well in order to gain his approbation]; but men of leisure are so very rare, that it is hardly worth while to speak of them." Ultimately the mother's influence is the more important, as "Men can seldom, if ever, make a home by themselves."[11] Yonge's vision of the ideal father apparently correlated exactly with her vision of her own father; even so, she was prescribing for rather than describing the ordinary family, in which, her comments suggest, the reason for the father's role as the object of love and striving is his very distance from his children's daily lives.

By the century's end, "supreme authority" had apparently yielded to simple uninterest. Emma Churchman Hewitt complained in 1897, "The new man seems to feel but little responsibility in household and family matters"; in other words, he lacks that quality of involvement so central to the maternal personality. While men plead the press of business to escape household duties, they demonstrate ever less competence even in the public sphere: "Many a girl is also called upon to-day to help meet family expenses with which her father can no longer cope."[12] In such a situation, of course, male influence must be minimal. Hewitt's compatriot President Charles W. Eliot of Harvard was more tolerant. Although Eliot remarked that "It is obvious at the start that the man is of necessity away from home much more than the woman, and therefore has much less opportunity than has the woman to exert a direct influence hour by hour on the children of the family," he added that a father may still complement and "reënforce the moral and intellectual influence of the mother with the children" by making sure the latter understand that he is "earning the livelihood of the family by punctual, assiduous, productive labor. Such an example is in itself a valuable educational influence on children." [13] Here the mother influences by presence, the father (like Yonge's worker) by absence, an argument at once excusing and recommending paternal separation from the family. But while they stand on different sides of the question, both Eliot and Hewitt see the father as a void within the home.

Less commonly—and particularly in the mid-Victorian period—writers on paternal influence fought to deny this model of absence, working to revive an ever less meaningful model of the patriarchal family. According to an anonymous contributor to *Fraser's* in 1861, not women (who are merely the arbiters of manners) but men have the power "to raise or depress the moral standard, and with the moral standard, the social condition and well-doing of the people" through their control over education. The real source of influence in this formulation is force of character rather than gentleness and purity: "There are few [strong natures] who have no influence over the minds and natures of others; few who, by raising their own standard of virtue, honour, or integrity, do not unconsciously give a higher tone to the society in which they live." Along the same lines, this writer laments the nonhierarchical practices currently in fashion, whereby "it is not unusual to hear a parent discussing with a mere infant the whys and the wherefores, the pros and the cons, of everything which it is required to do," and seeks to replace them with the "laconic 'do this,' and 'do that,' of a [patriarchal] day gone by." [14] The *Fraser's* model was reprised in the *Pall Mall Gazette* of 10 June 1868, which, deeming men to be women's "superiors in every sense in which one class of beings can be superior to another," remarked that "families are in the nature of small governments, and . . . the constitution of these governments should be monarchical, the head being king." [15] Advocates of men's greater influence and worth, however, were decidedly in the minority by this time.

More common, given the strength of the companionate ideal of marriage, was the suggestion that fathers who wanted to do so could certainly make themselves a presence within the home. For this school, paternal influence worked along the same lines as maternal influence, if it did not always have the same force. Those who supported such "mirroring" (who, significantly, tended to be either women or male sympathizers with women's goals) envisioned both "the fathers and [the] mothers of the future generation of sons and daughters" working together to shape the children "while the character is impressionable and habits are still unformed." [16] Not all were as pessimistic as Caird and Hewitt about the level of male interest in the home. "Men's brains are absolutely necessary to progress in domestic matters, and in a hundred ways their influence is seen, from the introduction of machinery to the government of a child's temper," commented the conservative *National Review* in 1889, recommending that fathers concern themselves with the details of children's food and clothing as with the task of character development.[17] Indeed, the involved father was endorsed in every sort of periodical and especially in those catering to woman readers, from the advanced *Englishwoman's Review* ("as man and woman are the two halves of one whole, so the child needs and has a right to the influence both of father and mother") to the more domestic American magazine *Cosmopolitan* ("there [is] something left for [the father] to do which no one else can do so well, and which will supplement and strengthen the influence of the mother on the child").[18]

But just as women predominated among the commentators who argued that paternal influence is an underdeveloped national treasure, women also formed the majority of those who held that paternal influence is generally maleficent. The basis of this criticism was that men could not control their sexuality, a position that gained adherents as the strength of the social purity movement increased. (The movement was fed by the controversy of the 1860s–80s surrounding the Contagious Diseases Acts, designed to save sailors from syphilis by abrogating the civil rights of accused prostitutes; by muckraker W. T. Stead's revelations in 1885 about the white-slave trade and child prostitution; and by a variety of sex scandals involving prominent men, most notably Oscar Wilde.[19]) Thus "A Woman" charged in the *National Review* that church and state conspire to encourage bad fatherhood by absolving men of responsibility and the need for self-control. The 1884 St. Paul's Christmas sermon, she instanced, had made "absolutely no appeal whatsoever to fathers to be original in well-doing, to institute a new order of things, in endeavouring to save their sons from a life of nineteenth-century barbarism." Brought up by ill-disciplined fathers, sons in their turn become faithless husbands and examples of infamy for their children.[20] If male sexuality is poorly regulated, undiscerning, and selfish in its impulses, can paternity rise above these origins?

On the opposite end of the political spectrum from the *National Review* (and considerably more marginal), the feminist publication *Shafts* was likewise doubtful about the quality of paternal influence. A subscriber signing herself "Bereft" wrote in February of 1894 to warn, "Fathers bring home to their children most undesirable thoughts—and so the subtle barriers rise up—the thoughts which draw them into the vortex." The editor, Margaret Sibthorp, held similar views, arguing "that men from boyhood are never taught self-restraint, that they are allowed to acquire all sex knowledge from their own impulses, and the more or less depraved talk of their fellows," whereas women are saved not by an inability to experience desire but by "developing the maternal." Developing the paternal, it would seem, was more rare. While "Motherhood and fatherhood through pure and high love may help us greatly" to achieve utopia, Sibthorp and most of her contributors doubted that fathers, at least, find purity easy.[21]

It was precisely this fear of the "vortex" represented by dissolute fatherhood that caused *Shafts*, like many other periodical voices of the day, to define the sexual education of both genders as the mother's responsibility. Again and again this magazine insisted that the mother should be "the teacher and guide of her children—both girls and boys— in this matter. No other human being is so fitted to instruct in these matters as a mother."[22] Founded in the 1890s, *Shafts* appeared at the right time both to inherit a tradition of debate about sex education for children and to participate in a previously unparalleled amount of discussion on the issue on the part of periodicals. And while *Shafts*, as a radical publication aimed at women and the working classes, never sought to express mainstream opinion, its comments on gender and domesticity echo (at most, amplify) those of writers considerably closer to the political center. In its discussion of sex education, then, this magazine is more unusual in its frankness than in its stance.

The question of who should be in charge of explaining sexual matters to children had long been a delicate one. Mid-Victorians such as Margaret Oliphant, noting the existence of sex manuals that arrogated to themselves the instruction of brides, expressed dismay that "our tender young girls, the margin of innocence, and, if you will, ignorance . . . fringing the garment of the sadder world, should be . . . put up to every possible emergency of all the relationships between men and women."[23] F. W. Newman (brother of the cardinal and himself a prominent classicist and humanitarian), on the other hand, applauded such books for sparing the innocence and ignorance of the *parents*, whose responsibility this instruction would otherwise be: "parents seldom feel themselves strong enough in knowledge to converse freely with their children" on the more "fundamental" aspects of marriage.[24] Similarly, an unnamed contributor to the *British Medical Journal* also supported teaching children about sex while deeming both parents unqualified to "warn and instruct on themes which require the most cautious and delicate handling, and which the rough touch of those who work at second hand and with only partially scientific instruments would inevitably make suggestive rather than deterrent"; the logical provider of firsthand and wholly scientific information should rather be the headmaster.[25]

But for most commentators sex education was a family matter. As male sensuality came increasingly under fire, such training often became the particular concern of the mother, as the parent more likely to understand that sex is for procreation rather than recreation, altruistic rather than selfish. Organizations such as the Social Purity Alliance found her the logical teacher, presumably because, as "A Woman" argued, the father would approach the task "only half convinced that [men] have the same chances of purity as women," while no such doubts would impair his wife's persuasiveness.[26] This assignment of sex education to the female was sufficiently widespread to draw the fire of Eliza Lynn Linton, who found it "just one of the lines of demarcation between the sexes which is becoming blurred and obliterated in the present moral attitude of women"; she chided, "A son would not retail the story of his youthful immoralities to the mother he truly honoured, though he would confide in his father, seeking advice and assistance from the experience and sympathy of sex."[27] A perennial supporter of the double standard and of complementary gender roles, Linton differed from most sex educators in seeking to eliminate not boys' "youthful immoralities" but women's right to discuss them, which she described as prurience masquerading as morality.

Besides institutional and maternal sex education, the other common pattern in this period was for fathers to instruct boys and mothers to instruct girls.[28] Significantly, while many periodical writers thought that mothers should teach even sons about sex, I have found no example of a recommendation that fathers should teach daughters. This anomaly would seem to have had two major causes. First, the form of the instruction usually differed for the two genders. Boys were typically enjoined to continence—or, one might argue, to absence—alike in homoerotic, heteroerotic, and autoerotic circumstances, a lesson that could be expressed vaguely enough to be appropriate when delivered by mothers or before large audiences in a school. Girls were initiated into the secrets of the female physique, perhaps via botany or apiology.[29] Boys, in other words, were learning about sex, girls about motherhood, in the suggestive opposition that pervaded the thinking of the day. Apparently, fathers seemed ill equipped to comment on the latter mystery: sex is an action subject to the nongendered Victorian virtue of self-control, while motherhood is a state of being in which, as I suggested in chapter 1, even women who had never borne children were thought to participate. A second reason for the discrepancy is the significant shrinkage of the father's role as family instructor in all areas during this period, of which his exclusion from this most intimate of topics is but one example.

Overall, indeed, periodical writers indicated that fathers can't, don't, or shouldn't instruct children on any subject.[30] Whereas theorists of the late seventeenth and early eighteenth centuries had held, Demos notes, that fathers "must be centrally concerned in the moral and religious education of the young," even to the exclusion of mothers, the Victorians reversed that principle.[31] Young children, especially, fell to their mothers' tutelage. Thus while Dorothea Beale (principal of Cheltenham

Ladies' College) praised husbands for "generally understand[ing] better
[than wives] the value of education" and approvingly quoted the remarks
of the *Christian Remembrancer* on paternal influence that serve as the
epigraph to this chapter, she denied firmly that "men [can] teach young
children nearly as well as women."[32] This idea had particular force in
the context of pleas for maternal custody of children in cases of legal
separation; for example, claiming that the father "can do hardly anything for [his offspring's] moral or mental welfare until several years are
past," an unidentified commentator in the *Westminster Review* observed
in 1885 that even after a child has left infancy, "The best of fathers has
as a rule, little time to give either to the physical or mental training of
his child."[33] And fathers who make the time may be courting disaster,
an Edwardian writer warned in *Blackwood's:* "I am inclined to think the
father who personally undertakes the daily instruction of his little son
is embarking upon a very hazardous experiment"—partly because boys
resent study, partly because fathers make poor teachers.[34] Whether they
assumed a lack of time or a lack of talent, periodicals typically suggested that men deem primary education a female task and secondary
education a matter for professionals. In other words, men were often
viewed as being absent from the schoolroom, just as at an earlier stage
of the child's life they had been absent from the nursery.

To be sure, examples drawn from life often contradicted this pattern.
In the capsule biographies of notable women that sometimes appeared
in *Shafts*, for instance, fathers might play a prominent part in their
daughters' instruction. Thus the father of educators Matilda and Emily
Sharpe was their primary intellectual influence, "his cultured mind and
mature thought helping and encouraging them to strenuous endeavour
and abiding effort," and their French colleague Elisa Grimailh Lemonnier "always gratefully recognised how much she owed to the way in
which [her father] had awakened in her mind the desire for an active
life of inquiry."[35] But examples of upstanding real-life fatherhood could
not satisfy the commentators on this subject. Pleas for more active male
involvement in child rearing abounded, from Linton's 1869 hope that if
a boy's father should die "a stalwart uncle" might accept the duty of ini-
tiating the child into manly sports and thereby save him from the effemi-

nacy that is the inevitable lot of a widow's only son, to Jean H. Bell's 1910 complaint that for fathers to leave all religious teaching to their wives was "a most unfair shelving of responsibility."[36] Overall, even writers taking the old-fashioned view that it is through the spiritual and temporal "guidance of an earthly father . . . [that children] may be led to a knowledge of their Heavenly one" felt that, in reality, most fathers viewed their didactic responsibilities with "comfortable indifference."[37]

Many commentators held that such "comfortable indifference" is somehow inherent. Where the home was concerned, moreover, this apathy represented not so much "otherness" as incapacity. Some writers saw the problem almost as a physical lack: men are constitutionally incapable of feeling parenthood as deeply as women do. Others argued that the male role in the marketplace precludes significant involvement in the home. "Man can only display the fulness of his character in public life," noted the *Chronicle* in an essay reprinted in the *Victoria Magazine* in 1867, remarking that while the father might be the titular master of the home, "the mastership is of little importance."[38] Another voice in the *Victoria* proclaiming men's incompetence in child rearing was that of the Reverend Charles Dunbar, whose 1872 article comments scornfully, "Fancy a man managing the nursery! As Nature has not provided him with the power (to put it elegantly) 'of nourishing and bringing up children,' he is evidently there as much out of place as a stork would be on the rugged tops of the steep 'high hills'!"[39] The simile suggests that mother's milk is part of a complex system of physical and spiritual nurturance of which, due to his biological deficiencies, the male can be only the recipient, never the supplier. In such a system, gender roles cannot be shared. Even the suffragist J. E. Cairnes, debunking Goldwin Smith's 1874 rebuttal of John Stuart Mill on the grounds that overly separate spheres militate against happy marriages, found convincing "all the substantial reasons of convenience, natural aptitude, and taste, which . . . make it desirable that women should, as a rule, take charge of the domestic half of the world's work, and men of that which is transacted out of doors."[40]

Later writers are as likely as their predecessors to deny men's capacity for deep parental feeling, and again this argument spans political and

gender boundaries. Compare novelist Dinah Mulock Craik's 1887 assertion that men are at once ignorant of "the claim of child upon mother and
mother upon child" and "in general quite incapable" of the demands
of child rearing, "a closer bond and a stronger duty than that towards
any husband," to that of an anonymous writer in *Shafts*, "Fatherhood
is momentary; motherhood prolonged," to that of Nat Arling in 1898,
"A man, not being so necessary as a mother to young children, cannot
exhibit the tender ways of motherhood," and to that of Florence Hayllar
in 1909 that "motherhood and the capacity for motherhood have had
an infinitely greater effect upon women than fatherhood has had upon
men."[41] The respective authors are using these remarks to argue against
divorce, against Old Testament sex bias, for the New Woman, and for
the employment of (maternal) spinsters in the reformation of society—
which diversity suggests the extent of the era's doubt that fatherhood
could have anything like the emotional significance of motherhood.

Clearly this doubt was both result and continuing cause of the doctrine of separate spheres, which located the power of both sexes in men's
virtual exclusion from the home and women's near separation from the
public world. This vision found widespread and varied support, num-
bering among its endorsers not only the Queen but also many prominent
evangelicals, scientists, politicians, and feminists. Nor was it absent
in the details of daily life. For instance, sartorial fashion reinforced it,
exaggerating and hobbling the female shape while replacing the leisure-
oriented male garb of the eighteenth century with the drab uniform still
retained by today's businessman—and emphasizing, as Joan Burstyn
notes, how "All men had come to be valued for their diligence at work."
Historians focusing on the affluent classes have made similar points
about domestic architecture at the height of the period.[42] Although those
feminists whose enthusiasm for the home was beginning to wane might
argue like Caird that parenthood was not a power to be cherished but
a burden to be shared,[43] the belief that mothers have unique talent for
child rearing was far more common. While most Victorians were convinced that the home was essential to the well-being of the father, they
often doubted the converse.

Fears about women's incursions into the public realm were therefore usually expressed not in terms of the havoc women would wreak upon male institutions but in terms of what would happen in the home if women left it. Once the mother's influence faded, it must be replaced with the father's or with nothing. In either case, commentators warned, the result would be chaos: "Man has no aptitude for domestic duties"; "Making mamma attend the law-courts and Exchange . . . while papa stays at home to cook the dinner and nurse the babies, would assuredly be very bad, if not for himself, for the dinner and the babies"; "If the nursing of babies were given over to men for a generation or two, they would abandon the task in despair or in disgust, and conclude it to be not worth while that mankind continue on earth."[44] It is man's incompetence, not women's, that is at issue in such arguments, which indeed often follow an acknowledgment that women could function successfully in Parliament or in the hospital ward. Cartoons in periodicals such as *Punch* also implied that women could go public much more easily than men could go private. As Patricia Marks observes, caricaturists depicted New Women as strong, independent, and analytical, worthy denizens of the public sphere wholly unlike the men who, faute de mieux, take over the domestic space and find that their sojourn in sewing room and nursery has diminished them both in size and in capability.[45]

The ultimate source of this nervousness would appear to be a fear of effeminacy. If sexuality was the true male analogue to motherhood—and Victorian writers saw nothing strange in this idea[46]—then competent, active fatherhood might be analogous to female sexuality, which for many commentators simply did not exist. Could the good father remain potent, especially given the purity reformers' threat to virility? Hence emasculation was one of Linton's perennial concerns: for instance, the widow's sissy son in her 1869 article "Apron-Strings" was reborn in the husband of the working woman or the cigarette-smoking woman in her 1893 "A Counter-Blast," which warned that "with the increased masculinity of women must necessarily come about the comparative effeminacy of men." Another example from Linton is the child of the educational faddist she described in "Viewy Folk" in 1896, who "keeps his son at home, tied to the apron-strings of women—educated by women—his playmates, girls—his toys, dolls—his amusement, worsted work, till, at fourteen, he is emphatically no more a boy in essential manliness than are his sisters."[47]

Likewise, in 1871 William S'Arrac wrote in the correspondence column of the *Englishwoman's Domestic Magazine* that England risks defeat at the hands of an army of androgynes "which in times to come will, unless prevented, immerse for ever in a flood of effeminacy the last remnants of the Anglo-Saxon race."[48] This fate had evidently already overtaken France, to judge by Frederic Marshall's comments in *Blackwood's* the same year; Marshall sketched a society in which maternalism is so pervasive that boys are essentially girls, since "women do not suffice to make men."[49] Goldwin Smith was more sanguine in 1888 as to the likelihood of gender merging in England:

> It is worthy of note that while all these female reformers are exhorting women to become masculine, nobody exhorts men to become feminine. Hector is not bidden to take up the distaff, though Andromeda [*sic*] is incited to grasp the spear. Women themselves appear particularly to dislike and despise an effeminate man. This looks like an involuntary tribute to the judgment and good taste of nature in giving us not one, but two sexes.[50]

To such commentators as Linton and Smith, male domesticity could seem the prelude to Sodom.

Conversely, those writers who supported active fathering and a manly ideal that shared much with womanliness took pains to explain that they were not urging effeminacy.[51] Arguing that "the real individual, the ego, is neither male nor female," for instance, John Ablett urged coeducation in order to heighten the similarities between the sexes and encourage the development in men of the maternal qualities of "gentleness, sympathy, delicacy of feeling, considerateness, [and] self-abnegation." But a major benefit of this exercise, he explained, would be the extinction of "the perverted and abnormal sexuality which is so prevalent among us at the present time," by which he meant not only heterosexual incompatibility but also public-school autoeroticism and homoeroticism, both often thought to undermine virility.[52] A generation earlier, the *Daily News* had analyzed the difference between "womanly" and "womanish," noting that to apply the latter term to a man "is to hold him up to the bitterest contempt. Effeminacy, cowardice, spite, and petty viciousness, are all conjured up," while the former, with its connotations of "goodness of heart, of a nature unspotted by the world, and of trustworthiness unsullied and complete," is complimentary to either sex.[53] The effect is to reassure readers that the "womanly" man, whose characteristics are those of the mother, has no points of contact with his "womanish" alter ego, whose characteristics are those of the negatively stereotyped homosexual.

Such commentary reflects the continued pressure on men during the nineteenth century to display virtues that had become exclusively domestic and consequently exclusively feminine—as long as it was clear that the feminized man was not a homosexual.[54] A number of historians of masculinity have noted that mid-Victorian ideals of Christian manliness, as expressed by (say) Thomas Hughes, were in many ways androgynous in that they valued feeling, piety, self-sacrifice, and other qualities also appropriate to womanliness;[55] Edwardian models of manliness were generally much more sex specific, in part because discussion of homosexuality had become better articulated and thus more threatening. Nevertheless, in the proper circumstances—those in which one's masculinity could not be impugned—it remained possible to endorse old-fashioned androgynous manliness. The question was merely that of defining those circumstances.[56]

But as I argued at the beginning of this chapter, the separate construction of the separate spheres made male androgyny potentially both troubling and essential. If most Victorians were sure that women should remain women, that men had no qualities a good woman ought to want, they were much less sure about the corollary to this rule. Within the home, at least, perhaps a man *should* participate in "feminine" values, helping to rear his children in a gentle, altruistic, sympathetic fashion. This suspicion helped to establish the father as a locus for conflict, placing his two roles in the two spheres at odds, suggesting that his sexual and family lives might undermine each other, creating the consciousness of absence and lack that has dominated much of the rhetoric of fatherhood we have been examining thus far in this chapter. Until now I have concentrated on areas in which the father might be seen as

mirroring maternal functions: moral influence, education. In neither of
these areas, I have contended, could men expect to compete successfully with the ideal of womanhood; nevertheless, many commentators
asked them to try. The remainder of this examination of the father in the
domestic setting will explore ways in which the maternal ideal infiltrated
areas that would traditionally have been considered masculine: work,
discipline, and provision for the family. These "male" provinces, too,
were affected by the new moral primacy of the values of the feminine
private sphere.

The most obvious separation between the middle-class paterfamilias
and his wife was that his forum was the workplace, hers the home. The
question of how well the domestic ideal of selflessness could thrive in the
alien commercial environment—sometimes pessimistically framed, as
in Charles Dickens's *Dombey and Son* (1847–48), to emphasize the extent to which commercial selfishness could infiltrate the home—was of
perennial interest to Victorian commentators. It had special resonance
for two groups. The first consisted of those concerned with the increasing number of working women, who variously feared that motherhood
might lose its virtue or promised that "public mothers" would reform
the marketplace. The second, more relevant here, consisted of those
concerned with defining the benefits or limitations of fatherhood.[57]
One of the latter number, the Scottish historian and essayist John
Skelton, suggested in an 1858 issue of *Fraser's* that it is precisely the
conflict between the male power to earn and the domestic power to expend that creates virtue in the financially challenged father. The shabby
man condemned by a censorious society as a probable wastrel is in
reality "not a bit impoverished; but has gathered love, and pity, and reverence, and grown rich with the years." It is this willingness to give up
comfort for children that saves both fathers and mothers from "the demon
of respectability"; without it, "the best of our young men and women
will continue to grow up into hard, one-sided, calculating machines,
on whom the most potent reformatory influence that Christianity recog-
nises, the family life, is never permitted to act."[58] Likewise, Frances
Power Cobbe also employed a metaphor of opposing influences to con-

trast "the centrifugal force of LOVE, which carries us out of and above ourselves" to "the centripetal force of SELFISM, which brings us back to our own personal interests and desires." While a man yoked to the wrong kind of wife risks becoming "wife-selfish, child-selfish, interested for those who belong to him," love is properly gendered female: unlike spinsters, bachelors can neither make a home nor form deep friendships, as the preeminent male virtue is not love but knowledge. It is thus only through establishing a family life in which money is a matter of indifference that men can attain true feeling.[59]

Many mid-Victorian writers characterized the marketplace as inimical to morality because of its emphasis on success and the ego. Others, however, argued that it need not undermine domestic virtue but might provide the husband and father with the opportunity to practice that unselfishness so central to the ideal Victorian home. Essayists who held this view thus found it possible to support a status quo in which men's perceived self-sacrifice while absent from the home excused a certain amount of self-involvement while present. The *Cornhill Magazine*'s anonymous writer on "Toleration" (1869), for instance, conceded a variety of unattractive male qualities, including apparent lack of feeling and heaviness of mind, but linked them to the demands of the public sphere. Wearisome and worrying, unsympathetic in time of sorrow, the marketplace enforces a persona as unappealing as public life itself; the paterfamilias, the editorialist observed, nevertheless deserves not blame for his deficiencies but understanding for his altruism in facing this debasement for the sake of his children.[60] If such a man cannot fit into the home, he nonetheless enables its existence; indeed, his sacrifice may even be greater than his wife's, since she is not called upon to give up the right to participate fully in family life.

Thus while some who believed in the working father's selflessness argued that his employment for the sake of his family demonstrates his ability to feel all the parental love that characterizes his wife, others contended that it not only demonstrates that ability but kills it. Oliphant, for instance, compared the father's activity as breadwinner to the mother's passivity as "the fountain of life." While both roles demand altruism and the abdication of the adult's "natural liberty," motherhood

changes women fundamentally as fatherhood cannot change men, since
the bachelor and the paterfamilias must both focus their energies on
earning money. Indeed, married men need more money than do the unmarried.[61] Craik was still more specific: Man has nothing corresponding
to woman's "abstract mother-instinct," as his love for children is limited
to his own offspring. But, she noted, this very lack is an important part
of masculinity: "His very selfishness, or, call it selfism, his hardness
and masterfulness, are, in one sense, a necessity, else he would never
be able to fight his way and protect those whom he is bound to protect."
Moreover, his role as protector comes at considerable cost, since for all
his inherent egocentricity ("a thoroughly unselfish man is almost a *lusus
naturae*"), he is liable to be found "toil[ing] all his life at a trade he
hates, yet which happens to be the only calling in which he can earn
the family bread." His sufferings, however, never fit him to play any
role beyond that of provider; Craik omitted all discussion of his possible
interaction with his children.[62]

Still other commentators denied any link between earning and selflessness. Linton's "young man of the period" is wholly a creature of the
marketplace who "resents affection and proclaims home a bore." Far
from learning what work is really for, "he grudges the birth of children
as an additional expense."[63] A generation later, in 1892, Lady Mary
Montgomerie Singleton contended that the man's "more selfish nature"
renders marriage and paternity uninteresting to him; in the first flush
of love he may enjoy the novelty of self-sacrifice, but it will rarely out-
last the beginning of the engagement.[64] Likewise, Arling wrote in 1898
that even in the paternal role, selfishness is man's salient characteristic. To be a father is to be a negative creature, an embodied absence
who takes feeling rather than giving it. Thus fathers of all classes refuse
to spend the money they earn on their daughters—understandably, as
father-love, based on the aggressiveness required for a family's "maintenance and defence," barely exists: "the self-communion, the suffering,
the joy of possession, the feeling of being all in all to another, these
are experiences fatherhood can never touch."[65] And Elizabeth Wolstenholme Elmy, reviewing Frances Swiney's *The Awakening of Women, or
Woman's Part in Evolution* in 1899, approvingly cited Swiney's dictum

that only by leaving their sex behind and understanding "the supreme unselfishness and sublime abnegation of motherhood" can men "emerge from self-centred masculine individualism to the far loftier discipline of a tender sympathetic Altruism."[66] So innate is egotism to the male animal and his activities that only by putting the public sphere behind him and becoming a "mother" can man be saved.

Like influence and instruction, the (un)selfishness of the father outside the home was variously constructed as echoing, complementing, or combating the altruism of the mother within it—an altruism whose existence seemed far more certain, as pregnancy and lactation had shown it to be inherent in the female body, while male physiology appeared to be centered on the self. But the definition of the father's role became still more problematic when men were viewed in the context of the home. In the domestic setting it was considerably harder to depict mothers and fathers as occupying separate spheres; when fathers interacted with children, they came into direct competition with mothers (as opposed to the indirect competition exemplified by the dichotomy between bread-winning and nurturing). Androgynous behavior, with all its terrors for commentators fearing the end of masculinity, became much easier to see, and different roles for the two parents became more difficult to define. Some writers, to be sure, saw nothing distressing in this situation and cheerfully recommended a thoroughly maternal model of fathering; others tried to set the father apart in any way they could. Overall it was the former group whose views became dominant: insofar as men paid attention to their children, this group held that it should be similar to the attention women paid the young. But there was sufficient concern about feminine men and doubt as to the domestic competence of men in general to prevent a wholesale endorsement of involved, androgynous fathering, and many writers assumed that men would have little to do with their children, not simply from want of time but also from want of desire.[67]

The evolution of theories of home discipline over the late nineteenth century exemplifies the shift in assumptions about fatherhood. As Patricia Branca observes, discipline was a vexed question for Victorian child-rearing theorists; after heated debate on both sides (Branca places the

peak of this discussion in the late 1860s), those favoring gentle guidance
and soft remonstrance gradually emerged as the victors.[68] But while the
firmer methods of discipline were likely to be administered by fathers,
the gentler ones were often considered the province of mothers. Thus
while some fathers depicted in periodicals accept the trend toward kindness and adapt their behavior according to a new model of companionate, androgynous parenting, others reject their erstwhile responsibility
and simply yield this territory to their wives.

Middle-class England changed its patterns of discipline concurrently
with changes in its conception of the childish mind. As experts began to
see children as something other than pocket-size adults and to acknowledge the child's right to its own style of behavior and beliefs instead
of insisting on a reproduction of adult styles in everything from clothing to fiction, severity began to lose ground. The doctrine that parents
were responsible to an unbending God for children's sins had encouraged adults to aim at complete control of juvenile minds, leading not
only to a "spare the rod and spoil the child" mentality but to less violent
though equally severe methods of coercion. By 1850, however, when
the *Family Economist* published an extract from Harriet Martineau's
Household Education outlining disapprovingly a father's well-meaning
efforts (in a disciplinary process lasting a full day) to break the will
of his eleven-month-old infant, the style of child rearing described in
the popular evangelical novel *The Fairchild Family* was giving way to
leniency.[69]

Thus when Dinah Mulock (later Craik) commented on this topic in
Chambers's Journal in 1857, she explained that childish misbehavior actually reflects adult faults and thus merits only gentle treatment.
Over-harsh discipline, especially, creates the very flaws it attempts to
address: "Does ever any man or woman remember the feeling of being
'whipped'—as a child—the fierce anger, the insupportable ignominy,
the longing for revenge, which blotted out all thought of contrition for the
fault in rebellion against the punishment?" Mulock offered instead the
example of a man who had brought up three children with "his authority unquestioned, his least word held in reverence, his smallest wish
obeyed" and who attributed his success to "*love*"; what child rearing

demands, she continued, is "purity and truth, self-control and self-denial." The combination of these newly fashionable androgynous traits with the older model of the authoritative father—as well as the assertion that "this law of love" is especially necessary for boys, since they will have to leave the home eventually—suggest an attempt to integrate the new feminine influence into the old hierarchical control.[70]

Andrew Halliday's article on "Fathers," published in *All the Year Round* in 1865, indicates that this combination of companionable influence and authoritarian hierarchy had proved unworkable: the former element, in his view, had overtaken the latter. Comparing modern fathers with their old-fashioned counterparts, who "conducted themselves towards their children as if they, the children, were a lower class, a dangerous class, which it was necessary to suppress and keep down, lest it should obtain universal suffrage and swamp the paternal class altogether," Halliday found that "The British father has undergone a great metamorphosis of late years." Whereas once "almost every father in Great Britain kept a strap, or a cane, for the special purpose of correcting his children," the modern parent "has relaxed his old severity of aspect, and become more human. . . . Love and sympathy and intelligent communion have taken the place of a cold and senseless severity." The class structure operating within the families of the writer's childhood has given way; love has proved a leveling force, and children are no longer "taught, like servants and humble dependents, to know [their] place."

It is important to note that the replacement of the "three-tailed strap" by the "heart" represents the triumph of nature over artifice. While Halliday compared children living under the former system to dogs and mechanical toys, present-day children are fully human in the essay's metaphorical structure. "There is no doubt," the piece concludes, "that the relations which now subsist between parents and children are more in accordance with nature than they have ever been at any previous period of the world's wisdom." It is not the egalitarian father, androgynous in his sympathy and gentleness, but the patriarchal father who is unnatural and anomalous.[71]

Herbert Spencer was also among those attempting to replace authoritarian fathers with more kindly ones, less for the sake of the children's happiness than for the sake of meaningful parental influence. In 1858, a few months after Mulock's article appeared, Spencer commented in the *British Quarterly Review* on the folly of showing anger toward a child: "It weakens that bond of sympathy which is essential to a beneficent control. . . . Hence the numerous cases in which parents (and especially fathers, who are commonly deputed to express the anger and inflict the punishment) are regarded with indifference, if not with aversion." Focusing on the control in preference to the sympathy, Spencer was in full accord with the fashions of the preceding century. (Indeed, his theories draw on those of John Locke.) His ideal father, however, seems softer than his eighteenth-century counterpart, as Spencer's man "makes himself thoroughly his children's friend. . . . possessing their perfect confidence and affection, he finds that the simple display of his approbation or disapprobation gives him abundant power of control." Nor should "abundant power" be unlimited; the friendship between parent and child is one "which avoids needless thwartings, which warns against impending evil consequences, and which sympathizes with juvenile pursuits."[72] If control was still the ultimate aim, sympathy had become indispensable. Making no distinction between the approaches of the two parents (a characteristic also of Halliday's essay), Spencer was replacing a model of specifically paternal punishment with one of androgynous influence.

But even though Victorian opinion in general was tending toward softness in the nursery, it was by no means certain that individual periodicals would consistently take any one side in the debate over the value of a firm approach. For instance, *Fraser's Magazine*, a conservative but tolerant publication, followed "Manners and Morals" with A. K. H. Boyd's "Concerning the Sorrows of Childhood" in 1862, which remarked, "You hear a great deal about parents who spoil their children by excessive kindness, but I venture to think that a greater number of children are spoiled by stupidity and cruelty on the part of their parents," and then with "Our Modern Youth" in 1863, whose unnamed author expressed the contrary fear that parents have abdicated too much of their authority: "Moral discipline . . . is enfeebled by the relaxation of parental rule."[73] It was the latter view, however, that gave ground.

The debate did not confine itself to the issue of corporal punishment, although this question continued to excite interest well into the period. While Mary S. Hartman notes that by the 1840s theorists of child rearing such as Sarah Ellis "were urging that corporal punishment should only be a last resort," she observes also that "harsh canings and psychological humiliation" were common practice for girls as well as boys—a practice reflected in the flurry of letters to the *Englishwoman's Domestic Magazine* in the late 1860s and early 1870s on the propriety of flogging daughters.[74] (One exchange in the *EDM*'s correspondence column, locus of this periodical's debate on the issue, makes a gendered distinction between "mamma's whipping [i.e., spanking]" and "papa and the big rod" before concluding that corporal punishment of any kind should be reserved for lying and then should be inflicted by someone other than the parent.[75]) But as Boyd's article in *Fraser's* suggests, not only "the big rod" but also a variety of psychological disciplines, such as shaming, were coming to seem inappropriate. To be sure, they had always had their detractors; Locke, for one, opposed shaming. By the mid-Victorian period, however, those who preferred the gentle approach were becoming (at least in theoretical circles) the majority. As companionship between parents and children became preferable to hierarchical order, so firm authority gradually gave way to influence as an ideal.

Most writers of the period seem to have been well aware that this shift in child-rearing fashions had replaced the "law of the father" with the gentler rule of the mother. Thus suffrage advocate Millicent Garrett Fawcett argued in 1870 that patriarchy and the new family are incompatible, as "command is blighting to the affections, and . . . where anything approaching the ideal of domestic happiness at present exists, the subjugation of all members of the family to the husband and father is not enforced."[76] Writing at about the same time, barrister Edward A. Carlyon held rather that it is a father's particular responsibility to require obedience, and that modern fathers, who neglect this duty, wrong their families: "Men treat their dogs more considerately than they do their children. They *make* their dogs obey, and the animal is happier for having learned his lesson."[77] Again, at the turn of the century journalist Stephen Gwynn conceded, "I will say this for the modern parent—that this evil [ruling by fear] is far less common than it would appear to have been even half a century ago; the father is not that awe-inspiring person he once was." [78] In each case discipline and authority belong to the father and are perceived to be waning; only the interpretation differs.

By Edwardian days, the trend away from strictness was well established, to the point where some commentators felt that neither fathers nor mothers but children had the upper hand. Among these was novelist Edward H. Cooper, who in a 1903 essay on "The Punishment of Children" observed with a touch of regret that since the founding of the Society for the Prevention of Cruelty to Children (SPCC) violent punishment had become impossible except at boys' schools; in the modern era "Love and patience are the last secret of child management." [79] The exception made for the public schools, usually considered a rigidly hierarchical environment in which women had no overt role, is interesting insofar as it suggests the linkage of male-dominated environments and harsh discipline, as well as the extent to which mainstream family ideology, embracing "love and patience" rather than the cane, had ceased to be male dominated.

Corporal punishment had in fact become a feminist issue, with writers such as Caird contending that it establishes a chain of abused sons who grow up to become abusive fathers and husbands in their turn. Because "the very nursery has been, from time immemorial, the school of violence and brutality," society has imbibed a false ideal of manliness consisting merely of "a spirited willingness to inflict pain and injury on those who cannot hit back." [80] Caird and her fellows feared that by convincing children that force rather than love is the basis of family order, whipping creates a dystopian (and masculinist) domestic paradigm that encourages wife beating and the subjugation of feminine values. Feminist journals were thus particularly apt to report that "love, reason, the putting of things clearly before children, in teaching them and allowing them to find out by youthful experience when they had done wrong, [form] a much more convincing method than birching." [81] Conversely, such commentators as Reginald Brabazon, earl of Meath, who feared that England was becoming soft and feminized, called for a return to "strict and unquestioned discipline in the earliest years, enforced if necessary by what used to be called the wholesome 'encouragement of a slipper'"; Brabazon's watchword was "'the rod and reproof.'"[82] In either case, harsh discipline was associated (for good or ill) with masculinity, gentleness with the ideals of motherhood. Clearly the trend was with the latter.

If the father's role was not to be that of disciplinarian, the most distinctively male function left to him within the family was that of provider.[83] I have described above the ways in which theorists of the period viewed the juxtaposition of home and marketplace created by the father's earning power; it now becomes important to examine more specifically the ways in which fathers were expected to spend their earnings on their children in particular (beyond the requirement that they finance the household in general). Chief among these applications, and another major issue for feminists of both political and domestic stripe, was the education of daughters.

Victorian commentators assumed, with reason, that middle-class fathers fully understood their responsibility to educate their sons. Education—in gentlemanliness rather than in scholastic attainments—was the basis of social rank, and any man who proved unable or unwilling to establish his son on at least the level in the class structure that he himself occupied had failed in his most basic duty as a father. As the *Saturday Review* put it in 1858:

> For a man who has had the prolonged and elaborate education of an English
> gentleman, there could hardly be a greater mortification than to see his
> sons growing up around him under circumstances which would prevent
> them from understanding him, or which would force him to descend to a
> lower level, moral and intellectual, than that to which he was bred.[84]

Family pride and paternal affection are intertwined here: loss of honor is measured by the extent to which communication between father and sons has become difficult.

But while a gentleman's education was intended to fit him not only to meet the "moral and intellectual" demands of his particular level but also to take up a career, at the beginning of this period a lady's commonly taught her only to fill unlimited amounts of leisure time.[85] To be a wife and mother was the only career a conventional middle-class girl expected, and wives and mothers, in the popular view, should not *act* but *be*. Moreover, as most professions were then closed to women, a respectable father who prepared his daughter to earn her own living was almost invariably encouraging her not only to unwomanliness but also to social descent. Thus when *Punch* observed in 1852 that "benevolent men and fathers of families, in England, for the most part, bear too much love and too much respect for their daughters to think of allowing them to walk the hospitals, and wield the scalpel," the point was not merely that only an immodest woman would study anatomy, but also that a self-supporting woman could not be considered a lady.[86] Partly as a response to the changes in assumptions about parental roles, however, the periodicals' stance on this issue was about to reverse itself.

One problem, as Caroline Cornwallis observed in 1857, was that mothers educated to be "mere drawing-room ornaments" were incapable of exercising adequate authority over their children. In her analysis of family dynamics, fathers are marginal: it is the lack of a strong *mother* that leads sons to "run a wild career of vice and folly, which a prudent female adviser might have prevented" by advising sexual continence.[87] Girls should be brought up to understand business but still more to reach their full potential as the more strong-minded sex, the better to reform both their families and society as a whole. By implication, then, mothers are being educated to take on the role formerly arrogated to fathers, principally because fathers no longer seem to be filling this position. Even writers who disagree that women should be encouraged to operate in the public sphere, such as the author of the 1862 *Fraser's* article "Female Labour," often conceded mothers' dominance: "If they stand apart from the busy throng, it is only that they may appeal more loudly to all that should be mightiest over the soul of man."[88] Given such a destiny, a girl must clearly be trained to more than the simple exhibition of accomplishments. What she now had to provide was not performance but direction.

If one school of thought regarding female education focused on fathers' impotence and the need for strong mothers to fill the void, another focused on fathers' selfishness or shortsightedness. Writing in 1857, Mulock disparaged the practice of bringing daughters up to be merely "papa's nosegay of beauty to adorn his drawing-room," pointing out that "the Father of all has never put one man or one woman into this world without giving them something to do there, in it and for it." The biblical disjunction visible here between Mulock's earthly father, burying his daughters' talents in the home, and the heavenly Father whose intentions were quite otherwise, suggests the significant shift that by 1857 has moved us away from earlier family hierarchies: the father is no longer God's simulacrum in the home but his faithless steward.[89]

Similarly, numerous writers commented on fathers' criminal folly in believing marriage to be the inevitable fate of daughters. The widening gender gap in Britain's middle-class population (caused in part by the exodus of eligible bachelors to participate in assorted foreign and/or imperial adventures) meant that an increasing number of women could expect never to marry. "What shall we do with our old maids?" was not simply a catchy headline but a serious concern. Thus Irish barrister H. J. Wrixon, for one, explaining that it is a father's responsibility to bring his daughters into the family business, inveighed in 1862 against "the pernicious idea that marriage is with us, in this nineteenth century, the only business of women in life—the final cause of their creation"; circumstances have shown that this is not the case, and the only solution is to ensure that women can find employment compatible with membership in a family.[90] Martineau, on the other hand, was one of a substantial group of strong-minded women less concerned with the maintenance of the working woman's femininity than with the maintenance of the woman herself. Observing in 1864 that "there must be tens of thousands of middle-class women dependent on their own industry," she accused English fathers of parsimony and partiality: they "grumble over paying five-pound notes for their daughters' educations, while cheerfully spending hundreds a year for their boys," and die leaving the daughters both destitute and helpless.[91]

The fear that fathers would prove incapable of providing for their families undercut two of the most important qualities commonly considered masculine during this period: financial acumen and the sense of justice. Women's advocates complained that it is as "cruel and careless of a father to neglect to teach his daughter a trade, if he cannot leave her a fortune, as if he had left his son similarly unprovided."[92] The implied accusation of arbitrariness and lack of foresight denied the male's traditional claim to a fair-mindedness not found in women. Men who exceeded their income were deemed criminal, as in Maria Theresa Earle's comment in 1904 "that the father who lives in luxury in spite of debts and conceals this fact from his children is quite as much to blame as the son who spends money behind the father's back, hoping to rob his sisters and pay his debt."[93] In such formulations money has become not something men supply for their families but something men prevent women from acquiring, not the fruit of competition but the wellspring of independence.

Specifically, of course, it is independence from men that is at issue: the economic mark of a bad father is that he seeks to keep his daughters forever children,[94] preventing them from fending for themselves and forcing them into the power of husbands (in this context operating as surrogate fathers) who may also prove irresponsible. Justice, as women's advocates pointed out in a variety of contexts, demands equality. Furthermore, as I shall argue in a later chapter, a major tactic in the fight for women's legal equality was the publicizing of images of bad fatherhood. The proliferation of comment about men's reluctance to provide for their daughters the same opportunities that they provided unquestioningly for their sons was an important factor promoting the education and employment of women. At the same time, this reluctance would not have been considered worthy of note if fatherhood (or male responsibility in general) had not already been under siege. Only a widespread sense that men might be "absent from fatherhood"—unwilling or unable to perform their appropriate economic function—could allow the proposal that daughters as well as sons should be trained to occupy the paternal role of breadwinner.

Clinical psychologist Jonathan Bloom-Feshbach has theorized that "societies in which mothers dominate early childrearing may create strong feminine identifications in males and foster more authoritarian expressions of power in adult men—a cycle that would lead to further paternal reluctance to engage in nurturant parenting behavior."[95] This hypothesis helps to explain the tension between the Victorian quest for moral androgyny (for instance, in social-purity campaigns) and the simultaneous fear of male effeminacy and female aggression as the separate spheres began to collide. But the situation in Victorian and Edwardian England is complicated because, as an examination of periodical articles shows, the deification of motherhood was so intense as to discourage the "authoritarian expressions of power" that men might have used as a counterbalance. Rather, men were urged again and again to behave more like mothers in both the private and the public sphere and to acquiesce in women's efforts to share and to adapt male power (for instance, in household discipline and access to careers). Nor do these injunctions seem to have fallen on deaf ears; recently historians have begun to provide examples of Victorian families that appear—insofar as contemporaneous evidence can be trusted—to have conformed to ideals of paternal nurturance.[96]

While the question of the extent to which individuals may have lived up to the new ideals of fatherhood falls outside the scope of this inquiry, it remains necessary to consider more specifically the techniques by which these ideals were made to appear attractive. We have seen many examples of negative reinforcement at work, all driving home the idea that fathers have no right to anything but nominal domestic authority because they have no talent or no time to exercise such power. But the task of positive reinforcement—persuading fathers at once to abandon their authority and to remain involved with their children under maternal direction—was more delicate. Such men had to believe that their surrender of power would be recompensed by the discovery of new springs of feeling, new avenues of communication. These could occur between husband and wife, as the man's acknowledgment of women's abilities (underscored by his abdication in the home) made possible a companionate marriage; they could occur between father and child, as the old regime based on fear gave way to a new one based on trust; or they could occur internally. Boyd Hilton notes that the evangelical attitude toward charity answered "at least as much the spiritual needs of the giver as the material needs of the poor";[97] the same could be said of the supporters of paternal nurturance, who emphasized not only the greater happiness possible to children under this system but also the new enlightenment possible to fathers who supplied their own lacks by imitating maternity.

In the antihierarchical structure of the new family, writers promised, men would find salvation. It would come not merely from the altruism fostered by working to support others but also from the contact with the purity and innocence of childhood. The credo Boyd professed in 1862—"Oftentimes, I believe, when the worn Man is led to [Christ] in childlike confidence, it is by the hand of a little child"—found expression again and again throughout the period.[98] Such salvation was not always couched in religious terms: thus Linton saw "the sweeter influences of the family" as a lotus-land after "a hard day's struggle in the arena"; Frederic Adye promised "chasten[ing] and elevat[ion]" from being near children (at the same time wondering, "From how many a virile mind has a certain grace been missing through lack of some such refining influence?"); and philosophy professor James Sully noted simply "the humorous banquet which nature has provided for us in child-talk."[99] Commonly, these benefits cannot coexist with masculine domestic power; the father who insists on acting as disciplinarian or divinity is prepared neither to be influenced nor to be amused.

It is not enough, then, to observe that the ideal of the father seemed to be waning in power during this period. What Barbara Fass Leavy astutely describes, in her examination of the mid-century *British Mother's Magazine*, as "a growing conviction of his passivity and relative ineffectualness"[100] was also, in some instances, a recommendation: the more passive the father, the more likely that he would accept the guidance of his wife and even his children, to the benefit of himself, his family, and society at large. By constructing the paterfamilias in terms of absence and lack, in other words, cultural commentators could rewrite him in terms of the much stronger presence, that of the ideal mother. Writers thus often made clear, in the *British Mother's Magazine* as elsewhere, that the advice they offered to mothers applied to fathers too.[101] The power struggle that was occurring was further complicated by the Victorian ambivalence toward power, which for many appeared synonymous with moral danger and corruption. True power, perhaps, was worldly powerlessness, as the force of the "Angel in the House" icon makes evident. In short, ideals of power were themselves changing; it was no longer authority but influence that was wanted, and not control but true feeling would be its reward.

3

Science
and the
Father

With man, then, both paternity
and love of children were borrowed
factors, supported and moulded
by social or sentimental necessities
which were chiefly created by woman,
and which took ages to develop
into sufficient coherence to make him
co-operate effectively with the primitive
woman in the career of child-care,
which is the basis of the family. . . . To
this day it is the fathers who
abandon their young.

If Victorian and Edwardian domestic commentators differed as to the degree of involvement appropriate to fatherhood, their scientific and medical counterparts experienced much less doubt on this issue. In the shadow of Charles Darwin, paternity was first and last a matter of biology. The burning question of the age was that of heredity; and if children simply recapitulated the characteristics of their forebears near or remote, parental influence became more or less trivial once the children had left the womb. Science—overwhelmingly the province of men—thus stood in opposition to the more humanist and woman-oriented school of writers on the home, who saw environment as the most significant factor in shaping the life of any individual. For Darwin's heirs family had to give way to lineage or race.

While science minimized the family environment, it treated inactive fathering as normative, holding, as Jonathan Bloom-Feshbach puts it, "that fathers were comparatively unimportant in family functioning and childrearing."[1] Thus anthropologists traced the evolution of marriage customs to kinship patterns in which the father was invisible; students of instinct explained that while the maternal instinct was the basis of civilization, the paternal instinct was a late and trivial acquisition; eugenists preached that fatherly responsibility is at its peak before fatherhood is achieved. While social-purity agitators touched the fringes of the medical world with their discussions of (predominantly male) sexuality, proffering the mother as a model of virtue for both genders, the medico-scientific establishment as a whole assumed both the preeminence and the uninterest of the father, constructing personal influence as insignificant for the family in comparison to the blind tide of genetic inheritance.

All of these strands perhaps ultimately had their source in constructions of sexuality. Victorian interest in the mother was overwhelmingly
directed toward her ability to create a psychological environment for
her family; in contrast, nineteenth-century science saw the father's contribution as biological. Thus when the medical establishment, for instance, considered paternity, it primarily focused on creating the best
possible circumstances for fertilization, and the major areas of debate
were the effects of nonreproductive sex (such as homosexuality, masturbation, or contraception) and parental ill health (whether the wages
of sin or the wages of poverty) on the unborn. But medicine was more
likely to consider mothers in terms of their existing children, sometimes
by castigating women for the maternal ignorance that supposedly lurked
behind rising infant mortality, sometimes by joining with them in an
attempt to control "unhealthy" behavior in older children through equat-
ing immorality with physical weakness.[2] Doctors thus reinforced the
idea that the mother is the only significant parent in the child-rearing
process; in Victorian medical opinion, the father's effect on the child's
health typically ended at conception.

Given the intensity of Victorian and Edwardian concern about childhood and social reformation, impregnation and its antecedents became
scientifically fascinating on a newly grandiose scale. The sexual drive,
usually considered in its relation to masculinity, appeared as a social
force of awesome destructive power, leaving in its wake prostitution, disease, and overpopulation, to name only a few evils. Observers tied these
abuses of sexual energy to men's inability to limit their reproductive
drive to the family context. Social critic W. R. Greg, for one, depicted
the patrons of prostitutes as well-to-do men unwilling to abandon "the
habitual indulgences of a bachelor's career, for the fetters of a wife,
the burden of responsibility of children, and the decent monotony of the
domestic hearth. They dread family ties more than they yearn for family
joys." Conversely, suffragist Florence Balgarnie speculated in 1887 that
women's greater ability to control their "animal passions" resulted from
their greater sense of parental responsibility: "they suffer the consequences in child-bearing."[3] While for middle-class women domesticity
and sexuality were inseparable, middle-class men were all too likely to

bring sex into the public sphere, in another (and crucial) manifestation of the male "absence" from paternity that chapter 2 broached. Men's inability to commit themselves wholly to domesticity, their oscillation between home and marketplace, appeared as both effect and cause of a male sexual drive that often linked sex and finance and separated sex and parenthood.

Significantly, when men could be brought under institutional control, aberrancies might be addressed by attempts to impose "feminine" sexual patterns and family roles. Hence David Pivar notes the support of woman doctors for the castration of rapists, which would "free the sex offender from criminal drives."[4] "Criminal drives," perhaps, were common to all men; the impulse behind rape was thought to be not one of violence, as we perceive it today, but merely an extreme level of desire. (To those Victorians who denied that normal women could experience desire, indeed, any sexual advances toward women were necessarily a form of violence.) The issue was not so much that most Victorians denied the existence of a female sex drive as that they found female sexuality qualitatively different from its male counterpart. Men, they argued, sought release; women sought to provide pleasure or to become pregnant.[5] The same "take and give" dynamic operated in the bedroom that distinguished masculinity from femininity in the world at large. And again, femininity often seemed morally superior and socially preferable. For women, then, parenthood redeems sexuality; for men, sexuality blights parenthood.

Another suggestive case is the Alabama Insane Hospital (opened in 1861), which, as John Starrett Hughes explains, sought to treat not only patients but their friends and families by placing both male and female inmates in a mock-domestic setting, thus providing a " 'feminine' example [that] might reform society as well as the individual deviants."[6] Even when prostitution or syphilis were not at issue, unchecked male sexuality was thought to destroy both its objects and its hosts. Alabama psychiatrists were not the only professionals to deem the male sex drive a major cause of insanity; physicians on both continents had long warned that masturbation, among other nonprocreative sexual practices believed to be more typical of boys or men than of girls or women, led to mental illness. Thus the *British Medical Journal,* inveighing in 1882 against public-school "immorality," explained "that real insanity is often caused in this way, and that mind-disease short of actual alienation often results from what Dr. Mortimer Granville . . . calls 'mental debauchery.' " [7] Even unfulfilled desire was enough to drive men mad.

Periodical writers joined in the general condemnation of male sexuality as antidomestic. Attacking the double standard, poet and feminist Louisa Shore asked in an 1874 *Westminster Review* whether, if men were not kept from creating and patronizing prostitutes, readers could be "so very sure that even this one-sided purity will always be maintained? Is it certain that no moral contamination from men's earlier associations ever enters [the home]? Are we sure that the house built on such a foundation will always stand firm?" [8] Shore depicted men as the agents of a sex-based pollution gradually corroding the feminine institution of the family; she argued that sex is a form of aggression that renders impossible the gender equality that should underlie both the home and the nation.

Such rhetoric typically assumed equivalences between the male, sex, and selfishness and between the female, family values, and altruism. Thus "A Woman" contended in the *National Review* some ten years after Shore's article had appeared that the double standard, reinforced by generations of male immorality, had led to the deterioration not only of the masculine character but also of domesticity:

> Had generations of fathers and masters but fulfilled their duty towards the youth placed under their charge, the philanthropist's suggestion of a Wife-beaters' Bill and a Disowned Childrens' [*sic*] Act would now be needless, the files of the Divorce Court would be less full, and men blessed with fine generous qualities, would less frequently prove themselves to be bad husbands and unsafe guides to youth. Few men allow themselves to reflect that the responsibility of the nation for hideously monotonous vice rests on the heads of successive generations of careless fathers and guardians. [9]

Male sexual responsibility, in this formulation, mainly consists of enjoining sons to continence, a duty fathers have refused to perform, thus forcing mothers to take it on. Men can only be integrated into the successful family, it would seem, by preferring maternal purity to paternal license. Or as another woman writer put it in *Shafts* in 1893, "We women must be true to our motherhood, and teach men to be true to their fatherhood, and fight the demon of life in married life as [well as] outside its bonds."[10]

Nor was this vision of male sexuality as the home's enemy limited to women. Herbert Jamieson, for one, applauded in 1899 the sexual knowledge of the modern wife, which enabled her to keep her husband under tight control instead of naively allowing him to "wade to [his] rope's end of impurity"; the most important result of women's new sophistication (achieved not through practice but through novel reading and social frankness) was that "finer sincerity between man and woman, on which the happiness of married life depends."[11] Greg's *Westminster Review* article on "Prostitution" half a century earlier suggested that the transaction concerns "a brutal desire on the one side only, and a reluctant and loathing submission, purchased by money, on the other"; his prostitutes (at worst frail, at best saintly) are often working only to save their families from starvation in a desperate manifestation of "filial and maternal affection." It is the seducer or customer, not the "girl," who betrays purity, nature, and family values.[12] Similarly, W. T. Stead's "Maiden Tribute of Modern Babylon" 1885 *Pall Mall* series was shocking not only because of its titillating descriptions of bound virgins and its appeal to proletarian rage but because it too placed moral responsibility for the fragmented working-class families discussed (even those in which the parents willingly sold their children into sexual slavery) primarily with the "respectable" male customer.[13]

Some purity reformers concentrated their fire on sex outside the marriage bed—on prostitution, masturbation, homosexuality, and illegitimacy—feeling that desire within marriage was desire controlled. They often tried to persuade men to virtue via arguments centering on fatherhood. Perceived as the daughters of men whom poverty, drink, or crime had deprived of control, prostitutes served as the objects of an analogous but more reprehensible lack of control on the part of middle-class men. In victimizing such women, men not only committed a form of symbolic "incest" by abusing the power bestowed on them by their greater

wealth, position, and probably age (reformers usually depicted prostitutes as young women in their teens or early twenties) but also brought
the consequences of their failure in self-government back to their own
families in the form of venereal or moral disease. The latter risk applied
also to masturbatory or homosexual activities, even when these took
place years before marriage. Perhaps their most publicized danger was
that the boy who engaged in them was jeopardizing his ability to father
healthy children.[14] As for illegitimate offspring, the law recognized only
their mothers' responsibility and claim; the man who sired a child outside marriage was the ultimate absentee parent, being legally no father
at all.

But because it was clearly the most usual of sexual forums, other reformers focused their efforts on sexuality within marriage. Again it was
men who posed the danger, because it was men who were assumed to
initiate sex. Their hunger for gratification brought with it the possibility
that their wives would become pregnant, and, as both reformers and
physicians were aware, excessive childbearing was a major strain on
women's health and a principal cause of sickly children. (In the words
of Frances Albert Doughty in 1903, "More vital energies, moral, mental, and physical advantages . . . will be transmitted to posterity by
three or four highly individualised, well-equipped representatives of a
family, than by eight or ten poverty-stricken weaklings and degenerates."[15]) The same was true when marriage occurred too early; Greg
voiced prevailing opinion in observing that "the power of procreation in
the human animal, consistently with the conservation of full vigour in
the parent and the transmission of due vigour to the offspring, is rarely
attained before twenty-five, and never before twenty-one."[16] In addition,
children were becoming increasingly expensive in monetary terms, and
many writers expressed concern about the average middle-class father's
ability to provide adequately for a large family.[17]

To be sure, not all commentators believed that men should add to their
families late and seldom; some argued that the moral benefits for men of
early marriages and many children—the purifying influence of domesticity, the encouraging of sacrifice—outweigh any drawbacks. For those
who did see a need for checks within the family, however, the question

was whether these should be internal, in the form of moral control, or external, in the form of birth control. In other words, Victorian family planners were having to choose between a model of sexuality they perceived as female, in which sex was primarily reproductive, and one they considered male, in which sex existed for pleasure and should have no consequences. The first was the pattern of the ideal mother, the second that of the irresponsible bachelor.

To writers who acknowledged women's moral superiority, birth control seemed a national disaster, a license to libertinism. The anonymous author of "Chastity: Its Development and Maintenance" (1880) warned that

> the difficulty of enforcing male astriction has been that paternity has carried with it no physiological responsibilities, and now it is proposed to reduce woman to the same irresponsible condition by making her, artificially, neuter. . . . Obviously, immunity from procreation and parental responsibility will invite the multiplication of ephemeral partnerships, and, hence, a gradual social change will supervene which must have very profound results, especially on child-care.[18]

Likewise, when Geoffrey Mortimer published an article in *Shafts* arguing that the answer to sexually demanding husbands was birth control, an anonymous respondent objected to the idea that the wife should employ "'scientific checks' to enable the husband to indulge himself without restraint"; the real remedy was "the extermination of . . . lust . . . the teaching of true chivalry and purity of life." Birth control would undermine the ethical superiority of womankind: "Hitherto wives, at least, have been taught the true doctrine that the wonderful gifts of motherhood were to be kept for use alone and not profaned to sensual purposes . . . though men have been permitted to degrade their corresponding gifts of fatherhood."[19]

But if the feminist impulse was often to reject the sexual revolution promised by advances in contraception, in some cases—notably that of Annie Besant, who with Charles Bradlaugh was convicted on obscenity charges in 1877 for publishing a birth-control manual entitled *The Fruits of Philosophy*[20]—feminists accepted "scientific checks" eagerly as a way to liberate women from excessive maternity. Science, likewise, was of two minds; while physicians warned that birth control (like masturbation) would lead in women to "unsexing," madness, or death, eugenists such as Montague Cookson (later Crackanthorpe) contended that "such [family] limitation is as much the duty of married persons as the observance of chastity is the duty of those that are unmarried."[21]

Meanwhile, the rising sales figures of birth-control books (Besant's, for instance, sold 40,000 in its first three years and 175,000 by 1891) and the falling birth rate suggested to Victorian and Edwardian commentators that either contraception or continence, and perhaps both, had come to stay.[22] Noting that "family size declin[ed] from about six for couples married in the decade of the 1860s to about four for the 1900 cohort," F. M. L. Thompson suggests that late-Victorian spouses were practicing not only coitus interruptus and its rarer, more technological counterparts but also abstinence; illegitimacy rates were falling, too.[23] The subject of contraception during this period is both complex and well-traveled.[24] But for the purposes of this discussion, let it suffice to note that while social reformers (many feminists among them) usually recommended continence and imperialists tended to call for unchecked family growth, medicine was reluctant to endorse either the "unnatural" solutions of artificial birth control and abstinence or the expensive and dangerous one of large families, and younger scientific movements such as eugenics and sexology generally applauded birth control as a means of preventing undesirable pregnancies and of legitimating male desire. Each position exemplified a different way of looking at parenthood; of them all, the last most strongly implied a minimal role for the father within the family by subordinating paternity to husbandhood.

Furthermore, writers with scientific pretensions were increasingly wont to combat criticisms of masculine desire with criticisms of feminine "repression." As Margaret Jackson notes, the work of sexologists such as Havelock Ellis "can be interpreted as part of a response, however unconscious, to the threat to male power posed by the feminist onslaught on male sexuality."[25] Ellis and his confreres sought to justify existing patterns or at any rate to prove that the fetish of social purity was at least as much a warping of natural behavior as male sexual aggression was. If both conservatives and feminists usually held, like Dinah Mulock Craik, that "Mercifully for the world, very few women can in the least understand that side of a man's nature, in which the senses predominate over or are perpetually fighting with the soul,"[26] the new biology of the 1890s thought otherwise. Again, the battleground was often not the general one of "nature" (male or human) but the particular one of parenthood. What role, writers wondered, does sexuality play in the family?

The novelist and writer on popular science Grant Allen, for instance, maintained in his controversial article "The New Hedonism" that the sex instinct is not the enemy but the source of family delight, to which "we owe the paternal, maternal, and marital relations; the growth of the affections, the love of little pattering feet and baby laughter; the home, with all the associations that cluster round it; in one word, the heart and all that is best in it." While Allen held that a father's first duty is not nurturance but self-development—"to make his own muscles, his own organs, his own bodily functions, as perfect as he can make them, and to transmit them in like perfection, unspoilt, to his descendants"— he saw this concern with biology as equally binding on mothers.[27] The new family was primarily a physical rather than a moral unit. Likewise, calling for "Education in Sex" in 1904, Vere Collins condemned not only the "arid voluptuousness" of uncontrolled masculine desire but the "repressed instincts" of overly pure wives: "what should be regarded as natural and wholesome becomes associated with morbid introspection, leading often to ugly and morose secrecies," prostitution, and "domestic misery."[28] The ideal mother, one gathers, is as dangerous to the home as the anti-ideal father.

At least until Sigmund Freud became a household name, to be sure, such claims were by no means dispositive. Physicians could still argue, like Elizabeth Blackwell, that the health of father and child alike depends on men under twenty-five remaining chaste; purity reformers such as Ellice Hopkins could invoke medical authorities to prove that the reason "insurance offices value a young man's life at twenty-five . . . at exactly one-half of what it is worth at fourteen" is the deadly effect of "the indulgence of the passions in youth."[29] Nevertheless, the general ten-

dency of scientific theory was toward an acceptance of male sexuality as
healthy and even as the cornerstone of human society. Precisely because
a "feminine" absence of desire had been constituted by social reformers as the ideal rather than the norm, "masculine" desire appeared to
scientists as natural. And increasingly, what interested scientists was
not the family decreed by God but the behavioral patterns decreed by
nature.

While some purity reformers began to counter this trend by arguing that all desire was in fact unnatural, others recognized a need to
focus their warnings not on the unhealthiness of the male sex instinct in
general but on venereal disease in particular. Like sperm, the syphilis
bacillus was seen as requiring an active partner (male) and a passive
partner (presumably female) for transmittal; syphilis was therefore a
useful metaphor for male sexuality as well as a direct reminder of the
wages of sin. And like the cautions about sexuality, the cautions about
syphilis centered on its effect on the family. Disease became for purity
reformers a symbol of adult male irresponsibility toward wives and children, a vehicle by which fathers destroyed their offspring. Merging
with and overtaking the mid-Victorian anxiety about prostitution, it also
became a rallying point for the feminist and purity movements.[30] The
"Great Scourge" that radical suffrage leader Christabel Pankhurst tried
to parlay into the vote was the subject of an international conference in
Brussels in 1899 and a major focus for eugenist concern about national
degeneracy.

Richard Davenport-Hines juxtaposes quotations illustrating the development of thought on syphilis from the mid-Victorian period to the
early twentieth century. In 1860 Samuel Solly, a prominent surgeon
and professor of medicine, could record in the *Lancet* his belief that
the disease is "a blessing . . . inflicted by the Almighty to act as a
restraint upon the indulgence of evil passions." But by 1904 another
physician, Sir Victor Horsley, was focusing on its effect on the race, as
medical advances were permitting more syphilitics to "produce stunted
and diseased offspring"; Davenport-Hines remarks that "he stopped
short of advocating that they be forcibly sterilized, 'though I think they
deserve to be.'"[31] The switch in emphasis from individual morality to

racial health is emblematic of the change in medical thinking on purity, which, Edward J. Bristow writes, mirrored "the contemporaneous shift from 'internal' social Darwinism, the doctrine relating to competition between individuals, to 'external' social Darwinism, which emphasised the struggle between nations."[32] Increasingly, science was moving the bounds of the family outward, reassigning the father's importance from his immediate circle to the empire.

The link between male sexuality and disease, as Angus McLaren has noted, became the most potent weapon in the feminist arsenal. While some eugenists still argued that syphilis was best countered through the suppression of prostitutes, public opinion generally held that the answer lay in controlling men. McLaren hints at the reason for the success of the feminist and reformist stance when he cites Charles N. L. Shaw's "The Supreme Menace," published in the *Penny Illustrated Newspaper* on 10 September 1910: "the 'father of the race' was depicted as picking up germs in the underworld and passing them on to his innocent loved ones."[33] Prostitutes, in the popular stereotype, were not mothers; that their customers were perceived as the nation's future fathers literally brought the threat home.

Although it reached its peak at the turn of the century, concern over the ability of sinning fathers to poison not only their children but their remote heirs was in evidence throughout the period. Writing in 1857, Caroline Cornwallis warned that the young man who leaves his home because of financial pressures "learns at length to waste his strength and his means upon harlots, and hands down an uneradicable taint in the blood of his unfortunate descendants, which may undermine the health and the faculties of his posterity for generations to come."[34] Such statements pervaded mid-Victorian rhetoric. Physician and *Westminster Review* editor John Chapman, for instance, applied to syphilis in 1869 "the terrible declaration that 'the sins of the fathers shall be visited on the children to the third and fourth generation.' . . . [syphilis] is slowly, but surely, destroying the health and strength of the British people"; Craik pleaded in 1887 for legal separation in cases where fathers have brought into the family "an hereditary curse, which may not be rooted out for generations."[35] And as Gail Savage has shown in her study of divorce between 1858 and 1901, the general sense that men rather than women were the nexus of disease in the domestic context gave wives who wished to end their marriages a rare legal advantage: women's suits were much more likely than men's both to complain of venereal disease and to succeed if disease was cited.[36]

Given such a level of concern, whether about the father within the family or about the father as a factor in imperial strength, the popularity of the eugenics movement is hardly surprising. Negative eugenics—the effort to discourage the unfit from reproducing—had a particular advantage in that it appealed at once to feminists' suspicion of male sexuality, to purity reformers' desire to keep the family free of carnal taint, and to the medico-scientific establishment's inclination to separate "natural" masculinity from the sentimental bonds of the Victorian domestic ideal. In contrast, positive eugenics—the effort to encourage the fit to breed—had a narrower audience drawn primarily from the last-named group. Because it ran to suggestions such as that of Grant Allen in "The Girl of the Future" (published in the *Universal Review* in May 1890) that women should reject traditional marriage for serial monogamy in order to maximize their chances of bearing perfect children, it had limited attractiveness for conservatives or for those interested in widening women's opportunities in the public sphere.[37]

But although the popularity of eugenic thought relied partly upon older movements having little to do with science and much to do with ideals of domesticity, both strands of eugenics were heavily colored by their scientific pretensions, which in turn helped to reinforce the eugenists' rejection of active fathering as irrelevant. The movement's undoubted charm for women (out of a council of twenty-three listed on the masthead of the first number of the *Eugenics Review*, eleven were women) related not to any endorsement by eugenists of nurturant motherhood as a psychologically meaningful act but rather to a biologically based acknowledgment that childbearing has a social significance denied to male activities such as soldiering or commerce. If eugenists limited maternal power insofar as they minimized womanly influence (arguing, in Daniel J. Kevles's summary, "that heredity determined not simply physical characteristics but temperament and behavior"[38]), they also affirmed, as women's advocates had long argued, that marriage is the basis of all human progress.

The foundation stone of eugenics, the argument that ability is inherited, was laid in Francis Galton's influential work "Hereditary Talent and Character," published in *Macmillan's* in 1865 and expanded four years later into *Hereditary Genius: An Inquiry into Its Laws and Consequences.* A cousin of Darwin's and, ironically, himself a childless husband,[39] Galton was trying to scotch the popular notions that mothers have more than fathers to do with the intelligence of children and that one genius in a family generally means that its other members will lack ability. Examining 603 notable men (and two women, Queen Elizabeth and Madame de Staël) who flourished between 1453 and 1853, he observed that 102 of his subjects were related to others on his list and concluded "that talent is transmitted by inheritance in a very remarkable degree; that the mother has by no means the monopoly of its transmission; and that whole families of persons of talent are more common than those in which one member only is possessed of it."[40] (The possible role of the nonbiological inheritance of advantage and power was more evident to Galton's critics than to Galton himself.[41])

Galton's first recommendation was for positive eugenics.[42] "What an extraordinary effect might be produced on our race," he mused, "if its object was to unite in marriage those who possessed the finest and most suitable natures, mental, moral, and physical!" What comprised a "suitable nature," however, differed for male and female. Although he conceded that "the transmission of talent is as much through the side of the mother as through that of the father," his requirements for the perfect mother in his eugenic utopia were "grace, beauty, health, good temper, accomplished housewifery, and disengaged affections, in addition to noble qualities of heart and brain."[43] The contributions of the perfect father are less clear, but Galton's list of 603 desirable male specimens suggests that men would be selected primarily or even exclusively for their intellects.

Galton's model, in other words, retained the doctrine of separate spheres; women would make happy homes while men controlled public success. But womanly influence, which relied on the idea that women's

talent for personal relationships renders them morally superior, would
be set aside; to Galton, family affection was merely a Darwinian survival characteristic.[44] No virtue could inhere in a quirk of biological
programming. Nor could women continue to claim the dominance over
heredity that popular myth assigned to them. The distinction between
the contributions to heredity Galton expected from men and those he
expected from women became still clearer in the third installment of his
Macmillan's series, in which he examined the family networks of two
centuries of English judges, all of whom he presumed to be talented.
His conclusion, "that judicial ability passes somewhat more through the
male line than through that of the female," was linked to his conception of ability as mirroring a Victorian stereotype of masculinity. Most
judges "are vigorous, shrewd, practical, helpful men; glorying in the
rough-and-tumble of public life, tough in constitution and strong in di-
gestion, valuing what money brings, aiming at position and influence,
and desiring to found families." What we see here is an early version
of the turn-of-the-century public-school alumnus, well adapted to public if not to private life and ideally suited to pass along to (male) heirs
the "capacity, and zeal, and vigour" essential to talent.[45] In contrast,
women selected for beauty and grace presumably exist simply to encase
this talent in an attractive package.

Eugenic theory was useful to feminist marriage reformers, who invoked this blend of science and politics to show that the empire would
be best served by allowing divorce on the grounds of alcoholism, insanity, and diseases ranging from cancer to consumption.[46] Nevertheless, those at the center of the eugenic movement continued to emphasize masculinity, whether directly or through their diction. The rhetoric
of such leading enthusiasts as Montague Crackanthorpe (*né* Cookson),
president of the Eugenics Education Society, was larded with prom-
ises that "race regeneration" would render "the component parts of the
nation more healthy, more virile, and, by consequence, more effective";
such phrases implicitly constructed maleness as the final good.[47] Again,
Galton, writing on "Eugenics as a Factor in Religion" in 1909, used
a preponderance of words connoting stereotypically feminine values—
"social duty," "philanthropy," "home," "personal kindness," "love," and

other terms central to the Angel in the House tradition—but concluded resoundingly, "In brief, eugenics is a virile creed, full of hopefulness, and appealing to many of the noblest feelings of our nature."[48] And in a lecture reported in the first number of the *Eugenics Review*, Dr. C. W. Saleeby hinted that women who develop their talents are either masculine or asexual: "The woman acrobat, whether of muscle or of mind, tended towards sterility. . . . That education which taught a girl to despise motherhood, whilst making her incapable of it, was not 'higher' but 'lower' education."[49]

Since eugenics rested on the belief that heredity outweighs environment in its influence on society, the movement could both assert male dominance (by privileging stereotypically masculine characteristics, such as physical strength or commercial savvy) and retain mid-Victorian views of woman's role. The *Eugenics Review*, for instance, was interested not only in the biological contributions of both parents but also in the environmental influence of the mother. In a typical essay, Saleeby remarked that in "a generation consisting only of babies who were loved before they were born"—and he had earlier established that the ability to love children is much more an instinct of women than of men—"there would be a proportion of sympathy, of tender feeling, and of all those great, abstract, world-creating passions which are evolved from the tender emotion, such as no age hitherto has seen."[50] Such nods to womanly influence, however, did not diminish the power of the male. Eugenics was a convenient way for men to come to terms with the Victorian belief that fathers have less significance than mothers in child rearing; why not, when child rearing is so much less important than child breeding, and when the most desirable genetic characteristics are male?[51]

Edwardian eugenists calculated, like Ethel M. Elderton (who assisted Karl Pearson in running the Galton Eugenics Laboratory), that heredity had at least five times the power of environment in determining human character.[52] In making such statements, scientists invoked a supposedly dispassionate logic of statistics (a specialty of Pearson's) or empirical evidence such as Galton's twin studies, countering the "sentimental" environmental hypotheses associated with meliorist social theory.[53] Contrastingly, mid-Victorian writers of humanist stamp had taken for

granted, as Henry Thomas Buckle put it in 1858, that "the really important events occur after birth";[54] given the assumed dominance of women
in child rearing, environmentalism naturally emphasized the effect of
the mother. Later reformists found themselves forced to grant the importance of heredity on physical well-being but postulated a progression in
which, to quote the unnamed author of "Chastity: Its Development and
Maintenance" (1880), "as we proceed from the physical to the moral, the
dominion of environment enhances" and heredity becomes ever less important. Again, such theories typically placed the mother at the acme of
morality, surrounded by stereotypically female virtues such as chastity
and tenderness toward children.[55]

Thus in the first decade of the new century, at the height of scientific claims about heredity's importance, writers with social agendas
sometimes noted, like Maria Theresa Earle, that "the power of heredity
was considered a more overwhelming influence [a generation previously]
than seems to be generally accepted now." To Earle the modern trend
was "to regard the effect of heredity as almost incidental compared to the
greater forces of individuality, training, and associations"; not coincidentally, she was also arguing for mothers' primacy in child rearing.[56]
Likewise, Bernard Houghton, writing on "Immorality and the Marriage
Law" in 1907, contended: "The weight previously ascribed to heredity in
the making of a good citizen is as a result of modern investigation found
to be a steadily diminishing quantity; the environment during childhood
is . . . assuming a greater and greater importance."[57] Such claims do not
reflect the views of the scientific establishment in general. Eugenics was
a dominant influence of the time, and writers in professional journals
such as *Mind* countered the humanists' recollections of the quaint days
of hereditarianism with reminiscences of bygone generations' folly in
accepting Lamarckism and other theories that left open the possibility
of environmentally based change.[58] Rather the reformers seem painfully
aware that hereditarianism meant the downfall of the meliorist—and
mother-centered—ideals for which reform had long striven.

Partly because of the reformist unwillingness to view heredity as
primary, post-Darwinian science felt great pressure to determine the
mechanism by which traits passed from one generation to the next;

an explanation of this process was clearly essential to the Darwinian model. But even the 1900 rediscovery of Gregor Mendel's work on peas did not immediately lead to scientific agreement that his experiments would reveal the basic principles of genetics. Neo-Lamarckism and August Weismann's germ-plasm theory remained important and seemingly irreconcilable currents in heredity theory throughout the Edwardian era (though the former, which allowed for the inheritance of acquired characteristics, began to lose ground after 1890). Professional and lay scientists alike admitted that no one really knew how heredity worked. Throughout the period under discussion, then, folk wisdom about biological inheritance had nearly as strong a footing in articles relating to the field as did scientific explanations. The lack of accurate knowledge about genetics, Stephen Kern observes, caused both popular and technical writers to feel particular concern about degeneration, the theory that evil characteristics, once acquired, remain in the germinal cells forever, snowballing destructively through the generations.[59] Plainly, without reliable information about how implacable heredity might be, it behooved society to take care.

At the beginning of the period, writers on heredity often addressed the question of the respective contributions of father and mother. Summing up the state of inheritance theory in 1856, G. H. Lewes expressed the frustrating uncertainty of the inquiry, noting that "although the male influence is sometimes seen to preponderate in one direction, and the female influence in another, yet this direction is by no means constant, is often reversed, and admits of no absolute reduction to a known formula." Further complicating the situation was the phenomenon of atavism; not only parents but grandparents and even remote ancestors could affect the embryonic child. Lewes remarked the popular desire to simplify matters by ascribing limbs to the father's influence and organs to the mother's, which could mean that biologically as well as environmentally the mother would predominate in forming her offspring's character. His own theory, however, was that "it is only on the supposition of *both* individuals transmitting their organizations, and the one modifying the other, that [observed] anomalies are conceivable. When the paternal influence is not counteracted, we see it transmitted."[60]

Mid-Victorian scientific thought, as this example suggests, was strug-
gling to credit fathers with significant biological influence upon children's minds. Lewes's rejection of maternal primacy was followed by
Galton's in 1865 and 1869; subsequent scientific constructions, such as
Henry Maudsley's 1886 article on "Heredity in Health and Disease,"
usually did not treat hereditary characteristics as sex linked, instead
giving equal weight to both parents. But humanist discussions of this
point worked otherwise, in the apparent hope that society had a better
chance if maternal rather than paternal influence dominated in biology
as in the family. Finding the "theory that we derive our intellectual
qualities from our mothers, while we are indebted to our fathers only
for our physical attributes . . . most agreeable to all the natural instincts of man," Andrew Halliday asserted in *All the Year Round* in 1865,
"Genius is not hereditary through the fathers, but through the mothers."
He added that "we are more nearly flesh of their flesh, and blood of
their blood."[61]

Such views appeared at all points on the political spectrum. Four
years after Halliday's article, a letter in the feminist *Englishwoman's
Review* pleaded for women's education on the Lamarckian grounds that
"children inherit more of the mental qualities of the mother than of the
father." Similar points can be found in the conservative *National Review* in 1887 ("Without fail an able man has had an able mother, while
with the male sex the reverse is the case: clever men rarely have clever
sons") and the *Fortnightly Review* in 1892 ("It is generally admitted that
a man inherits his brains from his mother, and the daughter her figure
and disposition"), although the theory had lost ground by the end of the
century.[62]

This perception generally appeared in connection with arguments for
women's rights, the primacy of the domestic sphere, or various types
of social reform; proponents of such ideas were typically more interested in environment than in biology, and invoked science only to add
a technical ornament to a nontechnical discussion. Humanist critics of
scientific endeavor were also likely to remind readers of the importance
of proper child rearing and the difficulty of separating prenatal from
postnatal influence. Reviewing Galton's *Hereditary Genius* in 1870, for

instance, political economist Herman Merivale commented, "The truth is that the success in life which leads to distinction is due to two causes, the one consisting in natural aptitude or ability, the other in surrounding circumstances"; he acknowledged as well that while one might generalize that overall intelligence comes from the mother and specific aptitude from the father, "again, there are reasons quite independent from any 'hereditary' theory."[63]

Similarly, schoolmaster and novelist F. W. Farrar complained that until science gained insight into the mechanism of inheritance, Galton's lists of bygone examples could contribute little: "at present our views on that subject must be regarded as . . . but little in advance of popular empiricism." Galton, Farrar maintained, had failed to prove that nature overpowers nurture.[64] Again, in an 1871 *Edinburgh Review*, W. Boyd Dawkins (an anthropologist and geologist) faulted Darwin's account of human evolution for its insistence "that the mysterious law of reproduction, with the passions which belong to it, is the dominant force of life. He appears to see nothing beyond it or above it." Ethical beliefs—Darwin's "social instincts"—come from training, Dawkins held, and are not "transmitted in the same unerring way. . . . [as] the impulse by which a bird builds a nest."[65]

Nevertheless, science increasingly minimized postnatal influence. In part this was accomplished by the slow abandonment of the combination of environmental and biological influence represented by neo-Lamarckism, whose theoretical importance in the 1870–90 period diminished under the combined fire of the supporters of Galton, Weismann, and finally Mendel. Outlining "Weismann's Theory of Heredity" in an 1890 *Contemporary Review*, scientist George J. Romanes observed that among its chief attractions was its denial "that any acquired character can, under any circumstances whatsoever, be transmitted to progeny." So strong was germinal continuity that "no external influences or internal processes can ever change the hereditary nature of any particular mixture . . . save and except its admixture with some other germ-plasm."[66] While Darwin, as Jeffrey Weeks has noted, inspired as much interest in Lamarckism as in determinism,[67] late-century scientific refinements of the Darwinian model tended to emphasize such elements as pangenesis, the theory that all cells contain from the outset a blueprint for the cloning of their parent organism and are therefore normally incapable of transmitting changes created by the environment, or to adopt Weismann's theory that reproductive cells are entirely distinct from their "somatic" counterparts and are not affected by the influences that affect the latter. Thus, writing in 1908, Marcus Hartog cited Darwin, Romanes, Herbert Spencer, and Hartog's fellow zoologist Ernst Haeckel as Lamarckian sympathizers but noted that younger men—including Darwin's codiscoverer Alfred Russel Wallace—had "rejected this factor as non-existent," some even going so far as to deny "that differences of nutrition of the body may affect the germ-cells, and consequently the stock."[68]

Writers whose primary interests were social continued to employ Lamarckian arguments despite the tendency of science to move in the opposite direction, just as they also exhibited more respect for nonhereditary influence. Mona Caird's 1894 article in the *Westminster Review* on "Phases of Human Development," for instance, repeated the "sins of the (grand)fathers" plea, warning that "every man, woman, and child—stupid, weak, ignorant, as each may be—is busy forming the forces of heredity." Simultaneously, she disputed the theory that "mankind is . . . the slave of primitive [sexual] instinct, except when mankind so wills it."[69] Frederick Maurice, whose 1903 views on national degeneration represented common fears, worried about the might of an army composed of the grandchildren of city-dwellers, "who, after two or three generations, [have] deteriorated in physical vigour" to the point where they are no longer "able to rear a healthy family."[70] And turn-of-the-century theosophists held, in the words of an anonymous feminist partisan in *Shafts*, that whatever heredity's importance to the body, nothing "so mundane and physical as heredity could affect a *soul*"; reincarnated over many lives, each being retains the wisdom it has won in scores of environments, in a kind of super-Lamarckian inheritance of the development of the ages.[71]

Other reformers invoked both hereditarianism and folklore in arguing for social purity. The author of "Enforced Maternity" (*Shafts* 1893) drew on an idea long popular in the United States in noting the need for parental continence: "When we remember the marvels of heredity, and how the mood of the parents at the moment of generation, and their habits of life, are inherited and reproduced in the mental equipment of their offspring, this is evident."[72] Akin to the popular belief that a pregnant woman's terror at some sight could mark her unborn child, arguments about the importance of the parents' mental state during conception were clearly more useful to purity reformers. Responsible coitus was performed calmly, without passion, and with not pleasure but parenthood uppermost in the partners' minds; in other words, it catered to stereotypes of feminine rather than masculine sexuality in hopes of ensuring that the resulting child would duplicate the maternal ideal.

Furthermore, writers such as E. I. Champness extended this hereditary psychic influence to the full nine months of pregnancy, writing, "Science may yet have to determine whether, not only the thoughts, but the sub-conscious brain action of the mother . . . may not be able to fill some of the gaps left by the theory of heredity." While Champness also believed in the possibility of telepathic influences on unborn children—thus permitting fathers' voices to be heard, providing that their interest is "manifes[t] in the home life at all"—clearly speculation of this type in all its forms challenged what had become dominant in scientific thought by assuming the primacy of the mother before, as after, birth.[73] Science, in turn, sought to lay such theories to rest, although by the time Havelock Ellis published "The Psychic State in Pregnancy" as part of *Studies in the Psychology of Sex* (1897–1910), he could only remark that "while the influence of maternal impressions in producing definite effects on the child within the womb has by no means been positively demonstrated, we are not entitled to reject it with any positive assurance."[74]

Had the supporters of hereditarianism sought to demonstrate the father's psychic (as opposed to physical) importance to the child, they might have begun by establishing the paternal instinct as equal in force to its maternal counterpart. The periodical writings of the day, however, reflect no such effort. As Stephanie A. Shields notes, late-nineteenth- and early-twentieth-century science "only infrequently considered" the paternal drive, and when it was discussed it was typically viewed in nonparental terms as an aspect of possessiveness, sexuality, or chivalry.[75] Theorists considered, indeed, that male chivalry is directed less at the helpless infant than at the child's equally dependent mother; of the two parents, it is she who feels any innate connection to her offspring.

As I suggested in chapter 2, man's supposed lack of parental feeling was an important aspect of the argument about keeping women out of the public sphere. Writers drew on this assumption of Victorian science to contend, like the anonymous author of "Biology and 'Women's Rights'" in 1878, that civilization would founder "were the duties of the two sexes confounded together, or, still more, were they inverted—the female, for instance, going forth to face danger or to hunt for prey, while the male was left to nurse the young."[76] Women's advocates, on the other hand, argued that the maternal instinct is the source of woman's moral attainments and entitles her to operate in any sphere that attracts her. Following the leads furnished by biologists and anthropologists, both sides agreed that the paternal instinct (if it exists at all) is a function of civilization, a product of marriage patterns that curtail men's instinctive promiscuity or of labor patterns that compel men to abandon their natural desire for freedom in order to support their families. Because it has no ongoing biological source analogous to pregnancy, childbirth, and lactation, paternity "lacks that profound impress which is produced by maternity."[77]

Providing a history of the maternal instinct in comparison with male experience, Julia Wedgwood, for instance, drew on an 1867 work by anthropologist A. Giraud-Teulon *fils* (a member of the "Mutterrecht" school) entitled "La Mère chez certains Peuples de l'Antiquité" to argue that "the first *man* who undertook the responsibilities of paternity was . . . 'un homme de génie et de coeur, un des grands bienfaiteurs de l'humanité'" ("a man of genius and heart, one of the great benefactors of humankind"). Significantly, however, both Giraud-Teulon and Wedgwood suggested that this original father was acting against the normal male instincts in behaving in a way fully congruent with femininity. According to Wedgwood and her sources, involved fatherhood is a sophisticated moral impulse, akin to philanthropy and only possible in an advanced culture; in contrast, woman "is, from the first, consciously a mother."[78]

Millicent Garrett Fawcett spoke for one type of humanism when she criticized Frederic Harrison for implying that "only abnormal men . . . have the strong clinging affection for their children that most women have. This is not true for human nature as I have observed it. At least, I have never considered those men abnormal or 'unsexed' in whom family affection was strongly developed."[79] She and her cohorts hoped to foster domestic impulses in husbands and fathers in order to advance women's cause; the more pessimistic, such as *Shafts* contributor Miss Gay, traced judicial wrist slappings in cases of child rape, wife beating, or other gender conflicts to the fact that "in the large majority of men [including judges and legislators] the sexual instinct always triumphs over any paternal feeling."[80] If society were to be reformed, clearly the one must be controlled and the other enhanced.

But science offered little support for the idea that the paternal instinct might eventually conquer male desire. It had wagered too much against innate fatherliness to support this concept. Thus James Sully's 1899 study of children's doll play demonstrated a real reluctance to confront the evidence that boys may feel something akin to the maternal instinct. While Sully acknowledged that boys may adopt dolls, sacrifice their own meals in order to "feed" these surrogate children, and otherwise exhibit tenderness toward them, he argued on the unexamined ground that boys prefer their dolls to take unusual or animal shapes that "this boyish feeling seems to be different from the girl's" in that it exhibits "less of the warm fondling element." Boys then dropped out of the study, Sully contending that "the doll is emphatically the *girl's* plaything," a "nursling" eliciting "the germ of the maternal impulse."[81] Likewise, the hereditarian physiologist G. Archdall Reid found, "It is very doubtful whether the human male has any 'natural affection' for his children. There are indications that he acquires his love for them, as he may acquire a love of country or of a particular religious system, through the incitements of his imitative instincts."[82] What was thought to be innate in man was the sex urge, which, as we have seen, was often seen as inimical to the family. In its pronouncements on paternal instinct, science thus both responded to and did much to construct the concept of male antidomesticity.

The debate over fatherly feeling was an important one for Victorian anthropology, which was keenly interested in tracing the history of the family. As Rosalind Coward reports, the question of whether the world had ever been without the patriarchal family "provoked the most violent controversy. It engaged virtually every social theorist writing in the second half of the nineteenth century," not only in Britain but in the United States and on the Continent.[83] For Britain the leaders of the opposing schools of thought were barrister and sociologist John F. McLennan, who believed patriarchy to be the end product of lengthy social and historical processes, and legal historian Henry Maine, who held that the primacy of the father was intrinsic to human community. For all the heat of the argument, however, in some ways what was at issue was a distinction rather than a difference; both groups agreed that patriarchy was the proper system for humanity and that power was the basis of the father's rule, although some scholars suggested that power might be transmuted into love. Anthropology thus often worked to ratify the same hierarchical and authoritarian family structures that Victorian child-rearing ideology (as we have seen) was discarding, creating one more fissure between science and reformist social thought and reaffirming humanist fears that the father was too rigid and too fearsome to be integrated into the utopian family of the future.

Maine's 1886 article "The Patriarchal Theory," for example, opposed the views of McLennan and the American Lewis Morgan, arguing that comparison of the laws of various cultures (among them the Roman, German, and Hindu) demonstrates a universal heritage of patriarchal power. To Maine, however, the recent course of English law and custom indicated that the ancient hegemony of the father was fast disappearing, as "the practical domestic authority of an English Father in his own household was once vastly greater than it is now." Manners and modes of address no longer stress the ceremony and respect with which the father should be treated; the absolute legal right over the disposition of children and property has vanished. Power, in fact, is not what it used to be, for "the institution [of English fatherhood] . . . is a Patria Potestas in decay."[84] The note of wistfulness in this explanation suggests a fear of societal degeneration, an anxiety that the father's abandonment of absolute power might mean the dissolution of English society rather than—as more optimistic social thinkers imagined—its apotheosis.

In the post-Darwinian environment, other researchers considered the family an evolving rather than a largely static form. Journalist William Schooling's "Marriage Institutions" drew on Spencer's *Principles of Sociology* (1876–96) in describing the journey from primitive promiscuity through polygamy to monogamy, women's concurrent acquisition of status and value, and men's gradual acceptance of fatherhood's impor-'tance. Schooling noted of the polygamous stage that owing to financial considerations and indicating an improvement in morality, "exercise of care and sacrifice on [women's and children's] behalf gives rise to sympathy and parental feeling, and the dawn of marriage and fatherhood is at hand." Of future refinements on monogamy, he speculated that "with the parent less and less a master, more and more a friend, will go a deep lasting influence, and mutual love."[85] A similar outline was provided by Effie Johnson in "Marriage or Free Love," which held that the "admitted responsibilities and varied obligations [of acknowledged fatherhood] . . . constituted no slight contribution towards *spiritual* Evolution."[86] Such explanations suggest the uses to which reformers adapted the insights of anthropology; Johnson, for instance, employed her synopsis to argue for marriage reform and against free love, on the grounds that parental love and involvement are essential to the progress of civilization.

Conversely, the work of scholars such as Edward Westermarck (Swedish-born professor of sociology at London University), whose *The History of Human Marriage* appeared in 1891, helped to confirm the beliefs of social-purity activists by contending that sex antagonism was natural, the result of conflict between the male's desire to procreate extensively and the female's commitment to child care.[87] Anthropological explorations of the origins of religion likewise suggested the friction between the father and the family; Aberdeen biblical scholar W. Robertson Smith's *The Religion of the Semites* (1889) found that most forms of worship stem from the child's feelings for the mother, not the father, while James G. Frazer's *The Golden Bough* (1890) indicated, in its exploration of sacrificial rituals, that the parricidal urge is both wide and deep.[88]

Feminists mined such research for ammunition in their calls to overturn the status quo. An article in *Shafts* in 1899, for example, noted the cumulative effects of woman's prehistory as man's slave: "her finer organisation and quality of brain, developed by the devotion she lavished upon her children, had the effect of endowing her with a certain intuitive perception by which she learnt in a measure to counteract the tyranny of mere brute force."[89] The distinction between a noble mother-hood based on love and a brutish fatherhood based on strength had been sharpened not just for a few generations, but for millennia. Clearly it was time to redistribute power and let the more deserving govern the family and the world.

Some anthropologists, notably J. J. Bachofen (Swiss author of the influential 1861 tome *Das Mutterrecht*), postulated that between the primitive promiscuity of earliest society and the rise of patriarchal mo-nogamy had intervened what Ellis termed "a free primitive community in which women ruled since they alone were recognizable as parents."[90] British scientists tended to discount this idea under the influence of McLennan, who defined the matriarchal period as merely an era of po-lygamy in which the impossibility of establishing paternity had caused matrilineal descent to prevail but denied that significant power had ac-crued to women.[91] But feminists accepted the theory eagerly. To Frances Swiney, for one, "the history of old civilisations is simply the struggle of the man to supplant the matriarchate by the patriarchy, as soon as he had learned from the woman the first principles of social life, of industrial invention, of aesthetic art, and primitive culture." His suc-cess introduced persecution, bigotry, and the subjugation of women, "with what dire results, the state of society at the present day but too tragically shows."[92] Again, mother rule connotes cooperation, beauty, and productivity; fathers, in contrast, are only concerned with imposing hierarchies of force.

Swiney's assertions would not have seemed extreme in the context of her day. Even male scholars, Ellis among them, could comment that polygamy "was peculiarly favourable to women," who had equal politi-cal power, controlled "the arts and industries of peace," determined kinship ties, and owned the household property. It was men's desire to arrogate this latter privilege to themselves and their sons that cre-ated patriarchy and lowered the wife to slavery: "Thus arose the modern status of women."[93] Save that Ellis seems considerably less disturbed about this historical process than Swiney, the two outlines show little difference in content; the distinction is one of emphasis. Feminists saw motherhood as the creative impulse of civilization, while the anthropological establishment thought fatherhood more important.[94]

But despite anthropology's emphasis on fatherhood, one of its often inadvertent contributions, as Elizabeth Fee has pointed out, was its suggestion that the patriarchal family of Puritan tradition "was dictated by no law of nature."[95] The father's power was merely an accident of history, if one took the McLennanites' argument to its logical conclusion; the family hierarchy once thought to have been ordained by God now seemed a product of local circumstance, helped along by male arrogance and greed. This realization vastly expanded the possibilities for utopia. To discard conventional family models seemed much less radical than had been the case a century earlier. As Caird wrote in an 1890 article on "The Emancipation of the Family," scholars had shown "how completely our notions of family ties are matters of the moment, historically considered, and not of eternity." Using this premise as a starting point, she outlined the way in which the father had usurped maternal power ("paternal rights take their rise in the ownership of the mother, and not in the relationship to the children or the support which the father may afford them") and suggested that " 'human nature' need not be a perpetual obstacle to change." Whereas under existing law "Father and mother are to share pleasantly between them the rights and duties of parenthood—the father having the rights, the mother the duties," in the future woman might regain power to match her responsibility.[96] While some writers saw the patriarchal father as the shining product of millennia of natural selection, less sympathetic critics could suggest with equal justification that he was on the brink of extinction.

Like other scientific disciplines, then, anthropology generally upheld the image of the father as distant and authoritarian, at best contributing to his children's support without having much to do with their upbringing. But it also shared in the one area in which science reflected the idea of certain domestic writers that the father's role should complement that of the mother in ways beyond the purely financial. The scientific analogue to domestic commentary about the father's unique contribution as influence or instructor was the late-Victorian and Edwardian belief

that the intellectually curious father might act as a scientist within the
nursery. Masculine logic and masculine dispassion in family matters
could enable men to achieve special insight even within the "feminine"
domestic environment.

Beginning in the 1870s, child study came to be regarded as an appropriate area for scientific research.[97] It received the imprimatur of no
less an authority than Charles Darwin, who in 1877 published in *Mind*
a report of a journal he had kept on one of his infant sons in 1840. The
description exhibits Darwin as at once loving parent and neutral scientist; accounts of trips to the zoo and games of peek-a-boo alternate with
clinical data on the baby's reflexes, emotions, and linguistic capacity.
The two sides appear simultaneously in the father's reports on his son's
moral development:

> The first sign of moral sense was noticed at the age of nearly 13 months:
> I said "Doddy [the child] won't give poor papa a kiss,—naughty Doddy."
> These words, without doubt, made him feel slightly uncomfortable; and at
> last when I had returned to my chair, he . . . shook his hand in an angry
> manner until I came and received his kiss.

This eliciting of affection through baby talk and appeals to the conscience sits somewhat oddly with the impersonal tone Darwin creates
with his use of passive voice and his air of clinical observation (already
well established when, for instance, he compares his son's understanding of mirrors with that of the "higher apes"). But plainly the range of
effects is part of the point: the tender and involved father, whose conformity to maternalist doctrine is evident ("As this child was educated
solely by working on his good feelings, he soon became as truthful, open,
and tender, as anyone could desire"), still finds it possible to retain his
scientific objectivity.[98] Domesticity can provide a forum not merely for
sentiment but also for research.

Darwin's *Mind* article was but one of a number of child-centered
accounts appearing in that journal from its inception, ranging from a
translation of "M. Taine on the Acquisition of Language by Children"
(April 1877) to psychologist Alexander Bain's series "Education as a
Science" (1877–78). Some called for an understanding of child psy-

chology in order to increase the effectiveness of education; others found children interesting primarily because they were thought to recapitulate the primitive development of humankind. The latter theory, whose proponents included such influential men as Spencer, Wallace, and the American child psychologist G. Stanley Hall,[99] turned children into a kind of tribal group in which culture was determined by age, making them objects of particular interest to linguists and anthropologists. The social scientist who happened also to be a father need no longer leave home to do his fieldwork.

James Sully, the professor of philosophy at University College, London, who produced the "dollatry" study discussed above, explained in the *English Illustrated Magazine* in 1884 why "of late quite a number of scientific fathers have been taking notes of the first utterances of their children," following the fashion set by Darwin. Whereas mothers have perennially taken a personal interest in their children's speech acquisition because "Language . . . binds together child and mother by new bonds," fathers claim to be concerned with their offspring as "psychological specimens. . . . some light [may] be thrown on the early growth of the closely connected powers of thought and speech by a careful consideration of the child's first tentatives [*sic*] in linguistics." Men, in other words, as creatures of logic and learning, purport to be immune to the emotional (over)involvement of mother and child. After a lengthy discussion of one father's scientific interaction with his infant son, however, the real point of the essay becomes clear: "the object of this article will be attained if it reminds other parents how much pure pleasure may be derived from a close daily observation of any ordinary specimen of the baby mind." [100] Scientific discovery is not, after all, the aim of such interaction between father and child, but the lure to promote it. The article's movement from intellectual snob appeal to charming anecdotes of babyhood is also to be the trajectory of the reader; Sully seems to have suspected that the intelligent man would want to provide himself with an unimpeachably male cover before venturing into the maternal domain.

The publication of "Baby Linguistics" in a broad-based lay magazine of no academic pretension may have affected the essay's message, a message that other recapitulationists repudiated in more serious journals. Louis Robinson, for one, erstwhile resident surgeon in a children's hospital and author of several articles on the atavistic tendencies of children's mental and physical characteristics, remarked in 1891 that parenthood and scientific observation are usually incompatible, as mothers are too close to their children to be dispassionate and fathers are too hampered by family constrictions to do sound work. Even Darwin was not above this failing:

> The fact that such important and easily ascertained characteristics . . . should have been passed over by one so keenly observant of all phenomena bearing upon his theory might suggest that the great man was scarcely so supreme in his own nursery as he was in the wider field of research, and that his opportunities for investigation were to some extent limited by the arbitrary and inflexible rules of this household department.[101]

While Robinson valued childhood because it "preserv[es] for us, in an almost unchanged form (like ants in the resin of the tertiary epoch or mammoths in the frozen tundra of the quaternary), relics of the thoughts and customs of long ago"—the ability of month-old infants to hang from horizontal bars proving our arboreal origins, for example—he suggested that separation from the family is essential to good observation.[102] Fatherhood, in short, precludes the best science.

In the earnest *Fortnightly Review*, however, Sully again recommended that fathers engage in child study. Here his emphasis reversed that of "Baby Linguistics"; while "The New Study of Children" begins with an invocation first of maternal tenderness and next of poetry and sentiment ("As we with hearts chastened by many experiences take a peep over the wall of [the child's] fancy-built pleasaunce, we seem to be carried back to a real golden age"), it moves quickly to the value of establishing "by a careful study of infancy the way in which human life begins to take its characteristic forms" and of witnessing, "in a diminished, distorted reflection no doubt, the probable condition of primitive man." Again the father-scientist is to learn through the mother the importance of childhood, but he is not to mirror her approach absolutely. Women are unlikely to set aside "baby-worship" to do real scientific work, so that "It is for the coarser-fibred man, then, to undertake much of the earlier experimental work in the investigation of child-nature. . . . enlisting the mother . . . as collaborateur, or at least as assistant." While women will prove invaluable in the collection of data, they will find that "the sentimental or aesthetic attraction of the baby is apt to be a serious obstacle to a cold matter-of-fact examination of it as a scientific specimen." For all his new appreciation of childhood, and even of the poetry of childhood, the father will suffer from no such handicap.[103]

Nevertheless, the new scientific interest in the young still provided one of the few intellectually endorsed avenues for the connection of adult male and child, one of the few opportunities for selected men to merge public and private identities. Whether scientists were watching infants hang from rods like Robinson, immersing them in baths to test their atavistic swimming skills like the American efficiency expert Frank Gilbreth, analyzing the similarities of their vocalizing to Polynesian languages like Gilbreth's countryman Charles Johnston, or arguing like geologist S. S. Buckman that "the vocabulary of the present-day human baby at twenty months old approximately represents the speech of adult pre-human ancestors," they were at least acknowledging infancy as important.[104] In so doing, as Miriam Lewin points out, they adopted much of the very maternalist ideology that the science of the day generally contravened.[105] While enterprises such as linguistics insisted on the need for specialized knowledge typically available only to men, they simultaneously focused on the family relationships that had become the province predominantly of women. Norman Vance, for instance, notes that linguistics' emphasis on the Indo-European languages as a *family*—advanced particularly through comparisons of words for "father," "mother," and so on—confirmed a sense that "the language of family had been important even at the dawn of history." [106] If women prided themselves on their intuitive understanding of that language, recapitulationists and linguists sought to establish their superior credentials in intellectual terms as its mappers and definers.

It is important to note, then, that science was becoming increasingly concerned in all its aspects with questions relating to fatherhood. Nevertheless, in repudiating environment as the most crucial influence upon childhood (and recapitulation too, of course, saw children

as the repositories of inherited information rather than as individuals responsive to present-day stimuli), scientists continually minimized
what domestic theorists were simultaneously upholding: women's right
to power through their role as mothers. Perhaps partly in response to
some women's hopes of using that power to gain entrance to the medical profession,[107] science in general preached biological determinism
more fervently than did the population as a whole. Lay reformers who
encroached on medical or scientific ground, as we have seen, saw environment as all-powerful and gender as fluid; the more "scientific" and
impersonal the approach of the professional researcher into these matters, on the other hand, the more likely it was that biology would be
destiny. The effect was to justify the doctrine of separate spheres and
often to fortify as well the idea that fathers are predestined to distance.
While some researchers agreed that family affection was important even
for men, in general their attention was primarily directed away from
emotion and toward depicting fatherhood as pollination. The result was
to give a scientific imprimatur to the view, already present in much Victorian periodical writing, that fatherly responsibility was something of a
contradiction in terms.

4

The Law
and the
Father

The fundamental principle of
English law is, that the father
alone is entitled to the custody and
disposal of his children; that
this right inheres totally irrespective
of his moral character or fitness
for the charge; and that it will
be confirmed and enforced by
the court, though he be an open
and notorious evil-liver.

The early-Victorian court system was a male preserve. Not only were all judges, barristers, solicitors, and court officials men—women did not gain admission to the English bar until after World War I—but more, under English law married women were ineligible to bring suit, own property (unless, in the case of the upper classes, appropriate marriage settlements had been arranged), or otherwise act as legal entities in their own right. Indeed, even when local statutes extended voting or office-holding privileges to qualified "persons above the age of twenty-one," throughout the century the courts rejected the petitions of both *femes sole* (spinsters) and *femes covert* (wives) to be allowed to partake of these privileges: women, they held, were not persons.[1]

As jurist and anthropologist Henry Maine explained, English law was based on the principles of patriarchy. By this tradition women and children were not separate individuals but parts of the corporate entity of the family; it was their representative, the paterfamilias, whose rights the legal system was designed to protect. Thus according to the legal code the early Victorians inherited, if the Englishman's house was his castle, his wife and minor children were serfs. Victorian feminists were quick to point out that a man could legally squander his wife's earnings against her will, forcibly remove their children from her guardianship and send them to be brought up by his mistress, and generally dispose of the family belongings (children included) with utter unconcern for the feelings or welfare of anyone but himself.[2] It was the father who determined how his children should be raised, the father who could expect to have custody of them should the couple separate.

This principle of total paternal control reflected an increasingly out-
moded view of children as economic assets whose earnings reverted to
the male holder of the pursestrings. In this formulation, children, as
actual or potential wage-earners, were high-yield investments; and because God had clearly ordained that men rather than women should
control property animate and inanimate, English family law provided,
in the words of William Blackstone's *Commentaries* (1765–69), that "a
mother, as such, is entitled to no [legal] power, but only to reverence
and respect."[3] But as children came to be seen as emotional assets and
financial liabilities (rather than vice versa), legal precedents began to
seem correspondingly misjudged. The moral importance of the mother,
reformers argued, could not be reconciled with her legal insignificance.
What mattered about the Victorian conception of the family was not economics but ethics. Consequently, the "reverence and respect" that were
the mother's due gradually acquired a modicum of legal power, while
the law was slowly forced to come to terms with the negative images of
fatherhood that reformers consistently put before it. Indeed, the success of many legal reforms depended in large part on the widespread
acceptance of such images as true to life.

Originally, Ivy Pinchbeck and Margaret Hewitt observe, "the rights
of the father as against the mother were so absolute that the courts did
not in fact have the power to grant a right of access to her children to a
mother whose husband had not granted it himself."[4] In contrast, before
the 1873 Custody of Infants Act, the courts both possessed and exercised the right (according to a writer in the *Dublin Review* in 1879) to
nullify clauses in separation agreements giving custody to mothers, "as
contrary to public policy."[5] Still, a father's power to determine the fate of
his children was eroding. Mary Lyndon Shanley dates the first break in
legal patriarchalism to 1763, when the case of *Rex* v. *Delaval* established
that the courts could deprive fathers of their "natural" custody rights
under certain conditions; the man in question had sought to apprentice
his daughter to a prostitute.[6] It is important to note, though, that what
Michael Grossberg has observed of the United States also applied in
Britain: the judicial system did not reassign paternal rights to mothers
but absorbed them. Judges were not presiding over a shift toward a legal

matriarchate, which many feminists hoped to see, but over a shift away from the private family, a lessening of "the rights of parenthood itself." [7] But if the courts finally became the embodiment of the British patriarch, they did so slowly, owing their every new increment of paternal power to the continual publicizing of the examples of bad fathers who came before the bench—and whom judges were often loath to chastise.

The first Victorian to spotlight men's abuse of their legal power over the family was Caroline Norton. Upon separating from her husband in 1836, Norton found herself unable to get a divorce or to retain control of her inheritance, literary earnings, children, and reputation; her resentful spouse hauled the prime minister, Lord Melbourne, into court charging adultery (the suit failed), curtailed her financial support even though most of their joint property had come through her, and seized their three young boys. Norton's anger was matched by her rhetorical powers. Over the next decades she used her pen and her connections to good effect, writing pamphlets, articles, and petitions in a dogged quest for justice. Her labors bore fruit in the 1839 Custody of Infants Act, which permitted women of probity separated from their husbands to petition Chancery for custody of their children under age seven and access to their children under age sixteen, and the 1857 Matrimonial Causes (Divorce) Act, which gave separated women the legal rights of spinsters and established a divorce court. (Husbands could obtain divorces by proving adultery against their spouses; wives had to prove not only adultery but also desertion, cruelty, or sexual criminality.) Neither act satisfied most reformers, as the first provided no charter for mothers' rights and the second acquiesced in the double standard, but the two did give women a forum in which to air marital grievances. And once women gained even so small a voice in the courtroom, the legal system increasingly found itself confronting, critiquing, and suborning the paternal role.

Throughout the period the center of the legal debate over fatherhood was the question that had also been one of the focal points of the Norton controversy, that of custody. Carol Brown argues from a Marxist perspective that the gradual shift toward maternal rather than paternal custody should be seen primarily in economic terms: "children themselves and

the labor required to rear them have changed from a valuable family asset that men wished to control to a costly family burden that men wish to
avoid."[8] Whatever the accuracy of this diagnosis for today's "deadbeat
dads," it has little relevance for the Victorian middle class. The economics of child rearing were indeed undergoing drastic revision over the
nineteenth century, with children becoming more and more expensive
as standards of living and expectations about education rose. But at the
same time, childhood was experiencing an equally drastic redefinition
as a moral asset, an unparalleled source of spiritual renewal for world-
weary adults. If children were costly, this seemed only right: the values
of the marketplace *should* be reversed in the nobler atmosphere of the
home. Whether or not the fathers in Victorian custody cases expected
to realize these intangible moral gains, they certainly saw custody as
a privilege, a social acknowledgment of their own superior rights and
status rather than an onerous duty.

If men considered paternal custody an affirmation of their hierarchical power within the family, women supported instead the concept of the
nonhierarchical family. Money and status might be male perquisites, but
they were coming to seem irrelevant in a domestic ideology that newly
emphasized the heart. As mothers, not fathers, were typically seen as
the wielders of influence and the voices of the Christian ethic, any system allowing fathers to usurp the primary parental role during a child's
formative years must jeopardize children, mothers, and society alike.
Significantly, women's challenge to the tradition of paternal custody of
children succeeded earlier than their challenge to the tradition of male
custody of family finances; the various Custody of Infants Acts (1839,
1873, 1886)[9] extended the possibility that mothers could be granted a
voice in their children's upbringing before the Married Women's Property Acts (1870, 1882, 1893) affirmed wives' rights to control their own
money. Clearly men's claim to the role of breadwinner struck Victorian
reformers as stronger than their claim to be the primary influence within
the family.

Pleas for legal reform thus usually emphasized women's right to their
own property not as a matter of abstract justice but as a necessity of good
motherhood: women must be permitted to defend their children against
the rapacity of wicked fathers. In this context, writers tended to depict

men as entirely lacking in paternal feeling. Children seem to belong
only to their mothers. Nor do women in these articles ask for male action
of any kind, for instance in child support; rather they beg that men will
refrain from interfering in the mother-child relationship, a tie that men
seem incapable of respecting. As Eliza Lynn (later Linton) remarked in
her 1854 defense of Norton in *Household Words*, what women want is
only "the recognition of their natural rights as mothers, the permission
to them to live . . . untaxed by the legal Right and moral Wrong of any
man to claim as his own that for which he has not wrought—reaping
where he has not sown, and gathering where he has not strawed."

Linton's essay (which fictionalizes the Norton situation somewhat and
rechristens the participants) emphasizes that the products of a mother's
industry include not only money but also children, "those who had lain
beneath her heart, and drunk of her life." The worst sin of the heroine's
husband is to have deprived her of the boys, passing them to his dragon-
like sister, "who flogged the eldest child, a sensitive and delicate boy of
six years old, for receiving and reading a letter from his mother. . . . The
yet younger was stripped naked and chastised with a riding-whip." [10]
Plainly the children's punishment and humiliation, with their obvious
sexual component, symbolize no mere difference in disciplinary style or
child-rearing philosophy but the husband and sister-in-law's desire to
punish and humiliate the wife. Because the sons have "drunk of [their
mother's] life" without, apparently, having imbibed anything from their
father, they literally serve as whipping boys in this domestic war. The
father can distance himself from them, sending them to live elsewhere
and authorizing their harsh treatment; in contrast, the mother at first
bears her many trials patiently in order to stay near them and then
keenly feels their every torment after the separation.

The debate over the Divorce Act and its unsuccessful rival, the
Married Women's Property Bill of the same year, focused attention on
women's claims to their own earnings, but also on the purported differences between male and female attitudes toward children exemplified in
such descriptions of the Norton case. The 1856 petition sent to Parliament in support of the Property Bill—whose more than three thousand
signatories included Elizabeth Barrett Browning, Jane Carlyle, Elizabeth Gaskell, Harriet Martineau, feminist educator and author Barbara

Leigh Smith (later Bodichon), and Bessie Rayner Parkes of the *English Woman's Journal*—noted that at present society could not combat "the selfishness of a drunken father, who wrings from a mother her children's daily bread. . . . the law, in depriving the mother of all pecuniary resources, deprives her of the power of giving schooling to her children, and in other ways providing for their moral and physical welfare."[11] Here again the mother is the real parent, serving in both the feminine capacity of moral guide and the masculine one of breadwinner and payer of school fees; the father is not part of the family but its enemy. As Caroline Cornwallis commented, the public has every right to protect children from neglect, "but as, from the very nature of animal instincts, this is more likely to take place on the part of the father than the mother, so the despotic power granted to the husband over the wife's property and earnings is little calculated to attain its ostensible object."[12] Although giving men absolute rights over property and offspring had failed to conquer the "animal instincts" that always impel them to selfishness, Cornwallis argued that to give *women* equal rights would only augment their greater natural sense of familial responsibility.

Where paternal custody was defended, it was usually defended on grounds of tradition: to undermine the father's power over his family was to undermine the principles on which society rests. Law, jurists argued, must uphold order, not sentiment. A very few commentators did appeal to feeling in proclaiming a father's right to keep his children. Margaret Oliphant, for instance, held that there can be no justice in custody cases because father and mother must long equally passionately for their offspring:

> God has not given to the mother a special and peculiar claim. It is hard, but it is true. The law might confer upon her the right to bereave her husband of this dearest possession, as it now gives him the right to bereave her; but the law can only, by so doing, favour one unfair claim to the disadvantage of another; for in this matter right and justice are impossible.[13]

Far more common, however, was the assumption that family feeling was entirely on the mother's side—that she did indeed have a "special and peculiar claim," as she alone of the parents could be trusted to behave tenderly and responsibly toward her children or even to bring them up herself rather than designating some teacher or female relative to take them in charge.[14] Once the husband has escaped his wife's influence, most writers implied, fatherly instinct vanishes.

In and out of political contexts, the custodial father was a figure of evil. An episode of W. M. Thackeray's *Roundabout Papers* in the *Cornhill Magazine* in 1860, for example, recorded the novelist's encounter in Germany with two well-dressed boys and an adult woman and his second sighting of the boys a month later in "bare-footed squalor in Venice," where they were accompanied by an ill-favored man. Admitting to no knowledge of the facts of the case, Thackeray was yet able to deduce all: "The mother was gone, who had given them the heaps of pretty books, and the pretty studs in the shirts, and the pretty silken clothes, and the tender—tender cares; and they were handed to this scowling practitioner of Trente et Quarante," whom we are to identify as their father. The article ends with questions clearly rhetorical in intent: "Had the father gambled away his money, and sold their clothes? . . . Who will read this riddle of The Two Children in Black?"[15] So strong are the cultural assumptions about paternal custody underlying the anecdote that the riddle is no riddle at all. While mothers give, fathers take. Not only do they treat their children as possessions, but they subvert the children's belongings to their own use. And only a father, Thackeray implies, has both the desire and the legal power to behave so badly.

Given this paradigm of paternal selfishness and maternal selflessness shaping the articles on custody, woman writers were especially bitter about the judicial belief that only the father has a "natural right" to the children. The rhetoric of feminists such as Lydia Becker, a staunch supporter of married women's property legislation, was more impassioned on this subject than on any other. Criticizing the 1839 Custody of Infants Act in 1872, Becker argued that to permit a wife in certain cases "to keep—not her children—oh no! the law does not recognise them as hers—but . . . her husband's children until they are seven years old" is at least as cruel as the original refusal to give her custody at all. The law arranges the situation thus

that she may have all the care, trouble, and anxiety of their helpless infancy, and the—it may be—profligate father be relieved from the same,

and the torture and the uprooting of her heart be all the more cruel at the
end of the seven years, when the fiat of separation goes forth. What that
torture is, none but a mother can know. It is probably the greatest that a
human being can suffer. And the law sanctions the infliction of this torture
on Englishwomen at the irresponsible will and pleasure of a man who may
be a cruel and heartless scoundrel.[16]

Oppositions of this kind—the mother's "heart" and the father's
"heartlessness," her "torture" and his indifference, her concern for her
children and his "irresponsibility"—pervade feminist writings on custody. Some women, like Becker, saw the vote as their only redress.
Responding to Eliza Lynn Linton's "The Future Supremacy of Women"
in 1886, for example, "A Peeress" castigated "the monstrous law which
declares, in so many words, that a mother is no relation to her own child,
and that enables a man to take away her daughters from a blameless
mother and give them to his own mistress," arguing that to leave the law
in exclusively male hands is to destroy motherhood.[17] Similarly, humanitarian and feminist Frances Power Cobbe charged in "Wife-Torture in
England" (1878) that men were using their physical and legal power
to minimize rather than uphold motherly influence. For all "the fine-
sounding phrases perpetually repeated about the invaluable influence
of a good mother over her son," Cobbe asked: "How is a lad to learn to
reverence a woman whom he sees daily scoffed at, beaten, and abused,
and when he knows that the laws of his country . . . deny to her the
guardianship of *himself*—of the very child of her bosom—should her
husband choose to hand him over to her rival out of the street?" Only the
suffrage would enable the passage of legislation to protect wives from
domestic violence and to secure maternal custody rights.[18] But what
Cobbe termed "heteropathy"—the hatred of the weaker Other—clearly
not only perverted the fatherly and husbandly instincts of the working-
class brutes who formed the ostensible subject of her article but also
perverted the law.

What especially angered many feminists, Becker among them, was
that even when the law resigned itself to giving a child into a woman's
keeping, it did so "not in consideration of the natural right or parental
feelings of the *mother*, but solely out of care for the supposed interest of

the *child*."[19] When the Judicature Act of 1873 moved custody cases out of the purview of the common law and into that of Equity (permitting the court to consider the child's welfare and not simply the father's rights), women gained no legal power. Rather, control simply shifted from one male institution to another, the brutish father giving way to the arbitrary judge. At the bar as in the family, radical politician Arthur Arnold noted in *Fraser's* in 1878, a mother had to concede that her right to her children depended upon masculine authority. To win custody of her offspring from "a vicious and profligate father," a woman "must exhibit the fact that it is not hers by law; she must petition a Judge of the Chancery Division, who '*may*' thereupon order that her claim, founded on natural right, upon most obvious equity, and fraught with nothing but the clearest benefit to the infant children, shall be acknowledged."[20] The law of England, in other words, directly conflicted with the law of nature, as the latter had been defined time and again through the doctrine of separate spheres. If women's and children's place was indeed at home, as the rulers of the public sphere insisted, there could be no justification for removing the children from their mothers' care to give them into the power of either their fathers or the courts.[21]

Despite this paradox, periodical writers observed that judges continued to uphold fathers' rights to what many found a dismaying extent. The *Englishwoman's Review* made it a point of honor to draw public attention to such cases as *Beattie* v. *Beattie* (1883) or the Lilley case of 1877, in each of which an abusive husband in Scotland gained custody of an infant born after his wife had left him; neither the man's cruelty nor the baby's needs proved to the court's satisfaction that separation from its mother and "association with its father would be detrimental either to the physical or moral welfare of the child."[22] Although papers such as the *Scotsman* and the Dundee *Advertiser* decried such decisions, Scottish law required that the father be deemed unfit before custody could go to the mother, and Scots judges seemed particularly reluctant to believe that violent husbands might not make adequate fathers.

The *Scotsman* of 20 November 1883 explained the reasoning behind such decisions: judges hoped that bad husbands might yet be reclaimed as family men through the innocent influence of their children. Frances

Hodgson Burnett's *Little Lord Fauntleroy* (1886) had yet to appear, but the *Scotsman*'s gallery of judicial quotations prefigured the portrait of redeemed masculinity presented by that novel and its imitators:

> "How often has the presence and society of a child been the means of pre-venting a father from going wrong, or of reclaiming him after he has gone wrong?" "If we take a man's children from him, we leave him a solitary being, and deprive him of the most powerful inducement to amendment of life." "To leave his wife"—admitted blameless—"with the defender, were to subject him to an influence exciting, and tempting him to vio-lence towards her; to leave his little child in his house is, or may well be, to introduce a soothing influence to cheer the darkness of his lot"—he had knocked his wife insensible—"and bring out the better part of his nature." [23]

While the *Scotsman* writer conceded that the "wholesome and ele-vating influence" of children upon wayward parents is "happily an im-portant truth," the courts' optimism overlooked a still more crucial issue: "The violation of the family relationship through the action of the hus-band is thus emphasised and sustained by a violation of the maternal relationship to gratify either the parental instincts . . . [or more probably] the desire of the husband still further to annoy the wife." [24]

Judges and commentators alike, then, saw women as preserving family values and men as destroying them; the difference was that judges were reluctant to take the radical step of wholly removing unsatisfac-tory fathers from the family. Men merited custody precisely because it was men, not women, who were in need of redemption, a stance that would have seemed alien to the patriarchal courts of the early eigh-teenth century. To the still less conservative commentators, however, this reasoning seemed not to encourage domestic order but to strike at its very roots. An anonymous essayist on "The Law in Relation to Women" in an 1887 *Westminster Review* quoted two of the decisions that had also caught the eye of the *Scotsman*. The judgment of Lord Neaves, for one, struck the *Review* as morally indefensible. Neaves had written that to deprive a father of his children is to "deprive him of the most powerful inducement to amendment of life. It is not that he has committed faults, but that he teaches, or is likely to teach, evil to them, and to corrupt their morals, that can alone entitle us to interfere"—which seemed a pharisaical opinion, given that the father in the case had debauched the boys' seventeen-year-old nursemaid. To the Victorians, sexuality never affected simply the individuals directly concerned; the father's actions thus could not appropriately be defined as the peccadilloes natural to masculinity, but must be seen as one more contribution to the male-created moral malaise poisoning British society. Deprived of their mother's influence, the boys wouldn't stand a chance.

Similarly, the decision of Lord Ardmillan about the father's need for "a soothing influence to cheer the darkness and mitigate the bitterness of his lot" met the same writer's wrath as "sickly sentimentality and unmitigated nonsense . . . surely strong proof that he had great difficulty in giving any reason for his judgment at all." The implication was that Ardmillan and Neaves alike were motivated by feelings of male solidarity, their gender at once making them indulgent toward the failings of their sex (violence, sexual misconduct) and keeping them from comprehending the importance of children to mothers. On losing their offspring, women will frequently suffer "what is literally and with no exaggeration a broken heart"—in contrast to men, who, occupied with their professions, "will not spend [their lives] in useless lamentation either for wife or child."[25] Judges too are bad fathers, to the children in their courtrooms as (probably) to the children in their homes. The blindness of male authority to the true nature of domestic justice requires women, the writer concluded, to obtain and use the vote in order to bring about a more equitable arrangement.[26]

After the Norton case, the most publicized custody matter in Victorian Britain was the Agar-Ellis litigation, begun in 1878. The couple concerned had agreed before marrying that any children would be brought up in the mother's faith, Roman Catholicism; some fourteen years afterward, however, Ellis had repented his decision and decreed that the daughters should begin accompanying him to a Protestant church. The children, of whom the oldest was eleven at the time of the first trial, rebelled with their mother's support; the father ultimately removed them from her sphere of influence. His wife sued for religious control, citing the prenuptial agreement, but her suit was denied on the grounds that the contract had been invalidated by the marriage, which had turned the couple into a single legal entity, and that a husband, as the head of the house, clearly had the right to determine his children's location and education. In 1883 one of the daughters petitioned the court for the right to meet her mother freely. This petition too was denied, Sir John Pearson explaining for the appeals court "with great regret" that "he could not in the absence of any suggested fault on the part of the father, interfere with the right which the father had to control the custody and to decide upon the proper residence of his own children."[27]

The Agar-Ellis case "revolted the public conscience" (in suffrage leader Jessie Boucherett's phrase)[28] on two counts: the decision that men need not keep bargains made before marriage and the affirmation of the legal convention that fathers, not mothers, should determine their children's religion. The abuses of trust made possible by the former point were obvious to all; the latter was if anything still more discordant in the context of dominant late-Victorian thought about the roles of the two parents. As the *Dublin Review*'s unnamed essayist described the problem, the father's shepherding of his daughters to church could only be a matter of form, "while the mother's influence was allowed to work on their plastic minds during the remainder of the week. It is not difficult to foresee the side to which victory must inevitably incline as the result of this training."[29] Given the assumption throughout the period that maternal influence is the strongest moral force available to humankind, that mothers rather than fathers are the type of the divine, the ruling that fathers should control their children's religion seemed little short of bizarre. "Is it the ideal created in a child's mind by the father that usually acts as the spur to nobler effort in after life? Is it man or is it woman that has kept the reverence for a Supreme Being amongst us and implanted in each rising generation the sense of a moral ideal?" asked Frederick Thoresby in 1906.[30] That he phrased his argument about woman's moral supremacy as a series of rhetorical questions needing neither proof nor answer suggests the hold these ideas had come to have.

The Agar-Ellis case provided additional evidence about the comparative religiosity of men and women in that the husband's faith had come upon him only in middle age, whereas the prenuptial agreement demonstrated that religion had always mattered to his wife. Moreover, that the principal effect of Christianity on Ellis had been to cause him to break the promise exacted from him as the condition of the marriage suggested to critical observers that his ethical sense was not yet all it might have been. The maternal role, on the other hand, struck many Victorians as practical religion embodied in "each act of patience, self-abnegation, tending and guidance," as Nat Arling put it: "Through suffering, introspection, and their close association with innocence and helplessness, women have developed a more vivid sense of things spiritual than is gained by men in their ordinary career of sport, warfare, or business." Given this paradigm, men's claim to custody or to educational and religious control over their children was clearly rooted in might, not right, what Arling referred to as "heavy blackmail for their accorded protection."[31]

Women's legal powerlessness to determine the circumstances of their children's moral educations—for instance, the courts decreed that a child should follow its father's religion rather than its mother's even in cases where the father had died without expressing such a wish—thus existed against a presumption, shared by most periodical writers, that fathers were "frequently ill-qualified to fulfil that duty."[32] Instances where a father might be deemed the morally superior partner thus received almost no attention in journals and reviews. After Annie Besant's obscenity conviction for publishing information on contraception, for example, her estranged husband Frank, a minister, successfully sued for custody of their seven-year-old daughter, then living with Besant under the terms of the couple's separation agreement. (The husband already had custody of their son, who was slightly older than his sister; Besant was effectively separated from both children until they reached adulthood, when, much to their father's chagrin, they allied themselves with her.) Presumably afraid that publicizing either the obscenity or the custody trial would link the feminist cause to sexual immorality, women's advocates generally ignored Besant's difficulties, even though the jury in the first trial had affirmed its belief in her honor and good intentions.[33] Still more to the point, however, there seems to have been little effort on the part of conservative periodical writers to use this case as evidence that fathers could indeed be more reliable religious and ethical guides than mothers, an omission that suggests the extent to which the culture assumed the truth of the opposite stance.

Fathers' presumptive rights to custody included, as we have seen, the right to be the sole arbiters of the details of their children's lives. In practice, of course, women would typically not only direct religious education but have considerable say in secular education as well. (According to officials of Westminster School in London, for example, mothers' concern over the institution's unhealthy location lost Westminster many prospective pupils.) In law, however, such privileges belonged wholly to men. Only if a father had "forfeited his parental rights" by what Nigel V. Lowe terms "gross moral turpitude, abdication of parental authority, or seeking to remove the child from the country" would the court reassign them to the mother;[34] again, even in such a case the mother could expect nothing by right but only by the favor of the court. Even so, Shanley observes that by the 1880s, doubtless influenced in part by the public outcry that was likely to follow any too tender consideration for paternal rights, judges were becoming more ready to accept evidence of fathers' moral turpitude and more willing to intervene in family life to serve what they saw as the child's best interests. She quotes an 1884 article in the *Journal of Jurisprudence* to the effect that "it seems natural to a woman to take care of children; it does not seem so natural to a man."[35] Nevertheless, in accepting the responsibility of determining what constituted the child's interests, the courts were increasingly "taking care of children" in a peculiarly masculine (paternal) way.

Judges' initial reluctance to curtail fathers' "natural rights" seemed to one 1885 commentator in the *Westminster Review* to stem from an unwillingness to burden the judicial system with custodial responsibilities: "it is assumed that if the Court interferes with the authority of the living father, it will have to take upon itself the duty of seeing to the education of the child." As this essayist pointed out, however, the choice was not simply

> between the father and "judicial machinery," but between the father and
> the woman, who is at least equally responsible for bringing the child into

the world, who has been generally supposed to have had some faculties bestowed upon her for bringing it up, and who in the world's ordinary course has much more to do with its bringing up than its father has.[36]

Faced with delinquent fathers, in other words, the response of a legal system used to conceiving of women as nonpersons was to treat those fathers as the sole parents available. The choice seemed to rest between leaving the children to the care of men whose irresponsibility might be offset by the blood tie or turning them over to court-appointed guardians whose worth might be undermined by the impersonality of the legal connection. As a class, mothers were beneath the notice of the law; the arguments of commentators as to the primacy of the mother-child bond fell on deaf ears because mothers had no legal standing as parents.[37]

To acknowledge the individual existence of married women seemed to the courts and to Parliament a still more radical step than to take a quasi-paternal role by intervening in the private proceedings of family life. Thus during the debate in the House of Lords before passage of the 1886 Custody of Infants Act, Lord Ashbourne complained that the bill gave women too much power, albeit a power inferior to that of the judges presiding over domestic cases. As the *Englishwoman's Review* summed up his objections, he worried that it seemed possible "for the mother having different views from her husband as to how the children should be brought up to ask the opinion of the Court whether she or her husband was right. That was a very dangerous power to give the wife, and might lead to litigation, confusion, and unhappiness in families." His quarrel was not with the judge's right to express an opinion, but with the mother's; family "happiness" was incompatible with anything but the strictest of family hierarchies.[38] Similarly, in response to complaints that irresponsible fathers could miseducate, mistreat, and otherwise ignore their duties to their children, legislators generally curtailed fathers' rights in preference to expanding those of mothers.

The only regard in which Victorian law did accept a mother as the primary parent was in cases of illegitimacy. Under the Bastardy Act of 1834,[39] the burden of maintaining illegitimate children had been shifted from the father to the mother, whose word was no longer adequate to establish paternity and claim a maintenance allowance.[40] To feminists the law's leniency toward unmarried fathers served as a striking example of legal support of the sexual double standard, as men would have no financial incentive to refrain from sexual activity outside marriage. When the Bastardy Law Amendment Act was passed in 1872, its aim, as the *Englishwoman's Review* noted, was "to provide more stringent means than at present existed for compelling seducers to maintain their illegitimate offspring. . . . [and] to alter the bastardy law in favour of the seduced person and her offspring . . . in accordance with sound principles of public policy."[41] Under the new law women gained the right to sue their children's fathers for limited support if the children were born after the act's passage. Reformers of the 1890s, however, still more imbued with social-purity principles of sympathy for fallen women and anger toward fallen men, found the 1872 law inadequate. Arguing that "the law should not punish the child for the fault of its parents," barrister D. F. Hannigan contended that all children have the right to maintenance and education "as far as [the parents'] means will allow."[42]

To such authors the root of the illegitimacy problem was men's irresponsibility toward women and children alike. Elizabeth Wolstenholme Elmy, for instance, inquired in *Shafts*, "Do men really not see that the recognition and substantial enforcement by law of *paternal* duty and obligation towards children, whether born in or out of marriage, is *the* remedy needed?" Baby-farming and other such ills, she noted, could never be cured except by addressing men's sexual and parental irresponsibility—precisely the factors to which male legislators were likely to be blind.[43] Similarly, historical novelist and writer on women's issues Matilda M. Blake noted that while the father of an illegitimate child might sometimes be made to pay the paltry sum of five shillings in weekly maintenance,

> he has *no* legal obligations whatever to the child. If the mother dies, his liability ceases. Nor is the case altered if he voluntarily admits the paternity, and brings up the child; he can repudiate it when he chooses. The magnitude of this freedom from responsibility, and the recklessness it induces in men, may be gauged by the fact that some 50,000 illegitimate children are born annually in the United Kingdom.[44]

Male writers concurred. Herbert Flowerdew, for one, criticized the unsatisfactory nature of a law that not only seeks "no undertaking from the
father that he will contribute to [his child's] support" but requires him
at best to pay "not an adequate sum for the upbringing of his child, but
the maximum amount that can reasonably be expected from him as the
penalty of a peccadillo."[45] To define sexual and parental irresponsibility
as unimportant for men could only encourage such behavior.

Perhaps in part because it was the father, not the mother, whose legal
duties toward illegitimate children were seen as insufficient, articles
of this sort were concerned with securing for these children not emotional but financial rights—the "support and educat[ion]" of Hannigan's
essay. But British law generally resisted such attempts to impose an
economic penalty on fatherhood, preferring (or so critics charged) to
safeguard the property of the strong from the depredations of the weak.
Hence inheritance law, too, was significantly less friendly to women
and children than to adult males. While barrister and *Tablet* editor John
George Cox expressed in 1883 the "general principle, that in every case
where the distribution of property is concerned the law ought to stand *in
loco parentis*, and make such a distribution or arrangement as an ordinarily good parent would make,"[46] most periodical writers found that
the law failed this test on a number of counts.

In an article supporting Locke King's bill against primogeniture, for
instance, an anonymous legal critic of 1870 (tentatively identified in the
Wellesley Index as the barrister, poet, and diarist A. J. Munby) commented on the flaws of a system that in cases of intestacy awarded the
entire estate to the oldest son: "Certainly it is not the common practice
of those who make wills to leave their whole property to one child, and
leave the rest to starve; and it is, surely, not too much to require that
a man who intends so monstrous an injury should clearly express the
intention."[47] The law, in other words, was designed to protect the property at the expense of the children, and in doing so proved more callous
than most men. A subsequent intestacy law, the Intestates' Estates Act
of 1890, confirmed that it was the husband's property rights that mattered: designed as a reformist measure, the act gave the first £500 of a
man's estate to his widow before dividing the remainder along the lines

then customary (a third to the widow and two-thirds to the children, or, if no children existed, half to the widow and half to the next of kin or the Crown). In cases where it was the wife who had died intestate, however, the widowed husband would inherit her entire estate; children, next of kin, and Crown had no claim.

Many feminists sought a reversal of the legal philosophy expressed in such legislation, arguing that contrary to the assumption of the law in general, father and family were not identical. Harriett M'Ilquham expressed the opinion of a significant faction among women's advocates when in 1902 she proposed that widows and children should have a legal right to a deceased paterfamilias's property even in cases where he had willed it elsewhere. Claiming that "the true head of the family is he or she who most ably holds the home together," M'Ilquham castigated men for the "selfish carelessness" and familial irresponsibility that impoverished their dependents; because men could not be trusted to do their duty unsupervised, she called for legislation to ensure their equitable contribution to the home.[48] By way of a sequel, M'Ilquham asked in October 1907 that adultery be deemed sufficient cause to grant divorce to a wronged wife and criticized the Intestates' Estates Act of 1890 on the grounds that husbands were likely to will their first wives' property to their second wives, passing over the children who by rights should inherit.[49]

Another issue in dispute between feminists and the courts was that of paternal maintenance in the case of legitimate children. To the former it seemed obvious that given the limitations on women's ownership, employment, and child-custody rights, men should at least be legally required to support their children in appropriate style. But again, there was considerable reluctance on the part of lawmakers to curtail the man's right to spend his money as he saw fit.[50] Feminist writers on this question and on that of the Married Women's Property Acts thus constructed an image of improvident fatherhood as negative as the corresponding image of custodial fatherhood discussed at the beginning of this chapter. Women's political journals, such as the *Englishwoman's Review* and *Shafts*, were particularly prone to provide their readers with examples of runaway husbands whose deserted families, left without means of support, had no recourse but prostitution or starvation.

Thus the author of "The Property Earnings and Maintenance of Married Women," published in the *Review* in 1867, enumerated the woes of such working-class families and observed bitterly that "the husbands escaped all punishment, and were not even subject to the inconvenience of being tried."[51] In a similar vein, some thirty years later Elmy commented in *Shafts* on the Summary Jurisdiction (Married Women) Act of 1895, which permitted wives who fled from cruel or neglectful husbands to apply for separation orders after the fact without being deemed guilty of desertion, thereby giving them a chance to win from the court the custody of their children under sixteen and a maintenance order of up to two pounds a week. In Elmy's view what was really needed was an amendment to "enable a wife, whilst living with her husband, to enforce his presumed legal obligation to contribute to the maintenance of what the law, in every other connection, calls *his* family."[52] If men were to enjoy the privileges English law accorded to male heads of households, such writers opined throughout the period, they should at least pay for them.

That fathers and husbands were capable of abusing these privileges, editorialists (although perhaps not all judges) agreed; while estimates as to the prevalence of such behavior varied, I have found no example of a denial that any male Briton could willingly leave his family to starve. There were, however, three schools of thought as to how the problem might be solved. The first was expressed in Dinah Mulock Craik's 1887 *Contemporary Review* article "For Better for Worse," which argued that delinquent fathers should be exiled from the family so completely that they should not even be asked to contribute toward its support, since "a bad father is worse than none." The virtue of mothers, Craik asserted, is such that almost all would

> prefer the hardest poverty for themselves and their children, rather than
> the misery of a home in which the name of husband and father is a mere
> sham; where—sharpest pang of all—they have to sit still and see their
> little ones slowly contaminated by one to whom the hapless innocents owe
> nothing but the mere accident of existence.[53]

In this view, a man *is* his money; if the former is tainted, so is the latter. So thoroughly has Craik embraced the spiritual values of femininity and influence that the home can apparently exist completely independent of the marketplace. Indeed, it should, if the mother otherwise risks prostituting herself to a despicable husband.

The second view was articulated by Mary C. Tabor in the same periodical a year later. Observing, "It is a matter of constant occurrence that a family of children are kept from starvation by the ceaseless, slavish toil of the mother alone, while the father consumes in vicious indulgence the whole of his earnings, not one penny of which can be claimed for the children's support [without going through the unsympathetic Poor Law authorities]," she called for a "Sustenance and Protection of Children Act" to enforce and define parental responsibility. The model for the act was to be the Education Act of 1876, in which by instituting compulsory paid schooling "the idea of *duty* was for the first time recognized as an element in the parental relation." While she conceded that mothers as well as fathers might abuse their children, the economic focus of her article made clear that the primary neglecters of duty are fathers, as nature has decreed that mothers shall provide "nourishment and tendance" and fathers "protection and support." It was support, not "tendance," that she hoped to mandate.[54] When a limited Prevention of Cruelty to and Protection of Children Act was passed the following year, the focus was again largely economic. The act's definition of cruelty included making children work at undesirable occupations such as street selling, and an important aspect of this piece of legislation was that after the mistreated children had been remanded to the courts' care, parents would still be liable to pay up to five shillings per week maintenance.

The 1889 act sought at once to remove children from irresponsible parents (probably fathers) and to train working-class adults to a better sense of parental duty even in their children's absence. Parents would learn what constituted a reasonable sum to expend on their offspring, without getting the chance to plume themselves on having shifted their financial burden over to the state. Conversely, the courts would occupy the enviable position that had formerly belonged to fathers, in that they would have all the say in the disposition of the children and none of the monetary responsibility. The third school of thought about maintenance, however, sought to follow to its logical conclusion the general trend toward turning the state into the ultimate paterfamilias. As Vere Collins put the argument in a 1905 *Fortnightly Review*, fathers are dispensable except for their wallets: in cases of marital unhappiness "it is opposed to reason and experience to believe that the offspring will be better off with the two parents than with one." Furthermore, he continued,

> Various considerations mark out the woman as the natural guardian, except in cases when she can be proved unfit. The child belongs to her more than to the man. . . . up to the seventh or eighth year children's needs make them more dependent on the mother's care, and after that age the male influence that a boy stands in need of is to a considerable extent supplied by school life.

The problem with revising custody arrangements to privilege the mother, of course, was that the father could not be depended upon to provide financial support if his "natural rights" had thus been curtailed. Collins's solution, backed by the authority of George Bernard Shaw's *Man and Superman* (1903), was to remove the mother's "dependence on a particular man" by giving all mothers an allowance from the public coffers. This sum could at the court's discretion be augmented by the requisitioning of additional funds from the father to allow for the maintenance of class distinctions, but in either case the ultimate father would be the state, which would take over the paternal functions of paying for a child's upkeep and deciding what kind of education that child should receive.[55]

In their separate ways, then, both the legal system and outside commentators upon that system saw the father-child relationship in material terms. Family law generally viewed the child itself as property, from which the father (or, later, the state) had the right to benefit; commentators tended to suggest that the father's contribution to the child's upkeep was mainly financial. The latter stance also informed the Victorian and Edwardian debate over divorce, a major focus of which was the question of whether it was better for parents to "stay together for the sake of the children" or part company in the hope of minimizing domestic conflict and other damaging influences.

Before the passage of the 1857 Divorce Act, the termination of a marriage (as opposed to legal separation) could only be effected by ecclesiastical annulment or by the passage of an individual act of Parliament for each case; Brown notes that the total number of divorces ever granted in the latter fashion was only 317.[56] In contrast, Allen Horstman reports that in 1858 no fewer than 253 petitions for divorce were filed, ninety-seven of which came from women despite the greater legal difficulties the act placed in their way. The number was more than ten times that anticipated by the Lord Chancellor,[57] a discrepancy that helped to establish divorce, for all its statistical insignificance compared to modern-day figures, as an important Victorian concern.

As Horstman points out, the impetus behind the Divorce Act was largely the desire to encourage marital morality: a wronged middle-class spouse would now have a legal recourse earlier granted only to the wealthy.[58] The newspapers' fascination with divorce-court proceedings was also intended to have a deterrent effect by making prospective petitioners reluctant to enter the public arena (although Queen Victoria spoke for the faction that held this effort counterproductive when she complained that such reportage was "pernicious to the public morals"[59]). The Victorian liberalization of divorce, in other words, did not signal a new acceptance of serial monogamy; it was rather a signal that the sexual license of patriarchal tradition would no longer be tacitly endorsed.[60] And insofar as it confirmed the ideology of separate spheres,[61] it gave another imprimatur to the idea that men were less emotionally involved with the family than women.

To those who wrote in support of the 1857 act, male sexual immorality was an important concern. While he conceded that women's adultery was especially dangerous to society because of the possibility that illegitimate children might be inserted into the family, William Stirling-Maxwell (a Scottish M.P. and historian who would marry Caroline Norton in 1877) argued that "it is surely illogical and unjust to say that because the infidelity of the wife deserves a heavier chastisement than that of the husband, the husband's breach of vow is in every case to be reckoned venial."[62] To make divorce accessible to the poor and to women, he concluded, was essential for the public good. From a woman's point of view, such condemnation of male adultery hardly went far enough. Thus Cornwallis, for one, observed in 1857 that "the husband's infidelity wastes on his spurious offspring the property which ought to have benefited the legitimate children of his marriage, and very probably injures the unfortunate and innocent wife in health no less seriously than in property," given the risk of venereal disease.[63]

Once the Divorce Act had passed into law, attention swung to the question of the circumstances under which it should be used. As Craik remarked, "in most cases of unhappy marriage the first thing to be considered is *the good of the children*"—which, she held, is best served by placing them in their mother's sole custody through a legal separation.[64] Other commentators believed that whatever the merits of separation, divorce is unconscionable. Lyman Cobb, writing in the American periodical *The Nation* in 1869, worried that divorce weakens even the parent-child tie, since children learn to view the family as temporary and "to jeer at the 'sacredness' of the relation" between husband and wife.[65] From Britain, historian and political writer Goldwin Smith claimed in 1874 that American women were beginning to recognize divorce as an evil, knowing "that marriage is pre-eminently a restraint placed on the passions of the man in the interest of the woman . . . and that to the children divorce is moral and social ruin."[66] However a man may struggle against the "restraint" of marriage, in other words, it is dangerous for children and for society at large to learn that this restraint may be broken.

Cobb's and Smith's stances represent the dominant arguments against divorce—at least in its relation to parenthood—throughout the period. Smith's opposition of moral woman and degenerate man found an analogue in two articles by Elizabeth Rachel Chapman in the *Westminster Review* in 1888 and 1890, for example. The first of these, "Marriage Rejection and Marriage Reform," focused primarily on the differences between principled cohabitation (à la George Eliot) and its revolutionary counterpart (exemplified for Chapman by Jean-Jacques Rousseau or Percy Shelley). While according a grudging respect to the former movement, she castigated free-love radicalism as masculinist in its sensuality and parental irresponsibility. Divorce, to Chapman, served as another example of these latter evils. Not only did British law wink at male infidelity, but the male court system compounded the fault by awarding child custody to guilty husbands in preference to innocent wives. To put married or unmarried love on a merely temporary basis could only gratify base male instincts at the expense of feminine ideals. To reject divorce, then, was "in the interest of the community" because the rejection would privilege women's drive toward permanence, order, and responsibility, helping to contain men's drive toward instability.[67]

Chapman's second essay, which focused more specifically on divorce, dismissed the argument that dissolving a marriage may be the best thing for the children. Divorce, she explained, "is based on universal selfishness, and proceeds on the assumption that ease—not endeavour, comfort—not duty, happiness—not goodness, are the highest human ideals." This is no ethic for children to absorb. Rather, the principled parent will bear any pain, any humiliation, not only to "avert outward scandal and protect, as far as may be, the happiness and the innocence of the children" from a social standpoint, but also to inculcate children with appropriate ideals of sacrifice and parental devotion. Again, Chapman made clear that this kind of fortitude was largely a specifically maternal characteristic, noting that "divorce was instituted solely in the husband's interest . . . historically speaking, [it] has been but another name for the subjugation of women." Men, in other words, lack the sense of family responsibility that imbues women; divorce panders to the male impulse to flee committed husbandhood and fatherhood.[68]

While Chapman's argument most closely resembles Smith's in that both are gender-based, it also bears some similarity to Cobb's in its assumption that the most unhappy marriage could yet teach children valuable lessons about the holiness of matrimony. This stance, too, remained important into the late-Victorian and Edwardian period. Thus Susan Harris, countess of Malmesbury, complained in 1892 that the easy dissolution of marriage leads to "the entire loss of the moral influence of both parents over the rising generation." Similarly, in 1907 G. Willett Van Nest feared that "Divorce granted between parents must have a bad effect on the children, and too liberal divorce laws for parents are sure in future generations to prove injurious to the community where they are too readily granted." The same year, Bernard Houghton judged that divorce undermines children's right "to healthy and sanitary surroundings, to kindly home influences, and sufficiency of education. . . . surely that State has in the future the greatest chances of success which best safeguards the up-bringing and education of the young," otherwise jeopardized by the "notoriously inferior" care provided by stepparents.[69] If Van Nest and Houghton seemed more concerned about the state's interests than about the individual's, the same assumptions about "family influence" were still present that were so crucial in the mid-Victorian years. Such arguments, however, were noticeably less rooted in gender than the views of Smith and Chapman; moral faults do not necessarily develop along biological lines.

The arguments in favor of readily available divorce likewise often centered on the ethical upbringing of children. Here again, when men were singled out as morally different from women, the advantage went to the latter. A lecture by Irish novelist Mabel Sharman Crawford on wife beating, reported in *Shafts* in 1894, thus cast men as the aggressors and women as the victims in what amounted for boys to "a training school in crime. The lessons learnt in childhood where the mother was a tyrant's slave, exerted an influence for evil far more powerful than any influence for good that could be brought to bear upon them"—presumably by the battered mother. The only hope of breaking this nefarious male influence was that of separating boys from brutal fathers.[70]

Likewise, M'Ilquham's 1907 *Westminster Review* essay criticized existing divorce law for failing to hold men to a high (female) standard of sexual morality. To grant only separation, not divorce, to "insulted wives . . . greatly degrades the ideal of marriage," while male-biased custody arrangements discourage mothers from ending unions so degraded. Because

> No true mother would wish to soil the minds of her children with her wrongs, she therefore invariably has to let her character and aims lie under a cloud, for the father is generally allowed great latitude in seeing his children. I do not know of any case in which an erring wife has been allowed to have her children spend part of the year with her, but there have been instances where such favour has been granted to very erring husbands.

Mothers avoid contaminating their children with the knowledge of male sin; fathers not only embrace corruption but feel no compunction about

exposing their offspring to it.[71] There seems little question as to which
parent behaves more responsibly toward the family and toward society.

Other critics avoided blaming one gender or the other while still focusing on the bad effects of unhappy unions on children. In her rebuttal
of Chapman's "Marriage Rejection and Marriage Reform" in December 1888, Jane Hume Clapperton became one of the few feminists
to join hands with Linton over any issue; she approvingly quoted the
latter's September 1888 *Universal Review* article, "The Philosophy of
Marriage," which noted, "Surely nothing can be worse for the morals of
children than to bring them up in an atmosphere of dissension, of mutual
hatred, of mutual recriminations, and disrespect between father and
mother, where, too, they are forced to take sides and be partisans." To
Linton, as to Clapperton, "divorce is a better state of things than domestic unhappiness, wherein the passions have it all their own way, and the
dignity of human nature is lost in the turmoil of dissension. . . . the well-
being of the children [demands it]." Combining eugenics with theories
of nurture, Clapperton argued that "forces of reproduction, heredity,
and training" crucial to future generations depend on the present avail-
ability of divorce. Until it permits the dissolution of unions, humanity
will never evolve into a race "capable of spontaneously forming life-
unions of ideal perfection."[72] Dissent, passion, and dysgenic forces,
however, apparently emanate from either parent.

Similarly, an essay signed "E.M.S." and entitled "Some Modern
Ideas about Marriage" (*Westminster Review*, 1895) claimed to take
a middle-of-the-road stance between what it defined as the woman-
centered reforms proposed by social-purity groups and the masculinist
reforms advocated by sexual-freedom apologists such as Grant Allen.
Calling simultaneously for an "extension of [woman's] influence" over
sexual morality and for more relaxed marriage laws, E.M.S. noted that
while the existence of children must discourage frivolous divorce, "not
even the mutual care of children can be said to justify the enforced
perpetuation through life of a loveless and uncongenial marriage, nor
can the home influence of such a marriage fail to be baneful to their
upbringing."[73] Although the essay clearly implied that women are more
chaste than men, the invocations of parenthood—the "mutual care" it

represents, the interest both partners feel in remaining with their children—as clearly suggested that fatherhood no less than motherhood is an important emotional force.

Articles drawing on the principles of eugenics likewise made little distinction between the behavior of the two parents. Holding that "epilepsy, insanity, moral perversion, incurable viciousness of temper, habitual drunkenness, criminal conduct of any sort, or habitual laziness and shiftlessness, ought to render divorce not merely obtainable, but obligatory," Woods Hutchinson made clear in "Evolutionary Ethics of Marriage and Divorce" (1905) that both partners in a marriage should have but one object: "Husband and wife unite not to enjoy themselves, but to rear and train healthy, happy, worthy offspring. Any flinching from this purpose and aim, on personal or selfish grounds, is biologically immoral." To be sure, the exigencies of men's lives might put them at greater risk than their spouses of dysgenic attributes, and in acknowledgment of this likelihood Hutchinson suggested that society subsidize women's flights from "drunken or criminal" husbands. At the same time, however, he remarked that fatherly indifference is primarily a characteristic of savages, not of civilized men; in general, then, monogamy and paternal involvement go hand in hand, and men as well as women are liable to feel the pull to stay married (or to divorce) for the sake of the children.[74] Similarly, eugenist Montague Crackanthorpe concurred in 1910 that any inheritable weakness ought to be grounds for divorce, since it is the parents' biological influence over the children that is paramount in marriage. Emotionally, too, friendly divorce is best for the well-being of the young, as it creates an atmosphere of healthy frankness about sexual matters and reduces domestic tensions that may injure growing minds.[75]

To summarize, then: The debate over custody arrangements or parental control opposed the question of the feelings of the mother (and, in general, only the mother) to that of whether social order could be maintained if fathers' rights were curtailed. In contrast, advocates on both sides of the divorce debate invoked family well-being and the importance of parental influence to prove their points. But even within the discussion of divorce, the overall attitude commentators took toward fathers was negative: men are sexually wild and morally contaminated, or at best not *necessarily* their wives' ethical inferiors; they are never women's betters, never superior influences upon children. The divorce law itself seemed to codify these pessimistic sentiments by implying that any husband may be unfaithful and that a wife has cause to complain only if her husband unites infidelity with some darker sin.

The rights and responsibilities of fatherhood were naturally never far from any discussion of marriage-law reform in the Victorian and Edwardian era, and the marriage question was one of the most frequently disputed. Wives' desire to retain legal "personhood" was inseparable from the custody issue, free love from illegitimacy, divorce from its effects on children. Even what W. S. Gilbert described in the finale to act 1 of *Iolanthe* (1882) as "that annual blister, / Marriage with deceased wife's sister" was seen in terms of fatherhood; a widower, proponents assumed, would wish to remarry at the first opportunity in order to give his children a mother's care, and what more suitable stepmother than an aunt? Significantly, the corresponding question of the "deceased husband's brother" received little attention, implying that while a mother's care might be essential, a father's is not.[76]

Judicial intentions often to the contrary, the tendency of family law in this period was to confirm the impression that fathers are likely to be a maleficent influence and that male power should operate as little as possible within the domestic sphere. Nevertheless, women's claims to custody rights, control over their children's lives, child support, and the ability to rid themselves of abusive husbands were answered with an increase not in the amount of power granted to mothers but in the amount of power granted to the courts. The latter gained the rights of deciding children's residence and upbringing, ordering the payment of maintenance, and agreeing to separations, all of which had once been the province only of the private (male) citizen. What seemed to many reformers the high-handed and even immoral attitude of the law in the use it made of these new privileges at once confirmed that the domestic power of actual fathers was dwindling and symbolized the domestic irresponsibility of male institutions as a class. In its gradual assumption of the paternal role, the judicial system upheld the patriarchal principles of English law without successfully convincing women's advocates that even surrogate fatherhood could be compatible with domestic justice. For all that the law did begin to grant mothers recourse against unsatisfactory husbands, metaphorically it proved in the eyes of many feminists to be the worst father of the lot.

5

"Alma Pater": Fathers and the School

Over and over again have I noticed,
and I know my testimony will be borne
out by men of experience, that
all the exertions and energies brought
to bear for good on a boy at school
are undone by the home. It is a strong,
a terrible, indictment to bring against
home life; but it is true. . . . The
schoolmaster reads the boy from alpha
to omega; the parent is often
profoundly ignorant.

In his classic study *Godliness and Good Learning*, David Newsome notes that the first generation of reformist Victorian headmasters inherited an educational system that was in many ways spiritually bankrupt. Regency critics, led by the humanitarian essayist Sydney Smith (cofounder of the *Edinburgh Review*), blasted the public schools for their brutality on the one hand, their lack of moral or intellectual standards on the other. Barely supervised in class (given the low faculty-student ratios) and wholly unsupervised outside it, a boy's significant contact with his teachers might well be limited to the occasional flogging; graduation found all but the gifted ignorant even of the classical studies that constituted their entire curriculum.

While aristocratic fathers, having weathered exactly this academic experience in their own years at Eton or Harrow, were willing enough to see their sons endure it too, middle-class men were less tolerant. And it was the flourishing bourgeoisie—the Quantity rather than the Quality—that the public schools had to serve if they were to survive. In Newsome's formulation: "There was wanting an ideal; and, to save the public schools from the wholesale desertion of the middle class, this ideal had exactly to express the wishes and sentiments of the parents whose sons the schools needed to retain and attract."[1] But matters did not end in a simple mirroring of ethics. In its adaptation of the domestic and religious ideals of the Victorian middle class, the public school (and later, the girls' school and the state-run school as well) presented itself as not the servant of but the substitute for the home. In the artificial "family" of the boys' school, the headmaster clearly represented the father. Because of the virtual absence of mother figures in this con-

struct, however, male teachers were enabled to claim superiority over
real fathers by taking on a mantle of androgyny, asserting their power in
terms of both masculine authority *and* feminine moral influence.[2] While
the bourgeois family split these roles along gender lines, schoolmasters
could join public and private spheres into a unified whole, playing out
a type of masculinity that, like the Victorian Christ's, went beyond the
usual male confines and obsessions to perform its allotted tasks. As suc-
cessive reforms reshaped nineteenth-century education, the image of
the ideal educator drew ever closer to that of the ideal mother.

The beginning of the public-school reforms is usually placed at
1828, the year Thomas Arnold became headmaster of Rugby. Arnold's
approach recalls that of any Victorian missionary set down amidst a
primitive and warlike tribe; he sought not only to civilize and educate individuals, but also to bring divine light to a backward society
by reorganizing Rugby's government, recreations, and overall aims so
that school culture might instill noble (and in many ways androgynous)
manliness even in boys unlikely to come directly under the headmaster's
eye. Wresting new autonomy from the trustees of the school, Arnold
worked to disseminate this power along orderly and effective lines by
shaping a tightly knit cadre of masters and sixth-form boys loyal to his
vision. As Rugby graduates and faculty members rose to head other institutions, his views gained ever wider currency in the world outside; as
Rugby dormitories and studies gradually turned away from chaos and
violence, his values trickled downward from the prefects to the lowest
forms. And while Arnold's death in 1842 predated the real revitalization
of Victorian education, nevertheless the findings of the Public Schools
Commission of 1864, the debates over the Education Acts of 1870 and
1902, and the tenor of commentary on schools of all sorts throughout the
period served to ratify and reinscribe his pedagogy of morals.

It is no part of my project to argue that Arnold's ideology survived
unchanged until Edwardian days, or even that the public schools of
the early twentieth century were significantly gentler than those of the
late eighteenth. Certainly grafting athleticism and patriotism onto the
public-school stem yielded fruit far removed from the Christian gentlemanliness so dear to Arnold's heart; as historian of education J. A. Man-

gan has observed, "The [late-Victorian and Edwardian] public school world was often a godless world of cold, hunger, competition and endurance. There was frequently little kindness and less piety." (Indeed, Mangan finds that the sufferings endured by schoolboys of this period resulted not from "adult indifference," as had been the case before 1850, but from "adult calculation"; the unstated ideal was one of privation.[3]) Rather, I am concerned with the terms in which the education question was discussed—not what actually happened in the schools but what critics claimed was happening. To a great extent, the rhetoric they employed was the rhetoric of domesticity, of the same evangelical values of moral purity and personal influence that also formed the basis of the ideal woman's spiritual power. The consistency with which writers presented headmasters and housemasters as symbolic parents may not provide accurate insight into how schools actually functioned, but it says a great deal about the ideal of parenthood such writers had internalized.

To be sure, the schools' image depended from the first on the very patriarchal structures that Victorian culture was coming to distrust. John R. Gillis observes that the new power over both students and faculty that Arnold and his successors gained from the trustees of the various public schools was crucial to the development of the paternal metaphor within Victorian pedagogy. Only after the virtual anarchy of the pre-reform school had given way to a pyramidal hierarchy, its pinnacle occupied by the headmaster, did it become "possible to think of the school as a proper substitute for the family, the teachers serving as surrogate fathers. By the 1860s it could be said that the Master was *in loco parentis* in the full sense of that term."[4] Likewise, Arnold established his moral influence within the school in part by using the values of the public sphere: he gave his teachers higher salaries and his prefects more power. Concurrently, male instructors' status began to improve, while education was becoming more generally defined as a profession. In an era before the widespread formal higher education of women, the credentials needed for success in academia belonged almost exclusively to men, just as the authority the headmaster wielded within the school mirrored the common-law privileges of the father within the family.

But if the headmaster's power could not have been solidified without this appeal to the authoritarian economy of the public sphere, his status required a simultaneous appeal to what was deemed feminine and private. An unsigned allegory on "The Two Guides of the Child," which appeared in Charles Dickens's magazine *Household Words* in 1850, struck what was fast becoming the dominant note in the rhetoric of education: the invocation of explicitly maternal tenderness and understanding. The sketch of childhood first depicts happy infants romping with their mothers in the Child Valley and then introduces a harsh male teacher who "seizes an unhappy, shrieking child" in order to inform it "about two languages spoken by nations extinct centuries ago." Neither the knowledge nor the accompanying beating adequately prepares the child-victim for adult life, and the graduates of this system "wander among men out of their fog-land, preaching folly." In contrast to the teacher-martinet, however, comes a smiling man whose educational approach is identical to the mothers' behavior: he "rolls upon the flowers with the little ones. . . . He frolics with them and might be first cousin to the butterflies." His lesson concerns not information but communication, not authority but sympathy. When *his* pupils enter the adult realm, they retain the loving ideals of the woman-dominated Child Valley and consequently may serve humanity.[5] The ideal teacher, in short, combines masculine professional standing with feminine nurturance; because he can operate in both spheres, he is best fitted to lead (male) pupils from one to the other. It is this "bilingualism," this combination of maleness and maternity, that consistently characterizes positive portraits of the Victorian educator.

"The Two Guides of the Child" prefigures the central theme of Dickens's *Hard Times*, which was to be serialized in the same periodical in 1854; both preach the understanding of the child mind, the unwisdom of a fact-based instead of a character-based approach to education. But Dickens and his contributors were by no means alone in arguing that the teacher-child relationship should depend upon love and sympathy rather than upon fear. While *Hard Times* was appearing in serial form, for instance, the philosopher Herbert Spencer used as his example of the ideal teacher the intelligent mother gently instructing her toddler about physical properties such as colors and textures; he reminded his readers "how efficient and benign is the control of a master who is felt to be a friend, when compared with the control of one who is looked upon with aversion." [6] To Spencer the qualities of the born teacher were encouragement, empathy, helpfulness, and an understanding of child psychology—all of which, of course, also characterized the stereotypical mother. The liminal figure of the schoolmaster, with one foot in the world and the other in the nursery, had to partake of the qualities of both genders.

Similarly, commentators on school reform in the 1850s stressed, like Arnold himself, that the best education is moral, so that the best goal of the public school is to build character rather than to force-feed information. This idea dominated even discussions of curriculum (it was claimed that the classics instilled ethics and were thus superior to mathematics, which only exercised the intellect) and was the major justification for the games craze: both as sexual sublimation and as symbol for the moral dilemma, sports stamped out sin. [7] In short, the school's primary responsibility was to inculcate the values usually associated with domesticity; worldly success was pronounced unimportant. [8] "The real object of a high-minded educator will be . . . to enlist the young hearts of his pupils on the side of what is good," wrote an anonymous editorialist on "Our Public Schools—Their Discipline and Instruction" in *Fraser's* in 1854. Such an end, Victorians theorized, is reached not by force but by love, and the writer added approvingly that under the Arnoldian system, "discipline is growing not less strict, but softer and gentler, the humanizing intercourse between boys and masters steadily increasing." [9] Reviewing *Tom Brown's Schooldays*, essayist Richard Ford (a product of Winchester) observed that Arnold was as conscientious about school housekeeping as about academic standards, while "his most earnest desire was to win [students'] hearts and stand to them *in loco parentis* rather than in that of a dreaded master. . . . His government of the school was no reign of terror, nor did he rely on the meaner motives of fear and punishment." [10] The ideal of the headmaster as domestic paragon and moral influence plainly lived even outside the pages of Thomas Hughes's novel.

Thus in the 1860s, when the public schools bore the scrutiny of both periodical writers and a parliamentary commission, one of the questions critics raised most often was that of the extent to which schools and masters lived up to their parental role. Matthew J. Higgins's negative portrait of Eton in an 1861 *Edinburgh Review,* which called for just such a Royal Commission as was soon to be established, accused the college of neglecting its pupils for its finances. Higgins, a journalist and Old Etonian, made much of the huge profits turned by Eton's provost and fellows in contravention of the founders' statutes; further, he estimated that Eton's turn-of-the-century headmaster John Keate had netted some £4000 a year from his post and that the contemporaneous headmaster, Thomas Balston, would be making more money yet. (One might usefully compare this figure with the £150 reported by the Schools Inquiry Commission in 1867–68 as the ceiling for headmistresses in girls' schools.[11]) Such profits depended in part on curtailing the staff so that there would be fewer people to share the wealth. While schools justified the system to parents by claiming that it promoted self-sufficiency and leadership, the result from the pupils' standpoint, Higgins argued, was neglect, "premature initiation into vice," and inferior teaching: "the general education to be had in the pauper school of the Slough union is considerably better and more useful to all sorts and conditions of men than the education to be had at Eton College." Only hiring more assistant masters could remedy matters. In the dormitories as in the classrooms, what the boys most needed was to "be subjected to the immediate personal superintendence of a sensible man" who would act "as their companion, adviser, and friend."[12]

Higgins's charges against Eton, reprised by Goldwin Smith in the wake of the commission's report,[13] suggested that the public schools' failure was directly linked to a rejection of family values. The hunger for money, which had no place either in these foundations as originally conceived or in the domestic circle, had made Eton and its competitors impersonal, immoral, violent, and irresponsible, the antitheses of all that either schools or families should stand for. Like the father corrupted by the marketplace, the school whose primary concern was profit had shown itself unfit to rear children. Only Rugby, with its post-Arnoldian emphasis on close supervision, personal influence, and Christian morality, seemed to rise above this pattern of greed and neglect.

To add insult to injury, the offending schools paid lip service to the very ideal they had betrayed. Summarizing the Public Schools Report in a series of articles in *Blackwood's* in 1864, clergyman and educational theorist W. Lucas Collins exposed the hollowness of Eton's and Harrow's claims to provide surrogate parenting:

> The tutor is said to stand to his pupil *in loco parentis;* this is the recognised phrase which nearly every Eton master uses to express the relationship; he is "his friend and impartial counsellor," says Provost Goodford; "his adviser, instructor, and friend," says Mr Durnford; they go to him in every "doubt, perplexity, and trouble," says Mr S. Hawtrey, who goes on to dilate upon this mutual confidence, "the pivot on which the whole system turns," at much greater length than we have space to follow him.

Collins juxtaposed these claims, tellingly, with headmaster Balston's evidence that he never had fewer than fifty-five students in his form, at which the following exchange took place between commission and witness: "'And you were able to be a father to them all?'—'*That is a rather puzzling question.*'"[14] One recalls here Victorian anthropology's dismissal of the tribal patriarchal family on the grounds that the father of fifty children is too distant to pay any child adequate attention; in the schools, too, critics exalted instead the model of the bourgeois, Christian family, in which love and character were at a premium and the profit motive was deemed inappropriate.

The Harrow masters reiterated what Collins belittled as "the *loco parentis* theory." But the report of Lord Clarendon's cross-examination of a Harrow tutor again reveals the skepticism of both chief commissioner and commentator:

> "Considering the great number of other calls upon your time, and the duties that devolve upon you, do you think that, with so many as sixty boys, you can really look after their individual character and moral conduct, and their particular fitness for certain studies, sufficiently to make you feel satisfied that you are *in loco parentis* to them?" "I could not do so if the boys

were left entirely to my charge. . . . but all the charge that is required from a private tutor, I hope I can undertake, or else I should not have done so." And we hope the Commissioners were satisfied. There is no going beyond that sort of answer, of course.[15]

In contrast, Collins singled out for praise the system that operated in a few Harrow houses, which did successfully mirror the British family. Here the number of boarders was limited to seven, who

> enjoy almost of necessity considerably more domestic and home-like supervision than would be either possible or desirable in large houses containing forty or fifty boys. It is usual for them to take all their meals with the master and his family, of which, in fact, they may be said to form a part. . . . Not only does this exempt a boy from many of the hardships of public-school life, but his moral character and general habits are more under observation and control.

Under these conditions "that old '*loco parentis*' formula, which seems to us so little applicable to the relation between tutor and pupil, becomes no longer a formula." [16] The lesson is clear: the good "parent" concerns himself not with finances but with child rearing, with personal influence over the few rather than cursory contact with the many. The ideals of the marketplace, profit and efficiency, have no place in the school, which should cleave instead to the tenderer ideals of the home.

To be sure, even in the 1860s there was doubt that the old regimen of harshness could be abandoned without jeopardizing manliness, the principal quality that Victorian boys' schools promised to instill. Collins, for one, conceded that "familiar and confidential relations" between boy and tutor could produce "a lamentable falling off" in the deference due masculine authority, even while it raised boyish morality to new heights. He warned of the small houses, "Plainly there are disadvantages in too much of the master's supervision, and the hardier and more independent elements of a boy's character may lose in development"—an argument long used by the laissez-faire defenders of dormitory anarchy.[17] Others, such as the teacher F. W. Warre-Cornish, hinted after the reforms were well established that "the power of self-control and the clear distinction between right and wrong [might] suffer"

from too much institutional kindness.[18] In general, though, the push
for masters' intimacy with students echoed contemporaneous pleas for
paternal closeness to children. In both cases the implicit model was the
mother, as sympathizer and friend rather than disciplinarian, despite
a certain anxiety about whether masculinity could be retained once the
less desirable trappings of patriarchy had disappeared.

The *loco parentis* movement continued to gain force after the public schools bowed to the need for reform. Nor did it have reference
only to prestigious foundations. A lead article titled "Public and Private
Schools" in the *Westminster Review* in 1873 chided some private schools
for failing to live up to the Arnoldian model of "high moral tone" and constant moral assessment; the answer, this anonymous writer found, was
greater supervision by masters, along the lines laid down by preparatory
academies.[19] In an essay on Roman Catholic education five years later,
William Petre (Vatican prelate and author of *Remarks on the Condition of
Catholic Liberal Education* [1877]) argued for limiting school size to an
intimate forty pupils so that *"personal influence"* could take precedence
over the less morally valuable task of *"surveillance."* Pleading for a still
freer rein for "that parental influence and tenderness which is the highest endowment, potentially, of the celibate educator," Petre explained
that the major contribution of Roman Catholic academies should be
"those advantages of personal and individual influence, combined with
minute and intelligent but elastic surveillance, and domesticity of life,
which are the special and peculiar characteristics of well-managed small
schools."[20] During the high-Victorian explosion of educational foundations, then, the small size and low profits often associated with private
facilities could be parlayed into advantages by invoking the domestic
metaphor. Similarly, a celibate staff could appear, paradoxically, as
"parental," a connection clearly dependent on the linkage of purity and
*mother*hood. The headmasters of such institutions, writers like Petre
implied, were better "fathers" than the more worldly, successful men
who governed the great public schools; in other words, true parenthood
mirrored femininity and ignored masculinity as far as possible.

But in general, more than any other professionals of the day, public-
school headmasters won laudatory comment in the periodical press. At

once clergymen, teachers, and statesmen within the school world, they embodied respected public roles; in addition, their work as nurturers and moral influences within the artificial family enabled them to wear as well the halo of ideal parenthood. This simultaneous expertise in public and private spheres carried with it a mantle of androgyny. Arnold was not the only man noted for his talent at guidance tasks more usually associated with mothers.[21] Indeed, writers seldom praised headmasters *except* in feminized terms. In an 1879 essay on Frederick Temple of Rugby, Arthur Sidgwick stressed, "Of the personal moral and religious influence of Dr. Temple we have neither the space nor the power to say anything adequate."[22] A contributor to the same series, Everard Thurn, chose G. F. L. Cotton as Marlborough's greatest headmaster; a man "of a gentle, kind, and sympathetic nature," Cotton's genius was his "complete influence" over students.[23] As late as 1910, J. E. C. Welldon (ex-headmaster of Harrow) eulogized J. J. Hornby (headmaster of Eton 1868–84, later its provost, and Welldon's former teacher) for his loving rule, his unconscious personal influence, and the lack of public ambition that resulted from his joy in "the calm serenity of home."[24] So common was the emphasis on the private sphere that French educator Pierre de Coubertin remarked in 1902: "I have noticed with some surprise that Englishmen as a rule see nothing but the moral aspect of the pedagogy of Thomas Arnold and Edward Thring." Far from combating this one-sidedness, he participated in it, praising the "moral revolution" effected by Arnold and Thring and contending that not intellectual or physical but ethical prowess (gained, of course, in the public schools) had enabled Britain to beat the Boers.[25]

Similarly, discussions of less exalted public-school teachers also tended to emphasize the feminine status and traits of these men. Classical scholar and headmaster J. F. Boyes commented in the *Cornhill* in 1861 on the schoolmaster's life in terms strikingly reminiscent of the experience of the middle-class woman, noting

his general want of large means; the main business of his life concerned with children and boys, not with men, and strongly leading him to trace the same eternal and limited circle, often real, always imagined; the confining

nature of his labours, generally keeping him in great measure secluded
from the world of men, and from a liberalizing mixture with general society.

Like the woman, too, the schoolmaster's task is to serve for his pupils
as "their highest moral type, model, and example"—a work that becomes especially difficult given the constrictions and humiliations that
may warp an inferior man. Character rather than scholarship is thus the
primary criterion in judging the pedagogue.[26]

In another *Cornhill* essay, Leslie Stephen, the magazine's editor and
a man who was in general no friend to androgyny,[27] presented in 1873
a similar portrait of the schoolmaster as housewife. Although his life is
tedious, subservient, and unremunerative,

> A master who does his duty thoroughly may flatter himself that he has
> done more good, counterbalanced by less evil, than he could have accom-
> plished in almost any other station in life. The cultivation of the growing
> crop of humanity which is so soon to succeed to our place is certainly a
> worthy employment of a man's best energies. . . . A schoolmaster who
> possesses the secret of really influencing his pupils' minds may, at any
> rate, feel that his energies have not all run to waste. Indeed, his danger is,
> that the consciousness of wielding a power so mysterious and undefinable
> may be rather too intoxicating.

Stephen concluded with the observation that "the vexatious duty of
superintending a household" is integral to the masters' "deeper influence upon the minds and morals of their youths."[28]

Such characterizations precisely mirror the homilies about ideal
motherhood so prevalent during this period. Given this resemblance, it
is striking that so few writers—or at any rate so few male writers[29]—
drew a direct parallel between the two. Headmasters and teachers were
not being overtly depicted as surrogate mothers; they were being defined
as surrogate fathers whose principal virtues happened to coincide with
pattern femininity. And although the power of the public schools largely
depended on headmasters' ability to present themselves as embodying
all the values of both halves of the Christian couple, and although attacks on educators were much more likely to highlight failures of nurturance than failures of scholarship or authority, commentators sometimes

sought to distance the schools from "real" domesticity. This impulse seems to have had its roots in the fear of effeminacy; teachers, some feared, could go too far in abjuring the old authoritarianism in order to display a Christlike androgyny.

Thus Margaret Oliphant's 1894 profile of Eton science master Edward Hale distinguished him from those instructors "whose delight it is to cultivate, almost as if in a hot-house, with sedulous observation, intercourse, and influence, the characters, as they think, of the boys under them, uniting a kind of maternal, half-feminine intimacy and tenderness to the ruder bonds." A passable description of Arnold as imaged by late-Victorian hagiographers, one might say, but Oliphant preferred a more overtly masculine ideal: "the genial father of English life, not so overwhelmingly devoted to his children as to cut off his own individuality, not feminine in any absorption of sympathy: but all the more a tower of strength on that account."[30] Along the same lines, a writer for *Macmillan's* in 1883 applauded the master who responds to a boy's question by "talk[ing] with a caressing tone—probably with his arm over the lad's shoulder," but assured readers that such a teacher "has nothing soft or sentimental about him."[31]

The apparent removal of women from the formal education of boys had a variety of effects. For one thing, as we have seen, it freed male teachers to adopt "feminine" nurturing behaviors toward the children in their care while still permitting them to define these behaviors as "manly." (The schools, significantly, were at the epicenter of the debate over what constituted manliness.) As Nancy F. Cott writes in an American context, the Victorian separation of spheres "made the home-sanctioned virtues *oppose* the worldly ways of getting and making— made the attributes of the mother *not* those of the father."[32] Were men to exhibit qualities associated with the opposite gender, then, they would plainly find it easiest to do so in a milieu in which women were invisible. While effeminacy was a major concern in the public-school domain, without women to model what was not masculine it must have been difficult at times for boys and teachers alike to be sure of what "effeminacy" might be.

At the same time, the masculinized public-school environment worried a small but vocal group who feared that no all-male institution could inculcate morality as well as the family could. (Their concern gives weight to historian J. R. de S. Honey's contention that in fact the school was not, for all its publicists' claims to the contrary, an artificial family but a rival to the family with its own "alternative values."[33]) Thus Henry Lee-Warner's 1885 "A Few Last Words on Day-Schools and Boarding-Schools" asks, "Is it not an astounding fact that in these days, when women are so carefully educated, mothers think it necessary to send their boys away from home, very often at the age of eight, to be brought up among strangers, in an atmosphere where the prevailing tone is set by a knot of bigger boys?" To Lee-Warner, a Rugby master, schools are the enemies of domesticity:

> Parents who only receive their little boys for the holidays have lost the character of being educators. . . . [They] should take more personal interest in the education of their sons, and not be content to pay large sums to have the trouble taken off their hands, if by any sacrifice they can undertake it. . . . such sacrifice improves the whole tone of family life.[34]

As Lee-Warner's diatribe suggests, writers of this stamp saw educators as usurping what was primarily the mother's role. Thus another member of this party, the unnamed author of "The Apple and the Ego of Woman" (1889), condemned women who "hand over their most powerful function to the nurse, governess, and schoolmaster . . . chancing altogether the most dangerous part of the moral character in their boys; expecting, on a mere supply of cash, a finished and flawless article to be supplied them."[35] And L. Vansittart de Fabeck stated flatly in 1896, "The woman who prefers school to home education for her child confesses herself either unable or unwilling to assume the responsibilities of motherhood."[36]

Although writers treated the matter delicately, the maternal responsibilities in question were in large measure sexual. Mid-Victorian adults were under no illusion regarding the practices common in public-school dormitories; in the era of the double standard, the pre-reform academy was permissive to the point of libertinism. Jonathan Gathorne-Hardy notes that from the sixteenth century through Arnold's day, homosexuality, while presumably common, was rarely made an issue. As for expressions of heterosexuality, "In the early 19th century Eton ran a sixth-form brothel, and Lord Hinchingbrooke's being served with a bastardy order by a woman in Windsor was regarded as no more serious than missing an absence."[37] In the post-reform era, in which feminine standards of purity gained new dominance, the overt expression of any kind of sexuality was strongly disapproved. Moreover, critics did not hesitate to blame masturbation and homoeroticism upon the boys' enforced and "unnatural" absence from home and from womanly influence.

Thus, for instance, Lee-Warner cautioned that immorality is especially prevalent "where boys are not related to one another" and when they must submit to "absolute unnatural separation from mothers and sisters and all female society for the greater part of their growing years"; other writers merely hinted at "the moral effect of aggregating boys together, and isolating them from the other sex."[38] By the century's end, feminists were replying to such fears by urging that schools' moral standards be raised by employing women. Answering Harrow headmaster Welldon's "admission that grave faults are inevitable with boys who are living apart from female influence," "Another Educator" called in *Shafts* in 1893 for taking on "women teachers in place of men for the younger boys, women as heads of schools, with women subordinates, who could scarcely fail to impart their own high tone to their charges."[39]

Of course the public schools had no intention of hiring women, even though their all-male composition was the source of the anxiety over rampant sexuality—due less to fears about homosexuality, although these were certainly present, than to the assumption that boys (and men) lack the self-control typical of women. But it had long been suggested that schools might defuse such concern by giving a feminine cast to faculty-student interaction. If the surrogate fathers could behave toward their charges more like mothers, purity—a largely feminine virtue—would gain ground. As early as 1857 (before fear about school sexuality reached its peak), inspector general of military schools G. R. Gleig remarked upon the difficulty of contemplating "the years spent in the cadet barracks [at the Royal Military Academy at Woolwich] except with disgust." The problem, he held, was poor supervision, resulting from authoritarian officers' inability to provide "moral training. Rarely do they draw the cadets towards them and become their advisers; more frequently repel them by a harsh dictatorial manner."[40] Insofar as it differed from the family and from maternal morality, the school fostered sin.

But while some commentators saw schools as undermining the family and endangering both souls and bodies, still others believed that schools represented an advance on conventional domesticity. Predictably, many used this argument particularly against working-class families. To gain support in the 1890s for school-organized savings banks catering to poor children, Agnes Lambert presented London parents as a second and more unruly set of children; she lamented "the inadequacy of our present educational system to supply these deficiencies [technical, housekeeping, and moral skills] in the education of the parents." To Lambert the elementary schools served as substitute families, guarding pupils against their improvident seniors and properly socializing an otherwise unreclaimable group.[41] Still more contentiously, the anonymous author of "Elementary Education" wrote in 1888: "The school ought to be the antidote to the [working-class] home, the high moral ideal of the one counteracting the low visible examples of the other."[42]

Still, such rhetoric was by no means limited to discussions of the less privileged classes. Perhaps inspired by Nathaniel Woodard, whose 1848 *Plea for the Middle Classes* led to the founding of eight boarding schools for tradesmen's sons and who explained, "The chief thing that is to be desired is to remove the children from the noxious influence of home," not a few commentators focused their arguments on the shortcomings of even comfortable domesticity.[43] Some, like the author of the 1854 *Fraser's* article on "Our Public Schools," held that the trouble within the middle-class family was the absence of the father, which might create an atmosphere too feminine and circumscribed for a boy: "the wise father knows that, in all probability, other duties will compel him to neglect his boy . . . he feels that a sterner discipline and a wider field [are] desirable, than his quiet home and his sisters' society can give."[44] Even were the father present, others implied, overly gentle parenting techniques might work to the detriment of boyish character. A *Contem-*

porary Review article in 1866, for instance, inveighed against giving boarders individual studies, as the practice represents "a transference of home to school"; any undercutting of the communal spirit encourages the eccentricity and vanity so often fostered by "the indulgent tenderness of parents."[45] Again, the advantage of the schoolmaster was often that he seemed to combine the virtues of both genders, excluding neither femininity nor masculinity.

Critics of conventional domesticity were not always so mild. An editorialist in the *British Medical Journal*, denouncing boys' sexual immorality in 1882, noted "that home-influences too often present a somewhat inharmonious contrast with the best kind of school-teaching"; the purity inculcated by school sermons could be eradicated by careless and cynical parents.[46] Likewise, the author of the *New Quarterly Magazine*'s 1879 profile of Harrow accused the parents of day scholars of running "a kind of sanctuary where the school criminal may take refuge from the law," furnishing their young visitors with tobacco and "a large lending library of cribs," and facilitating the boys' intercourse with "doubtful characters." The alumnus who has spent his school years as a boarder rather than as a "home-nurtured youth," the article concludes, will be " 'More skilful in self-knowledge; even more pure / As tempted more; more able to endure / As more exposed to suffering and distress; / *Thence also more alive to tenderness.*' "[47] In this formulation neither home nor school is characterized by the purity and tenderness that editorialist and poet find essential to manliness, but home combines temptation with indulgence rather than with privation and discipline. Inasmuch as it offers neither feminine innocence nor masculine self-control, it fosters the worst of both spheres. School, in contrast, provides the best.

A similar point of view is evident in Walter L. Bicknell's *National Review* articles on schoolboys, from one of which essays the epigraph to this chapter is taken. Arguing that the upper classes are irreligious, uncontrolled, and irresponsible, Bicknell, himself both a parent and a headmaster, considered the preparatory and public schools the nation's last best hope: "frequently all the good which the boy gets is got at school, and most of the evil which he gets is got at home. . . . I believe the secret but real reason of this to lie in the fact that the parents are incompetent to deal with the child of their own creation." As amateurs of child care, parents feed their offspring improperly, get swept up in fads, misjudge their characters and needs, and in any case have little interest in them. Fathers are especially at fault, since they "have often a quiet way of shuffling out of such responsibility" and provide their sons with neither attention nor discipline.[48] And while Bicknell admitted, "The natural offices of the mother are but ill fulfilled by another," the father's case is different. Rather, his "duty and privilege and yearning should be to build up his boy into a man by combining in every way with the schoolmaster," who is both more qualified and more devoted.[49]

Parental and particularly paternal irresponsibility, the centerpiece of Bicknell's accusations, was a focus for many other writers on education during this period, in part because of changes in the lifestyle of the newly affluent middle class. On the one hand, as Bryan S. Turner notes (drawing on the work of Philippe Ariès), bourgeois fathers belonged to a group that had not traditionally sent its sons away to school. Such men— who were spending increasingly less time at home anyway, while their wives' role in the home simultaneously gained status—were likely to re- gret "their loss of control over the moral development of their offspring," reacting with suspicion to the influence wielded by the headmaster.[50] On the other hand, Honey draws attention to the indifference common among certain well-to-do parents, who "were only too ready to abandon to the school the upbringing of the children which earlier in the century they would have abandoned to the nursery and the servants."[51] There was thus ample room both for guilt on the part of fathers who feared that they had somehow shirked their home duties and for resentment on the part of teachers facing parental "interference" on the one side or parental noninvolvement on the other.

Both these currents are apparent in periodical articles after the mid- Victorian boom in public-school attendance. In an 1879 *Fraser's* essay, for instance, C. A. Vansittart Conybeare, a barrister, refuted an earlier writer's contention that parents should not invariably defer to the school- master's professional authority since "the parent is as likely to be right as the Master." Conybeare stated bluntly that "if any parent persisted in interfering in the course of instruction given to his son, he would very

soon be compelled to withdraw him altogether"—save in the debased
arena of the prep schools, "which, as depending for their maintenance
on the goodwill of their patrons, must necessarily fawn upon parental
idiosyncrasies."[52] Conversely, Lee-Warner mourned parents' inability
to "see what they stand to lose when they pass over their responsibilities," adding in a later article that "it is necessary to remind good homes
and the ever increasing body of well-educated mothers of the power
they possess, and the duties they cannot delegate."[53] And Sidgwick
complained in 1879 that parental irresponsibility mandates the medical
vetting of arriving students, since parents often display "foolish reticence or even want of candour" in admitting that a child is delicate: "if
the boys require protection against their own parents, it is surely the
imperative duty of the school . . . to protect them."[54]

For many writers the ideal was one of cooperation between parent and
school, in which both parties would conscientiously educate themselves
about the details of the boy's curriculum on the one hand and his character on the other. Thus schoolmaster, father, and perhaps even mother
would *all* partake of the dual public/private privileges that characterized the androgynous teacher; adults, too, could learn from schools.
Bicknell balanced his attack on the dangers of home life under ignorant
parents with an account of the good parent's role:

> He ought to combine with the schoolmaster; he ought to take the greatest
> pains in choosing, so far as he can judge, the right school; he should keep
> himself (of course, what applies to one parent applies at least equally to
> the other) *au fait* with the doings of his boy; he should in every way see all
> he can of, and do all he can for, him when at home.[55]

Similarly, in his 1897 article "The Responsibility of Parents for the
General Failure of Modern Education," educator William K. Hill blamed
parents for the prevalence of competitive examinations and the dearth
of teacher training. The responsible father, he noted, visits prospective schools to approve their facilities and to meet teachers and pupils.
After selecting a school, the parent should support it not only by paying
the fees but also by reinforcing its dicta about discipline and work; he
must "strive constantly to educate himself in the science of education,

so that his judgment of the educator may be just and his help effective."[56] And a 1902 writer who signed himself "B.A. (Oxon.)" added more contentiously, after complaining about distant headmasters, poor housekeeping, and unfit housemasters,

> I feel bound to say that the [apathetic] attitude of parents and guardians is not a little answerable for any abuses or defects which still survive in our public schools. . . . Does it never occur to that father to try and discover for himself first-hand whether his son is really "well educated" in its fullest sense at the school of his own choosing?[57]

The schoolmaster's role *in loco parentis*, then, took a variety of forms, but each manifestation of this ideal suggested directly or indirectly the flaws of real-life parents, especially and sometimes exclusively fathers.[58] If the teacher was scorned as distant and money-grubbing, as in the reports on the Public Schools Commission's findings, the same point could be made about the father who had entrusted his child to such a man; if the teacher appeared as a concerned expert, the father dwindled into a bungling or careless amateur. In either case paternal instinct seemed insignificant. Writers on education, however, found it impossible to ignore what was deemed women's inborn talent for child rearing. Accordingly, side by side with the discussion of school as family went a discussion of teaching as a naturally womanly pastime.

Nineteenth-century educational theory supported a typically "feminine" approach to pedagogy, especially in the case of young students. Some writers cited John Locke in this regard: "whilst [children] are learning, and apply themselves with attention, *they are to be kept in good-humour, and everything made easy to them, and as pleasant as possible*"[59]—a picture recalling rather the Child Valley of the 1850 *Household Words* allegory than normal practice. The ideas of kindergarten founder Friedrich Froebel and Swiss reformer Johann Pestalozzi also flourished in Britain after mid-century; as Anne M. Boylan has written, "women claimed a special competence" in the methods of these educators, which were predicated "upon an understanding of the child's 'nature' and the achievement of 'empathy' between teacher and pupil."[60]

Thus in her discussion of kindergarten needs in 1905, one K. Bathurst diagnosed the problem as "the absence of the quality known as 'mother-liness'" and prescribed "the appointment of women inspectors, espe-cially those with a Froebel certificate, to supervise the infant schools of this country." While she saw women as innately more talented in dealing with young children than men (who want "military rather than maternal" discipline), she was also alive to the value of Froebelian theory in en-hancing, or simply endorsing, women's skills.[61] In elementary teaching, where prestige and salaries were low and certification often unimpor-tant, theoretical trends combined with feminist pressure and women's entry into the white-collar job market to create equal numbers of male and female elementary teachers by 1870 and a heavy preponderance of women in the field by 1896.[62]

Again, while even in the elementary schools (and certainly in the pub-lic schools) women did not invariably teach boys, the ideal of the edu-cator was much affected by the increased respect given to motherhood and by pressures on men to become more "feminine" in their dealings with children. A case in point is the evolution of attitudes toward school discipline, which mirrored trends in domestic discipline. George Behl-mer observes that the trend was against ruling by terror: "By 1880 the flogging of scholars in both public and school board schools had dimin-ished appreciably. . . . Increasingly, even 'mild' scholastic punishment evoked public anger."[63] With Arnold's stress on gentlemanliness and reason came a general sense that violent measures should be a last re-sort against childish misbehavior. Commentators on education, among them Herbert Spencer, denigrated extreme corporal punishment as bad for the child, the teacher-student relationship, and even the nation: the discipline of the public schools, Spencer complained, "is much worse than that of adult life—much more unjust, cruel, brutal. . . . And chiefly recruited as our legislature is from among those who are brought up at these schools, this barbarizing influence becomes a serious hindrance to national progress."[64]

But after the public-school reforms had begun to take hold, fewer and fewer critics located such brutality in the present. Increasingly, ac-counts of savage punishment became an essential part of descriptions of school life many years past, a way to turn pre-Victorian headmasters

such as Keate of Eton into figures of mythic proportions. As one fictionalized memoir put it, "flogging was meat and drink to Dr. Keate . . . he
would sooner, Brutus-like, flog his own son than not flog somebody."[65]
In contrast, although Collins praised Rugby's Dr. Temple for his firm
hand ("In opposition to the soft-spoken modern theorists who will hear
of nothing but 'reformatory' processes, he understands that one great
object of punishment is—to punish"), he remarked simultaneously that
floggings occurred at Rugby on an average of only eight times a year.[66]
Collins was not alone in treating the relaxation of discipline with some
regret, but no nostalgia is apparent in autobiographical accounts such
as "Greenwich School Forty Years Ago" (*Fraser's*, 1874). Comparing
this school for the sons of naval officers to Dickens's Dotheboys Hall,
the memoirist shuddered at the "shameless brutality which prevailed in
every department of the school," the "fiendlike" temper of the flogging
headmaster, the "hunger and cruelty . . . unparalleled in any school
in England": "So much for the good old times, which many pretend to
regret who never knew their injustice and hardship."[67] While corporal punishment had by no means vanished, commentators consistently
suggested that sadism was no longer part of the mid- and late-Victorian
educational ethic.

   The wistfulness sometimes implicit in accounts of epic floggings certainly emanates in part from the thrill of such scenes (the drama, the
sexual component, the opportunities for stoicism and bonding among the
boys), but it also suggests a longing for the harsh discipline of the van-
ishing patriarchal family, another manifestation of the occasional calls
for a return to paternal autocracy observed in chapter 2. But as in the
domestic context, such voices spoke for the past, not the future. Much
more common was the point, entirely in line with maternalist doctrine,
that an authority based on mere physical strength not only damages students but demonstrates the moral inferiority of masters. Sidgwick noted
that the old "indiscriminate flogging [was] the offspring (and probably
the parent) of a general coarseness of tone about education," a flaw that
Arnold had remedied not by force but by "the intensity and strength
of his own personality and character."[68] The official policy of the Education Department in 1883 with regard to elementary school discipline

was "that the more thoroughly a teacher is qualified for his position by skill, character, and personal influence, the less necessary it is for him to resort to corporal chastisement at all."[69] And feminist Ben Elmy spoke for many when in 1902 he praised Arnold "for discarding the fossilised habit of treating boys as irrational beings, amenable only to the argument of the stick"; Arnold's preference of milder methods "elevates not alone the pupil, but the preceptor also—an action with an ever-widening circle of consequence."[70]

As in the case of arguments about the proper application of pedagogical theory, male feminists and women were more likely than other writers to make an explicit link between gentle discipline and femininity. Elmy's plea for greater general respect for women's capabilities and characteristics recalls Mrs. C. G. B. Corbett's 1890 *Macmillan's* essay on "The Education of Children," a plea for extending Froebelian principles to the treatment of middle-school pupils. "Nothing satisfactory can be accomplished by a teacher without close sympathy with and love for the child. An attempt to further the development of a human being by harsh rule and stern command, with threats of punishment, is like pulling the branches of a tree to make them grow," Corbett claimed. And while she used the male pronoun in referring to her ideal teacher (who "never takes up the position of a cold and rigid martinet"), she not only described a teaching style that approximated Victorian femininity more than masculinity, but also noted that the "true sympathy with children" essential to good teaching is more likely to be found in women than in men.[71]

Again, all this is not to suggest that late-Victorian school discipline actually consisted primarily of quiet appeals to children's better feelings, even in girls' schools or kindergartens. As an ideal, however, this position gradually achieved the dominance it may have lacked in practice. Pleas for teacher training, coeducation, and female faculty in elementary schools invoked a softer milieu as one of the principal benefits to be achieved; seldom do such essays suggest that readers might think a gentle environment undesirable. And while they resisted any changes in the composition of their staffs or their student bodies, public schools nevertheless sought to persuade parents that the era of harshness was past. One might argue that headmasters had always been *in loco parentis*, but the parental model, once patriarchal, distant, and authoritarian, was transmuting into its own opposite as it began to blend feminine attributes with masculine.

In this sense Arnold committed an act of no little symbolic significance when in 1831 he established a new tradition by combining the headmastership of Rugby with its chaplaincy. The immediate function of this innovation, which became the norm among the influential public schools, was to underscore what Newsome describes as the "pastoral nature" of the Arnoldian headmastership at the expense of its disciplinary aspect.[72] To the Westminster graduate Rev. W. J. Conybeare, in the article "School Sermons" published in an 1855 *Quarterly Review*, Arnold's example had transformed the master's relation toward his boys into something "no less a cure of souls than that of the parochial minister."[73] To be sure, there were some objections. For instance, Charles Kegan Paul, editor of the *New Quarterly Magazine*, argued that it is preferable to have a separate chaplain, as boys will listen more readily on spiritual matters to one who has not flogged them (a statement that is also illuminating in light of the changing attitudes toward discipline already discussed).[74] But most commentators gladly accepted the implication that the public school would be a theocracy.

The terms in which headmasters might be praised shifted to reflect the pedagogue's new role as priest. Thus, for example, the anonymous author of "Our Public Schools: Harrow" described H. Montagu Butler, who had become headmaster of Harrow at twenty-six, in words that might equally well have applied to a headmistress or a mother. Although Butler was a noted cricketer and a fine scholar, it was his spiritual qualities that seemed especially worthy of notice:

His intensely religious character and lofty moral purpose cannot but make themselves powerfully felt by all who are brought into immediate contact with him. In private intercourse, and especially in times of moral distress or difficulty, his unusual directness, honesty, and simplicity of faith have often done his pupils incalculable good. To his sermons in chapel many will feel that they owe a permanent debt for guidance and encouragement.[75]

The question was no longer simply one of temporal authority; concurrent with the father's loss of his pre-Victorian role as God's simulacrum within the family and the mother's new status as spiritual guide, the headmaster was gaining those functions within the school. By the time Arthur C. Benson contributed "Religious Education in Public Schools" to the *National Review* in 1906, it was possible for him to depict the public schoolmaster as the fount of all religious education for the young, the heir to the role of instructor in Christianity abandoned by incompetent parents.[76]

For state-supported schools in the era of the Education Acts, religious education was a matter of considerable controversy. Roman Catholics, Jews, Dissenters, freethinkers, and other religious minorities quarreled with the suggestion that the law should compel them to send their children to Anglican schools if they could not afford to make other arrangements. Voluntary (that is, denominational) schools did not profit from taxation to the same extent as did the neighborhood board schools (those governed by school boards and open to all). And the educational establishment countered the suggestion of John Stuart Mill and his supporters that state schools should be secular by arguing that some religious component is essential to compulsory education for the working classes: first because religion's omission will only privilege atheism, second because most working-class parents are incapable of instilling religious principles themselves.[77]

The debate over religion in municipal schools, in other words, centered on justifying its presence and defining its form. The public schools, which drew their students from a far more homogeneous pool, were much less concerned with such questions; while they might be subject to pressure not to ally themselves too firmly with Low or High Church factions within the Anglican establishment, they had no need to cater to other religions or even denominations. The discussion of religious questions and religious roles in the public schools, accordingly, had little to do with overt issues of politics and class. Rather, it focused on matters "closer to home": not only the implications of combining spiritual leadership and secular discipline but also the best strategies for bringing an unruly congregation of boys to the divine light. Predictably, writers suggested that this goal could only be accomplished by combining weekly sermons to the entire student body (which would degenerate in some men's hands into impersonal harangues serving merely to emphasize the discrepancy in power between speaker and auditor) with more intimate parental talks to a group of no more than two or three.

As a pastor, then, the ideal headmaster was to be not only an authority figure but a friend. Just as was the case with his role as teacher or disciplinarian, he was expected to fulfill the goals and approaches at once of masculine and feminine economies by both directing and sympathizing, highlighting his superior knowledge without losing sight of the boy's spiritual equality. In this connection it is valuable to note that the headmaster's spiritual fatherhood echoed contemporaneous changes in the conception of the spiritual parenthood of God. Eighteenth-century theology had customarily defined God as the supreme patriarch, a not always nurturing father seated at the pinnacle of a hierarchy in which caste and chastisement were the chief signs of the divine presence. While such views had by no means vanished by the mid-nineteenth century (for instance, Jenifer Hart finds them still characteristic of the sermons of Anglican clergymen between 1830 and 1880), they came to exist concurrently with the competing idea of God as the ultimate androgyne. A divinity who combined strength and tenderness, fatherhood and motherhood, could no longer be seen as angry and unapproachable; as Boyd Hilton notes, the vindictive God postulated by the doctrine of the Atonement gave way to a God able to meet humankind's perplexities with perfect understanding.[78]

This androgynous vision was naturally highly attractive to nineteenth-century feminists, who were also exploring gender-neutral alternatives to orthodox Christianity, such as theosophy. *Shafts*, for one, ran a multitude of items preaching that "Jesus Himself owed His power to the spiritual development of His dual condition [as male and female]"; that "the Mother is involved in the Fatherhood of God, equally the Father in the Motherhood"; and that "the God of many of the Theologians is more nearly akin to Juggernaut and to Moloch than to the Parent, which He of Nazareth told about."[79] Similarly, John Shelton Reed has provided a persuasive reading of the "alternative to feminism" represented by

Anglo-Catholicism, which consistently offered "at least symbolic opposition to the patriarchal Victorian family."[80]

One might equally cite male opinion on the subject. Most famous,
perhaps, is the conclusion to *Tom Brown's Schooldays* (1857) describing God as "[He], in whom alone the love, and the tenderness, and
the purity, and the strength, and the courage, and the wisdom of all
these [men and women] dwell for ever and ever in perfect fulness." Norman Vance reminds us also that "Victorian religious painters such as
Holman Hunt and apologists of Christian manliness such as S. S. Pugh
stressed both the masculine strength and the womanly tenderness of the
Christ." By the end of the century, indeed, as John Springhall recounts,
popular preachers found it necessary to place themselves in opposition
to what one described as the widespread notion "that if you become a
Christian, you must sink your manliness and turn milksop"—one fear
that the fierce pre-Victorian God would not have inspired.[81]

This confluence of Victorian revivalism and a new valuation of
women's qualities, as I have suggested elsewhere, was an extraordinarily
potent mixture; each gained strength from the other. Together the two
were a major factor, even *the* major factor, in the transformation of the
Victorian family. And in turn, the family provided a ready-to-hand context for the discussion of religion. Thus in his review of a treatise by one
of John Henry Newman's disciples, F. W. Faber's *The Creator and the
Creature, or The Wonders of Divine Love* in 1857, theologian Frederick
Oakeley (himself a convert and former member of Newman's community at Littlemore) singled out for special praise Faber's use of family
diction, which, he argued, creates a new bond between worshipper and
worshipped:

> Father Faber has conferred a far more important benefit upon religion
> [than a purely stylistic one] by consecrating to its uses the affectionate
> vocabulary of domestic life in the place of an overstrained and pompous
> phraseology which tends to remove all matters of the supernatural world
> from the region of our ordinary thoughts and feelings. Why, for instance,
> should we seek for any more appropriate epithet to denote the claims upon
> our affection of Our Lord or His Mother, than that simple one of "dear-
> est," which, till Father Faber took pen in hand, was, we believe, generally
> excluded from religious language as bordering upon undue familiarity?[82]

A similar mental and linguistic shift was occurring among Protestants, for example in Charles Kingsley's use of domestic relationships as figurations of divine "antitypes," or in what Vance terms "F. D. Maurice's theological adaptations of the language of family." As Walter E. Houghton has written, it was through such interpretations that "the moral authority of the church was being transferred to the home without any apparent break with the Christian tradition."[83]

Given this current of thought, fatherhood became for many critics a prerequisite for ordination. Kingsley (whose hatred for Roman Catholicism owed much to his instinct that unmarried priests must be effeminate) was not alone in asserting, "Fully to understand the meaning of 'a Father in Heaven' we must be fathers ourselves." Along similar lines, an anonymous *Saturday Review* essayist claimed in 1869 that bachelordom "has a natural tendency to foster selfishness," while the "refinement and chivalry of character" that mark the husband and father are "especially valuable in those whose mission it is to [ad]minister consolation to the sick, the sorrowful, and the erring."[84] Another writer, chaplain G. C. Swayne, observed that "it is hard to substitute a vague general interest in the wellbeing of one's kind, for the particular interest one ought to feel in one's own flesh and blood," adding, "It is the nature of man, not of woman, when cut off from the natural fountains of sympathy, to grow more lazy and selfish every day."

If such descriptions seemed to emphasize feminine ideals of altruism, nurturance, and empathy, Swayne like Kingsley took care simultaneously to emphasize masculine potency: celibate priests "are poor, puling, unable mortals, utterly unfit . . . to supply spiritual strength to the flocks confided to their care. . . . as for the shaven, stubble-chinned, petticoated priests of the Roman Church, I have no patience with them. They are neither masculine, feminine, or neuter."[85] Analysis of the literal and symbolic fatherhood of the clergy, then, might draw not only on the maternalist model of fathers as full participants in domestic virtues but also on a competing view of fatherhood as an expression of virility. By 1906, indeed, Welldon was combining a portrait of the rector as domestic father with an appeal to eugenics and its masculinist ideals. Not only are clergymen more likely than most men to spend time teaching their children and cultivating their "high moral qualities," but "the law of heredity" decrees that such fathers will transmit "gentleness, sympathy, refinement, cultivation, humanity, piety" to future generations. Personal and biological influence alike are responsible for the moral and worldly success of the clergy's heirs.[86]

The linkage of the minister's position to that of the father served in part, as these variations upon the theme suggest, to confirm that the former was not sexually suspect: not only was he not effeminate, but he used his virility responsibly by begetting children, who in turn would cement his devotion to his family and to the larger "family" of parishioners. Nevertheless, for the Victorians the pastor's position, like the educator's, was often inherently androgynous, both because of his public role as spokesman for a God increasingly viewed as both male and female, and because within the family it was the mother who was thought to be the natural teacher of religion. At once through example and precept, as countless periodical writers made clear, mothers were to control their children's discovery of God. This function depended partly on the assumption that mothers spend more time with children than fathers do, partly on the belief in mothers' moral superiority, and partly on the same "soft" approaches to educational theory that also underlay the idea of women's affinity for kindergarten teaching. In a typical article on "The Religious Education of Children" appearing in the *Westminster Review* in 1875, for instance, the anonymous author rejected overly doctrinal, terror-laden, or sentimental teaching techniques in favor of an individualistic Froebelian method. And while the chief religious teacher might prove to be a nurse or governess rather than the mother, the essayist implied that she would surely be female.[87]

When in following Arnold's lead the public schools increased their attraction for the middle classes by appealing to bourgeois ideals of religion and morality, they found that one way to show conformity to these ideals was to image headmaster as father. But even while the schools claimed as their primary goal the inculcation of manliness, the head's role as pastor and caregiver suggested that his own manliness, at least, would take an androgynous form. In order to demonstrate his difference from prereform predecessors, he had to present himself as personally involved, morally influential, and incapable of the inappropriate, unfamilial desires manifest in greed or sadism. In addition to the public role of successful professional, the headmaster and his staff—like teachers in state-supported schools and indeed like those in girls' schools, although the latter fall outside the scope of this discussion—had to prove themselves in the private role of nurturing parent; indeed, the one seemed impossible without the other. While the law and its representatives often met attack for excessive attachment to increasingly discredited ideals of masculinity, then, schools and educators could attribute much of their success to their adaptation of femininity's strengths.

Parenthood
and the
Motherland

In caring for the children of the
State [the woman school board
member] is only walking in the steps
of every mother from the earliest times.
No infringement here of man's ancient
rights; rather it is he who intrudes
when he tries to play the double rôle of
father and mother simultaneously.
Of course he does not do it well. All public
institutions elected in the interests
of both sexes need *mothering* as well as
fathering, and those institutions most
need it which exist entirely in the
interests of children.

The second half of the nineteenth century witnessed an unprecedented amount of legislation dealing with issues once believed to be properly the concern of the (male) individual. Some laws intervened between employer and employee, such as the Chimney Sweepers' Regulation Acts of 1840, 1864, and 1875, or the Factory Acts of 1850, 1867, 1874, and 1878, each of which restricted the hours or scope of women's or children's workdays. Others addressed matrimonial questions, most importantly the Married Women's Property Acts of 1870, 1882, and 1893, which slowly established wives as economic entities separate from their husbands. Still others concerned the treatment of minors; these ranged from the wide assortment of mid-century legislation on the proper disposition of juvenile delinquents or young vagrants, to the Education Acts, to late-Victorian laws designed to protect children from cruel treatment or sexual misconduct, to the Provision of Meals Act that arranged in 1906 for the feeding of disadvantaged London schoolchildren at taxpayers' expense.

One cannot, of course, assign a single cause to this large array of enactments and reforms. Clearly the impetus behind (say) the Factory Act of 1850, which limited women and children to a sixty-hour workweek and thus sought to ensure, among other goals, that adult men would dominate the workforce, differed from that behind the 1870 Married Women's Property Act, which gave women legal title to the sums they might earn after marriage. Nevertheless, one of the few common threads binding together the divergent and sometimes contradictory elements of Victorian and Edwardian social legislation was an increasing distrust of what we might term the private patriarchy of factory or family, a general sense that individual men are liable to abuse authority.

Moved by this anxiety, Victorian lawmakers gradually displaced many powers formerly vested in the paterfamilias (and also in the employer, although the latter issue is less relevant to this study) onto the nation. That the state was taking on a parental role was acknowledged by many social commentators, whose references to "this paternal affection of Parliament," "the duties of a paternal Government," and "grandmotherly legislation" were not mere rhetorical flourishes but an apt choice of metaphor.[1] As with the contemporaneous discussion of domesticity, however, there was considerable debate over how this role might best be carried out—in other words, whether paternity, maternity, or something else altogether might best characterize the state's social action. Should government be nurturing or punitive toward "undesirables"? To what extent can impersonal institutions redress ills resulting from family dysfunction? And how far may children be said to be the proper business of the state in any case? Such questions, which are central to the burgeoning Victorian bureaucracy, recapitulate the doubts and concerns of nineteenth-century attitudes toward parenthood. In Parliament and on school boards, from philanthropic offices to the strongholds of the antivaccination movement, the family drama was replayed. But because upper- and middle-class rhetoric usually cast the working classes as either the subjects of irresponsible parenting by individuals or the objects of irresponsible "parenting" by government, thus projecting a personal concern onto a putatively alien group, domestic life and especially paternity could be covertly criticized as well as endorsed.

As Gertrude Himmelfarb observes in *Poverty and Compassion*, the late nineteenth century was characterized by both a sharp rise in the public services afforded to the working classes and a still sharper rise in the expectations about such services; although reforms and new programs were proliferating, demand for such innovation outstripped supply.[2] This trend represented a departure from beliefs prevailing earlier in the century. (The 1834 Poor Law, for instance, provided minimal relief and forced the poor into workhouses in an attempt to winnow out the desperate from the merely lazy.) Children served as a fulcrum for the accomplishment of such shifts in policy: theories of education, public health, and social amelioration in general all depended on the conviction that bad conditions breed worse ones while good conditions breed better. Only by arresting poverty, ignorance, feebleness, and vice in childhood could reformers hope to cure the nation's ills. But it seemed to many activists (although by no means all) that the lower-working-class family had reached such a pass that only outside intervention— even, sometimes, the severance of all ties between endangered child and depraved parents—could remedy matters.

These dire pronouncements often owed more to fear than to fact. John R. Gillis's portrait of British marriage suggests that in reality, working-class domesticity in the mid-nineteenth century generally hearkened to middle-class ideals. Monogamy "became virtually mandatory"; the separate-spheres doctrine took on increasing importance, slowly removing women from the workforce; and "children were at home for a much longer part of their lives and their relations with parents, especially with mothers, were more intense."[3] And while Gillis observes that working-class men, fearing accusations of effeminacy, avoided participation in household tasks, Trevor Lummis argues of turn-of-the-century East Anglian fisherfolk that men did share this burden (although accounts written after the fact often deny it, due to the influence expectations have over memories) and that "fathers were a very positive influence in domestic affairs."[4] In other words, even the model of the nurturing, androgynous father, which was by no means all-powerful in the middle classes, had its working-class analogue. District-nurse superintendent M. Loane, for one, wrote in 1905 of the degree to which "libelled" working-class men conform to middle-class models of involved parenting; while "The ideal of fatherhood is less developed among the poor than the ideal of motherhood," still fathers may be "tender and assiduous nurses" who lavish affection on their young children. These regard them "as companions, as abettors of many forbidden practices, and as protectors from the occasional slaps and rather frequent reproofs [administered by] the acknowledged ruler of the family," not as figures of authority or abuse.[5]

Of course, Loane's profession would have given her long acquaintance with working-class family life and positioned her as her clients' helper rather than their adversary. Those bourgeois Victorians and

Edwardians who had this type of personal contact with the less privileged were often ready enough to profess their kinship and respect,
suggesting that there was no need for drastic intervention (as opposed
to friendly assistance) in the family life of the poor. In 1908 Frank J.
Adkins, seeking to create a fresh-air fund for urban children, praised
the working-class father for "sacrificing his life to industrial necessity;
he has his reward in his children's occasional freedom from the conditions he himself is obliged to endure."[6] Similarly, pioneering sociologist
Charles Booth, author of the seventeen-volume *The Life and Labour
of the People in London* (1889–1902), observed that "the simple natural lives of working-class people tend to their own and their children's
happiness more than the artificial complicated existence of the rich."[7]

But as Himmelfarb notes, Booth was writing in that instance about
the upper tier of working-class families, not about the destitute (of whose
domestic relationships he painted a darker picture). And the destitute
had the greater effect on the image of family life among the poor. It was
not until late in the century that the "pauper class ceased to dominate
the public imagination" in discussions of poverty.[8] Used to thinking of
the poor in terms of Bill Sikes and Fagin, many Victorian social commentators depicted them as uncivilized and even subhuman, a criticism
having especial urgency for child rearing: ill-disciplined, oversexed,
abusive, and unhealthy, working-class adults would make the worst
possible parents. The fear was an enduring one. If Benjamin Disraeli
charged in 1845 that infanticide and incest are common among the poor
and that "the domestic principle wanes weaker and weaker every year
in England," Winston Churchill's outlook was no more positive when he
warned in 1910 that "the seeds of Imperial ruin and national decay" are
planted in "the want of proper discipline and training in our [working-
class youth] . . . the physical degeneration which seems to follow so
swiftly on civilised poverty."[9]

As Jeffrey Weeks has observed, reformers as disparate as Lord
Shaftesbury, Friedrich Engels, and "Dr." Thomas Barnardo urged social
change on the ground that poverty renders proper family life impossible,
in particular because it causes the breakdown of parent-child relationships.[10] Even the prominent philanthropist Octavia Hill, a founder of

the Charity Organisation Society committed to considering the poor "as members of families," held that district visiting is beneficial because middle-class women may thereby play a maternal role for the untrained and feckless working classes, teaching them to save their money, to keep a sanitary home, and to behave responsibly toward their children; for the poor, it would seem, family membership means eternal childhood. If the privileged classes want the domestic lives of their "inferiors" to run smoothly, they must oversee these lives themselves; experience and instinct come into play only for the well-to-do.[11] That such beliefs had wide currency meant that among the poor, both fatherhood and motherhood were subject to middle-class activism. Neither the father's traditional role as ruler of his family's destiny nor the mother's newer role as moral influence was sacrosanct.

The assumption of family incompetence among the needy appears again and again in periodical articles urging particular social projects. An unsigned article on "Public Nurseries," published in *Fraser's* in 1850, is typical. Here the author described the children of the poor as "accustomed to misery, ill-usage, and privation, from their earliest infancy; their spirits are broken from the cradle . . . worse than all, they never have their feelings touched by the softening influence of parental love." But if "the hand of their natural protectors is too often raised against them," this circumstance arises not from "peculiar depravity" but from "the grinding poverty which checks [parents'] natural impulses, and turns them from good to evil."[12] Because it is environment, not heredity, that is at fault, it is clearly the duty of the more fortunate to provide day-care centers to counteract the topsy-turvy world of poverty, wherein love turns to hate, domestic peace to strife, and nurturance to abuse.

Such articles made clear that poverty is not simply the lack of money but the overturning of all principles of normal family life, a point of view suggesting that many Victorians suspected domestic bliss to be much more fragile and circumstantial (less "normal," in fact) than iconographers of Home might concede.[13] A subsequent (1854) *Fraser's* piece on the Great Ormond Street pediatric hospital implied that the patients were there to be cured not of physical illness but of the contagion of poverty or the deficiencies of their family life. Thus middle-class children's ailments are best left to a "mother's solicitude" in the comfort of home; poor children, in contrast, have neither comfortable homes nor mothers trained in caregiving. The failure of domesticity among the working classes forces a chain of inversions: sickness means that one leaves home rather than staying in bed; strangers, not parents, provide the cure; and the most important "medicine" administered at the hospital addresses family deficiencies by instilling morality and discipline. Thus "Children who enter the wards rude, dirty, and fractious, speedily, under the influence of kindness and firmness, acquire habits of order and cleanliness, which we may hope will prove of lasting benefit to them."[14] They may in fact be able to teach their parents what they have learned, so that if the contagion of poverty passes from parent to child, the antidote of middle-class mores passes from child to parent. The latter reversal of hierarchy, of course, suggests that not only the "disease" but its cure will turn the family order upside down. At any stage of the interventionist process, it is the parent-child relationship that is to be the target of middle-class activity.

With the rise of eugenics, the linkage of low social status and disease took on a scientific cast, while parenthood among the poor came in for still heavier criticism. In an 1883 *National Review* article entitled "Hereditary Pauperism and Boarding-Out," statesman Gathorne Gathorne-Hardy (Lord Cranbrook) invoked "those who have never known a parent's love or care,—the deserted, desolate children whose very physical frames bear the marks of inherited disease" and who may be saved only by "good influences from good hearts."[15] His plea encompassed only those children already separated from their parents and institutionalized, but it was easy to conclude from such essays that even in intact families, disadvantaged children are unlikely to meet with the "good influences" essential to moral and physical health. By 1905, a representative piece by Charles Rolleston in the liberal *Westminster Review* warned, "It is clear that children brought up under the present unwholesome conditions especially prevalent in the slums of our large towns must become moral, mental and physical degenerates." In "a typical home of one submerged," Rolleston wrote, "moral sense [and] training" are alike absent; starved of good food and proper guidance, "children take to begging or stealing naturally" and turn to drink. Unless the state intervenes, such families will destroy their children and finally Britain itself.[16] Similarly, M. K. Inglis apostrophized the well-to-do in the *Fortnightly Review* in 1908, predicting that unless the problems surrounding working-class childhood are solved, "you will rouse yourselves to find your stock so deteriorated that it has become almost valueless."[17]

Writers with a feminist agenda extended concern about the working-class family upward from the stratum of the destitute to that of the respectable poor. Thus "A Woman" (*National Review*, 1887) castigated laboring men for their selfishness vis-à-vis the family, claiming that the typical husband and father spends the housekeeping money on "his beer and tobacco . . . his amusements, his society in the public-house or music-hall" instead of on educating his children and feeding his family on the same fare he himself enjoys.[18] Feminist periodicals teemed with reports of cases in which idle men seized their wives' earnings, diverting them from responsible (usually child-oriented) uses in order to waste them on vice. Such pieces were plainly designed to forward passage of the Married Women's Property Bills; at the same time, however, they played a significant role in building up a picture of working-class domesticity as fragmented and damaged.

Nor was selfishness the only problem feminists identified in the workingman's attitude toward family and children. Allying themselves with the Society for the Prevention of Cruelty to Children (SPCC) and with housing reformers, women's advocates and purity workers fought for the passage of a law against incest and for the establishment of an appropriate age of consent. The latter rose to sixteen under the Criminal Law Amendment Act of 1885, after a lengthy campaign publicizing child prostitution and English law's inability to protect the innocent; after a twenty-five-year battle, the former was achieved with the passage of the 1908 Punishment of Incest Act, the first law on this subject since the abolition of incest legislation at the Restoration. Presumably sexual abuse was as prevalent in the upper reaches of society as in the lower, yet for the Victorians it was linked to the overcrowding and underdiscipline of working-class life, and indeed public attention was first riveted on incest with the 1883 appearance of the anonymous pamphlet on slum housing *The Bitter Cry of Outcast London*.[19] Thus the president of the International Women's Union, Mrs. A. Warner Snoad, fulminated in *Shafts* in 1895 about the early age at which "the children of the poor of both sexes are tempted to immoral acts. . . . with female children, it is often the result of violence, and, horrible as it is to write, many of the betrayers are the fathers—the wretched drunken fathers, who almost invariably escape punishment."[20]

Incest and pedophilia alike were seen as acts visited by adult men on young girls, a tragedy specifically of working-class fatherhood and the latter's characteristic stigmata, brutality and alcoholism. To be sure, the Incest Act defined incest as occurring between a female victim and her brother or son as well as her father or grandfather. But as Sheila Jeffreys observes, it was father-daughter incest that most concerned the SPCC and the National Vigilance Association (a purity organization with many feminist members, founded in the wake of W. T. Stead's white-slave series in the *Pall Mall Gazette*); both were "involved in large numbers of prosecutions of fathers" under rape or age-of-consent laws. Significantly, the SPCC noted in 1910 that "It has been one of the evidences of the low moral understanding of many parents that in many cases of incest the fathers have claimed a right to their actions, and in others the mothers have acquiesced in what was being done."[21]

This understanding of the dynamics of incest, which closely resembled the SPCC's reading of child labor and physical abuse, suggests one way to look at the late-Victorian "discovery" of the phenomenon: what we have here is a rejection of the (il)logical conclusions to which the patriarchal family and the "law of the father" might come. In the SPCC's incestuous family the problem is literally the unnatural closeness of the father to his children, enabled by the corresponding distance and apathy of the mother.[22] Were the situation reversed—the mother passionately demonstrative, the father absent—no one would cavil (especially because maternal sexuality was seen as qualitatively different from its paternal counterpart). The incestuous father is thus yet another of the apparent inversions of normalcy that plagued the working-class family. At least with regard to the private sphere, commentators on proletarian domesticity consistently implied, the predominance of men or masculine values is the hallmark of unhealthiness and impurity. That incest was one apparent result of the diversion of domestic power from women to men helped to underscore the validity of the maternalist ideology even while it employed a line of argument that the middle class hesitated to direct against itself.

Sexual deviance, however, was seen more as a symptom than as the root of the problem. And if there was a general sense that the lower-working-class family was in grave danger, there were various opinions as to what principally threatened it. Some writers located the danger in poor training, others in poor heredity, still others in poverty itself. For feminists and child-welfare advocates, it often seemed to lie in masculinity (the unemployed lout who spends the family's grocery money on gin and sex is clearly the blood brother of the aristocratic monsters populating the child-custody cases discussed in chapter 4, just as the father who forces his daughter into incest is closely akin to his richer neighbor who visits syphilis upon his unborn children). All these causes were theoretically open to cures enabled by applications of money or morals or model housing on the part of outsiders. But yet another group of commentators—and these by no means the least influential—saw middle-class interference as a major cause of the splintering of working-class family life.

Thus in an 1889 *National Review* article, one Mrs. F. M. Foster pilloried female do-goodery for helping to lure laborers from their homes. While "Father's place for the evening would seem to be in the elbow-chair, with his feet spread out to the fire, and the 'littlest' child on his knee," philanthropic women refuse to leave him in that paternal position, insisting on arranging "concerts, picture-shows, choir-practice, readings, recitations, dramatic performances" and making city life all too attractive to youths who might better have stayed on the farm.[23] Similarly, in a 1907 *Macmillan's* Henry Iselin remarked of the working classes, "The duties and responsibilities of parentage are approached with the same shiftless irresolution which marks the attitude of the poor towards all the other responsibilities of life," but he also contended that "the State and philanthropic agencies . . . do their part in encouraging the parents to evade their responsibilities."[24] While working-class parents tend to be bad disciplinarians in any case (that the children contribute to the family purse undermines adult authority), he explained, the social-service machinery only reinforces adolescents' rebellion against those whom they should obey.

In constructions such as Iselin's and Foster's, in short, the working-class father was doubly troubling. On the one hand, he was deemed incapable of financing and ruling a "normal" (middle-class) home, in which he was the only wage-earner and in which domestic/maternal principles of unselfishness, tenderness, and peace could therefore flourish. On the other hand, if state or private philanthropy attempted to supply what the father could not, it risked pauperizing him, creating a welfare-addicted underclass to which family values, as opposed to institutional values, could never be restored. While interventionist reformers sometimes saw the working-class father as all too strong, indulging his improper appetites without the checks that arise from a sense of social and domestic responsibility, their anti-interventionist counterparts feared that he was weak and liable to become weaker.

It was for this reason, and not because most doubted that the working-class family was indeed unsatisfactory, that many legislators remained reluctant to interfere with the father's perceived rights over his family: the right to discipline his children (or his wife), for instance, or to educate or apprentice them as he saw fit. Ivy Pinchbeck and Margaret Hewitt observe that parliamentary bills designed to counter cruelty to children faced opposition because "In the minds of many—including [arch-philanthropist] Lord Shaftesbury himself—to undermine parental responsibility was to undermine family stability and thus the stability of society itself."[25] To supporters of children's rights such as Cardinal Manning and Benjamin Waugh (who founded the SPCC in 1884), this sentiment licensed evil, even though the bills were not the only way to bring adults to account for violent acts directed at children.[26] In a joint contribution to the *Contemporary Review* in 1886, for instance, Manning and Waugh cited the stance of one father arrested for abuse: "He denied none of the charges, and boldly claimed his right; his children were his own he said. And one of the papers, quoting his remark, took occasion to warn the readers that we might have another of those

Societies whose business it was to interfere with parental rights."[27] For Waugh, who later wrote, "To allow bad parents to be unjust to their children makes their arbitrariness and worthlessness worse," not parents' rights but children's were the primary concern; for many of his contemporaries, however, this stance represented a disquieting reversal of natural order.[28]

Thus as George K. Behlmer notes in his study of turn-of-the-century child abuse, child labor laws had a considerably easier passage than did laws against cruelty: "To patrol industry on behalf of the young was England's Christian duty. To patrol the home was a sacrilege."[29] By the 1830s, Parliament was already prohibiting the employment of young children in factories and mines; subsequent acts expanded such legislation and moved it into such fields as chimney-sweeping (1840, 1864, 1875), farming (1867, 1876), brickmaking (1871), and acting, begging, and street vending (1889, 1894). Significantly, though, laws regulating how a parent could employ his child lagged behind those regulating the conduct of a master outside the child's family; "sweating" one's own child was legal until the 1870s, for instance, while begging and street vending withstood years of SPCC lobbying since such activities were so often directed by parents.[30] While many children's advocates believed, as political journalist and erstwhile Baptist minister Henry Dunckley wrote in 1891, that not only "the indifference of employers" but the "short-sighted eagerness of parents to make a premature profit out of their offspring" was the cause of child labor, Parliament preferred to address the workplace and ignore the home whenever possible.[31] The idea that parents often had no real need for their children's earnings—that they were irresponsible rather than desperate—was thus a necessary commonplace in the rhetoric of child labor's opponents. It was more palatable to suggest that the state should intervene against wanton cruelty (even on the part of parents) than to hold that it should prevent a father from feeding his children as best he could.

Thus Waugh, for instance, claimed, "The majority of street children maintain their parents, partly or wholly, as well as themselves"; Edith F. Hogg observed that it is by no means "the poorest parents who exact the hardest work from their children"; and reform M.P. John E. Gorst argued that "it is doubtful how much of the existing employment of chil-

dren is due to necessity, and how much to a greedy desire on the part
of unworthy parents to gain as much as they can, as early as they can,
out of the labour of their children." Gorst added reassuringly that while
such labor cannot be correlated to the parents' financial status, "It is
only a minority of the parents that require to be restrained by legislation." [32] But the evocation of vampiric parents living on the suffering of
their own children was a compelling one. In 1888, as Behlmer notes, the
London SPCC (and Waugh in particular) raised the specter of parents
murdering their offspring for a few pounds or even shillings in insurance
money. While the campaign to prohibit child insurance failed because it
angered the poor more than it saved lives, Edwardian commentators still
saw working-class parents as liable to do in their infants for what one of
them called "one day's swinish jollification at the Pig and Whistle, a reason for not going to work, and an excuse for not paying the rent." [33] Such
rhetoric presented the issue not as poverty but as perversity, justifying
interference on the ground of simple decency.

State intervention in child rearing seemed to trespass especially
on the father's preserves not only because of his role as the head of
the family, but also because such intervention usually took place on
financial or disciplinary levels, often seen as male territory. Himmelfarb remarks on the "subversive" qualities of reform and philanthropy,
which may be read at once as correctives and as condemnations of the
status quo. [34] Such subversion was particularly evident to Victorians and
Edwardians in the context of child-welfare efforts, which threatened to
destroy working-class paternity even as they sought to redress its shortcomings. One of the central concerns of the reform movement, then,
was that of fostering paternal responsibility among the very men whose
control over their families the reformers were consciously endeavoring
to undermine.

One attractive solution to the dilemma was to make parents pay at
least part of the expenses of the benefits their children received. Until
the passage of the 1870 Married Women's Property Act, "parents" in this
context meant exclusively fathers, while even after 1870 most commentators viewed such provisions as being directed toward men. This may
have been the case not merely because fathers were more likely than
mothers to work outside the home but also because assumptions about

paternal selfishness and maternal love extended to the working classes. Jane Lewis notes, "On balance, most [middle-class] observers agreed that mothers (unlike fathers) could be relied upon to exert themselves on behalf of their children and that [female] mismanagement resulted more from ignorance than vice."[35] For that matter, female ignorance could be read as a consequence of male vice: poor women were incompetent domestically because they were employed, and they were employed because their husbands or fathers were bad providers, either not working hard enough or diverting their earnings to other purposes. Furthermore, to extract maintenance payments from parents for the public care given their offspring was symbolically to place both parents in what Victorian society considered a paternal role (in the sense that their chief task in their children's lives would become financial rather than nurturant), suggesting that it was really the father whom the state had to keep up to the mark.

Maintenance clauses accompanied bills that allowed for removing children from their homes to place them in foster care or institutional surroundings. Important pieces of legislation incorporating the principle included the 1854 Reformatory Schools (Youthful Offenders) Act, which gave official status to the reformatory system; the 1889 Prevention of Cruelty to and Protection of Children Act, which empowered courts to remove children from the custody of abusive parents; and the 1891 Custody of Children Act, which declared forfeit the custodial rights of parents who had once abandoned a child. The reasoning of an anonymous writer in *All the Year Round* in 1870 is typical:

> To relieve bad parents altogether of the expense and trouble of bringing up their offspring would be a proceeding fraught with dangerous consequences, would be . . . in some sort offering a premium for the encouragement of parental neglect. We should, in fact, be gradually accustoming the lowest and worst-conducted classes among us to expect that their children should be brought up for them at other people's expense; a state of things which would be highly agreeable to this particular section of society, no doubt.[36]

Maintenance charges were intended as much symbolically as practically; the aim was less to reduce the burden on taxpayers than to stress the responsibility inherent in parenthood. (As Rolleston put it in 1905: "It is not to be supposed that the State could ever recover the full cost of maintenance from the submerged parents"; the point was to assert "the principle of the parents' liability."[37]) As such they represented a compromise between interventionists and their opponents, one that helped ensure the dominance of the former group because it accepted the principle that state control over the working-class family "for the sake of the children" was desirable. Indeed, insofar as the measures sought to educate parents in child rearing and assumed superior knowledge on the part of the state, they constructed the working classes as simply a larger set of children. Thus in ratifying the maintenance clauses, lawmakers simultaneously accepted and extended the negative stereotype of working-class parents explored above. But at the same time, the subtext of these enactments suggests a wider application.

The bills sought to address the problem of people who find it "agreeable" to have others bring up their offspring even though they may be fully capable of doing so themselves, people for whom a child represents a financial burden instead of a domestic delight. It may be no accident that such legislation coincided with the rise of the public schools and the expansion of household staffs among the well-to-do, at the time when the family ideal was at its zenith. One suspects that it sometimes represented a displacement of guilt on the part of writers and M.P.'s secretly aware that they themselves were avoiding the duties assigned to them by omnipresent Victorian ideals of home and family, just as the connection in the Victorian mind between incest and overcrowding suggests a certain distaste for the intimacy so dear to domesticity's advocates. By defining both excessive distance and excessive closeness as working-class problems, commentators tacitly defined the squirearchy as healthy.

To be sure, not all writers on the working classes approved the family situation of the more comfortably off. Police-court missionary and criminologist Thomas Holmes, for example, began an endorsement of Lord James's Youthful Offenders Bill in 1900 with an indictment of family life in all strata. While he went on to focus on the poor, his invocations of "the widespread desire that exists among parents to get rid of their children" by sending them to any likely institution and of parents' avoidance of their duty to oversee a son's "mental culture" and "moral culture" would have had wider resonance for many readers.[38] There is, of course, no knowing how often middle-class Victorians and Edwardians were moved to passionate discussions of the problems of working-class family life by an awareness that neglect—or incest or brutality or incompetence—is no respecter of social boundaries. Still, while the accusations such commentators leveled at the working classes were usually more dramatic than the criticisms aimed at middle-class parenthood (and the latter, as we have seen, were much more widespread than one might imagine), there is an unmistakable family resemblance between them.

Throughout the period, posing the question of the proper treatment of juvenile delinquents was an important way to voice such anxieties about parental responsibility.[39] It was a Victorian innovation to hold that youthful lawbreakers should be distinguished from adult criminals—first because the former might be reclaimed, second because they might be defined as the victims of parents who had provided both bad heredity and bad training. Given that the existence of a criminal child was often regarded as a sure sign of criminally irresponsible parenting, the state's duty to separate children and parents seemed obvious. In 1840 the first reformatory school opened at Redhill, Surrey; the passage of the Reformatory Schools Act in 1854 provided for the licensing of such institutions and authorized judges to commit juvenile offenders to them for two to five years if the children had served a fortnight in prison. Parents, meanwhile, could be made to pay up to five shillings a week for their children's maintenance at the reformatories.

W. R. Greg's laudatory 1855 essay in the *Edinburgh Review* revealed the assumptions behind the Reformatory Schools Act. He described youthful criminality as entirely a family problem. Not only are lower-working-class children often born to vice via illegitimacy, they are "driven forth into the streets" by the "brutality and drunkenness . . . harshness and destitution" of their homes or intentionally "brought up to depredation as others are brought up to shoemaking or spinning." Such children cannot be seen as villains, but only "as victims to be rescued and as patients to be cured"; while the law's first aim must be to protect society from their misdeeds, "the second object undoubtedly is to protect them against their antecedents and surroundings." This protection is best afforded by the substitute family of the reformatory, which wields "more healthy, more kindly influences. . . . softening and training, not crushing or terrifying." Because committing a delinquent to a reformatory "is the greatest kindness you can render him," the law should be extended to allow boys' incarceration until age twenty-one— always provided that the institutional atmosphere is characterized by "the absence of coercion," the exercise of "gentleness," and the display of "confidence." In paying toward a son's maintenance in such an institution, finally, "the father [is only paying] for the doing of that which he ought to have done himself."[40]

Notable in this description is that the reformatory works not by discipline but by love; while a father must pay, what he is buying is rather "maternal" nurturance than paternal firmness, just as the public schools promise to supply moral influence rather than scholarship. Similarly, Caroline Cornwallis's 1853 *Westminster Review* article "Young Criminals," which profiled both the children and the male philanthropists who had founded "Ragged Schools" (aimed at reclaiming waifs) to serve them, also described delinquents as "the children of parents who have been unable or unwilling to care for their comforts or their instruction." As a consequence, it is care that reformatories must supply. Again the way to retrieve these lost ones is via pleasure, not pain; "the utter inefficiency" of punitive measures stands in sharp contrast to the efficacy of the moral influence, self-sacrifice, and kindness displayed by the Ragged School pioneers.[41]

Cornwallis was writing before the passage of the Reformatory Schools Act; thus she characterized the state as cruel, parents as debased, and private philanthropists as nurturing. Subsequent articles on this topic, however, usually employed a bipolar model that contrasted evil parents to benevolent institutions both public and private. In such constructions, it is noteworthy that the parents are accused of the faults typically assigned to fathers in middle-class discussions of domesticity, while the agencies take on the virtues of the mother. This rhetoric permitted the equation of the institution with the family even while the biological family was being dismissed as harsh and cold, a mere training ground for crime. Thus, for instance, an article on "Reformatory Schools" published in the *Dublin Review* in 1864 noted that "mild and kind influences" are the key to reform, that even delinquent children respond best to genuine sympathy and interest, and that the Reformatory Acts are based on sound domestic principle: "they commit young criminals to the care of those who have feeling enough for them voluntarily to undertake the work of their reformation."[42] This strategy downplayed concern about the effects of outside interference in the working-class family by separating family virtues from the family itself; in this sense, to incarcerate the young was not to remove them from the mother's care but to restore them to it.

As the movement toward "public mothering" built up steam, reformers began to comment that if institutions existed to provide the nurture and feeling in which so many working-class families were proving deficient, such facilities should be run by women, not by men. Fathering, they implied, was inadequate; what the "children of the State" needed was mothering. When in 1881 Elizabeth Surr posed the question in the *Nineteenth Century* of what might be "the indispensable requirements of a young child" if it were to "grow up virtuous, well-behaved, and respectable," she concluded, "They are but *two* in number—a *good mother* and a decent *home*." She proposed that "criminal children . . . would derive even larger benefit [than orphan or vagrant children] from *womanly* care and management, whether boys or girls." Homelike institutions housing fifty or sixty children under the age of ten and run by women who exemplified all motherly virtues, Surr contended, would go far to cure the "infection" of crime; antimotherly, male-administered facilities such as prisons, in contrast, are counterproductive.[43]

Similarly, social reformer Henrietta O. Barnett, honorary secretary of the State Children's Association and longtime manager of a barrack school, explained in the *Cornhill* in 1905 the need for separate courts to deal with young waifs and criminals, a provision eventually included in the "Children's Charter" (Children Act) of 1908. Adult courts, Barnett argued, lack the expert knowledge of childhood boasted by those who spend their days dealing with children's issues; as a result, child offenders are remanded not "to some 'kindly woman's home,' but to an institution based on the foundation thought of discipline and restraint. . . . They want kissing at that age, not drilling; petticoats, not labour masters." Barnett concluded by quoting approvingly the president of the United States Council of Mothers, who observed that American juvenile probation officers are women: "Dealing as they do with the child and the mother, they come, we hold, into closer relations than can a man, for child care is ever women's work, the mother's work which the world needs."[44] In its encounter with children, in other words, the machinery of the public sphere should imitate the private sphere as far as possible—and mother figures, not father figures, are what is essential to children's well-being within that home.

Such theories had still more relevance to the question of appropriate facilities for "children of the State" who had committed no crime but yet had come into governmental custody through abandonment or abuse. Until 1853 young vagrants had gone to a multigenerational workhouse, where as Barnett put it in 1894, "They associated with the vicious and low" (presumably this category often included the children's parents), leaving only to "spread abroad the moral standards and lazy dodges" they had learned.[45] In 1853 reformers Edwin Chadwick, Carleton Tufnell, and James Kay-Shuttleworth established large district schools, also known as barrack schools, to segregate the children from contaminating influences and permit their better education. Subsequently, in 1857, ragged-school and reformatory pioneer Mary Carpenter had orchestrated an Industrial Schools Act allowing magistrates to send destitute children over the age of seven to these residential institutions until age fifteen. An 1866 act expanded the potential student body to include children found begging, homeless, associating with criminals, or beyond parental control; a sequel passed in 1880 at the urging of purity reformer Ellice Hopkins added association with prostitutes to the list; and the 1889 Prevention of Cruelty Act empowered courts to remove children from abusive homes. Over the second half of the century, in short, judicial control over the disposition of children and young teenagers mushroomed, due again to the belief (in Springhall's phrase) "that the welfare of the child and the protection of the social order required the separation of uncaring parent and neglected child."[46] Intervention seemed the order of the day.

Another major change had to do with the destinations to which such children were remanded. The 1891 Custody of Children Act and the 1899 Poor Law Act may be taken as emblematic of the trend of late-Victorian custody theory. The former law allowed judges to determine who or what ought to have the guardianship of a foundling; the contenders might be either a Poor Law board or an individual. The latter piece of legislation permitted a Poor Law guardian to take responsibility for vagrant children and to receive payment from local tax monies. Both suggest a personal and case-by-case approach, a way of thinking about the problem that privileged a private, "family" mindset over one more universalist and efficiency-oriented. Increasingly, the best interests of the child took precedence over the convenience of the institution, a shift also reflected in what Viviana A. Zelizer describes as the movement from "instrumental" to "sentimental" adoption: whereas in the mid-nineteenth century families took in foundlings for their usefulness as servants, by the 1920s what mattered was the emotional value of the child, who was now becoming part of the family and not part of the kitchen staff.[47]

Thus when in 1853 Cornwallis quoted the philosophy of John Ellis of the Brook Street Ragged School—"I recognized them as my children, and they looked upon me as their father"—she struck a note that would gain in force over the course of the next half-century.[48] What child paupers need, Cornwallis and her cohorts argued, is training not only in skills but in morality. And while institutional settings may efficiently teach trades, family virtues require a family atmosphere or something as close to it as possible. For the waif as for the delinquent child, this environment appeared to owe more to mothers than to fathers; descriptions of "cottage-school" schemes, wherein children lived in small groups under the supervision of houseparents, typically mentioned approvingly that women ran matters and that this practice fostered the home virtues and the personal touch.[49] Attempts to streamline public assistance by massing orphans in enormous, unhomelike institutions, in other words, increasingly seemed counterproductive.

For example, by 1875 George Eliot's stepson Charles Lewes was writing in the *Edinburgh Review* of the fate of the forty-eight thousand children in pauper schools in England and Wales, half of them permanently homeless, the other half shunted back and forth between institution and vicious parents. Neither group, significantly, speaks well for the system. The children who visit their birth families will "unlearn each time the little they have learnt during their sojourn in the school . . . coming back more and more 'versed in sin' "—a typical application of the contagion theory of working-class domesticity discussed above. But their counterparts who stay at school are no better off; lacking the moral anchor a good home life provides, they fall easy prey to the infection carried by their schoolmates, which "must have almost as pernicious an effect as contact with the adults in the workhouse." This situation should be intolerable to "the State in its relation of parent," since the parental role entails close attention to a child's associations and ethical education.

Lewes noted that in founding the district schools, Kay-Shuttleworth had proposed that such schools should mirror the respectable working-class home, so that girls would learn to cook, garden, and nurse under womanly supervision, while boys would receive "the natural training of a labourer's child under his father's roof, combined with intellectual instruction and moral discipline." (The mixture of guidance, involvement, and apprenticeship implied by this ideal would have been difficult enough for a real father to provide; that reformers believed the state could mimic it suggests how seriously they took the metaphor of the paternal institution.) But while the district schools' founders had originally planned to house forty pupils in a school, the average population was more like five hundred, rendering individual care impracticable.[50]

The impersonality of such a program convinced Lewes of the greater value of the Continental system, based on Pestalozzian theory. Here the children were divided into "families of boys and girls together," each headed by a superintendent "who discharges the duties of father" and whose wife acts as mother. Citing a Poor Law inspector as his authority, Lewes argued that these "families" should contain no more than twelve children (eight of them young) and that amateur rather than professional staff members—not "highly-salaried officials" but "persons of good character and domestic habits"—were chiefly desirable. Artificial homes of this sort, he concluded, could best work to stem the tide of degeneration evidenced in the "smallness of stature, sullenness and obstinacy of disposition, and apathy of mind" of the institutionalized child, traits resulting not from "any taint in the 'pauper blood' " but from the bad parenting and unnatural environment afforded by both the children's original homes and the unhomelike asylums of the state.[51]

Lewes's analysis contained all the elements that were to characterize subsequent articles on this subject. Again the home/institution opposition is inverted: it is the vicious home that represents the public sphere of sin and strife, the large institution that is vulnerable to the depredations of the poorly trained child (rather than vice versa), the imitation domesticity that is ultimately most real. One notices, too, the rejection of male-oriented science and economics in the twin assertions that environment is more important than heredity and that professional qualifications are less desirable than good hearts, both ideas running counter to trends that were becoming increasingly established in other contexts. Such reasoning was particularly hospitable to the further inversion that held that at least in situations involving children, women make the best public figures.

Thus Surr's urging of small group homes run by women was followed in 1883 by Maria Trench's praise of Irish industrial schools wherein nuns provided for the girls under their eye "a mother's care . . . a true motherly friend" and by Gathorne-Hardy's recommendation of "certified homes," in which "the matron is to represent a mother, and not to be burdened with a larger number of children than will admit of each receiving a due share of her affection and interest." Four years later Louisa Twining (a writer who specialized in women and poverty) suggested that "it was women's work to care for the helpless children of our Poor-Law schools," and that lack of supervision by those with "motherly instincts" is what causes crime among paupers. Philanthropist M. H. Mason stated the situation still more succinctly in 1910: "Men may be useful, but women are necessary." [52]

Predictably, feminist journals such as the *Englishwoman's Review* were particularly interested in furthering the idea that far more than men, women are qualified to assume responsibility for institutionalized children. The *Review* consistently argued, as in "Help for the Children" (1880), that Poor Law boards ought not to be "composed of tradesmen, whose chief attention is directed towards the diminution of the rates," but of women. "The system under which the children are herded and educated in regiments in large schools was a manly not a womanly device," the editorialist charged, adding that only women could fulfill the necessary parental function here: "To give a free child-life to all these forlorn little 'Children of the State' . . . to rouse in them affections, to train them to responsib[i]lity to the voluntary self-sacrifices of home, to moral individuality, is the task of women."[53] Or as Irish suffragist Isabella Tod put it in 1878, Poor Law guardians mirrored parents' functions:

> The masculine guardians represented the State in the function of providing the money—the raw material, as it were, of shelter, food, clothing, and teaching. The . . . feminine guardians, must represent the State in the function of seeing that money properly used, and in so doing seeing also that the wants of the heart and the soul are supplied likewise.[54]

As in similar constructions of parenthood, it is the surrogate mother who has the more delicate and specialized task. While the male contributes only money, the female contributes expertise; his presence may be dispensed with as long as the flow of money continues, but hers is essential.

It was in part this deep respect for motherhood, which implied no corresponding respect for fatherhood, that caused many reformers to see the "boarding-out system" (foster care) as the ideal solution to the problem of creating a home environment for destitute children. Writers such as Henrietta L. Synnot (in an article appearing in the *Contemporary Review* in 1875) found it "difficult to see how an institution can fill the place of parents to a child"—specifically, of course, the mother, since typically the child's "earliest thoughts and associations are chiefly connected with the mother," and it is she who provides the deepest love, the truest teaching, the strongest religion. "The very fact of bringing up children in large numbers," Synnot charged, "creates an artificial, *i.e.* a false, standard of truth" because it negates the individuality of the mother-child bond. Hence fosterage, which best mirrors the family and allows the re-creation of that bond, is preferable to institutionalization.[55]

While foster care struck most theorists as the best solution, in practice it proved difficult to implement. The *Englishwoman's Review* noted in 1888 that of 33,000 eligible children, 3,000 were boarded out, while in 1907 more than half of the 60,000 children identified as waifs were still in workhouses or barrack schools.[56] Many reformers accordingly proposed measures that would leave the needy child in the care of its own mother while rectifying the deficiencies of the father as provider. Such constructions assumed no lack of love on the mother's part; it was not she who had broken the implied domestic contract, but the father, who could not or would not keep the child in comfort. With the state as partner, the mother could look after her family in a manner impossible for a woman financially dependent on an individual man.

Along similar lines, some legislation sought to permit wives to function in public as well as private spheres, such as the Married Women's Property Acts. Once wives had legal title to their own earnings, they had an incentive to work outside the home and to keep control of the family finances, thus entrenching on roles usually seen as male. Given that many commentators assumed that gender roles among the working classes were more fluid than among the well-to-do (the paradigms of the helpless father and the masterful mother were widespread), the effect of the acts on the poor would have appeared less as a fragmentation of male authority than as an acknowledgment that many working-class women were already the keystones of their family economies. Underlying the acts' stance toward such families was a belief that women, much more than men, could be trusted to use their money to serve their children; the state, then, had only to sit back and let them do so.

But if in one sense the Married Women's Property Acts addressed the "family question" by permitting wives to unite the stereotypical roles of both parents (the moral responsibility of the mother, the financial responsibility of the father), at their most basic level they were concerned simply with the marriage question. The same cannot be said of the proposals that sought to insert the state directly into the family economy, not as mediator but as provider. These were more typical of the latter half of the period; writing in 1882, W. Stanley Jevons, a professor of political economy, was among the earlier periodical contributors to suggest Poor Law relief for deserted wives, noting, "In the long-run it would pay for the State to employ them as the nurses of their own children."

Jevons's assumption was that parental feeling is largely the result of propinquity. Mothers who put their infants out to nurse, or who leave them alone all day in order to work outside the home, "become more or less careless and indifferent about them" (again, the same charge could have been, and indeed often was, leveled at wealthy women for banishing their children to the care of a nurse). At the same time, however, he implied that most women would rather look after their families than work in factories and that the real problem stems from the "idle and dissolute" father who expects his wife to be the chief wage-earner.[57] It is the absent father who creates the absent mother; and while the latter fails through having to meet too many demands, financial as well as personal, the former meets none at all. It is thus his role, not hers, that the state should try to fill. Likewise, "A Woman" argued in 1887 for a new kind of income tax: "To subscribe to widow and orphans' funds, ought to be obligatory on all men who have to work for their living. . . . Working and professional men should be saved from their own improvidence," which so often forces their children and wives "to support existence by their own ineffectual efforts."[58] Here, while women and children are deemed inadequate in the public sphere, the real fault again lies with the men whose evasion of duty has jolted the former out of their natural existence in the first place.

By the early years of the new century, the idea of paying mothers for their services had become particularly popular among eugenists, socialists, and other "advanced" thinkers. Sidney Webb, for instance, argued for the "endowment of motherhood" on the grounds that the state might thus bring about "the production of healthy, moral and intelligent citizens."[59] In *A Modern Utopia*, serialized in the *Fortnightly Review* in 1904–5, H. G. Wells noted that "the Utopian State will pay the mother, and the mother only, for the being and welfare of her legitimate children"; he added that the normal father would nevertheless choose "to dispense some of his energies and earnings in supplementing the common provision of the State."[60] What is immediately evident about these proposals, of course, is their assumption that it is the mother who is primarily responsible for a child's "being and welfare," whether morally or physically; what a father has to contribute to the situation can be expressed in purely financial terms.

The same belief is apparent in criticisms of such reforms. The journalist John St. Loe Strachey, for instance, argued in the *National Review* in 1907 that while endowed motherhood would certainly benefit women and children, its impact on adult men must be deleterious. Working for his wife and infants "has upon the father the most beneficial effect"; removing the necessity of such labor "means merely relieving the man of duties which it is immensely to his advantage to assume." While women may show their devotion to the family in a variety of nonmaterial ways, Strachey implied, it is only through their financial contributions that men can demonstrate the "devotion to others and the need for self-sacrifice" that create not only a strong family but a strong state. Socialism, he concluded, can only demoralize the working-class family, not because of its effect on mothers but because it seeks to replace the father.[61]

While endowing motherhood remained a scheme for the future, the passage of the 1906 Education (Provision of Meals) Act appeared to some to represent a significant and present danger to the hegemony of the working-class father. The act permitted the London County Council to serve meals to schoolchildren at the council's discretion, paying for the food through charitable contributions or if necessary by the imposition of a tax. As Deborah Dwork observes, those in favor of the measure (which began to gather steam in the 1890s) relied upon eugenist and patriotic rhetoric: "the future of the race" or of the empire depended on the health of the children of the masses.[62] It was unwise, they argued, to trust working-class parents to feed their children adequately; poverty, domestic incompetence, and callousness or carelessness marked the catering arrangements of the urban proletariat just as they marked other facets of the group's family life.

One might suppose that the plan to provide hot dinners for schoolchildren was predicated at least primarily on assumptions about maternal incapacity. But most of those who opposed the Provision of Meals Act—and earlier, voluntary actions along the same lines, such as the efforts of the London Schools Dinner Association of the 1890s—spoke against it in terms directed, if anything, at fathers. Thus in an 1892 *Macmillan's* article, social reformer H. Clarence Bourne complained that the Dinner Association would sap parents' "sense of responsibility" and self-reliance, the same charges that were leveled against schemes addressing paternal shortcomings. Moreover, Bourne castigated this form of benevolence as misguided because it lacked the "personal element which distinguishes true charity from mere almsgiving." What he called for—"friendly influence" and intimate knowledge of recipients' circumstances—were those qualities the Victorians considered the great strength of women's philanthropy.[63] By implication, then, he criticized the mass provision of food in terms of "masculine" failings on the part of donors and recipients alike. Even the *Englishwoman's Review*, normally eager to support child-welfare measures, expressed concern in 1905 that while "The feeding of children by the State might possibly arrest the physical deterioration of a few," at the same time "it would certainly promote the moral deterioration of many" by pauperizing both parents and children.[64]

What prompted the *Review* writer's objection to the scheme seems to have been the sense that the state was usurping for evil the role of moral influence properly belonging to the mother. And other commentators, such as Mary A. Davies in a 1905 *Contemporary Review*, concurred that the real question was one of feminine capabilities; Davies saw the problem as insufficient home instruction in cooking, brought about by women's employment, and sought to cure two ills at once by suggesting that the free lunches should be produced by girls' cookery classes.[65] But the most vociferous exchanges on both sides of the subject centered on fatherhood. Gorst, the reform politician who was one of the measure's strongest supporters, noted in the *National Review* in 1905 that it is the father's "recognised obligation to feed, clothe, and otherwise maintain" his children, and that if he defaults on this duty, the state must step into the breach—"although it should do so in a fashion calculated to keep the sense of parental responsibility unimpa[i]red."[66] There is no place in Gorst's explanation for the mother, save as her husband's partner in financial delinquency. And even Clara Jackson's *Nineteenth Century* article of the same year, which blamed mothers for "the deterioration of the population" through poor hygiene and dysgenic marriages, considered that the real victim of the school-dinners movement was "the respectable man who does try to feed his children and bring them up properly."[67]

Himmelfarb has pointed out that the Provision of Meals Act was part of a wave of turn-of-the-century social-welfare legislation that sought to address not only the destitute but what Jackson called "the respectable man."[68] What policymakers hoped to do, in other words, was to extend state "paternalism" from families in desperate straits, upward to families who would earlier have been thought to be doing nicely on their own. It is in this context that we must also consider the growth of compulsory education, for instance, or (from 1853 on) the mandating of vaccination for schoolchildren. The aim of these latter movements was less to ameliorate the lot of the endangered few than to bring about equal treatment for all (working-class) children. To do so, of course, it was necessary to subordinate the traditional rights of the parent, and particularly the father, to the greater good of the state.

As this chapter has suggested, justifying this subordination of private patriarchy was made considerably easier by the vast quantity of rhetoric depicting the working-class family as damaged, even damaged beyond repair. While the problems of domestic life among the poor were variously described, most analyses traced matters to the lack of some central family authority: to the wife's need to earn money because of the deficiencies of her husband, to the husband's dearth of self-control or responsibility or tenderness, to the outsider's intervention in the household and consequent rearrangement of "natural" hierarchy. Because the Victorians viewed governance as part of the male gender role, in one sense it was almost always the father who was being found wanting, whether the problem was one of child maintenance, child abuse, or child delinquency.

But if this implicit or explicit criticism of the father provided an excuse for the state to impinge upon the working-class family in unprecedented ways, it also reflected upon the domestic situation of the more privileged. The concern of the social commentators cited in this chapter for symbolism—for instance, in the matter of maintenance payments for children removed to state control—may be viewed, as I have argued, in more than one light. Anxieties that writers glorifying the family ideal might have been reluctant to express in a middle-class context could break through tact-imposed constraints when the subject was the poor. In one sense the call for governmental intervention in working-class domesticity grew from a feeling that the imposition of the mores of the privileged upon the families of the less privileged might cure all social evils. In another, it reflected a longing on the part of the well-to-do themselves for a deus-ex-machina solution to their worries about their own family inadequacy. As the first chapter of this study suggests, much of this feeling of inadequacy was focused on changes in the ideal of femininity, demands regarding motherhood that often seemed to provide no corresponding blueprint for fatherhood. The frequent depiction of working-class fathers as perverse, sadistic, cruel, irresponsible, or simply incompetent, then, functioned as a sort of group "picture of Dorian Gray" to remind the middle- and upper-class father of his shortcomings, delinquencies, and ultimate helplessness in the face of larger social forces.

Conclusion

In her analysis of Charles Dickens's 1847–48 novel *Dombey and Son*, Lynda Zwinger perceptively notes that modern readers often cavil at Dombey's "surrender" to domesticity because "we all 'know' that domestic influence is not stronger than capitalistic power, that sentimental hierarchies are not superior to patriarchal ones. . . . Any suggestion that the world might well be perceived differently is much too close to a radical re-creation for comfort."[1] But this "radical re-creation" is not at all radical in the context of Victorian writings on parenthood, which so vociferously assert the claims of domesticity and feeling against those of money and position. Moreover, so firm was the cultural connection between the ideal of domesticity and that of womanhood that a man seeking to be the center of the family (in a literary work if not in real life) had to take on at least some "feminine" characteristics. The qualities that help a man succeed within the patriarchal realm, as Dombey discovers to his cost, are worse than useless in the home, which constructs its hierarchies along other lines.

It is the attempt to assess the adult male's standing within this alternate hierarchy based on motherly influence that typically concerns Victorian writers on fatherhood. Tainted as he is by the selfishness of the marketplace and even of his own body, how far can the father hope to achieve a feminine power? What does the achievement of that power demand of him? Having achieved it, what will become of him? And if he cannot achieve it, what will become of the world around him? Significantly, authors interested in such questions rarely doubt that domestic power will indeed conquer whenever it comes into conflict with more masculine endeavors. The redemptive myth of Dombey and Daughter was told and retold; we can trace it in *Silas Marner,* in *The Mayor of Casterbridge,* in *Little Lord Fauntleroy,* and in a host of less well-known fictions. And we can see its shadow throughout the host of periodical articles I have classified as "humanitarian" and "social-reformist," even as articles taking a different stance often regard such feminine incursions with horror.

As the preceding chapters of this study have argued, an examination of the periodical prose of the day reveals that many Victorians viewed fatherhood, at least in the abstract, with considerable ambivalence, anxiety, and even hostility. Typically, writers on domesticity presented fathers as ineffectual or uninvolved; writers on science did their best to distance men from the goings-on in the nursery; writers on law depicted fathers as the enemies of the family. Meanwhile, educators and social theorists usually saw the mother, not the father, as providing the best blueprint for child rearing and cultural engineering. However competent they might have been thought to be in the outside world, men appeared in the great majority of periodical nonfiction as mere amateurs in the home. Moreover, their failure to compete successfully within the domestic realm sometimes seemed to jeopardize their achievements in the public sphere, so that women's "innate" domestic excellence was proposed as a remedy for the muddle men had made of politics or poor relief.

The Victorian construction of the male as out of place in the home may be seen as both a cause and an effect of several interlocking trends, most of which were in place by the 1850s. These included new developments in theories of child rearing, the ratification of the ideology of separate spheres, concern about male sexuality as a destructive force, the scientific emphasis on heredity and the competing humanitarian emphasis on the feminine values of the home, the reformist impulse to expose abuses of paternal power in order to bring about social change, and the increasing willingness of the state to intervene in matters once defined as private. Looming largest of all was the mid-nineteenth century's glorification of maternity as woman's highest function, the capacity that defined her, limited her, conferred power upon her, and lifted her to a new spiritual level. In turn, each of these trends strongly affected the areas this study has examined.

Thus we see early in the period the establishment of an ideology of motherhood. As public and private life came to be viewed as separate, at least for commentators on domesticity, the family lost its hierarchical, pre-Victorian shape. Because it was not a public space, it could not work by public rules. In the context of the family, power no longer took the same form it had in the outside world. What mattered in the Looking-Glass Land of the Victorian home was not experience but innocence, to borrow William Blake's dichotomy. The child, then, became a creature to cherish and to mold through delicate influence rather than harsh discipline; the mother's authority became all the stronger for being covert. Once men acknowledged that each gender had its own power, they opened the door to a radical reordering of gender relations, as woman's power—which lay in gentleness, in influence, and in biological femininity itself—turned out to be infinitely expandable by virtue of its invisibility. Who can perceive the limits to an imperceptible force? Conversely, the more men did within the home, the more their performance could be critiqued because they were behaving in masculine ways in a space defined as feminine; yet male inactivity was likewise not an acceptable alternative, as what was read as moral force in women seemed sheer irresponsibility in men.

At the same time, the emphasis on mothers' influence over children permitted new speculation about the impact of maternity in the public world: domesticity-loving Victorians doubted that one could ever leave one's family behind. From that premise it was but a short leap to the feminist-inspired argument that if women were influencing the public sphere indirectly through their grown sons, women without sons should be allowed to improve the public lot directly, especially since so many social ills were clearly the product of a masculine excess untempered by feminine morality. Feminists made it their continuing project to attack institutionally sanctioned sexual license, brutality, and selfishness, all of which could be defined as male because they had so little relevance to the maternal stereotype. The argument that women needed equal rights in order to clean up the messes left by men did not, of course, convince all those who heard it; but it did convince many. Femininity and especially maternity duly crept more and more into the number of vocations that were becoming professionalized in the latter part of the century, as observers grew increasingly sure that the mother's complex and subtle duties warranted education and training. But while males also received training geared toward inculcating masculinity (consider, for instance, the rise of athleticism during this period), such pursuits seemed to have little relevance to fatherhood.

Writers on fatherhood, as I have contended, found it difficult to reach any kind of consensus about what fatherhood meant. The establishment of the ideal of separate spheres resulted in the construction of the home as the one place in which the will of the middle-class adult Englishman did not, and even should not, invariably prevail. Inevitably, many commentators voiced doubts about men's domestic abilities, suggesting that male influence over children was minimal, that fathers were important to the family only financially, and that while men should strive for more active involvement in the private sphere, the exercise was likely to benefit them more than their children, paternal nature being what it was. Other commentators fought a losing rear-guard action, seeking to reestablish the hierarchical home that was fast passing out of fashion if not out of practice. Meanwhile, as the specter of the bad father received more and more publicity from feminists and other social reformers and as fears about effeminacy mushroomed, the argument that fathers should try to behave like surrogate mothers lost ground: for many late-Victorian and Edwardian writers, the best contribution the father could make was to get out of the mother's way.

Scientific currents in the sixty years under discussion help to illustrate the difficulties facing the father. First came Darwinism, which was often used within the scientific establishment to suggest that environment plays a minimal role in shaping the new generation, so that a father who seeks to mold his children after conception is wasting his time. Later offshoots such as eugenics and genetic theory confirmed that breeding children, not rearing them, is of principal importance, and that the father's genetic contribution somehow predominates over the mother's. In tandem with the humanitarian emphasis on environment and maternalism, however, the scientific stress on biology merely reinforced the doctrine of separate spheres, casting the father as a sperm donor and the mother as the parent responsible for training the child. Next came developments in anthropological and social-evolutionary theory that displayed the family not as a stable unit perennially under patriarchal control, but as something fluid and liable to change, particularly in the method of its governance. What historical trends seemed to show was the increasing power of the mother over the ages, as promiscuity gave way to polygamy and polygamy gave way to monogamy; nor was there any reason to suppose that the process would end with the Victorian age. For some visionaries, the logical and desirable next step was the removal of the father from the family altogether. Once he had served his biological purpose, perhaps there was little reason to keep him around.

For science could discover no paternal instinct akin to the maternal drive; if it existed at all, it was because women's influence had created it in their male kin. Thus not only did fatherhood end where motherhood began (that is, at the moment of conception), but this limitation turned the father into the mother's child within the family context. If he were to be a concerned parent, she would first have to be his teacher. Science therefore helped to reinforce a movement already afoot in the legal world, namely, the exposure of men's indifference and irresponsibility toward their offspring. Child custody and control over child rearing became central issues within Victorian family law. Did not the child belong to the private sphere and thus to the mother's province? Was not the mother inherently more chaste, more loving, and more talented at dealing with children than her spouse? Then why, inquired reformers, could not matters be rearranged to conform to nature's dictates, so that in cases of legal dissolution of the family, each parent would make an appropriate contribution to a child's welfare, the mother providing nurture and the father financial support?

Makers and interpreters of the law, themselves male, proved reluctant to transfer the husband's traditional rights under English law to wives. Nevertheless, the portraits of evil fatherhood consistently drawn in periodicals' commentary on women's legal struggles were too powerful to ignore. While women did gradually achieve the financial rights formerly belonging only to *femes sole*, and had by the end of the period considerably more chance of gaining custody of young children than they had had at the beginning, the most radical shift in public policy during these years was not in favor of mothers but rather in favor of the state. Increasingly, the private man's loss was the public man's gain, as courts found it ever more possible and beneficial to remove the child from the father's control.

The same principle of growing state intervention was apparent in wider Victorian social legislation. Depictions of the working-class family as damaged by both poverty and immorality helped transform that family from a private to a public concern. Science again played its part: concerns about heredity and degeneration gained public attention, persuading late-century pessimists that without strong and immediate measures, the empire—which depended, many argued, upon a robust underclass—would collapse. Hence while the laissez-faire beliefs of the early Victorians rendered difficult any intrusion into the patriarchal family, late-Victorian and Edwardian distrust of patriarchalism bore fruit. By the end of the period, it was the state and not the father who determined whether children should attend school, what kind of employment they might undertake, and how they might be disciplined— all traditionally male decisions. The incapacity for domesticity that had so long been intrinsic to the stereotypical father had contributed to a widespread belief that the working-class father, at least, needed more help than the working-class mother could provide if his family, and the nation, were to survive.

That mid- and late-nineteenth-century legislation manifests a burgeoning willingness to see crisis within the working-class home—specifically, a crisis caused by a breakdown in paternal authority, competence, health, and feeling—may or may not signal a displacement of anxieties actually felt by the legislators themselves with reference to their own domestic situations. Certainly it is suggestive that proposals for reform (for "influence" over the family, one might say) were so often cast in maternalist terms, even while their parliamentary sponsors were necessarily male. Thus the trend in dealing with delinquent or unwanted children was generally nurturing rather than punitive, while state-sponsored institutions were depicted as motherly instead of masculine or impersonal. Meanwhile, opponents of governmental interference in domestic matters cited possible damage to fathers if paternal responsibility was reassigned to public authorities; readers were left to assume that maternal responsibility needed no repair or was impervious to tinkering.

I have suggested that one reason commentators might have felt ill at ease about their own domestic situations was their awareness that because of the popularity of the boys' boarding school, their relationships with their sons (or their parents, for that matter) lacked the intimacy supposed to be characteristic of the ideal Victorian home. The extension of the public school into the middle-class world offers a final and perhaps an especially provocative case study in the imaging of fatherhood during this period. Here we begin with a vision of surrogate, institutional paternity as all too stereotypically masculine. The Public Schools Commission of the 1860s, as periodical writers' descriptions made plain, exposed headmasters of the country's greatest educational foundations as profit-obsessed, irresponsible, distant, and hypocritical, just like the envisioned bourgeois fathers whom the headmasters offered to supplant. Within a few years, however, the rhetoric surrounding the public schools had caught up with the concerns of the nation in general. Whatever the realities of Victorian public-school life, writers claimed that headmasters, now invariably portrayed as noble, were tender influences, gentle disciplinarians, unselfish and high-minded guardians of the young lives entrusted to them. Like child-rearing practices overall, educational theory was tending toward the nurturing and maternal; and in the view of the periodical press, Victorian headmasters were in lockstep behind it.

Why did headmasters emerge from the fray so much better off than biological fathers? The answer, I would argue, is that unlike the father, the headmaster played his part on a stage on which *women* were the invisible gender. Women were not really absent from the late-Victorian public school: there were maidservants, matrons, masters' wives, just as the Victorian home was full of men. But the rhetoric surrounding schools presented femininity as an aporia into which the headmaster, already empanoplied in full masculine authority, might step. As we have seen, precisely the opposite was occurring with regard to the mother at home.

The school's great advantage was that it was a space simultaneously public and domestic, an institution that (after the embarrassment occasioned by the Clarendon Commission proceedings) promised at once to prepare boys for an imperial role and to instill family values. The headmasters preserved themselves from invasion by the "public mothers" by taking on the much rarer guise of "public fathers." Yet this expedient was only possible because it took place in an environment purportedly devoid of women.

The public schools, in other words, were a special case. As the example of the pre-commission headmasters suggests, nineteenth-century essentialists and social constructionists alike distrusted what they saw as the masculine tendency toward selfishness. The point of connection between the two groups—the scientists and the social reformers—was sexuality, which both constructed differently for male and for female. Biologists saw the one as active and energy-dispersing, the other as passive and energy-absorbing; for reformers, this opposition signified a moral distinction between men's selfish drive toward the pleasure of release and women's altruistic ability to nurture others. Thus women were viewed as biologically designed to care for children and husbands, while men seemed only interested in their own needs. And because men were not programmed for fatherhood as women were for motherhood, they could not be trusted to control their sexual drives enough to preserve the health of their wives, themselves, or their unborn children. Although science generally viewed male sexuality as a healthy instinct, then, reformers nevertheless were enabled to present it as socially damaging precisely because it was so strong and ineradicable a force: even conscience and reason could not invariably control it.

Moreover, this biologically constructed egocentrism was further encouraged by man's life beyond the home, where his profession so often stressed personal ambition and financial success over the more modest "living for others" to which women were enjoined. Such suspicions of masculinity, both inside and outside the bedroom, played a major role in placing maleness and domesticity at odds. If even conception depended upon the male's self-aggrandizement and loss of self-control, what were the father's chances of ever conforming wholly to the self-sacrificing discipline of the Victorian family ideal?

It is therefore not enough to say, with Dianne Sadoff, that the tensions surrounding the myth of the paterfamilias arose from a simultaneous "desire for its stability, decisiveness, and cultural validity" and a "hatred of its narrowness, stubbornness, and social domination."[2] As the articles we have examined illustrate, Victorian constructions of the paterfamilias were at once less stable, less narrow, and less dominant than our assumptions about them might allow. The problem was not simply that many fathers failed to conform to the stereotype; rather, it was that no one stereotype prevailed. "Cultural validity" was exactly what the paterfamilias lacked. Granted, insofar as the public sphere was concerned he still had power over the family: his was the vote, the money, and the legal authority, although his grip on all three was loosening. But his private power, his domestic influence, was much more doubtful.

As I have suggested throughout this study, anxiety about fatherhood took no single, easily classifiable form in the period we have been examining. There are no easy answers here, no smooth progression from one ideal (or anti-ideal) to another. Many of the concerns of 1850 are equally visible in 1910; on the other hand, one writer may see fatherhood's major problem as apathy while another, contemporaneous writer may see it as incompetence or poor training or biological destiny—or may deny that there is any problem, painting a rosy portrait of responsible paternity that all men may emulate if they will. Similarly, while many of the images and trends in place by 1910 still look familiar today, the deification of maternity has effectively vanished, so that the likenesses evident between Victorian fatherhood and fatherhood today do not necessarily carry the same meanings.

One may propose any number of reasons that the Victorians and their heirs should have become distrustful of fatherhood: changes in the performance of occupations, in the division between public and private, in ideas about sexuality, in the imaging of gender, all had their effect. Movements in evolutionary biology, theology, anthropology, and the legal system likewise had important (and unquantifiable) repercussions for the culture's construction of the family drama. So did agitation about child welfare, women's status, education reform, and a host of other issues. For all that many Victorians were horrified at the speed and extent of the changes taking place during their lifetimes, the radical revamping of society seems to have been the period's most longed-for goal. Nor can we afford to ignore class as a factor in how the father was conceived, even though the parameters of my own study are such that class has taken a back seat to gender throughout. Moreover, it is vital to bear in mind that one cannot readily separate cause from effect. If anxiety about fatherhood in part resulted from the societal shifts I have outlined (and from others that I have neglected), it also helped to create those shifts. Finally, my selection of one sixty-year time frame for the examination of some of the various phenomena of paternity, like my selection of texts, has necessarily been somewhat arbitrary, even though the period is certainly also one of major transition. While Victorian culture is in many ways distinctive, it is hardly anomalous; just as we can trace "Victorian" assumptions in present-day rhetoric, we can discern eighteenth-century (or Elizabethan, or even Roman) beliefs in the pronouncements of the nineteenth century.

In other words, no such study as mine can reasonably claim to provide any kind of definitive treatment of its subject, even merely as regards the particular years and body of evidence it employs. The impossible task nonetheless seems worth undertaking, if only by way of a corrective to a problem that still afflicts much research into Victorian patterns of thought. Scholarship has traditionally focused on men's achievements in public life; with the advent of feminist history and criticism, attention has increasingly gone to women's achievements as well. But while we are often ready to examine women in both their public and private roles— Florence Nightingale as nurse, Florence Nightingale as daughter—it is still comparatively rare for us to investigate men's place in the private world of the home. One suspects, indeed, that perhaps we too don't believe they have a place there. It is this exclusion, I believe, that so disturbed a great many of the nineteenth- and early-twentieth-century writers I have cited. The public sphere could work as prison, not only as privilege. Shut out of home and family, disconnected from the personal concerns that are the core of life, the stereotypical Victorian father remains an "invisible man." And while reality seldom approximates the stereotype, such images nonetheless have their uncomfortable impact on the real.

A Note on Sources

Any researcher into nineteenth-century British periodicals owes a debt to Walter E. Houghton and his coeditors, Esther Rhoads Houghton and Jean Harris Slingerland, for compiling the five-volume *Wellesley Index to Victorian Periodicals 1824–1900*, which provides capsule histories and biographies, reproduces tables of contents, and identifies an impressive proportion of the anonymous contributors to the generalist journals covered. It is with the *Wellesley Index* that I began my hunt for sources, reading through the collected tables of contents and noting down promising titles of articles. To move on to the actual periodicals, of course, was to discover serendipitously many articles whose titles gave little indication of the focus on fatherhood within the text and conversely to cross blind alleys off my list. My reliance on Houghton's invaluable reference has meant that, by and large, the parameters of his index are the parameters of my study; at some fifty thousand individual titles, the immensity of the Victorian periodical press is such that the largest sampling of journals must seem tiny in comparison to the available material, but he provides a useful digest of many of the most important monthlies and quarterlies, from *Blackwood's Edinburgh Magazine* to the *Westminster Review*.[1]

To the *Wellesley Index*'s compendium of journals I added a further handful, examining (sometimes thoroughly, sometimes sketchily) some of the major weeklies, such as *All the Year Round* and the *Saturday Review*; a few publications aimed primarily at women, especially the *Englishwoman's Review*, *Shafts*, and the *Victoria Magazine*; professional and scientific organs, including the *British Medical Journal*, the *Lancet*, and *Mind*; and some additional generalist and middlebrow titles, among them the *English Illustrated Magazine* and *Punch*. Inevitably, some periodicals have furnished a disproportionately high number of citations: the *Westminster Review*, my most heavily quoted source with sixty-six separate articles used, proved particularly fruitful because it united a long run with a wide scope. (The sheer number of topics explored in its pages meant that fatherhood would be invoked in a variety of contexts.) For the reader who may wish a more detailed overview of major sources, the following list offers a brief description of periodicals that provided ten or more articles cited in this study:

Blackwood's Edinburgh Magazine (1817–1980; monthly). Aristocratic, socially cautious, and among the most prestigious and influential journals of the nineteenth century, "Maga" was founded as a Tory rival to the *Edinburgh Review*.

The *Contemporary Review* (began publication 1866; monthly). The *Contemporary* was the brainchild of Alexander Strahan, the proprietor of a number of religious periodicals. It was created as a liberal Christian magazine focusing on philosophical and theological issues and generally speaking for the Anglican church. Like *Blackwood's*, it enjoyed an international reputation and a comfortable circulation, which swung from approximately two thousand in 1870 to eight thousand in 1876 under the guidance of a flamboyant new editor.

The *Cornhill Magazine* (1860–1975; monthly). A highly respectable and seldom controversial periodical, predominantly literary in focus, the *Cornhill* was the preeminent family magazine of its day, with an astonishing circulation in 1860 (when W. M. Thackeray was its editor) of 110,000 copies—which, however, dwindled to 12,000 in 1882 and still fewer by the end of the century.

The *Edinburgh Review* (1802–1929; quarterly). The most venerable of the nineteenth-century journals, the *Edinburgh* was founded in Scotland as a voice for Whig social reform. It moved to London in 1847, where, under the forty-year guidance of *Times* political writer and conservative Liberal Henry Reeve, it settled into a moderate Whiggery and a comfortable circulation (in the 1860s) of seven thousand, informing its readers on matters political, scientific, literary, and social.

The *Englishwoman's Review* (1866–1910; monthly). Consciously feminist in slant, the *Englishwoman's Review* succeeded another reformist periodical, the *English Woman's Journal* (1858–64), which had been conducted in tandem with the Society for the Promotion of the Employment of Women. The *Review* focused on political and economic issues, presenting itself as a watchdog for women's rights and women's dignity; for instance, it provided abstracts of legislative and judicial doings relevant to women's position. Although it was both comparatively long-lived and important in the development of Victorian feminism, it lacked the widespread influence of most of the other publications on this list.

The *Fortnightly Review* (1865–1954 [subsequently merged with the *Contemporary Review*]; originally fortnightly, it appeared monthly by November 1866). The brief inaugural editorship of G. H. Lewes helped put the *Fortnightly* on its course as a rationalist and progressive journal capable of establishing trends—such as its original stance (later relaxed) against anonymous contributions, a fashion quickly followed by some of its competitors. In 1872 its subscribers numbered some twenty-five hundred, but, as with all Victorian magazines, the actual readership would have been much greater; its proprietors at the time estimated the latter figure at thirty thousand.

Fraser's Magazine (1830–82; monthly). Modeled on *Blackwood's*, *Fraser's* was a progressive Tory publication focusing on politics, religion, and social conditions. It began prosperously with a circulation of eighty-seven hundred, but this fell to a mere five hundred by 1879, and the magazine closed its doors shortly thereafter.

Macmillan's Magazine (1859–1907; monthly). Like *Blackwood's* and the *Cornhill*, with which it may conveniently be classified, *Macmillan's* mixed political philosophy with literature. (Its emphasis on fiction, and the quality of the fiction it printed, grew markedly after a change of editors in 1885.) It purveyed a smorgasbord of topics and genres for the Victorian family, becoming known for its variety.

The *National Review* (1883–1960; monthly). Although the *National* had something of a reputation for dullness (especially among its political opponents), it drew readers with its big-name contributors. Its circulation hovered at around five thousand in its first decade, under the editorship of Alfred Austin, and climbed to over ten thousand in the Edwardian years. Its focus was predominantly political, with some excursions into literary realms, and its politics were uniformly conservative—as befit a journal founded at the suggestion of Benjamin Disraeli.

The *Nineteenth Century* (1877–1972 [title changed first to the *Nineteenth Century and After* and subsequently, in 1951, to the *Twentieth Century*]; monthly). With an early circulation of more than ten thousand and an estimated readership of fifty thousand, the *Nineteenth Century* was the largest of the journals of its type: a publication of political and scientific focus intended, like all the periodicals in this study, for an educated audience. While its politics were generally liberal, it usually endeavored to take a politically neutral stance by means of institutions such as its "symposia," which juxtaposed competing views by a variety of authors on particular topics. Strongly influenced in its initial years by the Metaphysical Society, the journal took its first editor from the *Contemporary* and its contributors, it would seem, from *Who's Who*.

The *Quarterly Review* (1809–1967; quarterly). Like *Blackwood's*, the *Quarterly* was intended as a rival to the *Edinburgh Review* and employed a similar format while taking a moderate Tory stance. By the middle of the century, it had outpaced the *Edinburgh* in influence, with a maximum circulation of thirteen thousand (it averaged around eight thousand, however).

Shafts (1892–99; variable frequency). Commencing as a weekly, *Shafts* became in turn a monthly, a bimonthly, and finally a quarterly—a progression reflecting the increasing inability of its editor and proprietor, Margaret Shurmer Sibthorp, to support it. The periodical provides a fascinating look at "advanced"—and often eccentric—feminism in the 1890s, reflecting through its correspondence columns, essays, stories, and poems the interests of a predominantly female circle caught up not only in the question of women's rights but also in vegetarianism, theosophy, antivivisection, and so on. (Unlike the *Englishwoman's Review*, *Shafts* offered little factual reportage.) But although *Shafts* lies some distance outside mainstream opinion, its difference is often one of degree rather than one of kind: it represents an extremist voice but not a unique one.

The *Westminster Review* (1824–1914; quarterly [monthly after 1887]). Founded by Jeremy Bentham and James Mill, and controlled between 1836 and 1840 by John Stuart Mill (when it was known as the *London and Westminster Review*), the *Westminster* continued throughout its existence to display the liberal-to-radical politics of its inception. While always financially troubled and relatively small in circulation—there were twelve hundred subscribers in 1840—the journal remained prestigious and influential, so much so that contributors put up with tiny or even nonexistent fees in order that their work might appear in its pages. Like the other publications of this class, such as the *Edinburgh*, the *Westminster* focused on political, literary, and scientific questions, seeking to educate its already highly literate audience in order to shape the society of the future.

Notes

Introduction

1. Exceptions to this rule usually take the form of articles rather than full-length studies. See, for example, David Newsome's chapter on Martin White Benson in his *Godliness and Good Learning: Four Studies on a Victorian Ideal* (London: Cassell, 1961); David Roberts's pioneering essay "The Paterfamilias of the Victorian Governing Classes," in Anthony S. Wohl, ed., *The Victorian Family: Structure and Stresses* (New York: St. Martin's, 1978), 59–81; and John Tosh's "Domesticity and Manliness in the Victorian Middle Class: The Family of Edward White Benson," in Michael Roper and John Tosh, eds., *Manful Assertions: Masculinities in Britain since 1800* (London: Routledge, 1991), 44–73.

2. Leonore Davidoff and Catherine Hall, *Family Fortunes: Men and Women of the English Middle Class, 1780–1850* (Chicago: U of Chicago P, 1987), 329.

3. For a discussion of men's "network of association" in the "age of societies," see Davidoff and Hall, *Family Fortunes*, 416–49. They also note the importance of women's "claim for a separate sphere" in the patriarchal world of eighteenth-century Britain (33).

4. For an account of the middle-class girl's entrance into the marketplace, see Sally Mitchell, "Girls' Culture: At Work," in Claudia Nelson and Lynne Vallone, eds., *The Girl's Own: Cultural Histories of the Anglo-American Girl, 1830–1915* (Athens: U of Georgia P, 1994), 243–58. Mitchell finds that whereas advice manuals and periodical articles viewed the working girl as a regrettable anomaly in 1880, by 1905 she had become normative.

5. [Anne Mozley], "Clever Women," *Blackwood's Edinburgh Magazine* 104 (October 1868): 410–27, 414.

Chapter 1: The Fascination with the Maternal

The epigraph is from [Andrew Halliday], "Mothers," *All the Year Round* 14 (9 September 1865): 157–59, 157.

1. Philippe Ariès, "The Family and the City in the Old World and the New," in Virginia Tufte and Barbara Myerhoff, eds., *Changing Images of the Family* (New Haven: Yale UP, 1979), 29–41, 32. See also, for example, Edward Shorter, *The Making of the Modern Family* (New York: Basic Books, 1975), for an extended discussion of the modern family as the product of "a surge of sentiment" and a gradual separation from the outside world (5). While revisionists have challenged the argument of a number of historians in the 1970s (Shorter included) that the devoted family is essentially a postindustrial phenomenon, it seems likely that expectations about the *display* of emotion within the family—although not, perhaps, about its existence—did undergo a change during this period. Linda A. Pollock provides in *Forgotten Children: Parent-Child Relations from 1500 to 1900* (Cambridge: Cambridge UP, 1983) a useful counterweight to Ariès, which is critiqued by S. Ryan Johansson in "Centuries of Childhood/Centuries of Parenting: Philippe Ariès and the Modernization of Privileged Infancy," *Journal of Family History* 12 (October 1987): 343–65.

2. See, for instance, Patricia Branca, *Silent Sisterhood: Middle Class Women in the Victorian Home* (Pittsburgh: Carnegie-Mellon UP, 1975), 102, and Judith Schneid Lewis, *In the Family Way: Childbearing in the British Aristocracy, 1760–1860* (New Brunswick, N.J.: Rutgers UP, 1986), 58. Lewis argues that the mid-eighteenth century saw the beginning of a domestic, mother-centered model among the aristocracy, a model that took firm hold as late as the 1830s (223).

3. [Julia Wedgwood], "Social Reform in England," *Westminster Review* 87 (January 1867): American ed. 68–78, 74. As Carl Degler notes in *At Odds: Women and the Family in America from the Revolution to the Present* (New York: Oxford UP, 1980), "it was to women's advantage to encourage this emotional concentration upon children within the family and throughout society, since in that way woman's own role would be enhanced" (74).

4. Quoted in Branca, *Silent Sisterhood*, 109.

5. Herman Lantz, Martin Schultz, and Mary O'Hara, "The Changing American Family from the Preindustrial to the Industrial Period: A Final Report," *American Sociological Review* 42 (June 1977): 406–21, 408. Invoking Leonore Davidoff and Catherine Hall's work on middle-class families from 1780 to 1850,

John Tosh has recently argued that women's control even over the home was largely illusory ("Domesticity and Manliness in the Victorian Middle Class," 50), a view contradicted by (among others) Jane Rendall in *The Origins of Modern Feminism: Women in Britain, France and the United States, 1780–1860* (Chicago: Lyceum, 1990), 211. Whatever may have been the practice in real life—and the increased emphasis in the latter part of the century on housewifery as a profession suggests that more and more wives were arrogating household power to themselves—the ideal presented in periodicals, with few exceptions, treated women's control as absolute.

6. "The Progress of Women," *Quarterly Review* 195 (January 1902): 201–20, 211.

7. [Eliza Lynn Linton], "Womanliness," *Saturday Review* 30 (6 August 1870): 166–68, 167. Such imagery was common on both sides of the Atlantic; in "Images of the American Family, Then and Now" (in Tufte and Myerhoff, *Changing Images of the Family*, 43–60), John Demos quotes William G. Eliot Jr.'s 1853 *Lectures to Young Women* to the effect that men worn down by "the corroding cares of business" would find in their homes "the healing oil poured upon the wounds and bruises of the spirit" (51, 52). See also Kirk Jeffrey, "The Family as Utopian Retreat from the City: The Nineteenth-Century Contribution," *Soundings* 55 (Spring 1972): 21–41, for an analysis of Victorian American families as utopian communities. Sennett's point will be found in his *Families against the City: Middle Class Homes of Industrial Chicago 1872–1890* (Cambridge, Mass.: Harvard UP, 1970), 217.

8. "The Ladies of the Creation; or, How I Was Cured of Being a Strong-Minded Woman," *Punch* 23 (1852): n.p.

9. Goldwin Smith, "Conservatism and Female Suffrage," *National Review* 10 (February 1888): 735–52, 741; Frederic Harrison, "The Emancipation of Women," *Fortnightly Review* n.s. 49 (1 October 1891): 437–52, 452; Carmen Sylva, "The Vocation of Woman," *National Review* 45 (June 1905): 611–24, 614.

10. Miriam Lewin, "The Victorians, the Psychologists, and Psychic Birth Control," in Miriam Lewin, ed., *In the Shadow of the Past: Psychology Portrays the Sexes* (New York: Columbia UP, 1984), 39–76, 63.

11. Thus Reverend Charles Dunbar pleaded that women who competed in the male arena would lose their moral purity and with it their ability to reform their husbands: "Once make woman the equal of man—no longer a being purer, softer, holier, and better than he is . . . not a woman, but a female man . . . no longer marked off by the reverent barrier of an innocence to which he may

not pretend but a being, who, having fallen from a greater moral height, will be spiritually even more shattered than himself; then . . . man, left without the companionship of those who are better than himself, will sink to the depths of the gates of hell" ([Charles Dunbar], "Answer to an Article Headed 'A Clerical View of Woman's Sphere,'" *Victoria Magazine* 18 [January 1872]: 237–46, 239).

12. Whose writers, Nancy Fix Anderson observes, were known as the "Saturday Revilers." Anderson's biographical study *Woman against Women in Victorian England: A Life of Eliza Lynn Linton* (Bloomington: Indiana UP, 1987) provides valuable insights into a major journalist and her market.

13. E. Lynn Linton, "The Wild Women: No. I, As Politicians," *Nineteenth Century* 30 (July 1891): 79–88, 79. Linton's own marriage was childless; her behavior toward her husband and stepchildren was never characterized by the gentle warmth she recommended to others; and her sexual identification appears to have been male (see Anderson, *Woman against Women*, especially 11–13). The element of self-criticism in her diatribes against what she labeled "*homasses*" may be related to her insistence on the inferiority even of feminine women, a somewhat exaggerated stance for her day.

14. E. Lynn Linton, "The Philistine's Coming Triumph," *National Review* 26 (September 1895): 40–49, 43.

15. H. B. Marriott-Watson, "The American Woman: An Analysis," *Nineteenth Century and After* 56 (September 1904): 433–42, 439–40.

16. "The Enfranchisement of Women," rpt. *Victoria Magazine* 9 (October 1867): 561–65, 565.

17. School chaplain B. G. Johns, writing anonymously on "The Education of Women" (*Edinburgh Review* 166 [July 1887]: 89–114), cited Maudsley's *Sex in Mind and in Education* (published as a pamphlet in 1874, the same year that it appeared in the *Fortnightly Review*) to the effect that menstruation places "special and peculiar demands on the strength of woman to which man is not liable, and which at times try her utmost resources. She is not *then* capable of further endurance without danger of utter exhaustion; and, if the mental training of men be planted on women, it cannot be done without positive injury to their general health and strength" (93). Given this climate of opinion, Sara Delamont reminds us, "It was *only* by continuing to glorify the Victorian domestic ideal, as the educational pioneers all did, that any educational progress could be made. . . . Women's education could only progress if the family was not threatened" ("The Domestic Ideology and Women's Education," in Sara Delamont and Lorna Duffin, eds., *The Nineteenth-Century Woman: Her Cultural and Physical World*

[New York: Barnes and Noble, 1978], 164–87, 184). For instance, women won the right to study medicine partly by promising to specialize in the suitably motherly fields of obstetrics and pediatrics.

18. Millicent Garrett Fawcett, "The Emancipation of Women," *Fortnightly Review* n.s. 49 (1 November 1891): 673–85, 676. For similar contentions, see the report in the *Englishwoman's Review* 3 (April 1867) of a "Lecture by the Rev. Ward Beecher on the Suffrage," 180–91, 186–87; Emily Pfeiffer, "The Suffrage for Women," *Contemporary Review* 47 (March 1885): 418–35; and Mrs. A. Warner Snoad, "A Plea for Justice," *Westminster Review* 138 (July 1892): 52–56. Both women counter the antisuffrage argument that women could not be full citizens because they could not be soldiers with the reminder that women's risks in bearing children are the moral equivalent of front-line service.

19. See, for instance, A. V. Dicey, "Woman Suffrage," *Quarterly Review* 210 (January 1909): 276–304, 297; Louise Creighton, "The Appeal against Female Suffrage: A Rejoinder," *Nineteenth Century* 26 (August 1889): 347–54, 348; J. Lionel Tayler, "An Interrogatory Note on the Franchise of Women," *Westminster Review* 167 (April 1907): 456–58, 457. Linton adds that according to science, "to admit women—that is, mothers—into the heated arena of political life would be as destructive to the physical well-being of the future generation as it would be disastrous to the good conduct of affairs in the present," and that the maternal instinct bred into women, translated into a political context, is a "tyrannous temper," the desire for an authority "so absolute, so irresponsible, as that of a mother over her young children" ("Wild Women: No. I," 86, 85). The latter point is echoed in G. K. Chesterton's "The Modern Surrender of Women" (*Dublin Review* 145 [July 1909]: 128–37), which contends that authority is "the perpetual repetition of the relation of mother and child. I would be much more willing to give women authority than to give them equality. I can imagine that a queen might really be the mother of her people without ceasing to be the mother of her babies"—a fate that must befall the woman who seeks equality (133).

20. L. Vansittart de Fabeck, "The Making of Woman," *Westminster Review* 145 (May 1896): 544–51, 545.

21. "Biology and 'Woman's Rights,'" rpt. in *Popular Science Monthly* 14 (December 1878): 201–13, 209.

22. Quoted in Mary Poovey, "'Scenes of an Indelicate Character': The Medical 'Treatment' of Victorian Women," *Representations* 14 (Spring 1986): 137–68, 145. Refusal of fatherhood, on the other hand, seemed beneficial; Dr. Lionel S. Beale, for one, linked male genius to male celibacy (see *Our Morality and the*

Moral Question: Chiefly from the Medical Side [London: J. & A. Churchill, 1887], 41).

23. George J. Romanes, "Mental Differences between Men and Women," *Nineteenth Century* 21 (May 1887): 654–72, 663.

24. Lucy Bland, "Rational Sex or Spiritual Love? The Men and Women's Club of the 1880s," *Women's Studies International Forum* 13.1/2 (1990): 33–48, 46, 42.

25. James Macgrigor Allan, "On the Differences in the Minds of Men and Women," *Journal of the Anthropological Society* 7 (1869), excerpted in Pat Jalland and John Hooper, eds., *Women from Birth to Death: The Female Life Cycle in Britain 1830–1914* (Brighton: Harvester, 1986), 22–23, 33–35, 35; M.A.E.L., "The Girl of the Future," *Victoria Magazine* 15 (September and October 1870): 440–57, 491–502, 441.

26. Taylor and Mill wrote in their unsigned "Enfranchisement of Women" (*Westminster Review* 55 [July 1851]: American ed. 149–61), "There is no inherent reason or necessity that all women should voluntarily choose to devote their lives to one animal function and its consequences. Numbers of women are wives and mothers only because there is no other career open to them, no other occupation for their feelings or their activities" (154).

27. Lady Jeune, "A Rejoinder," *Saturday Review* 79 (8 June 1895): 753–54. A prolific contributor to periodicals on women's subjects, Jeune was the wife of the divorce judge Sir Francis Jeune.

28. Julia Wedgwood, " 'Male and Female Created He Them,' " *Contemporary Review* 56 (July 1889): 120–33, 125, 132–33. Wedgwood, who in addition to her work as a journalist lectured at Girton College, was in 1848 a member of the first class to matriculate at Queen's College. Chapter 5 will include a discussion of paternity as a qualification for the ministry.

29. Frances Swiney, "Women among the Nations: Part I," *Westminster Review* 164 (October 1905): 409–19, 410, and "The Maternity of God: Part II," *Westminster Review* 165 (June 1906): 676–84, 677.

30. [Margaret Shurmer Sibthorp], "What the Editor Means," *Shafts* 2 (15 August 1894): 297–98, 298. Sibthorp, the proprietor of this small feminist journal, accepted theosophist belief in the transmigration of souls, holding that women's past experience of the lower plane of masculinity and their potential for motherhood require them to provide men and children with "teaching, leading, guidance, whether mothers in this life or not" ("What the Editor Means," *Shafts* 5 [September 1897]: 233–35, 235). For other quasi-religious rhetoric on

the subject of motherhood, see as examples the epigraph to this chapter and the anonymous "The Apple and the Ego of Woman" (*Westminster Review* 131 [April 1889]: 374–82), which envisions how the "magnificent emotional powers [of woman's "large maternal heart"] . . . will yet roll over the world in fructifying waves, causing also incalculable upheaval and destruction" (377).

31. [Margaret Shurmer Sibthorp], "What the Editor Means," *Shafts* 6 (September-October 1898): 145–48, 147–48. While *Shafts* did not cater to a mainstream audience, Sibthorp's rhetoric is no more extreme than similar exhortations published in more conventional journals, such as the *Westminster Review* (which indeed offered a forum to some of the same writers who contributed to *Shafts*).

32. Agnes Grove, " 'The Threatened Re-Subjection of Woman': A Reply to Lucas Malet," *Fortnightly Review* n.s. 78 (1 July 1905): 123–28, 127. Grove is among those who invoke Ward's *Pure Sociology*, quoting his belief that biologically speaking, women are "the primary and original sex. . . . naturally and really the superior sex" (124–25).

33. Carroll Smith-Rosenberg, *Disorderly Conduct: Visions of Gender in Victorian America* (New York: Knopf, 1985), 263.

34. [Frances Power Cobbe], "Celibacy v. Marriage," *Fraser's Magazine* 65 (February 1862): 228–35, 233.

35. [Helen Taylor], "The Ladies' Petition," *Westminster Review* 87 (January 1867): American ed. 29–36, 36.

36. "A Father's View of the Home," *The Independent* 61 (18 October 1906): 911–14, 914. The argument was a standard one among women. In Britain, suffragist Florence Bright not only described the woman's movement as animated by "the unquenchable maternal instinct; the Mother Heart brooding over her young" but also argued (somewhat unconvincingly) that radicals on the order of Christabel Pankhurst were best seen as "tender-souled women" who would really have preferred to stay in "the sanctuary of their homes . . . sheltered in their privacy" ("The True Inwardness of the Woman's Movement," *Fortnightly Review* n.s. 81 [1 April 1907]: 733–39, 739, 734).

37. For more on American feminism's expansion from child rearing outwards, see David J. Pivar, *Purity Crusade: Sexual Morality and Social Control, 1868–1900* (Westport, Conn.: Greenwood, 1973), esp. 6–7, 36–41, 79–80. By 1894 American politics, to a reformer writing in the *Woman's Journal*, "represented only two things, 'national and political housekeeping . . . and national and political child rearing' " (quoted in Pivar 206).

38. Joe L. Dubbert, *A Man's Place: Masculinity in Transition* (Englewood Cliffs, N.J.: Prentice-Hall, 1979), 83.

39. Quoted in Janet Horowitz Murray and Myra Stark, introduction to the facsimile edition of *The Englishwoman's Review of Social and Industrial Questions* (New York: Garland, 1980), v-xxxi, xxi. On the "socio-biological" position of late-Victorian feminists, see Barbara Caine, "Feminism, Suffrage and the Nineteenth-Century English Women's Movement," *Women's Studies International Forum* 5.6 (1982): 537–50, 546.

40. [Coventry Patmore], "The Social Position of Woman," *North British Review* 14 (February 1851): American ed. 275–89, 288, 279.

41. Henry Thomas Buckle, "The Influence of Women on the Progress of Knowledge," *Fraser's Magazine* 57 (April 1858): 395–407, 395, 398, 405.

42. [Reverend Adams], "Woman's Mission," *Westminster Review* 52 (January 1850): American ed. 181–96, 183, 186, 188, 189, 190.

43. To quote Sheila Jeffreys, Ellis believed "that sexual relations between women and men should take the form of male dominance and female submission. . . . [and supported] an ideology of the 'ideal' woman, which was represented as a form of feminism, and consisted of the glorification of motherhood" (*The Spinster and Her Enemies: Feminism and Sexuality 1880–1930* [London: Pandora, 1985], 129).

44. Arabella Kenealy, "The Talent of Motherhood," *National Review* 16 (December 1890): 446–59, 455.

45. [Montagu Burrows], "Female Education," *Quarterly Review* 126 (April 1869): 448–79, 453, 465. Burrows was a professor of history at Oxford.

46. [Margaret Oliphant], "Mill on the Subjection of Women," *Edinburgh Review* 130 (October 1869): American ed. 291–306, 299. Oliphant defined the sexes not as male and female but as mothers and nonmothers; childless spinsters "are as strong, as courageous, as clever as their masculine contemporaries" and have every right to operate within the public sphere, whether as workers or as voters (301). Fatherhood makes no corresponding change in the lives of men.

47. Johns, "The Education of Woman," 97. See also [Herbert Cowell], "Sex in Mind and Education: A Commentary," *Blackwood's* 115 (June 1874): 736–49, for an overview of opinions on the subject; Cowell, a barrister, was among those who contended that women's equality is incompatible with women's influence (749).

48. Havelock Ellis, "The Woman Question I: The Awakening of Women in Germany," *Fortnightly Review* n.s. 80 (2 July 1906): 123–134, 127; I. D.

Pearce, "The Enfranchisement of Women," *Westminster Review* 168 (July 1907): 17–22, 17.

49. "Female Labour," *Fraser's Magazine* 61 (March 1860): 359–71, 365, 370.

50. Taylor and Mill, "Enfranchisement of Women," 152.

51. Lydia Becker, "Is There Any Specific Distinction between Male and Female Intellect?" *Englishwoman's Review* 1 (July 1868): 483–91, 484. An anonymous critic responded in "Miss Becker on the Mental Characteristics of the Sexes" (*The Lancet* no. 2349 [5 September 1868]: 320–21) that "to apply the same system of education and training to both sexes alike . . . [would] diminish the usefulness and lessen the moral and spiritual influence which women unquestionably exert"; motherhood demands that women's physiology be oriented toward emotion, instinct, and a general "delicacy" of structure (320).

52. Charles Kingsley, "Women and Politics," *Macmillan's Magazine* 20 (October 1869): 552–61, 558. For Mill's influence on Kingsley, see Sylvia Strauss, *"Traitors to the Masculine Cause": The Men's Campaigns for Women's Rights* (Westport, Conn.: Greenwood, 1982).

53. Mona Caird, "The Morality of Marriage," *Fortnightly Review* n.s. 50 (1 March 1890): 310–30, 318. A prominent feminist writer, Caird was at the forefront of the marriage debate in the 1890s.

54. Patmore, "The Social Position of Woman," 283; Sarah Grand, "The New Aspect of the Woman Question," *North American Review* 158 (March 1894): 270–76, 273. Grand was the pseudonym of the feminist novelist Frances Clarke McFall, who is credited with having coined the term "New Woman."

55. I borrow this term from Kathleen Blake, *Love and the Woman Question in Victorian Literature: The Art of Self-Postponement* (Totowa, N.J.: Barnes & Noble, 1983), 133; see also 113. Nineteenth-century anthropological constructions of fatherhood will play a greater part in chapter 3.

56. Quoted in Susan Contratto, "Mother: Social Sculptor and Trustee of the Faith," in Lewin, *In the Shadow of the Past*, 226–55, 233.

57. Taylor and Mill, "Enfranchisement of Women," 159; "The Probable Retrogression of Women," *Saturday Review* 32 (1 July 1871): 10–11, 11.

58. T. Cave-North, "Women's Place and Power," *Westminster Review* 170 (September 1908): 264–67, 264–65, 265. The picture of mother as Svengali was a perennial favorite; compare, for instance, Sister M[ary] F[rancis] Cusack's "Woman's Place in the Economy of Creation" (*Fraser's Magazine* n.s. 9 [February 1874]: 200–209), which contends, "Her influence is apparently

circumscribed, but it is actually unlimited. The boy whom she is training for future life will influence hundreds, perhaps thousands, and he will be just what his mother has made him" (207).

59. Ben Elmy, "The Individuality of Woman: From a Masculine Point of View," *Westminster Review* 158 (November 1902): 506–14, 506.

60. Henry Maudsley, "Sex in Mind and in Education," *Fortnightly Review* n.s. 15 (1 April 1874): 466–83, 472; Thomas Case, "Against Oxford Degrees for Women," *Fortnightly Review* n.s. 58 (1 July 1895): 89–100, 99. For America, Nancy F. Cott dates "this unequivocal affirmation of the mother's predominance" to the 1830s ("Notes toward an Interpretation of Antebellum Childrearing," *Psychohistory Review* 6 [Spring 1978]: 4–20, 8).

61. I discuss androgynous ideals in boys' literature in *Boys Will Be Girls: The Feminine Ethic and British Children's Fiction, 1857–1917* (New Brunswick, N.J.: Rutgers UP, 1991). An insightful treatment of the conjunction of masculinity and religion is Norman Vance's *The Sinews of the Spirit: The Ideal of Christian Manliness in Victorian Literature and Religious Thought* (Cambridge: Cambridge UP, 1985).

62. Smith-Rosenberg, *Disorderly Conduct*, 118. She places this trend in the 1830s for America.

63. Carol Zisowitz Stearns and Peter N. Stearns, *Anger: The Struggle for Emotional Control in America's History* (Chicago: U of Chicago P, 1986), 47, 57.

64. "Espérance," "Woman's Place in Education," *Shafts* 1 (14 January 1893): 171; editorial addendum to "What Cradle-Rockers Might Do," *Shafts* 2 (March 1893): 9.

65. Branca suggests that we may interpret these publications as indicating "that the Victorian middle-class woman did not find motherhood as natural to her as it has been traditionally imagined." See *Silent Sisterhood*, 76. Rendall's discussion of "maternal education" at the beginning of the nineteenth century focuses on the effort to ensure that mothers would meet a certain level of general culture (*Origins of Modern Feminism*, 108–25); the conception of the home as laboratory was to arise later.

66. "Women and Sanitary Knowledge," *Englishwoman's Review* n.s. 11 (15 October 1880): 441–45, 444; M.A.B., "Normal or Abnormal," *Englishwoman's Review* n.s. 20 (14 December 1889): 533–38, 535. Richardson's lecture appears in the November 1880 issue of *Fraser's Magazine*.

67. E. Lynn Linton, "The Modern Revolt," *Macmillan's Magazine* 23 (December 1870): 142–49, 144. Similarly, Linton called in an 1868 *Saturday Re-*

view for more respect toward "practical housekeeping," which for middle-class women consisted of scientific cooking, economic marketing, and participation in the finer aspects of housework ("What Is Woman's Work?" Rpt. in [E. Lynn Linton], *Modern Women and What Is Said of Them: A Reprint of a Series of Articles in the* Saturday Review [New York: J. S. Redfield, 1868], 281–90, 284).

68. This description comes from Florence Bohun, "Back to the Home," *Englishwoman's Review* n.s. 41 (15 July 1910): 182–86, 184; see also Amy Strachey on the King's College course in domestic science, "Science and the Home," *National Review* 54 (October 1909): 282–89. The feminist and the conservative stances of these two periodicals appear almost identical here.

69. Frederick Maurice, "National Health: A Soldier's Study," *Contemporary Review* 83 (January 1903): 41–56, 42, 45, 51. Maurice was the son of the noted Christian socialist F. D. Maurice.

70. Helen Dendy Bosanquet, "Physical Degeneration and the Poverty Line," *Contemporary Review* 85 (January 1904): 65–75, 72. Anna Davin argues in "Imperialism and Motherhood" (*History Workshop* 5 [Spring 1978]: 9–65, 13) that the redefinition and professionalization of motherhood in the late-Victorian and Edwardian years reflects the dominance "of male over female" as well as "of ruling class over working class." It is important to remember, however, that the home visitors and domestic-science teachers were women, and that not only the administration of but the impetus behind these programs was largely female.

71. Patmore, "The Social Position of Woman," 287.

72. A. D. Edwards, "Evolution, Economy, and the Child," *Westminster Review* 171 (January 1909): 78–85, 82.

73. Clara Jackson, "Housekeeping and National Well-Being," *Nineteenth Century and After* 58 (August 1905): 298–305, 301, 299, 304.

74. I thank Lynne Vallone for drawing this connection to my attention.

75. E. Lynn Linton, "Modern Mothers," rpt. in her *Modern Women and What Is Said of Them*, 300–308, 302.

76. [Reginald Brabazon], Earl of Meath, "Have We the 'Grit' of Our Forefathers?" *Nineteenth Century and After* 64 (September 1908): 421–29, 422. A Christian philanthropist, Brabazon was involved in social-welfare projects that included sponsorship of the 1889 Indecent Advertisements Act, which forbade the advertising of condoms; his wife had been a leader in the National Association for the Promotion of Housewifery.

77. Quoted in J. A. and Olive Banks, *Feminism and Family Planning in Victorian England* (Liverpool: Liverpool UP, 1964), 62.

78. Joan N. Burstyn, *Victorian Education and the Ideal of Womanhood* (Totowa, N.J.: Barnes and Noble, 1980), 19.

79. Christina Hardyment, *Dream Babies: Child Care from Locke to Spock* (London: Cape, 1983), 79.

80. Joan Perkin, *Women and Marriage in Nineteenth-Century England* (London: Routledge, 1989), 244, 3–4.

81. Neil Smelser, "The Victorian Family," in R. M. Rapoport, M. P. Fogarty, and R. Rapoport, eds., *Families in Britain* (London: Routledge, 1982), 59–74, 66.

82. Two notable exceptions are David Roberts's essay "The Paterfamilias of the Victorian Governing Classes" and Barbara Fass Leavy's provocative "Fathering and *The British Mother's Magazine*, 1845–1864," *Victorian Periodicals Review* 13 (Spring/Summer 1980): 10–17; however, the brevity of both necessarily limits their scope. The situation is considerably better as regards the nineteenth-century United States, and some of the findings of scholars in this area can be generalized to provide insights into British life as well.

Chapter 2: The Father in the Family

The epigraph is from the *Christian Remembrancer*, quoted by "A Utopian" [Dorothea Beale], "On the Education of Girls," *Fraser's Magazine* 74 (October 1866): 509–24, 520.

1. In "Middle-Class Men and the Solace of Fraternal Ritual" (in Mark C. Carnes and Clyde Griffen, eds., *Meanings for Manhood: Constructions of Masculinity in Victorian America* [Chicago: U of Chicago P, 1990], 37–52), Mark C. Carnes provides an interesting analysis of American men's use of symbolic fatherhood in an all-male context, that of the initiation ceremonies of fraternal orders such as the Odd Fellows and the Improved Order of Red Men. He argues convincingly that such rites gave members the chance to play out fantasies of both fatherhood and sonship in a "family" that, because it rejected women, could redefine the nature and extent of paternal authority.

2. Effie Johnson [Richmond], "Capacity in Men and Women," *Westminster Review* 153 (May 1900): 567–76. See also Maria G. Grey's comments on "Men and Women" (*Fortnightly Review* n.s. 26 [1 November 1879]: 672–85) to the effect that while "tenderness and its outcome, pity, are as inseparable from true manliness as true womanliness. . . . human nature is substantially the same in both [sexes]"; the public/private dichotomy is nonetheless enforced by "the

one permanent and unchangeable difference between them, the physical one of function . . . which assigns to women motherhood and all this entails" (678, 679). In this formulation it would appear that men have the capacity but not the opportunity for parental tenderness since they are the providers rather than the caregivers for their offspring.

3. I take this phrase from one of the last but most important flowerings of Puritan child rearing, Mary Martha Sherwood's 1818 first volume of *The History of the Fairchild Family; or, The Child's Manual: Being a Collection of Stories Calculated to Show the Importance and Effects of a Religious Education*, 14th ed. (London: J. Hatcherd and Son, 1841), 260. For other examples of this mindset, see Davidoff and Hall, *Family Fortunes*, 89.

4. E. Anthony Rotundo notes that at that time, American mothers were commonly thought "too indulgent" to be permitted the major role in raising growing boys. See "Boy Culture: Middle-Class Boyhood in Nineteenth-Century America," in Carnes and Griffen, eds., *Meanings for Manhood*, 15–36, 33.

5. John Demos, "The Changing Faces of Fatherhood: A New Exploration in American Family History," in Stanley H. Cath, Alan R. Gurwitz, and John Munder Ross, eds., *Father and Child: Developmental and Clinical Perspectives* (Boston: Little, Brown, 1982), 425–45, 437. This phenomenon has been well documented in an American context: see also Degler, *At Odds*, 73; and Joseph H. Pleck, "American Fathering in Historical Perspective," in Michael S. Kimmel, ed., *Changing Men: New Directions in Research on Men and Masculinity* (Newbury Park, Calif.: Sage, 1987), 83–97, 84. Especially in this early period, there seems little difference between the United States and England on this particular point.

6. Davidoff and Hall, *Family Fortunes*, 107, 115.

7. I will discuss marriage only tangentially in this study, an omission that is by no means intended to imply that Victorian and Edwardian constructions of the husband's role precisely duplicated what was happening during this period to fatherhood.

8. Cott, "Antebellum Childrearing," 8. The advocates of paternal involvement included transcendentalist educator Bronson Alcott, who lamented in 1845, "I cannot believe that God established the relation of father without giving the father something to do" (quoted in Pleck, "American Fathering," 88).

9. "On Toleration: Part I," *Cornhill Magazine* 20 (August 1869): 246–56, 252. In *Child-Loving: The Erotic Child and Victorian Culture* (New York: Routledge, 1992, 86–87), James Kincaid identifies several earlier writers, among them William Cobbett, who argue to much the same purpose as the *Cornhill*

contributor; he notes that "such voices and their urgency may . . . suggest that it's a middle-class wilderness they are crying in." Cobbett's work first appeared in 1829, indicating that the perceived deterioration of parental responsibility was no new phenomenon. I would argue, however, that it gained strength over the period I am discussing.

10. Mona Caird, "The Future of the Home," rpt. in her *The Morality of Marriage: And Other Essays on the Status and Destiny of Women* (London: George Redway, 1897), 115–27, 126. Caird's warning also strongly resembles both the early-nineteenth-century American accusation that "paternal neglect" occurs when the father is "eager in the pursuit of business, toils early and late, and finds no time to fulfill his duties to his children" (quoted in Bernard Wishy, *The Child and the Republic: The Dawn of Modern American Child Nurture* [Philadelphia: U of Pennsylvania P, 1968], 29) and the statement of *The Revolution*, "Only when they two work lovingly together does the true home ever rise, and out of their union and wise interworking it never fails to come. And what our homes need to-day to make them perfect, is just this perfect union and blending of husband and wife in living helpfulness" ("Her Peculiar Sphere," rpt. *Victoria Magazine* 18 [December 1871]: 173–76, 176). Again, conservative and radical are at one.

11. Charlotte M. Yonge, *Womankind*, 2nd ed. (New York: Macmillan and Co., 1882), 129, 29, 264. While I quote for convenience's sake from the one-volume version, the book first appeared serially between 1874 and 1877 in Yonge's periodical *The Monthly Packet*, whose primary audience was young women.

12. Emma Churchman Hewitt, "The 'New Woman' in Her Relation to the 'New Man,'" *Westminster Review* 147 (March 1897): 335–37, 336. This criticism is echoed in H. Morgan-Browne's remark, "Man is wont to shirk his share of the trouble and responsibility of bringing up the children on the plea of much business. . . . [This circumstance] is in no sense the sole result of natural causes," but rather a matter of social custom and male laziness (in a review of Adele Crepaz's *The Dangers of the Emancipation of Women, Shafts* 1 [10 December 1892]: 89).

13. Charles W. Eliot, "The Part of the Man in the Family," *Ladies' Home Journal*, March 1908, 7.

14. "Manners and Morals, as Affected by Civilization," *Fraser's Magazine* 64 (September 1861): 307–16, 310, 315, 311.

15. Reprinted in "Public Opinion on Questions Concerning Women," *Englishwoman's Review* 1 (July 1868): 503.

16. Anonymous review of W. W. H. Robinson's *The Ethics of Love, English-*

woman's Review n.s. 12 (15 December 1881): 563–64, 564.

17. Annie M. Payne, "The Woman's Part in Politics," *National Review* 14 (November 1889): 401–18, 415.

18. Anonymous review of Frances Swiney's *The Awakening of Women, or Woman's Part in Evolution, Englishwoman's Review* n.s. 31 (17 April 1900): 130–32, 131; Harry Thurston Peck, "What a Father Can Do for His Daughter," *Cosmopolitan* 34 (February 1903): 460–64, 461. Another American example is T. S. Arthur's series on "Model Husbands" in *Godey's Lady's Book* 50 (January-March 1855): 37–40, 110–12, 206–8, which contrasts three types—the brutal, the insufficiently involved, and the good. The latter helps his wife by taking care of the baby, "sooth[ing] it with gentle tones and loving words," in an example of the "power every husband and father possesses [to create a pleasant household atmosphere]; yet how few use their influence, at all times, well and wisely!" (208). Overall the series serves to describe the three possibilities for male domestic life (the husband runs the gamut from the wife's adversary to her ally) and to note explicitly that the father who acts as the mother's assistant and stand-in is both the best and the happiest type of man. Arthur's stance on femininity and domesticity is explored in Judith Pascoe's "Stories for Young Housekeepers: T. S. Arthur and the Philadelphia Marketplace," in Nelson and Vallone, *The Girl's Own*, 34–51.

19. A symbolic manifestation of the fear of male pollution is provided in the broadsides of the female antitobacco agitators Eliza Lynn Linton described, whose author typically "set[s] forth the mysterious maladies of her infants and young children . . . which she finally trace[s] to their true source—their father's caresses, which were practically slow poison to her babes because of his baleful cigarette or still more destructive pipe" (Mrs. Lynn Linton, "A Counter-Blast," *English Illustrated Magazine* 21 [October 1893]: 85–89, 86). Linton saw the right to smoke, like the right to act on sexual desire, as exclusively male; any attempt on women's part either to curtail or to share these privileges is a blow against separate spheres, which represent "the grandest kind of beauty and harmony" (88).

20. "A Woman," "Chivalry, Marriage, and Religion: A Woman's Protest," *National Review* 4 (January 1885): 669–82, 673, 674–75.

21. "Bereft," "Correspondence," *Shafts* 2 (15 February 1894): 216; [Margaret Shurmer Sibthorp], "What the Editor Means," *Shafts* 5 (November 1897): 297–303, 301, 302.

22. Editor's response, "Correspondence," *Shafts* 1 (18 February 1893): 253. See also M. Lowthime, "Concealment—A Cause of Impurity," *Shafts* 2 (15 Sep-

tember 1894): 328; [Margaret Shurmer Sibthorp], "What the Editor Means," *Shafts* 2 (January–February 1895): 365; anonymous review of Edward Carpenter's *Sex Love, Shafts* 3 (October 1895): 97–99, 98; "For the Sake of a Pure Life," *Shafts* 6 (September–October 1898): 173.

23. [Margaret Oliphant], "The Condition of Women," *Blackwood's Edinburgh Magazine* 83 (February 1858): 139–54, 152.

24. F. W. Newman, "Marriage Laws," *Fraser's Magazine* 76 (August 1867): 169–89, 169. By the end of the century, sex-education manuals (such as suffragist Elizabeth Wolstenholme Elmy's pseudonymous *The Human Flower* [1892] and her 1895 book for still younger children, *Baby Buds*) were being produced for an increasingly youthful readership. It is unclear what part Wolstenholme Elmy's husband may have played in producing these works; see Sandra Stanley Holton, "Free Love and Victorian Feminism: The Divers Matrimonials of Elizabeth Wolstenholme and Ben Elmy," *Victorian Studies* 37 (Winter 1994): 199–222, 219n3.

25. "A Grave Social Problem," *British Medical Journal* 1 (14 January 1882): 55–56, 56. The writer's choice of instructor suggests a conception of sexuality as a moral rather than a medical matter; the "science" invoked here is not biology but ethics. That the proper place for sex education was the school rather than the home was an idea many teachers shared (while observing that they accepted the duty only because so many parents refused it). This controversy over location became particularly heated in 1913, when the headmistress of a Derbyshire elementary school introduced sex education into the curriculum without notifying local parents. Frank Mort records that it was mothers, not fathers, who felt that their role in maintaining their children's innocence had been usurped; they "protested that the teacher's disgusting and abominable information had undermined the sacredness of the home and the mothers' authority." See *Dangerous Sexualities: Medico-Moral Politics in England since 1830* (New York: Routledge & Kegan Paul, 1987), 160.

26. "A Woman," "Chivalry, Marriage, and Religion," 680. Edward Bristow discusses the stances on sex education of purity societies including the Social Purity Alliance and the Church of England Purity Society (later the White Cross Society) in *Vice and Vigilance: Purity Movements in Britain since 1700* (Totowa, N.J.: Rowman and Littlefield, 1977), 134–37. Nor were these views confined to the English groups of the 1880s and 1890s; Carroll Smith-Rosenberg notes their occurrence in the New York Female Moral Reform Society in the 1830s (see *Disorderly Conduct*, 119), although Charles Rosenberg's findings in "Sexu-

ality, Class and Role in 19th-Century America" (*American Quarterly* 25 [May 1973]: 131–53) suggest that American fathers of both permissive and continent stripes may have felt more pressure than their British counterparts to oversee their sons' sexual instruction.

27. E. Lynn Linton, "The Future Supremacy of Women," *National Review* 8 (September 1886): 1–15, 3.

28. See, for instance, Sarah M. Amos, "The Evolution of the Daughters," *Contemporary Review* 65 (April 1894): 515–20, 518; Sarah Grand, "The Modern Girl," *North American Review* 158 (June 1894): 706–14, 709; and the remarks of "A Public School Boy" on "Our Public Schools," *National Review* 56 (November 1910): 429–35, 433. Book-length formulations of this pattern include Eton headmaster Edward Lyttelton's 1892 *Mothers and Sons, or Problems in the Home Training of Boys*, which, as Anne Digby and Peter Searby record, argued that mothers should train boys in morality and self-discipline while fathers supplied what Lyttelton tactfully called "a few words of caution"; embarrassed fathers could delegate this task to the family doctor or to the publications of the White Cross Army, a major purity society (see *Children, School and Society in Nineteenth-Century England* [London: Macmillan, 1981], 105–8).

29. An illustration of such a lesson between mother and daughter occurs in Vere Collins, "Education in Sex," *Westminster Review* 162 (July 1904): 100–105, 104, where the provenance of a servant's baby and pollination are explained concurrently. The contrasting content and vagueness of what many boys were hearing is suggested in "Our Public Schools," whose author remarks of his schoolmates, "I have heard from many that their fathers had spoken to them on the subject [of manifestations of sexuality in the public schools] but that they had not understood what they meant!" (433).

30. One exception is the *Family Economist*, a mid-century periodical catering to the lower middle and upper working classes. In this environment—in which, for one thing, most children would have aspired at best to day schools and would thus have spent more time in their parents' company—fathers are depicted as sharing or taking over the children's education, for instance by reading history aloud to the family and interpolating appropriate moral glosses, or by curing a son's fear of shadows by explaining the scientific principle behind them. See the anonymous articles "Home Education," *Family Economist* 3 (1850): 127–29, 128, and "Suspicion and Caution," *Family Economist* 4 (1851): 82–87, 86.

31. Demos, "The Changing Faces of Fatherhood," 427.

32. Beale, "On the Education of Girls," 519, 520, 524. Beale did concede that men might have some success with older students. Other writers, however, sometimes defined instruction as a solely maternal talent; thus M. Loane, an Edwardian superintendent of district nurses, remarked: "Every woman is a possible mother, and therefore to some extent a born teacher, but a man can impart little to his wife" and presumably also to his children ("Husband and Wife among the Poor," *Contemporary Review* 87 [February 1905]: 222–30, 227).

33. "The Judicial Separation of Mother and Child," *Westminster Review* n.s. 67 (April 1885): 430–59, 432, 433.

34. "Boy's Home-Training," *Blackwood's Edinburgh Magazine* 176 (August 1904): 244–54, 245. This commentator does find, however, that fathers should impart informal instruction about the natural world and current events to supplement their sons' preparatory school curriculum and argues that even though "the higher sides of Boy's character" are of course shaped by the mother, a father may inculcate useful lessons in stoicism, industry, and resourcefulness (248–50, 251–54).

35. "Influential Lives: Miss Matilda Sharpe and Her Schools," *Shafts* 1 (3 November 1892): 3–4, 3; "Influential Lives: A Biographical Sketch [of] Elisa Lemonnier, Founder of the First Technical Schools for Women in France," *Shafts* 1 (26 November 1892): 50–52, 50. Readers will doubtless be able to add a host of additional examples of devoted and didactic Victorian fathers—who may not, however, have received credit for these efforts in the periodicals of their day.

36. [Eliza Lynn Linton], "Apron-Strings," *Saturday Review* 27 (1 May 1869): 576–78, 577; Jean H. Bell, "The Creed of Our Children," *Nineteenth Century and After* 68 (December 1910): 1076–81, 1081. Linton fears that the "mother's boy" will grow up domestic and delicate, with morals imposed from without by his mother rather than from within (presumably through the character-building effects of sports, uncles, and absence from home); Bell finds religious teaching a mutual concern, as the pupil "is, after all, the child of both."

37. M.C.J., "A Plea for the Little Ones," *Victoria Magazine* 12 (February 1869): 269–92, 290.

38. "The Enfranchisement of Women," 564, 563. The *Telegraph* concurred, explaining that while women might serve with entire competence in Parliament, "We prefer that, while men take the outdoor and public work, women should take the indoor and family tasks" of which men, by implication, are incapable (rpt. in "Public Opinion on Questions Concerning Women: Women on School

Boards," *Englishwoman's Review* n.s. 5 [January 1871]: 14–16, 15). See also the novelist George Whyte-Melville's unsigned "Strong-Minded Women," *Fraser's Magazine* 68 (November 1863): 667–78, which remarks that "out-of-doors, at least, [the father] is considered the head of the family; but his dominion, when analyzed, is found to be of a somewhat shadowy nature . . . his authority is by no means absolute" (667).

39. Dunbar, "Answer to 'A Clerical View of Woman's Sphere,'" 240.

40. J. E. Cairnes, "Woman Suffrage—A Reply," *Macmillan's Magazine* 30 (September 1874): 377–88, 387. See also Maria G. Grey, "Men and Women" and "Men and Women: A Sequel," the latter appearing in *Fortnightly Review* n.s. 29 (1 June 1881): 776–93; while the educator (another suffrage advocate) holds that personality is generally the product of environment, she considers parental feeling an exception. Enforced by nature and nurture alike, man's family role is merely that of breadwinner, his duty to his children consisting of giving them money rather than nurturance.

41. [Dinah Mulock Craik], "For Better for Worse," *Contemporary Review* 51 (April 1887): 570–76, 573–74; "Womanhood and Religious Mis-education," *Shafts* 1 (12 November 1892): 19–20, 20; Nat Arling, "What Is the Role of the 'New Woman'?" *Westminster Review* 150 (November 1898): 576–87, 582; Florence Hayllar, "The Superfluity of Women," *Westminster Review* 171 (February 1909): 171–81, 174.

42. Burstyn, *Victorian Education and the Ideal of Womanhood*, 14. F. M. L. Thompson notes that where wealth permitted spaciousness, houses were designed for separation: not only were employers removed from servants and children from parents, but gender-distinct terrain was carved out in the shape of boudoirs, gun rooms, and so forth (*The Rise of Respectable Society: A Social History of Victorian Britain 1830–1900* [Cambridge: Harvard UP, 1988], 156). See also Jenni Calder's observation in *The Victorian Home* (London: Batsford, 1977, 23) that aside from reading and singing, there was little in the way of male leisure activities that could be accomplished in the Victorian drawing room. The boom in feminine handicrafts ignored the adult male, assuming that his free time like his work life would be spent outside the home.

43. "Nature," Caird wrote in the introduction to her collection of periodical essays, "clearly has indicated fatherhood to man as much as she has indicated motherhood to woman, and it is really difficult to see why a father should not be expected to devote himself wholly to domestic cares; that is, if we are so very determined that one sex or the other shall be sacrificed *en masse*" (*The Morality*

of Marriage, 1–17, 7). The comment recalls Lydia Becker's remark that "if she had her way, every boy in Manchester should be taught to darn his own socks and cook his own chops" as a means of encouraging the equality of women (reported in "Events of the Month," *Englishwoman's Review* n.s. 8 [15 March 1877], 119–44, 127).

44. Respectively the views of W. Landels, quoted in J. A. and Olive Banks, *Feminism and Family Planning in Victorian England*, 46; Mulock, quoted in J. A. Banks, *Victorian Values: Secularism and the Size of Families* (London: Routledge & Kegan Paul, 1981), 37; and Henry Maudsley, quoted in Ruth Brandon, *The New Women and the Old Men: Love, Sex and the Woman Question* (London: Secker & Warburg, 1990), 252. To be sure, some writers held that neither sex is competent outside its proper domain. The inimitable Linton, for one, insisted: "As little as it is fitting for a man to look after the pap boat and the house linen, so is it for women to assume the political power of the State" ("The Wild Women: No. I," 88). Likewise, an anonymous *Saturday Review* article (reprinted untitled in *Victoria Magazine* 9 [July 1867]: 258–62) noted that "there are many spheres of action in which a woman is as much out of place as a man in a nursery." Ability is not the issue; fathers are "fully competent to determine the shape and material of frocks and pelisses, but custom has made male interference in some departments of human life unseemly and ridiculous" (261).

45. See Patricia Marks, *Bicycles, Bangs, and Bloomers: The New Woman in the Popular Press* (Lexington: UP of Kentucky, 1990), 206. Such cartoons long predate the invention of the phrase "New Woman"; *Punch* was interested in the beleaguered househusband as early as the 1850s.

46. See, for instance, Grant Allen, "Plain Words on the Woman Question," *Fortnightly Review* n.s. 46 (October 1889): 448–58, rpt. in *Popular Science Monthly* 36 (December 1889): 170–81. According to Allen (a masculinist sex reformer best known for his 1895 novel, *The Woman Who Did*), "A woman ought to be ashamed to say she has no desire to become a wife and mother. . . . as ashamed as a man in a like predicament would be of his impotence" (174–75). Smith-Rosenberg notes that nineteenth-century American physicians were likely to define women's sexuality solely in terms of reproductive capacity (puberty and menopause being " 'the two termini of a woman's sexual activity' "); men's sexuality, in contrast, was separate from any biological will to fatherhood (*Disorderly Conduct* 185, 183).

47. Linton, "A Counter-Blast," 88, and "Viewy Folk," *Fortnightly Review* n.s. 59 (1 April 1896): 595–604, 602. See also Linton's unsigned "Gushing

Men," *Saturday Review* 28 (4 September 1869): 315–16, and the husbands of the "Wild Women: No. I," who, depending for their glory on their wives, are "miserable," "pitiful," and "contemptible" (82–83).

48. Letter from William S'Arrac in "The Englishwoman's Conversazione," *Englishwoman's Domestic Magazine* n.s. 10 (April 1871): 256. The issue that particularly exercised S'Arrac was men's adoption of corsets, which he saw as a symptom of the way in which men were becoming "a mere tool in the hands of women." Domesticity was contraindicated in such cases; S'Arrac instead recommended the army.

49. [Frederic Marshall], "French Home Life II: Children," *Blackwood's Edinburgh Magazine* 110 (December 1871): 739–53, 749. The effeminacy and cowardice of the French boy are unimportant in the domestic setting, Marshall (a Paris resident by virtue of his post as councilor of the Japanese legation) concedes: "There is no denying that, like his sisters, he contributes wonderfully to the brightness of home. His intelligence is delicate and artistic; his capacity of loving is enormous; he possesses many of the sweeter qualities of human nature; and, provided he is not tested by purely masculine measures, he often seems to be a very charming little fellow" (751). But despite, or because of, his many feminine virtues, such a boy cannot grow up to be a good citizen in the public realm. Since its men, over-mothered and apparently under-fathered, are trained to the woman's part, France has no national strength.

50. Goldwin Smith, "Conservatism and Female Suffrage," 747. Another voice joining the chorus against blending or reversing gender roles was that of Friedrich Engels in *The Condition of the Working Class in England* (1844, translated into English 1892). Horrified to see Englishwomen working in factories while their unemployed husbands stayed home to mind the children, Engels denounced the practice as "virtual castration" (quoted in Thompson, *The Rise of Respectable Society*, 75).

51. Margaret Marsh theorizes that in part, the increased involvement of turn-of-the-century American fathers with their sons "was surely [intended] to balance the preponderant female presence in the lives of young children. . . . men became convinced that in order to have their sons grow up to be 'manly' they should involve themselves more substantially in their children's upbringing" ("Suburban Men and Masculine Domesticity, 1870–1915," *American Quarterly* 40 [June 1988]: 165–86, 176). This hypothesis may work less well in an English context, since fathers in that country were less likely to be urged to share specifically male activities with their sons and more likely to hear that they should try to reproduce maternal behavior.

52. John Ablett, "Co-Education," *Westminster Review* 153 (January 1900): 25–31, 30, 29.

53. "Womanly and Womanish," rpt. in *Victoria Magazine* 12 (February 1869): 350–51.

54. I discuss this pressure in the context of boys' fiction in *Boys Will Be Girls*.

55. See, for instance, Vance, *The Sinews of the Spirit*, 1, and Newsome, *Godliness and Good Learning*, 26–27.

56. Turn-of-the-century efforts at establishing the boundaries within which behavior then seen as feminine would be appropriate for men include, for instance, J. Tyrrell Baylee's "Army Nursing Reform and Men Nurses," *Westminster Review* 155 (March 1901): 255–57. Baylee called for male nursing recruits for the Boer War, explaining that the front is no place for women. While he conceded that women are generally more experienced nurses, he denied "any *inherent* inferiority resident in the male sex in gentleness, tenderness, and patience, or any *natural* superiority in capacity for nursing in the female sex. In fact, a thousand travellers' tales bear witness to men's devotion and self-sacrifice towards helpless comrades in emergencies of all kinds" (256). In the nondomestic arena of countries inaccessible to English women, men need feel no embarrassment at performing a function usually arrogated to the other gender.

57. These groups sometimes overlapped. Thus Becker's "A Reply" (*Englishwoman's Review* 12 [July 1869]: 245–47) responded to those critics who argued that women's home responsibilities preclude political involvement: "Have men no domestic duties? Surely they have a very important domestic duty. They have to bring grist to the mill, they have to work for the maintenance of the household—is not that a domestic duty? The part of the man in making his home happy is just as important and obligatory as that of the woman" (246). Here the father's role as public man is viewed in the context of the home in order to excuse the mother's aspirations to becoming a public woman; the happiest home, perhaps, is the emptiest.

58. "Shirley" [John Skelton], "People Who Are Not Respectable: A Lay Sermon," *Fraser's Magazine* 58 (December 1858): 719–29, 721. Half a century later, Frances H. Low echoed this line of thought as she took issue with Constance Smedley's assertion that fatherhood has no effect upon the character: "Let Miss Smedley question the next high-minded man she meets. Let her ask him what it was sobered him and gave him a sense of responsibility. Will he not tell her that [it was] the necessity and the sweetness of working for others and the sense of fatherhood[?]" ("The Parlour Woman or the Club Woman? A Reply

to Miss Smedley," *Fortnightly Review* n.s. 83 [1 January 1908]: 113–24, 123). The high-minded father of Low's imagination need have no direct involvement with the domestic sphere her article defends; it is enough that he knows his public activities to be dedicated to its maintenance.

59. Cobbe, "Celibacy v. Marriage," 229, 233, 235.

60. "On Toleration: Part II," *Cornhill Magazine* 20 (September 1869): 376–84, 376–79.

61. Oliphant, "Mill on the Subjection of Women," 297, 299. Sarah Ellis had expressed a similar idea in the 1845 edition of *Mothers of England* (first published in 1843): "Fathers of families in the present day, and the fact cannot be acknowledged without serious regret, are for the most part, too deeply engaged in the pursuit of objects widely differing in their nature from those which belong to the moral discipline of home" (quoted in Branca, *Silent Sisterhood*, 111). The problem is not simply that overworked fathers have little time to spend with their families, but that the world of men's activity is alien and probably antithetical to that of the home.

62. [Dinah Mulock Craik], "Concerning Men—by a Woman," *Cornhill Magazine* n.s. 9 (October 1887): 368–77, 370, 371, 376. See also the same author's "About Money" (also unsigned, in *Contemporary Review* 50 [September 1886]: 364–72), which comments that "the endless self-sacrifices demanded of a paterfamilias" are increased by the current fashion of indulging adolescents with no thought of adult pockets or health; here again the father is forced to degenerate "into the mere bread-winner of the family," the "victim" of a domestic lifestyle he has no time to share (366, 371, 367).

63. Eliza Lynn Linton, "Woman and the World," rpt. in Linton, *Modern Women and What Is Said of Them*, 93–100, 96. To be sure, the "young man of the period" represents not Linton's idea of the typical man but her idea of the appropriate mate for the "girl of the period," whose own reluctance to become a mother has apparently drawn the couple together.

64. Mary Montgomerie Singleton, "Two Moods of a Man: By a Woman," *Nineteenth Century* 31 (February 1892): 208–23, 208, 211. Singleton's article focuses on courtship but would seem also to suggest a pattern for marriage.

65. Arling, "What Is the Role of the 'New Woman'?" 578–79, 581. Arling blamed the ignoble traits of the male sex on "an age of money-making" and a tradition of excessive self-sacrifice among women; by entering the public sphere, New Women would correct both problems (576, 585). The selfish father discussed in this article, who refuses to give up his own pleasure in order to pay

for his daughters' training, is a common figure in feminist rhetoric of the turn of the century; see, for instance, Margarita Yates, "Should Women Work for Their Living?" (*Westminster Review* 174 [October 1910]: 424–29), where the father appears as "often either idle, selfish, or indifferent . . . entirely oblivious of the claims made upon him by any of the feminine members of his family" (425).

66. "Ignota" [Elizabeth Wolstenholme Elmy], "The Awakening of Woman," *Westminster Review* 152 (July 1899): 69–72, 71.

67. For instance, arguing that classes in domestic economy should be open to boys as well as girls, Becker remarked in a lecture on "The Teaching of Domestic Economy in Schools" that men "would be better husbands and fathers if they took more interest in their homes, and especially if they were able, when their wives were ill, or absent, or dead, to mind their children and attend to their houses, if necessary" (report on "Domestic Economy Congress," *Englishwoman's Review* n.s. 9 [15 July 1878]: 295–98, 297). The assumption here is first that fathers should be more involved in the home but also that even the most competent man will never be more than an understudy for his wife.

68. Branca, *Silent Sisterhood*, 110.

69. *The Family Economist* 3 (1850): 30. *The Fairchild Family*'s most notorious disciplinary scene is that in which Mr. Fairchild—from a disciplinary standpoint the more involved of the parents, who are both meant to appear concerned and sensible—takes his quarreling children to view the decomposed body of a gibbeted fratricide by way of an object lesson on the consequences of anger. While the father whips both his son and his daughters, the psychological approach (manifested also in confinement and lectures) is more important; nevertheless, the techniques Mrs. Sherwood recommends to her readers were passé by the century's end.

70. [Dinah Mulock], "A Woman's Thoughts about Women: Female Servants," *Chambers's Journal* 8 (1 August 1857): 68–71, 71. Mulock's use of a male example is particularly suggestive given her concurrent assumption that "women solely have the management" of young children (71). As she had written in an earlier article in this series, "Man and woman were made for, and not like one another," the one being intended to work " 'by the sweat of his brow'; the other, 'in sorrow to bring forth'—and bring up—'children' " ("A Woman's Thoughts about Women: Something to Do," *Chambers's Journal* 7 [2 May 1857]: 273–75, 273).

71. [Andrew Halliday], "Fathers," *All the Year Round* 14 (2 September 1865): 133–35. Halliday, at that time both a frequent contributor to the magazine and a

member of the editorial staff, is identified as the author of this and other pieces in Ella Ann Oppenlander, *Dickens' All the Year Round: Descriptive Index and Contributor List* (Troy, N.Y.: Whitston, 1984), 159.

72. [Herbert Spencer], "The Moral Discipline of Children," *British Quarterly Review* 27 (1 April 1858): 383–413, 398–99, 400, 406.

73. [A. K. H. Boyd], "Concerning the Sorrows of Childhood," *Fraser's Magazine* 65 (March 1862): 304–17, 311; "Our Modern Youth," *Fraser's Magazine* 68 (July 1863): 115–29, 120. Boyd, a Scottish Presbyterian minister, defined "stupidity and cruelty" to include denying children advantages, overworking them physically or intellectually, endeavoring to convince them of their own wickedness, and lacking the sympathy or imagination to understand childish phobias such as the fear of the dark—all of which might have been permissible or even necessary under the earlier forms of child rearing that tended to define children as inferior adults.

74. Mary S. Hartman, "Child-Abuse and Self-Abuse: Two Victorian Cases," *History of Childhood Quarterly* 2 (Fall 1974): 221–48, 239, 241. Calder notes in *The Victorian Home* the *EDM*'s 1868 publication of a piece suggesting that "unless a Mother uses her authority in this way [whipping girls] she loses all hold over her children, and when fear and reverence cease then good-bye to all affection"; she finds the "belief that fear was an essential component of love" typical of Victorian child rearing and Victorian theology alike (166).

75. "The Englishwoman's Conversazione," *Englishwoman's Domestic Magazine* n.s. 10 (May 1871): 320. The correspondent, who herself "was never punished but with a rod," inclined to the belief that mere spankings would be insufficient to end the naughtiness of her five-year-old daughter; the editor preferred a psychological approach, remarking, "Mere naughtiness may be cured by perseveringly making it more *disagreeable* to be naughty than to be good."

76. Millicent Garrett Fawcett, "The Electoral Disabilities of Women," *Fortnightly Review* n.s. 7 (1 May 1870): 622–32, 626.

77. [Edward A. Carlyon], "People's Boys," *Macmillan's Magazine* 23 (March 1871): 432–35, 434.

78. Stephen Gwynn, "The Modern Parent," *Cornhill Magazine* 3rd series 8 (May 1900): 662–78, 677. Gwynn applauds the increase in "parental responsibility" demonstrated by the shift from an eighteenth-century emphasis on children's good conduct (or even absence) to the late-nineteenth-century approval of childlike attributes.

79. Edward H. Cooper, "The Punishment of Children," *Fortnightly Review*

n.s. 73 (1 June 1903): 1060–67, 1065, 1066, 1067. Cooper's article drew fire
from Llewellyn W. Williams, honorary secretary of the Society for the Reform
of School Discipline, who denied that whipping is an appropriate punishment
for schoolboys; among the authorities Williams quoted was U.S. ambassador
Joseph Choate, who had recently observed, "Not very long ago the rod was
esteemed the best teacher of moral laws; but the wisdom of to-day is not the
wisdom of yesterday, and there is a growing tendency everywhere to avoid corporal punishment altogether." Both Choate and Williams took this tendency as
a mark of advancing civilization ("The Punishment of Children," *Fortnightly
Review* n.s. 74 [1 August 1903]: 373–74, 374).

80. Mona Caird, "Punishment for Crimes against Women and Children,"
Westminster Review 169 (May 1908): 550–53, 550. Corporal punishment had
long been a concern of Caird's; for instance, her 1890 essay "The Morality of
Marriage" had commented in an echo of Mulock's remarks of 1857, "It was once
thought impossible to bring up children without perpetual chastisement. This
idea has been found to be false and barbarous. Not only does it fail to restrain,
but it excites every evil impulse, and an inclination to repeat the transgression,
if possible without being found out" (318).

81. Anonymous, "Pioneer Club Records," *Shafts* 2 (15 June 1894): 276. See
also C. Olivia Orde Ward, "A School for Womanhood," *Englishwoman's Review*
n.s. 41 (15 April 1910): 98–107, which argues that it is "free happy *camarade-
rie*, by which the gulf which separates two generations is best and most safely
bridged" (103–4).

82. Brabazon, "Have We the 'Grit' of Our Forefathers?" 428, 429.

83. It should be noted that this role included not only the earning of money
but, for instance, the negotiation of daughters' marriage settlements, although
the latter issue became less important with the passage of the various Married
Women's Property Acts in the final third of the century.

84. Anonymous, "Love in a Cottage," *Saturday Review* 5 (23 January 1858):
85–87, 86.

85. Even in 1881, Janetta Manners (duchess of Rutland) noted that fathers
"willingly make sacrifices to obtain the benefits of University education for their
sons" because "this education is usually regarded as affording to young men
facilities for acquiring knowledge which will enable them to enter a profession."
The education of daughters, in contrast, often appears frivolous, as "fathers
cannot feel the same degree of assurance that treasures of knowledge, acquired
by sacrifices of much time and money, will prove investments that will bring

profitable returns to their fortunate possessor." See her unsigned "Employ-ment of Women in the Public Service," *Quarterly Review* 151 (January 1881): 181–200, 195.

86. "Doctors in Pettiloons," *Punch* 22 (1852): 208. In his unsigned "The Em-ployment of Women" (*North British Review* 26 [February 1857]: American ed. 157–82), military historian J. W. Kaye quoted a misgiving concerning father-hood and woman doctors expressed in the *Lancet:* "When the Mrs. M.D.'s are attending to patients in their boudoirs of consultation, or pointing out patho-logical nicknacks in their anatomical drawing-rooms, or going their rounds with stethoscopes in their bonnets, what are their husbands doing? Do they super-intend the perambulators, or are these hitched on to the professional broughams of the mammas? Is it a part of the husband's marital duty to manage the nurs-ery—in short, to attend to the domestic affairs generally?" (180). In this sketch (whose flippancy and stance Kaye disapproved) the problem is not the form women's work takes but their absence from the home, which forces a level of paternal involvement inappropriate to true men.

87. [Caroline Cornwallis], "Capabilities and Disabilities of Women," *West-minster Review* 67 (January 1857): American ed. 23–40, 25, 26. Women, Cornwallis explained, are more capable than men because their intellects are less likely to be obscured by passion; they therefore have every right (perhaps even a duty) to enter the public sphere in order to repair the damage wrought by male excess (34–36). The daughter of a country rector, Cornwallis herself had studied Latin, Greek, Hebrew, and German and had in 1853 won a prize offered by Lady Byron for the best essay on delinquency.

88. "Female Labour," 368. Other articles suggesting that an educated mother makes for a happier home include Beale's 1866 "On the Education of Girls" (512), M.A.E.L.'s 1870 "The Girl of the Future" (442), and Craik's 1886 "About Money" (368).

89. Mulock, "A Woman's Thoughts about Women: Something to Do," 274. Women writers were especially forthright in their comments about shortsighted fathers of this type. Feminist reformer Christina Bremner referred to them as "criminal," calling for family limitation in order to maximize the sums available for each daughter's training ("Woman in the Labour Market," *National Review* 11 [June 1888]: 458–70, 460, 469); Grand castigated them as caring more for "their own prejudices" than for the daughters they force "to lead an idle, use-less, and irksome existence" ("The Modern Girl," 708); Barbara Bodichon, in her 1857 pamphlet *Women and Work*, accused them of furthering "prostitution,

whether legal or in the streets" (quoted in Mary Poovey, *Uneven Developments: The Ideological Work of Gender in Mid-Victorian England* [Chicago: U of Chicago P, 1988], 150).

90. [H. J. Wrixon], "The Employment of Women," *Dublin Review* 52 (November 1862): 1–44, 34, 35, 18. An anonymous writer on "The Influence of Parents on Women's Work" (*Englishwoman's Review* n.s. 18 [April 1874]: 90–96) likewise suggested that the most appropriate employer for a woman is the family firm, but the emphasis here was different, focusing not on the need to keep daughters at least symbolically in the home but on the fact that fathers can protect their children from sex bias by giving "training which outside prejudice would refuse to a woman." Even so, this commentator holds out the promise that the family containing a self-sufficient woman will gain "that cheerful element now wanting in many homes of grown-up daughters," and even argues that "parents will materially assist, and not injure a daughter's chances of marriage, by making her independent" (95, 96). The *Review*, founded in conjunction with a woman's employment registry, considered job-training advocacy one of its primary responsibilities.

91. [Harriet Martineau], "Middle-Class Education in England: Girls," *Cornhill Magazine* 10 (November 1864): 549–68, 554, 567.

92. "Salary No Object," *Englishwoman's Review* n.s. 9 (15 January 1878): 1–7, 6–7. In contrast, men were more likely to see the establishing of daughters as a purely financial matter, as in J. E. Panton's 1889 comment, "Give the boys a good education and a start in life, and provide the girls with £150 a year, either when they marry or at your own death, and you have done your duty by your children" (quoted in John R. Gillis, *Youth and History: Tradition and Change in European Age Relations 1770-Present* [New York: Academic, 1974], 99).

93. Maria Theresa Earle, "Mothers and Daughters," *National Review* 44 (December 1904): 673–84, 683.

94. As Earle noted in pleading for the equal education and training of girls: "There are two things which, as a rule, fathers hate giving to their daughters—money and independence. And yet no young woman can enter the ranks of the bread-winners without at least one of these, and, in the well-to-do classes, generally both" ("Mothers and Daughters," 682).

95. Jonathan Bloom-Feshbach, "Historical Perspectives on the Father's Role," in Michael E. Lamb, ed., *The Role of the Father in Child Development*, 2nd ed. (New York: Wiley, 1981), 71–112, 80. Cott adds that the difficulty Victorian boys experienced in setting aside this early feminine identification

"might not only result in lasting guilty feelings about worldly pursuits, but also in male attitudes toward women in the nineteenth century, where glorification of women's value 'in their place' . . . warred with extreme hostility to and scorn for female endeavors in male-identified pursuits"; the drive toward separate spheres became more intense given men's need to achieve a sense of masculinity as distinct from motherhood ("Notes toward an Interpretation of Antebellum Childrearing," 16–17).

96. See, for instance, Norma Clarke, "Strenuous Idleness: Thomas Carlyle and the Man of Letters as Hero," in Roper and Tosh, *Manful Assertions*, 25–43, which describes what Carlyle considered a disgusting exhibition of continued fatherly involvement on the part of his friend Edward Irving in 1824; Olive Banks, *Becoming a Feminist: The Social Origins of "First-Wave" Feminism* (Athens: U of Georgia P, 1987), which comments of the early lives of 116 feminists of both sexes that fathers were more likely to be warm and encouraging even than mothers (26, 28, 154); or, for an American example, Degler's *At Odds*, which quotes an assortment of nineteenth-century letters from parents to suggest that fathers were typically loving, involved, and "gentle, even sentimental" (75).

97. Boyd Hilton, *The Age of Atonement: The Influence of Evangelicalism on Social and Economic Thought, 1795–1865* (Oxford: Clarendon, 1988), 102.

98. Boyd, "Concerning the Sorrows of Childhood," 317. Another example is provided by Celia Burleigh, "The Rights of Children," *Victoria Magazine* 23 (June 1879): 106–22, which argues that by keeping the "child-world" open to us, children provide "a Paradise which, [in] spite of the angel with the scythe and hour-glass who has driven us forth, we shall yet regain, and through all whose beatitudes a little child shall lead us" (122).

99. Linton, "The Wild Women: No. I," 81; Frederic Adye, "Old-Fashioned Children," *Macmillan's Magazine* 68 (August 1893): 286–92, 291; J[ames] Sully, "The Humorous Aspect of Childhood," *National Review* 27 (April 1896): 222–36, 235.

100. Leavy, "Fathering and *The British Mother's Magazine*, 1845–1864," 11.

101. For example, see Leavy, "Fathering and *The British Mother's Magazine*, 1845–1864"; Earle, who commented in "Mothers and Daughters" that "I do not at all wish to obliterate or diminish the equal responsibilities of the male parent. . . . Much that I shall say . . . applies equally to fathers" (673); and the turn-of-the-century effort to attract fathers to London mothers' clubs, described in Deborah Dwork's *War Is Good for Babies and Other Young Children:*

A History of the Infant and Child Welfare Movement in England 1898–1918
(New York: Tavistock, 1987), 154. Christina Hardyment notes in *Dream Babies*,
however, that for all the prevalence of attempts to encourage paternal involvement in childcare, in practice "the role of fathers seems to have remained
disappointingly distant" (122).

Chapter 3: Science and the Father

The epigraph is by the anonymous author of "Chastity: Its Development and
Maintenance," *Westminster Review* n.s. 58 (1 October 1880): 419–36, 423.

1. Bloom-Feshbach, "Historical Perspectives on the Father's Role," 102.

2. As Patricia Branca notes, Victorian pediatric medicine effectively did not
exist, at least in terms of preventive care; doctors had little interest in childhood
diseases and saw children's health as primarily dependent on maternal skill (see
Silent Sisterhood, 97–99). In *War Is Good for Babies and Other Young Children*,
Deborah Dwork discusses the increased interest on the part of the medical profession in diseases such as epidemic diarrhea (a major cause of infant death) at
the turn of the century, an interest concurrent with the embarrassing revelation
in 1899 that infant mortality was higher than it had been since 1861. For the
"alliance between doctors and mothers in the control of family morality under
the auspices of public health in the nineteenth century," see Bryan S. Turner,
The Body and Society: Explorations in Social Theory (New York: Blackwell,
1984), 219.

3. W. R. Greg, "Why Are Women Redundant?" *National Review* (April
1862), quoted in Banks, *Victorian Values*, 87; meeting of the Men and Women's
Club for May 1887, quoted in Bland, "Rational Sex or Spiritual Love?" 39.

4. Pivar, *Purity Crusade*, 156.

5. In this connection, it is interesting to note that Victorian erotica such as the
underground magazine *The Pearl* (1879–80) often depicts the female orgasm as
a moment of "spending." Such pornography, of course, does not depict women
as altruists (or as mothers) but as participants in a purely pleasurable or selfish
act. There is thus no way for these writers to imagine female sexuality except as
physiologically "male."

6. John Starrett Hughes, "The Madness of Separate Spheres: Insanity and
Masculinity in Victorian Alabama," in Carnes and Griffen, *Meanings for Manhood*, 53–66, 64.

7. "A Grave Social Problem," 56. In the 1880s schoolboy masturbation and schoolboy homosexuality were still often conflated; the latter seemed inimical to the family not because boys practicing such behavior would not father children but because they would make dangerously sensual husbands (and because they might have weakened their sperm, endangering the race). Edward Lyttelton of Eton, for instance, warned of public-school homosexuality that "the premature stimulus to the passions, [even if] only temporary, increases their strength in early manhood to a terrible degree" (*The Causes and Prevention of Immorality in Schools* [London: privately printed for Rev. R. A. Bullen, 1887], 21.

8. [Louisa Shore], "The Emancipation of Women," *Westminster Review* n.s. 46 (1 July 1874): 137–74, 170. Likewise, Mary Gove Nichols, an American physician who practiced in England, wrote in her 1854 handbook, *Marriage*, that "masturbation in children, and every evil of sensuality, spring from the polluted hot-bed of a sensual and unloving marriage, where woman is subject to a destroying sensualism during pregnancy and lactation" (quoted in Hartman, "Child Abuse and Self-Abuse," 242). Frances Swiney argued in the 1890s that "men's sexual impositions during pregnancy. . . . lead to eczema, skin diseases, eye disease and many more ailments in children" and that sperm is often contaminated not only with the poison of syphilis but also with alcohol and nicotine (Jeffreys, *The Spinster and Her Enemies*, 36). Throughout the period in question, it was not simply illicit sexuality but male sexuality in general that seemed to strike at the roots of the family.

9. "A Woman," "Chivalry, Marriage, and Religion," 679.

10. "Enforced Maternity," *Shafts* 1 (18 February 1893): 251–52, 252. Elizabeth Wolstenholme Elmy's "The Awakening of Woman," a review of Swiney's book by the same title, provides another example of this feminist sentiment. She quotes Swiney's hopes for "the new motherhood and fatherhood," in which "The lower animal instincts and passions of man will be held under control and ultimately eliminated. . . . Side by side, co-equal, in a holy bond of sympathy and love, shall walk down life's pathways the New Adam and the New Eve, and 'a little child shall lead them'" (72). Such expressions illustrate the appeal of theosophy for feminists, who were attracted by its promise to revise the sexual order by eradicating sex; Swiney's theosophy, for instance, implies that women have much less distance to travel to perfection than men, as the "new fatherhood" appears to be identical to the old motherhood.

11. Herbert Jamieson, "The Modern Woman," *Westminster Review* 152 (November 1899): 571–76, 573.

12. [W. R. Greg], "Prostitution," *Westminster Review* 53 (June 1850): 448–506, 450, 460.

13. [W. T. Stead], "The Maiden Tribute of Modern Babylon," *Pall Mall Gazette* 42 (6, 7, 8, 10 July 1885): 1–6, 1–6, 1–5, 1–6. Deborah Gorham contends in "The 'Maiden Tribute of Modern Babylon' Re-Examined: Child Prostitution and the Idea of Childhood in Late-Victorian England" (*Victorian Studies* 21 [Spring 1978]: 353–79, 355) that rhetoric like Stead's succeeded "because it did not threaten the images of womanhood, childhood, and family life that form an essential part of [the reformers'] world view"; I would argue rather that the construction of the middle-class adult male as a sexual predator victimizing girls made doubly helpless by their age and their economic status had considerable impact on Victorian views of family life.

14. Robert H. MacDonald observes in "The Frightful Consequences of Onanism: Notes on the History of a Delusion" (*Journal of the History of Ideas* 28 [July–September 1967]: 423–31) that the idea that masturbation weakens the sperm, leading to feeble or feeble-minded offspring, dates back at least as far as the early eighteenth century and continued to be influential into the twentieth century. MacDonald quotes the 1922 edition of R. S. S. Baden-Powell's handbook for the Boy Scouts, *Rovering to Success*, which warns, "You are throwing away the seed that has been handed down to you as a trust instead of keeping it and ripening it for bringing a son to you later on" (425, 431). E. H. Hare ("Masturbatory Insanity: The History of an Idea," *Journal of Mental Science* 108 [January 1962]: 1–25) likewise gives two hundred years as the duration of the belief "that every youth who masturbated endangered the vitality of his future children" (16).

15. Frances Albert Doughty, "The Small Family and American Society," *Nineteenth Century and After* 44 (September 1903): 420–27, 425. Doughty, a resident of Baltimore, was concerned not only with the parental duty to bear healthy and well-cared-for children but with the white duty to retain racial supremacy for the good of all (427). Small families for the ruling (white) class were essential to achieving this goal.

16. Greg, "Prostitution," 479–80.

17. One such was Christina Bremner, who in "Woman in the Labour Market" cried out "for temperance with regard to the number of a man's family. . . . Recently I urged upon the father of a large family of daughters the necessity for giving one of his girls a thorough education in art, necessary to develop her undoubted talent. 'What you say is very true, and I quite see it, but you know I have

SIX other daughters, and I cannot afford the outlay.' 'You should have thought of that before,' trembled on my lips, but I choked the words down" (469).

18. "Chastity: Its Development and Maintenance," 435. The article continues with a warning about degeneration: "Tampering with maternity must bring disease and exhaustion, it must fill the nation with surviving infants who are doomed to grow up emasculated, and unable to sustain the power of the race. . . . Already the prevalence of artificial intervention is giving the masculine evolution a preponderance in the formation of posterity, and the influence of muliebrity is restricted, so that there is being organized a formidable nucleus of moral lepers who, by a fatal and unscrupulous competition, exclude the best women from continuing the race" (436).

19. Geoffrey Mortimer, "Enforced Maternity," *Shafts* 1 (14 January 1893): 167; "Enforced Maternity," 251. Mortimer was later to publish a marriage manual, *Chapters on Human Love* (1898), which stressed the importance of pleasure for both sexual partners and the need for skill and knowledge in obtaining such pleasures.

20. In the same year she published a manual of her own, *The Law of Population*. Besant's various activities as birth-control pioneer, atheist, Fabian socialist, theosophist, and finally promoter of Indian self-government were united by her commitment to feminism, although her extremism sometimes rendered her embarrassing to those working to bring feminism into the mainstream of British thought.

21. Montague Cookson [Crackanthorpe], "The Morality of Married Life," *Fortnightly Review* n.s. 12 (1 October 1872): 397–412. In a much later sequel, the 1906 "Population and Progress," Crackanthorpe quoted "the well-known West London preacher, the late Mr. Haweis: 'You may say children are from God; I reply, so is the cholera. I suppose we are here, among other things, to determine when and how God's law shall operate'" (1016). As an example of the opposition to birth control on grounds of health, Eric Trudgill notes in *Madonnas and Magdalens: The Origins and Development of Victorian Sexual Attitudes* (London: Heinemann, 1976) that gynecologist "C.H.F. Routh lists, among *The Moral and Physical Evils likely to Follow if Practices intended to Act as Checks to Population be not strongly Discouraged and Condemned* (1879), metritis, leucorrhoea, menorrhagia and haematocele, hysteralgia and hyperaesthesia of the genital organs, galloping cancer, ovarian dropsy and ovaritis, sterility, mania leading to suicide, and nymphomania" (63). The *Lancet*'s review of Crackanthorpe's collected essays likewise complained that the author

"does not appear to have bestowed a thought upon the . . . possible influence of these [contraceptive] methods upon the health either of parents or of children" ("Population and Progress," *Lancet* no. 4377 [20 July 1907]: 170–71, 170).

22. Representative articles on this topic are Bernard Houghton, "Immorality and the Marriage Law," *Westminster Review* 168 (September 1907): 304–13, and James W. Barclay, "Malthusianism and the Declining Birth Rate," *Nineteenth Century and After* 59 (January 1906): 80–89. The former accepts birth control as a fact of life that serves at least to encourage early marriages (linked to low prostitution and low illegitimacy rates); the latter rejects the idea—earlier expressed by the Bishop of London, in an "imputation on the women of England, which a mere layman does not care to repeat"—that women are taking steps to avoid pregnancy, arguing instead that nature automatically limits the birth rate in an environment in which most people are well off (88).

23. Thompson, *The Rise of Respectable Society*, 56, 112. In "The Victorians, the Psychologists, and Psychic Birth Control," Miriam Lewin states that continence ("psychological means") was the major form of birth control for the Victorians (59). Whether or not this is the case—and it is notoriously difficult for historians to achieve an accurate sense of the secrets of bygone marriage beds—it is clear that the three million pamphlets that circulated, according to J. A. Banks's classic *Prosperity and Parenthood: A Study of Family Planning among the Victorian Middle Classes* (London: Routledge, 1954, 154), between 1879 and 1921 to proselytize for some kind of family limitation were having their effect.

24. See, for instance, the works of J. A. and Olive Banks; Angus McLaren's *Birth Control in Nineteenth-Century England* (London: Croom Helm, 1978); Richard Allen Soloway's *Birth Control and the Population Question in England, 1877–1930* (Chapel Hill: U of North Carolina P, 1982); and F. Barry Smith's "Sexuality in Britain, 1800–1900: Some Suggested Revisions," in Martha Vicinus, ed., *A Widening Sphere: Changing Roles of Victorian Women* (Bloomington: Indiana UP, 1977), 182–98.

25. Margaret Jackson, "Sexual Liberation or Social Control? Some Aspects of the Relationship between Feminism and the Social Construction of Sexual Knowledge in the Early Twentieth Century," *Women's Studies International Forum* 6.1 (1983): 1–17, 5.

26. Craik, "Concerning Men—by a Woman," 375.

27. Grant Allen, "The New Hedonism," *Fortnightly Review* n.s. 52 (1 March 1893): 377–92, 384, 381.

28. Collins, "Education in Sex," 101. H. R. Boyle concurred in "Sexual Morality" (*Westminster Review* 166 [September 1906]: 334–40), explaining that "love is in reality a synonym for lust" and that lust is "a perfectly natural, entirely healthy emotion, common, in greater or less degree, to every physically complete man and woman" (336). It is not desire but prudery, he charged, that creates prostitution and discourages informed parentage.

29. Blackwell is cited in Rosenberg, "Sexuality, Class and Role in 19th-Century America," 137; for Hopkins (and her authority, Dr. [William B.?] Carpenter), see Ellice Hopkins, "The Apocalypse of Evil," *Contemporary Review* 48 (September 1885): 332–42, 340. The guiding spirit of the purity society known as the White Cross League, Hopkins was the author of a continence tract entitled *True Manliness*, which sold more than a million copies (Bristow, *Vice and Vigilance*, 138). Blackwell, too, was predictably opposed to birth control, warning, "The very grave national danger of teaching men to repudiate fatherhood and welcoming women to despise motherhood and shrink from the trouble involved in the bearing and nurturing of children, demands the most serious consideration" (quoted in Jane Lewis, *Women in England 1870–1950: Sexual Divisions and Social Change* [Bloomington: Indiana UP, 1984], 129). Both women strove to extend the ideals of Victorian motherhood to fatherhood as a means of improving society.

30. Debate about prostitution became particularly heated during the controversy surrounding the Contagious Diseases Acts of 1864–69 (repealed 1886). The acts were based on the premise that prostitutes endangered the health of the military, since one-third of soldiers under medical care were suffering from venereal diseases. (The figure comes from Richard Davenport-Hines, *Sex, Death and Punishment: Attitudes to Sex and Sexuality in Britain since the Renaissance* [London: Collins, 1990], 167.) Thus any woman suspected of prostitution in certain garrison towns forfeited her civil rights. Whereas discussion of prostitution typically centered on the double standard and therefore is only marginally relevant to the study at hand, the Contagious Diseases Acts helped to highlight the effect of disease upon the unborn; discussion of syphilis thus shifted the burden of responsibility to men and put fatherhood at center stage.

31. Quoted in Davenport-Hines, *Sex, Death and Punishment*, 165, 162.

32. Bristow, *Vice and Vigilance*, 140–41.

33. McLaren, *Birth Control in Nineteenth-Century England*, 199.

34. Cornwallis, "Capabilities and Disabilities of Women," 30.

35. [John Chapman], "Prostitution in Relation to the National Health," *West-*

minster Review n.s. 36 (1 July 1869): 179–234, 218, 233; Craik, "For Better for Worse," 574. This is not to suggest that *only* remote generations were the focus of such anxiety; both Chapman and Craik, among others, also invoked the immediate families of the contaminated fathers.

36. Gail Savage, "'The Wilful Communication of a Loathsome Disease': Marital Conflict and Venereal Disease in Victorian England," *Victorian Studies* 34 (Autumn 1990): 35–54. As Savage notes, while the offensive quality of the Contagious Diseases Acts to many purity reformers was that they "presumed that women formed the reservoir of infection and ignored the role of men in spreading venereal disease, legal practice before the Divorce Court made the opposite assumption—that husbands rather than wives carried the disease" (49).

37. Cited in Lyndsay Andrew Farrall, *The Origins and Growth of the English Eugenics Movement 1865–1925* (New York: Garland, 1985), 36–37. Understandably, feminists were often uncomfortable with a social theory that confined women to the bedroom. As McLaren points out, the marriage of feminism and eugenics was never entirely happy; many eugenists held "that feminism actually posed a danger" to their cause (*Birth Control in Nineteenth-Century England*, 146).

38. Daniel J. Kevles, *In the Name of Eugenics: Genetics and the Uses of Human Heredity* (New York: Knopf, 1985), 71.

39. Kevles suggests that Galton's frustrated paternal instincts led to his "obsession with the eugenic propagation of Galton-like offspring" (*In the Name of Eugenics*, 9). Certainly Galton seems to have looked on the eugenics movement as his child.

40. Francis Galton, "Hereditary Talent and Character," *Macmillan's Magazine* 12 (June 1865): 157–66, 157.

41. See, for instance, [Herman Merivale], "Galton on Hereditary Genius," *Edinburgh Review* 132 (July 1870): 100–125, 110, and [F. W. Farrar], "Hereditary Genius," *Fraser's Magazine* n.s. 2 (August 1870): 251–65, 262.

42. The second installment of his article (Francis Galton, "Hereditary Talent and Character," *Macmillan's Magazine* 12 [August 1865]: 318–27) had more to say about negative eugenics. Finding that a "morbid susceptibility" to diseases physical and moral (contagion, alcoholism, gambling fever, criminality, "strong sexual passion") runs in families and that removing the children of such families or of "a low race" to a more admirable environment is insufficient to overcome their inherited proclivities, Galton suggested the necessity of discouraging socially undesirable breeding (320, 325–26).

43. Galton, "Hereditary Talent and Character," 165, 163, 165.

44. Galton, "Hereditary Talent and Character," 323.

45. Francis Galton, "Hereditary Genius: The Judges of England between 1660 and 1865," *Macmillan's Magazine* 19 (March 1869): 424–31, 426, 427, 430.

46. See, for instance, an essay by feminist Jane Hume Clapperton, "Miss Chapman's Marriage Reform: A Criticism," *Westminster Review* 130 (December 1888): 709–17; see also Laura B. Cameron, "How We Marry," *Westminster Review* 145 (June 1896): 690–94.

47. Montague Crackanthorpe, "Population and Progress," *Fortnightly Review* n.s. 80 (1 December 1906): 1001–16, 1016.

48. Francis Galton, "Eugenics as a Factor in Religion," rpt. in his *Essays in Eugenics* (New York: Garland, 1985), 68–70.

49. Lecture by C. W. Saleeby, reported in *Eugenics Review* 1 (April 1909): 9.

50. C. W. Saleeby, "The Psychology of Parenthood," *Eugenics Review* 1 (April 1909): 37–46, 43. See also Montague Crackanthorpe, "Marriage, Divorce, and Eugenics," *Nineteenth Century and After* 68 (October 1910): 686–702, which contends, "Eugenics, although it primarily means, as everyone knows, 'good breeding,' also includes good environment. It therefore lays very great stress on the happiness of the home, for happy homes make happy children, and happy children have [a] far better chance than unhappy children of growing into good and useful citizens" (694).

51. Perhaps because of the fluidity that permitted it to be adapted in support of social purity, women's issues, or men's noninvolvement with their families, the appeal of eugenics was extraordinarily widespread. Among the important figures who preached eugenic doctrines in representative periodical articles were Greg (in the unsigned "On the Failure of 'Natural Selection' in the Case of Man," *Fraser's Magazine* 78 [September 1868]: 353–62), Eliza Lynn Linton ("E.L.L.," "Our Civilisation," *Cornhill Magazine* 27 [June 1873]: 671–78), astronomer George Darwin ("On Beneficial Restrictions to Liberty of Marriage," *Contemporary Review* 22 [August 1873]: 412–26), Henry Maudsley ("Heredity in Health and Disease," *Fortnightly Review* n.s. 41 [1 May 1886]: 648–59), and political scientist H. J. Laski ("The Scope of Eugenics," *Westminster Review* 174 [July 1910]: 25–34). As Ruth Brandon reports, Havelock Ellis and his wife, Edith Lees, not only preached but practiced eugenist principles; they determined not to have children because of eccentricity in the Lees family, although Ellis claimed that "[his] heredity was as nearly as possible perfect" (*The New Women and the Old Men*, 106).

52. Cited in Farrall, *The Origins and Growth of the English Eugenics Move-*

ment, 166. This estimate dates from 1909; other Galton Laboratory researchers doubled Elderton's figure to suggest that heredity was as much as ten times more important than environment for humankind (Farrall 306).

53. Galton discussed his collection of anecdotal evidence on twins in "The History of Twins, as a Criterion of the Relative Powers of Nature and Nurture" (*Fraser's Magazine* n.s. 12 [November 1875]: 566–76), reporting, "I have not a single case in which my correspondents speak of originally dissimilar characters having become assimilated through identity of nurture. The impression that all this evidence leaves on the mind is one of some wonder whether nurture can do anything at all beyond giving instruction and professional training" (575–76). A more substantial study was Edward Lee Thorndike's *Measurement of Twins* (1905), which, as W. H. Winch commented, resembled Galton's work in showing "the great importance of natural powers as compared with the influence of varying environments" ("A Modern Basis for Educational Theory," *Mind* n.s. 18 [January 1909]: 84–104, 92).

54. Buckle, "The Influence of Women on the Progress of Knowledge," 405.

55. "Chastity: Its Development and Maintenance," 420. In this essayist's theory, men inherit desire from their "androgens" (forefathers) and its inhibiting factors from their "gynegens" (foremothers), the latter being bolstered by environment in the form of the boundaries family life imposes. Both individual male development and human history consequently follow a developmental pattern that "tends to ante-nuptial irregularity, then to monogamy with its resultant astrictiveness, and lastly to child-care with its steadying duties of labour" (432).

56. Earle, "Mothers and Daughters," 673–74.

57. Houghton, "Immorality and the Marriage Law," 309. See also Alex MacKendrick, "Heredity and Environment as Factors in Social Development" (*Westminster Review* 162 [August 1904]: 180–87), for a more cautious argument that although heredity remains an important (if frequently overstated) factor in shaping humankind, social reformers should bear in mind that they cannot influence it; they should therefore busy themselves with shaping an improved environment despite the genetic factors that may work against them (186).

58. See, for instance, Winch, "A Modern Basis for Educational Theory," 94.

59. Stephen Kern, "Explosive Intimacy: Psychodynamics of the Victorian Family," *History of Childhood Quarterly* 1 (Winter 1974): 437–61, 440.

60. [G. H. Lewes], "Hereditary Influence, Animal and Human," *Westminster Review* 66 (July 1856): American ed. 75–90, 84, 85, 80, 83. Carroll Smith-Rosenberg notes of the United States that some physicians of this period were

contending "that because male genes were stronger than female, the father's influence upon the fetus was greater than the mother's. . . . [H. A.] Storer went so far as to argue [in 1864] that the father's genetic influence on the fetus was far greater than the mother's" (*Disorderly Conduct*, 239, 341n66). Charles Rosenberg, however, holds that the general American tendency in the middle third of the century was to concede "the primacy of the mother in determining heredity and the need, therefore, to grant her dominion in the structuring of social relations" ("Sexuality, Class and Role in 19th-Century America," 149).

61. Halliday, "Mothers," 157. The experience of Osbert Sitwell, who was born in 1892, suggests that turn-of-the-century feeling on this point had reversed itself: he remarked in his 1945 autobiography that "the English tradition regards every child born in wedlock . . . as being solely his father's, descended from *his* father and his father's father. The mother's family do not enter in, bear no responsibility, and derive no credit. My father, however, frequently noticed, and never failed at the time to mention with distaste, traits, physical and otherwise, occurring in me which he had observed in members of my mother's family, directing attention to them, too, with a sour look, as though I had in some way broken all the rules of the game in heredity" (*Left Hand, Right Hand! Volume I, The Cruel Month: An Autobiography* [New York: Quartet, 1977], 4–5). I thank Gillian Adams for this reference.

62. Letter from C.I.C., *Englishwoman's Review* 11 (April 1869): 223–24, 224; "A Woman," "The Effects of Civilization upon Women," *National Review* 9 (March 1887): 26–38, 27; Susan Harris, countess of Malmesbury, "The Future of Marriage: A Reply," *Fortnightly Review* n.s. 50 (1 February 1892): 272–82, 275. A variation on the theory of maternal predominance suggested that sons inherited the mother's characteristics and daughters the father's; the failings of each gender might thus be constantly offset by being sifted through the other.

63. Merivale, "Galton on Hereditary Genius," 110, 122.

64. Farrar, "Hereditary Genius," 261. Farrar also took issue with Galton's slighting categorization of divines as sickly, unstable, and effeminate; although celibates might leave no biological mark, Farrar argued for their importance as an environmental asset in terms also relevant to asexual women: "ought it not in common fairness to be remembered that . . . the very fact of their stainless chastity gave them a direct and most powerful moral influence over the minds and characters of men?" (257). The reverend father here combines with the revered mother in an alliance resistant to scientific analysis.

65. [W. Boyd Dawkins], "Darwin on the Descent of Man," *Edinburgh Review* 134 (July 1871): 195–235, 235, 218.

66. George J. Romanes, "Weismann's Theory of Heredity," *Contemporary Review* 57 (May 1890): 686–99, 689, 697.

67. Jeffrey Weeks, *Sexuality and Its Discontents: Meanings, Myths and Modern Sexualities* (Boston: Routledge, 1985), 82.

68. Marcus Hartog, "The Transmission of Acquired Characteristics," *Contemporary Review* 94 (September 1908): 307–17, 315, 307, 317. Hartog argued for the likelihood of such transmission in certain cases, of which alcoholism is one example (310). Subsequent numbers of the journal contain assorted responses and rejoinders on this point, of which the first was G. Archdall Reid's "The Alleged Transmission of Acquired Characteristics," *Contemporary Review* 94 (October 1908): 399–412, which also took issue with Francis Darwin's Lamarckian address to the British Association at Dublin. While Lamarckism was by that time a minority view among scientists, it was by no means dead.

69. Mona Caird, "Phases of Human Development," *Westminster Review* 141 (January, February 1894): 37–51, 162–79. Rpt. in *The Morality of Marriage*, 195–239, 223, 239.

70. Maurice, "National Health," 50.

71. "Heredity," *Shafts* 1 (21 January 1893): 186–87, 187. An example of feminist Lamarckism occurs in "Espérance" 's "Woman's Place in Education" in the preceding issue, which argues that primitive woman's greater involvement in child rearing led her by degrees "to a higher life. . . . The qualities to which this care gave birth, developing and strengthening in herself, were passed on to posterity, and hence her daughters have become instinctively the best guides and fittest trainers of the young" (171).

72. "Enforced Maternity," 251. Carl N. Degler observes that in nineteenth-century American theories of conception, "physicians generally assigned to both parents an equal, if different, influence on the child" (*At Odds*, 81); one example is Henry C. Wright's 1855 *Marriage and Parentage* (rpt. New York: Arno, 1974), which suggested an equal and similar parental influence in its contention that children conceived in lust are degenerate, while children conceived in deliberate efforts at procreation are innately virtuous.

73. E. I. Champness, "Women and Purity," *Westminster Review* 166 (September 1906): 326–33, 333; E. I. Champness, "Heredity versus the Power of Thought," *Westminster Review* 168 (July 1907): 59–63, 63.

74. Havelock Ellis, "The Psychic State in Pregnancy," *Studies in the Psychology of Sex*, vol. 2 (New York: Random House, 1936), 225.

75. Stephanie A. Shields, " 'To Pet, Coddle, and "Do For" ': Caretaking and

the Concept of Maternal Instinct," in Lewin, *In the Shadow of the Past*, 256–73, 263, 264.

76. "Biology and 'Women's Rights,'" 208. Similarly, Frederic Harrison's 1891 "The Emancipation of Women" argued that maternity is "the dominant instinct of all women; it possesses women, whether mothers or not, from the cradle to the grave. The most degraded woman is in this superior to the most heroic man (abnormal cases apart). . . . In this central feature of human nature, Women are always and everywhere incontestably pre-eminent" (445). Women's innate educational and emotional talent, however, would not long survive a blending of gender roles (450).

77. "Chastity: Its Development and Maintenance," 423. A similar point occurs in Vere Collins, "The Marriage Contract in Its Relation to Social Progress" (*Fortnightly Review* n.s. 77 [1 March 1905]: 479–85, 484): "Not only is the parental instinct more closely associated with the amoristic impulse in the case of woman, but physiological facts produce in her an ante-natal cognisance of and affection for the child, while the father's love is of later growth." Feminist agreement on this matter is exemplified in Agnes Grove, "'The Threatened Re-Subjection of Women'" ("the instinct of fatherhood was a much later development [than the maternal instinct]" [125]), and Frances Swiney, "Women among the Nations: Part I" ("Paternal affection . . . is of gradual growth; for the man has to be taught the responsibilities of fatherhood; they are not instinctive" [414–15]). The debate here owes much to the influence of Spencer, who found that the paternal instinct is culturally a late development, dependent upon the practice of monogamy.

78. Wedgwood, "'Male and Female Created He Them,'" 125.

79. Fawcett, "The Emancipation of Women," 683.

80. "Libra" [Miss Gay], "The Legal Value of the Unrepresented," *Shafts* 1 (25 February 1893): 259–60, 259.

81. James Sully, "Dollatry," *Contemporary Review* 75 (January 1899): 58–72, 60, 71.

82. Quoted in C. W. Saleeby, "The Problems of Heredity," *Fortnightly Review* n.s. 78 (October 1905): 604–15, 614. This argument struck even the eugenist Saleeby as extreme; he was later to note in "The Psychology of Parenthood" that even though "the parental instinct is much less potent in men than in women," it nevertheless exists: "a society in which there was some development of the paternal instinct, in which the father's love and care came to help the mother's—which I take to be the essence of marriage—would have

superior survival value" (40). Accepting the possibility of "some development of the paternal instinct" was about as far as Edwardian science felt comfortable in going.

83. Rosalind Coward, *Patriarchal Precedents: Sexuality and Social Relations* (London: Routledge, 1983), 10.

84. [Henry Sumner Maine], "The Patriarchal Theory," *Quarterly Review* 162 (January 1886): 181–209, 186.

85. William Schooling, "Marriage Institutions," *Westminster Review* 135 (April 1891): 385–95, 388, 393.

86. Effie Johnson (later Richmond), "Marriage or Free Love," *Westminster Review* 152 (July 1899): 91–98, 95.

87. See Coward, *Patriarchal Precedents*, 89–90.

88. See Kern, "Explosive Intimacy," 448. The relationship between researches of this kind and Freud's later postulations about the oedipus complex is obvious.

89. Anonymous, "Woman's Mission," *Shafts* 7 (July–September 1899): 48–51, 48. See also "Espérance," "Woman's Place in Education," which notes that the reason that woman's talent as teacher is "not only not secondary to man's, but very much superior" is that "pre-historical woman ceased to be a nomad long before man became domesticated, and, in consequence, around her gathered the first home-life of humanity," while her mate was "occupied in the slaying of the brutes around him for the sustenance of himself and his dependents, and therefore not rising by equal steps to a higher life" (171).

90. Havelock Ellis, "The History of Marriage," in *Studies in the Psychology of Sex*, 2: 492–532, 503.

91. One exception was anthropologist Edward B. Tylor, who conceded that in matrilinear societies women might possibly (though not necessarily) wield more power than their husbands. He explained, however, that because of the instinctive drive to create a patriarchal family, "the maternal husband emancipates himself from his inferior position whenever the social pressure is removed, and he can become a paternal husband" ("The Matriarchal Family System," *Nineteenth Century* 40 [July 1896]: 81–96, 94).

92. Swiney, "Women among the Nations: Part I," 417, 419.

93. [Havelock Ellis], "The Changing Status of Women," *Westminster Review* 128 (October 1887): 818–28, 818, 819–20, 821.

94. See, for example, Woods Hutchinson, "Evolutionary Ethics of Marriage and Divorce," *Contemporary Review* 88 (September 1905): 397–410. In this

discussion of marriage in different cultures and on different levels of civilization, Hutchinson, an American physician, compared manifestations of paternal
feeling (from the indifference of the savage to the absenteeism of the harem
master—where "any paternal training of the young" is impossible—to the responsibility of the monogamist) to conclude that eugenic monogamy is the ideal
(401, 404, 407). The mother's interest in her children appears equally keen
throughout; it is the father's involvement that varies.

95. Elizabeth Fee, "The Sexual Politics of Victorian Social Anthropology,"
Feminist Studies 1 (Winter–Spring 1973): 23–39, 24.

96. Mona Caird, "The Emancipation of the Family," rpt. in *The Morality of
Marriage*, 21–59, 24, 50, 40, 57.

97. John Cleverley and D. C. Phillips point out in *From Locke to Spock: Influential Models of the Child in Modern Western Thought* (Melbourne: Melbourne
UP, 1976) that the child had become an object for empirical scientific study as
early as the late eighteenth century, through the influence of John Locke's work;
they date the real flowering of the movement, however, to the 1890s (71).

98. Charles Darwin, "A Biographical Sketch of an Infant," *Mind* 2 (July
1877): 285–94, 291, 290, 292.

99. John Springhall notes in *Coming of Age: Adolescence in Britain 1860–
1960* (Dublin: Gill and Macmillan, 1986) that Americans influenced by Hall
used the recapitulation theory to justify the emphasis of early-twentieth-century
youth movements on woodcraft and tribal ritual: to Hall adolescence represented
the barbarian stage in human development (30–31).

100. James Sully, "Baby Linguistics," *English Illustrated Magazine* 3 (November 1884): 110–18, 110, 111, 118.

101. Louis Robinson, "Darwinism in the Nursery," *Nineteenth Century* 30
(November 1891): 831–42, 832. Robinson's researches are further detailed in
"The Meaning of a Baby's Footprint" (*Nineteenth Century* 31 [May 1892]: 795–
806) and the unsigned "The Child and the Savage: A Study of Primitive Man"
(*Blackwood's Edinburgh Magazine* 151 [April 1892]: 568–72).

102. Robinson, "Darwinism in the Nursery," 831, 838–39.

103. James Sully, "The New Study of Children," *Fortnightly Review* n.s. 58
(1 November 1895): 723–37, 724, 725, 727, 733, 736.

104. S. S. Buckman, "The Speech of Children," *Nineteenth Century* 41 (May
1897): 793–807, 806. Gilbreth's experiments on his eldest daughter around
1905 appear in Frank B. Gilbreth and Ernestine Gilbreth Carey's 1949 memoir *Cheaper by the Dozen* (New York: Bantam, 1963), 103–4; for Johnston's

work, see Charles Johnston, "The World's Baby-Talk and the Expressiveness of Speech," *Fortnightly Review* n.s. 60 (1 October 1896): 494–505. Similar approaches include Buckman's "Babies and Monkeys," *Nineteenth Century* 36 (November 1894): 727–43, and (to provide a woman-authored example) Catherine Dodd, "A Study in School Children," *National Review* 32 (September 1898): 66–74.

105. Lewin, "The Victorians, the Psychologists, and Psychic Birth Control," 41.

106. Vance, *Sinews of the Spirit*, 114.

107. Medicine was the first licensed profession to admit women, which it did with reluctance in the 1870s, closing the loopholes that had allowed women to enter (in the statutes of the Apothecary Society, for example, and in granting privileges to doctors with foreign degrees) as soon as it became aware of them. For some years the woman doctors in Britain numbered four: Blackwell, Elizabeth Garrett Anderson (Millicent Garrett Fawcett's sister), and two others. But the presence of those four and the general sense that ministering to the sick was a womanly task made it inevitable that women would be admitted to practice.

Chapter 4: The Law and the Father

The epigraph is from [Lydia E. Becker], "The Political Disabilities of Women," *Westminster Review* n.s. 41 (1 January 1872): 50–70, 64.

1. For a discussion of "personhood," see Albie Sachs and Joan Hoff Wilson, *Sexism and the Law: A Study of Male Beliefs and Legal Bias in Britain and the United States* (New York: Free Press, 1979, ch. 1, esp. 5–6, 9–11), who contend that judges "manipulated the meaning of the word 'person' so as to produce results consistent with their picture of womanhood" (6).

2. The principle of male supremacy is well illustrated by the Cochrane case of 1840. Here a wife had left her husband, who four years later managed to entrap her back into his power and kept her confined. She succeeded in getting a writ of habeus corpus, but the judge dismissed her plea for freedom, confirming that Cochrane had a right to encourage her to do her marital duty by imprisonment and by force, so long as any beatings were not administered "in a violent or cruel manner." It was not until 1891 that the Jackson case (also known toponymically as the Clitheroe case) reversed this principle—but only on appeal.

3. Quoted in Nigel V. Lowe, "The Legal Status of Fathers: Past and Present,"

in Lorna McKee and Margaret O'Brien, eds., *The Father Figure* (New York: Tavistock, 1982), 26–42, 26–27.

4. Ivy Pinchbeck and Margaret Hewitt, *Children in English Society*, vol. 2: *From the Eighteenth Century to the Children Act 1948* (London: Routledge & Kegan Paul, 1973), 363. They note that the court of Chancery had slightly wider powers, being permitted to intervene "where [the father's] behavior might contaminate and corrupt the morals of his child; or where the child was likely to be inculcated with irreligious or athetistic beliefs which both law and society regarded as immoral, and dangerous; or where a father had deserted or refused to support the child" (364). It was Chancery that deprived the atheist Percy Bysshe Shelley of the custody of his children in 1817.

5. Anonymous, "Parental Authority in Matters of Religion," *Dublin Review* 3rd ser. 1 (January 1879): 208–23, 217. The author cited the cases of *Vansittart* v. *Vansittart* and *Hope* v. *Hope* as examples of this legal doctrine.

6. Mary Lyndon Shanley, *Feminism, Marriage, and the Law in Victorian England, 1850–1895* (Princeton: Princeton UP, 1989), 133.

7. Michael Grossberg, "Who Gets the Child? Custody, Guardianship, and the Rise of a Judicial Patriarchy in Nineteenth-Century America," *Feminist Studies* 9 (Summer 1983): 235–60, 236, 247. After the 1886 Infant Custody Act was passed, literary critic Augustine Birrell pointed out in an unsigned article that "it cannot now be said that infants belong to either parent. . . . and there are those . . . who rather dread the hour when the authority of the judges will be found like a veritable Aaron's rod, to have swallowed up both paternal and maternal rights" ("Woman under the English Law," *Edinburgh Review* 184 [October 1896]: 322–40, 338–39).

8. Carol Brown, "Mothers, Fathers and Children: From Private to Public Patriarchy," in Lydia Sargent, ed., *Women and Revolution: A Discussion of the Unhappy Marriage of Marxism and Feminism* (Boston: South End, 1981), 239–67, 242.

9. Custody legislation after the original act of 1839 included, in addition to a number of failed bills, the following: the Infant Custody Act of 1873, moved by Josephine Butler's Quaker ally William Fowler, under which separated wives (even adulterers) could apply for custody of their children under sixteen; the Matrimonial Causes Act of 1878, inspired by Frances Power Cobbe, under which chaste wives could apply for custody of their children under ten in cases where husbands had physically abused the women; the Infant Custody (Guardianship of Infants) Act of 1886, inspired by Elizabeth Wolstenholme Elmy, under which

women could apply for custody of their children under twenty-one and widows could serve as their children's legal guardians; the Custody of Children Act of 1891, which stripped parents of custodial rights over children they had previously abandoned; and the Summary Jurisdiction (Married Women) Act of 1895, under which wives who fled their abusive husbands could apply for custody of their children under sixteen without being considered guilty of desertion.

10. [Eliza Lynn], "One of Our Legal Fictions," *Household Words* 9 (29 April 1854): 257–60, 260, 259–60, 259. Linton's support for liberalized divorce laws was one of the few areas in which her youthful radicalism continued into later life.

11. Quoted in [Caroline Cornwallis], "The Property of Married Women," *Westminster Review* 67 (October 1856): American ed. 181–97, 185.

12. Cornwallis, "The Property of Married Women," 191–92.

13. [Margaret Oliphant], "The Laws Concerning Women," *Blackwood's Edinburgh Magazine* 79 (April 1856): 379–87, 383.

14. Novelist Herbert Flowerdew, for instance, argued in "Suggestion of a Substitute for the Marriage Laws" (*Westminster Review* 152 [September 1899]: 293–300, 299) that it was specious to contend that a change in custody rules would deprive children of a unique and invaluable influence: "the companionship and guidance of which they are bereft is that of a father who has no affection for their mother, and as a result most probably none for her children—who at the best has so little that it does not induce him to remain with their mother for their sakes. . . . Nor does the law make any attempt in the case of a happily married couple to make the personal supervision of the father compulsory. In the middle and lower classes his employment prevents him exercising such supervision, and in the upper classes it is usual to send the children to boarding-school, where the influence of the father is felt even less than among the middle classes. His chief function under existing circumstances is to provide money for their maintenance, and this would be ensured for them under the supposed regulation."

15. [W. M. Thackeray], "Roundabout Papers—No. II: On Two Children in Black," *Cornhill Magazine* 1 (March 1860): 380–84, 384, 383, 384. In interesting contrast to this article is Thackeray's treatment of paternal custody in *Vanity Fair* (1847–48), where—although the relationship between Rawdon Crawley and his son has redeemed Rawdon from moral mediocrity (it struck many Victorian critics as the most affecting aspect of the novel)—Rawdon's notion of responsible single-parenthood is to give the boy into his sister-in-law's charge

and take up a colonial appointment on the other side of the world. (Similarly, Thackeray himself sent his daughters to live with his mother in Paris after his wife was institutionalized.) For all the drawbacks of motherhood in Vanity Fair, children still need a woman's touch.

16. Becker, "The Political Disabilities of Women," 63.

17. "A Peeress," "Women and the Suffrage," *National Review* 8 (October 1886): 283–86, 285.

18. Frances Power Cobbe, "Wife-Torture in England," *Contemporary Review* 32 (April 1878): 55–87, 62, 80–82. The fear that a mistress could supplant a wife was frequently expressed in such articles; indeed, "A Peeress" charged that "this has been done in this generation" ("Women and the Suffrage," 285), although I have encountered no actual cases of this type.

19. Becker, "The Political Disabilities of Women," 65.

20. Arthur Arnold, "The Hon. Mrs. Norton and Married Women," *Fraser's Magazine* n.s. 17 (April 1878): 493–500, 495–96.

21. A point that was explicitly made by the anonymous author of the 1885 article "The Judicial Separation of Mother and Child": "We are constantly told by the party of stagnation, that a woman's duties are home duties, that she ought to devote herself to her children. . . . And yet when any question arises between father and mother as [to] the education of their children, we are also told that the father is the person to judge, and the law is appealed to in favour of his exclusive authority" (430–31).

22. The Beattie case is described in the anonymous column "Record of Events: Custody of Children," *Englishwoman's Review* n.s. 14 (15 December 1883): 552–63, 553; for a discussion of the case of the Reverend James Lilley and his wife, Maggie, see "Events of the Month," *Englishwoman's Review* n.s. 8 (15 March 1877): 141–42.

23. Quoted in "Record of Events: Custody of Children," 555.

24. Quoted in "Record of Events: Custody of Children," 555.

25. "The Law in Relation to Women," *Westminster Review* 128 (September 1887): 698–710, 703, 704, 705, 706.

26. An unsigned article in the *Englishwoman's Review* in 1872, for instance, commented on Parliament's indifference to redressing mothers' custodial wrongs: "a question involving the dearest right of every mother was not of sufficient interest to keep forty M.P.'s in the House!" ("'Eppure Si Muove,'" *Englishwoman's Review* n.s. 3 [October 1872]: 229–32, 231–32). Feminists also observed sex bias in the slight penalties meted out to rapists and wife-beaters

(see Gay, "The Legal Value of the Unrepresented," 259, and Anonymous, "Pioneer Club Records," *Shafts* 2 [November-December 1894]: 346–47). To many women the law seemed as corrupt as the men tried under it.

27. "The Agar Ellis Case in a New Aspect," *Englishwoman's Review* n.s. 14 (15 August 1883): 356–61, 357.

28. Jessie Boucherett, "The Agar-Ellis Case," *Englishwoman's Review* n.s. 9 (14 December 1878): 537–48, 547. Boucherett's article included an assortment of extracts from major newspapers—the *Times*, the *Morning Post*, and the *Standard*—all critical of the decision and of Mr. Ellis.

29. "Parental Authority in Matters of Religion," 211.

30. Frederick Thoresby, "Woman and Woman's Suffrage," *Westminster Review* 166 (November 1906): 522–30, 523.

31. Arling, "What Is the Role of the 'New Woman'?" 581.

32. "Parental Authority in Matters of Religion," 216. Even if they were qualified to provide their children's religious training, the anonymous writer continued, in practice they were unlikely to do so because of "want of leisure" or temperamental "indisposition." The same article quoted *Simpson on the Law of Infants:* "a child must be educated in the religion of its deceased father," even if the living mother's religious practices differed from her late husband's, and even if the man had left no directions to that effect (221).

33. This is not to suggest that Besant's case received no attention in periodicals. The author of the *Westminster Review*'s 1885 article "The Judicial Separation of Mother and Child" cites this custody dispute, as does the author of "Custody of Children" (*Justice of the Peace* 48 [14 June 1884]: 369–71; I thank Ann Sumner Holmes for drawing my attention to the latter article). Both writers argued for reform of the custody guidelines to benefit mothers. In addition, the newspaper Besant edited with Charles Bradlaugh, the *National Reformer*, retailed the history of the case (including legal documents) in 1878–79 (see Arthur H. Nethercot, *The First Five Lives of Annie Besant* [Chicago: U of Chicago P, 1960], 35n2, 133n2). Nethercot provides for this case a summary of newspaper coverage (most of it unsympathetic to Besant) but lists no articles in journals of the sort with which my study is primarily concerned (138). In general, newspapers were more likely than magazines to print reports on divorce, separation, and/or custody suits.

34. Lowe, "The Legal Status of Fathers," 27.

35. Shanley, *Feminism, Marriage, and the Law in Victorian England, 1850–1895*, 151, 192.

36. "The Judicial Separation of Mother and Child," 439–40, 441.

37. Witness the judgments quoted by the *Westminster Review* writer, taken from the Agar-Ellis case and similar custody disputes: "The father's right to the custody of his children is 'one of the most sacred of rights.' 'The rights of the father are sacred rights because his duties are sacred duties.' . . . 'The natural duties of a father are to treat his child with the utmost affection and with infinite tenderness. . . . The law does not interfere because of the great trust and faith it has in the natural affection of the father to perform his duties, and therefore it gives him corresponding rights.'" The essayist continued bitterly, "Will the law never have sufficient 'trust and faith' in the 'natural affection' of the mother to give *her* 'corresponding rights'?" ("The Judicial Separation of Mother and Child," 438–39).

38. "Record of Events: The Infants Bill," *Englishwoman's Review* n.s. 17 (15 June 1886): 262–65, 264. Ashbourne's proposed amendment, which would enable wives to petition the court only when the couples were living apart, was ultimately withdrawn. In a similar vein, see the speeches debating the Married Women's Property Bill, reported in *Englishwoman's Review* 1 in October 1868 (12–26); opponents of the bill feared that giving women control over their own money would foster family dissent. The text of the "Speech of Mr. Shaw Lefevre, M.P., in the House of Commons" for this bill (reprinted in the July 1868 number of the *Review* [504–14]) stressed that children would benefit if mothers as well as fathers could own property, as a father deaf to his "moral obligations" might be superseded by his more responsible wife (512); such arguments would only have heightened the anxieties of those concerned about women's increased power within the family.

39. Part of the New Poor Law, which sought to discourage undesirable behaviors (poverty among them) by punitive measures. The Bastardy Act placed the blame for illicit reproduction on the woman. John R. Gillis quotes a song from the 1830s, "My Grandfather's Days," which runs in part: "If a young man went a-courting a damsel meek and mild / And if she from misfortune should hap to have a child / By going to a magistrate, a recompense to seek, / They'd make the man marry her, or pay a crown a week. // But now by the New Poor Law he nothing has to pay / Nor would he, even if he got twenty children every day" (*For Better, for Worse: British Marriages, 1600 to the Present* [New York: Oxford UP, 1985], 240).

40. Joan Perkin notes that this law was liberalized in 1844, but that the increased mobility of the British population meant it was often hard to find the

delinquent fathers, so matters came to the same thing in the end (*Women and Marriage in Nineteenth-Century England*, 161).

41. "Events of the Quarter: Paragraphs," *Englishwoman's Review* n.s. 3 (July 1872): 226–27, 226.

42. D. F. Hannigan, "The Legitimacy of Children," *Westminster Review* 133 (June 1890): 619–24, 620, 622.

43. Elizabeth C. Wolstenholme Elmy, "Practical Work for Women Workers: Bills before Parliament," *Shafts* 4 (June 1896): 69–71, 70. See also A.H., "Purity" (*Shafts* 5 [September 1897]: 250–55, 254): "Make men responsible for their children, in or out of wedlock, and we shall hear less of miserable child-murders, or abandoned infants, of heartless mothers, driven desperate by their unshared burden of shame. Let the same social stigma be put on both partners in the sin, if it be a sin; or let society *accept* the lower conditions of polygamy."

44. Matilda M. Blake, "The Lady and the Law," *Westminster Review* 137 (April 1892): 364–70, 366.

45. Flowerdew, "Suggestion of a Substitute for the Marriage Laws," 296.

46. John George Cox, "The Changed Position of Married Women," *Dublin Review* 3rd ser. 9 (April 1883): 417–42, 423.

47. [A. J. Munby?], "Primogeniture," *Fraser's Magazine* n.s. 2 (December 1870): 783–92, 789.

48. Harriett M'Ilquham, "Marriage: A Just and Honourable Partnership," *Westminster Review* 157 (April 1902): 433–42, 440, 438. M'Ilquham also called for the removal from the Anglican marriage service of patriarchal language ("obey," "who giveth this woman," and so on). See also Blake's 1892 "The Lady and the Law," which complains that "the father who is invested with such enormous [custodial] powers is allowed, if he pleases, to will every farthing that he possesses away from his children, and to leave them helpless and destitute for the community to maintain" (366).

49. Harriett McIlquham [*sic*], "Some Necessary Marriage Reforms," *Westminster Review* 168 (October 1907): 398–403, 400, 401–2.

50. Gillis, for instance, recounts an 1872 Exeter case in which a woman sued her husband for maintenance of their two children; on the breakup of their marriage the couple had agreed that he would have custody, but he had since repudiated it during a quarrel with her. According to Gillis, "The court thought her conduct disgraceful and told her she must keep the children as part of her duties as a wife" (*For Better, for Worse*, 217).

51. Anonymous, "The Property Earnings and Maintenance of Married Women," *Englishwoman's Review* 1 (October 1867): 263–75, 271.

52. Elizabeth C. Wolstenholme Elmy, "The Summary Jurisdiction (Married Women) Act, 1895," *Shafts* 4 (February 1896): 7–8, 7. Elmy repeated this phrase in "Woman and the Law" (*Westminster Review* 168 [October 1907]: 394–97, 395) in connection with a recent case, reported in the *Daily Chronicle* by Florence Fenwick-Miller, in which a judge had ordered a wife's forty-pound nest egg, saved out of her housekeeping allowance, to be handed over to her husband on the ground that " 'she could not own any money at all if she had only worked in her own home' " (396). No matter how great their sense of responsibility and thrift, feminists worried, women constantly risked having their care for their families frustrated by their husbands.

53. Craik, "For Better for Worse," 574, 575.

54. Mary C. Tabor, "The Rights of Children," *Contemporary Review* 54 (September 1888): 408–17, 408, 412, 409, 413.

55. Collins, "The Marriage Contract in Its Relation to Social Progress," 484–85, 482–83, 485.

56. Brown, "Mothers, Fathers and Children," 248. Civil divorces were possible for a brief period during Oliver Cromwell's interregnum.

57. Allen Horstman, *Victorian Divorce* (New York: St. Martin's, 1985), 85, 86.

58. Horstman, *Victorian Divorce*, 63. Divorce actions remained outside working-class budgets; the poor had either to endure or to terminate bad marriages less formally.

59. Quoted in Davenport-Hines, *Sex, Death and Punishment*, 187. Another voice on Victoria's side was that of W. E. Gladstone, who in 1889 lamented that since the passage of the 1857 act, "the standard of conjugal morality has perceptibly declined among the higher classes of this country, and scandals in respect to it have become more frequent" ("The Question of Divorce," *North American Review* 149 [December 1889]: 641–44, 644). Similarly, Basil Tozer noted as late as 1909 that "the entire body of our modern mental specialists are of [the] opinion that the nation's high and increasing rate of insanity to-day is in a measure due to the surfeiting of what we complacently term the 'lower orders' with sensational descriptions of current crime," under which heading Tozer included divorce-court proceedings ("Divorce versus Compulsory Celibacy," *Nineteenth Century and After* 65 [February 1909]: 299–311, 310). Among present-day critics, Elaine Showalter argues in a study of the linkage of divorce reportage and sensation fiction that women novelists found fuel in the former to express a widespread "female discontent with the institutions of family life." She concludes, "The effects of divorce court proceedings and of sensation fiction

in undermining the sense of decorum, propriety and family secrecy, were considerable" ("Family Secrets and Domestic Subversion: Rebellion in the Novels of the 1860s," in Wohl, *The Victorian Family*, 101–16, 105, 113).

60. This is not to suggest that subsequent legal judgments always upheld the side of sexual rectitude, of course. One notorious case, *Reg.* v. *Clarence*, symbolized for many feminists and purity reformers the judicial mindset they were up against. The jury in this case had found Clarence guilty of grievous bodily harm for deliberately infecting his wife with venereal disease, but the court refused to accept the verdict.

61. In *A Woman's Issue: The Politics of Family Law Reform in Britain* (Westport, Conn.: Greenwood, 1982, 20), Dorothy M. Stetson observes that this ideology was responsible for the provision that "only the husband [would] be liable for alimony and child support, since the husband was the breadwinner and had the wife's property. Similarly, only the husband was permitted to sue his spouse's lover for damages."

62. [William Stirling-Maxwell], "The Law of Marriage and Divorce," *Fraser's Magazine* 52 (August 1855): 149–51, 150.

63. Cornwallis, "Capabilities and Disabilities of Women," 29. Combined with the complaint of the defenders of the rights of the illegitimate that men do not maintain such children, Cornwallis's stricture against men who wrong their legitimate children by supporting misbegotten offspring suggests that the father of two families can do no right.

64. Craik, "For Better for Worse," 576.

65. [Lyman Cobb], "The Decay of the 'Family Affections,'" *Nation* (15 April 1869): 291–92, 292.

66. Goldwin Smith, "Female Suffrage," *Macmillan's Magazine* 30 (June 1874): 139–50, 149.

67. Elizabeth Rachel Chapman, "Marriage Rejection and Marriage Reform," *Westminster Review* 130 (September 1888): 358–77, 367, 369, 376, 374.

68. Elizabeth Rachel Chapman, "The Decline of Divorce," *Westminster Review* 133 (April 1890): 417–34, 429, 428, 433.

69. Harris, "The Future of Marriage," 278; G. Willett Van Nest, "Divorce in the United States," *Nineteenth Century and After* 61 (January 1907): 119–26, 126; Houghton, "Immorality and the Marriage Law," 309.

70. "Pioneer Club Records," *Shafts* 2 (November–December 1894): 346–47, 347. Crawford's speech was clearly indebted to Cobbe's views on "Wife-Torture in England" (1878) and indeed cited Cobbe as the moving force behind the Matrimonial Causes Act of that year, which had established a husband's convic-

tion for aggravated assault against his wife as grounds for separation (although not divorce).

71. McIlquham, "Some Necessary Marriage Reforms," 400, 401.

72. Clapperton, "Miss Chapman's Marriage Reform," 711, 713, 711.

73. E.M.S., "Some Modern Ideas about Marriage," *Westminster Review* 143 (May 1895): 520–33, 526, 528, 531. The assumption that parents of children would be especially reluctant to seek divorce seems to be correct; Horstman notes for 1871 that a full "forty per cent of the [divorce] suits involved childless couples," in sharp contrast to the fertility rate for Victorian marriages overall (*Victorian Divorce*, 104).

74. Hutchinson, "Evolutionary Ethics of Marriage and Divorce," 408, 407, 409, 401.

75. Crackanthorpe, "Marriage, Divorce, and Eugenics," 698, 695.

76. Marriage with a sister-in-law became illegal with the passage of Lord Lyndhurst's Act in 1835 (such unions had earlier been voidable, but only if official attention was drawn to them while both partners were alive). The question of legalizing these arrangements was raised throughout the period, conservative divines quoting the Bible against the idea, liberals arguing, like Birmingham professor and religious writer Henry Rogers in an unsigned essay of 1853, that "The prohibition is especially oppressive to those classes whose children . . . must have their mothers' sisters for their protectors, or have none at all" ("Marriage with a Deceased Wife's Sister," *Edinburgh Review* 97 [April 1853]: American ed. 158–71, 170–71). The Deceased Wife's Sister Bill finally passed in 1907.

Chapter 5: "Alma Pater": Fathers and the School

The epigraph is by Austen Pember [Walter L. Bicknell], "The Religion of Our Boys," *National Review* 13 (August 1889): 738–49, 741.

1. Newsome, *Godliness and Good Learning*, 4. As J. R. de S. Honey points out in *Tom Brown's Universe: The Development of the English Public School in the Nineteenth Century* (New York: Quadrangle, 1977, 146–47), public-school attendance did not become the majority experience for the sons of the well-to-do until approximately the 1870s; he adds, "This phenomenon, involving as it did an important and general transfer of function from the parent to the school, is perhaps unique in modern history."

2. In fact, women were never absent even from boys' schools; as schoolmaster

W. E. W. Collins wrote in an unsigned article on "The Preparatory School" (*Blackwood's Edinburgh Magazine* 155 [March 1894]: 380–94, 394), the master's wife is "by no means the least important personage in many a modern preparatory school. If she be a wise and withal a womanly woman, her influence is thoroughly healthy, her share in the education in no sense trivial. . . . the lady's presence has a wholesome and a softening influence." If I seem to scant women's role in the public schools, it is because I am primarily concerned with image rather than reality. To Peter M. Lewis ("Mummy, Matron and the Maids: Feminine Presence and Absence in Male Institutions, 1934–63," in Roper and Tosh, *Manful Assertions*, 168–89, 169), the marginalization of women in this environment occurs because "The institution proscribes women and systematically disparages or devalues all 'womanly' traits and characteristics"; at least for the Victorian era, one might argue rather that the institution seeks to redefine these "womanly" attributes as "manly."

3. J. A. Mangan, "Social Darwinism and Upper-Class Education in Late Victorian and Edwardian England," in J. A. Mangan and James Walvin, eds., *Manliness and Morality: Middle-Class Masculinity in Britain and America, 1800–1940* (Manchester: Manchester UP, 1987), 135–59, 142, 143.

4. Gillis, *Youth and History*, 107.

5. "The Two Guides of the Child," *Household Words* 1 (7 September 1850): 560–61, 561.

6. [Herbert Spencer], "The Art of Education," *North British Review* 21 (May 1854): 137–71, 157–58, 171.

7. See Jonathan Gathorne-Hardy, *The Old School Tie: The Phenomenon of the English Public School* (New York: Viking, 1978), 147.

8. See, for instance, comments like those of Thomas Hughes in 1881: "The ideas and habits which those who have most profited by them bring away from our schools do not fit them to become successful traders" (quoted in Robin Gilmour, *The Idea of the Gentleman in the Victorian Novel* [London: Allen & Unwin, 1981], 96), or of R. H. Cheney in 1864: "Many parents, the [Public Schools] Commissioners observe with just reprehension, send their sons to school only for the purpose of 'making them gentlemen, and enabling them to form great acquaintance'" (unsigned article on "Public Schools," *Quarterly Review* 116 [July 1864]: 176–211, 188). In practice, of course, public-school attendance was fast becoming the major criterion for worldly success in the sense of instilling "gentlemanliness" (see Gilmour 182); but the ideal forbade frank discussion of the uses to which the old-boy network might be put, even

though the formation of useful friendships was presumably a major factor causing parents to expose their sons to the privations of public schools.

9. "Our Public Schools—Their Discipline and Instruction," *Fraser's Magazine* 50 (October 1854): 401–13, 410, 411. I will discuss school discipline at greater length later in this chapter.

10. [Richard Ford], "Tom Brown's School-days; Rugby Reminiscences," *Quarterly Review* 102 (October 1857): 330–54, 335, 341.

11. Quoted in Joyce Senders Pedersen, *The Reform of Girls' Secondary and Higher Education in Victorian England: A Study of Elites and Educational Change* (New York: Garland, 1987), 139. The £4000 does not, of course, represent Keate's base salary but the total reached after the addition of such traditional extras as the generous tips contributed by each departing student. The heads of girls' schools could also expect to supplement their incomes with capitation fees, but not to anything like the extent possible at an institution such as Eton.

12. [M. J. Higgins], "Eton College," *Edinburgh Review* 113 (April 1861): 387–426, 387, 420, 406, 407.

13. See [Goldwin Smith], "Public Schools," *Edinburgh Review* 120 (July 1864): 147–88. Smith found that the major public schools had "stubbornly resisted" Arnold's influence and that Eton, in particular, had become too large and too impersonal, a problem that he saw as the root of its readiness to use flogging as a first resort in controlling its population (151, 183). "It is not possible that one head master should know anything about eight hundred and fifty boys," he complained; "it is scarcely possible that they should form in any real sense one school" (182).

14. [W. Lucas Collins], "The Public Schools Report: Eton," *Blackwood's Edinburgh Magazine* 95 (June 1864): 707–31, 728, 729; italics in original. By the 1890s, commentators on the Eton system displayed none of the doubts about its efficacy that characterized the Public Schools Report. Thus, for instance, in "Eton College: As a School" (*English Illustrated Magazine* 14 [July 1890]: 721–23), lawyer and statesman Alfred Lyttelton noted that the tutorial plan "secures to every Eton boy permanent relations of a very close and confidential character with one master, selected at the outset of the boy's career, and who throughout his schooldays is to him really, and not nominally, *in loco parentis*" (723).

15. [W. Lucas Collins], "The Public Schools Report II: Harrow and Rugby," *Blackwood's Edinburgh Magazine* 96 (August 1864): 219–40, 224.

16. Collins, "The Public Schools Report II," 227.

17. Collins, "The Public Schools Report," 710, and "The Public Schools Report II," 226.

18. [F. W. Warre-Cornish], "Old Eton and Modern Public Schools," *Edinburgh Review* 185 (April 1897): 355–81, 360.

19. "Public and Private Schools," *Westminster Review* n.s. 44 (1 July 1873): 1–32, 26. This article's endorsement of private schools represented a minority view; most commentators found the system of continual supervision by ushers (who were not regarded as trained professionals) overly Continental and liable to foster underhandedness and talebearing. The majority favored the public schools' system of giving the older boys authority over the younger. Masters thus served as ultimate rather than primary controls—although, as I have argued, the ideal master's moral influence reigned even in his absence.

20. W[illiam J. P.] Petre, "Large or Small Schools," *Dublin Review* n.s. 31 (July 1878): 98–105, 104, 98, 105. English Protestant authors, to be sure, sometimes associated "surveillance" with Catholicism and foreignness and distrusted it accordingly (one thinks of Charlotte Brontë's description of Belgian practices in *Villette* [1853]). Still, the trend was overwhelmingly toward greater supervision, particularly in preparatory schools.

21. Some headmasters, such as J. E. C. Welldon (whose tenure at Harrow ended in 1898 after a pederastic scandal), contributed to the production of such rhetoric. In a lecture given in Tokyo in 1906, Welldon explained the "unique responsibility" of the public-school tutor: "He looks after [the boy's] physical, intellectual, moral, and spiritual welfare. He is to him, or is supposed to be, all that a parent, when the boy is at home, may be and ought to be. No profession, perhaps, makes a larger demand upon tact or insight or sympathy. . . . Not authority alone, but sympathy, is the secret of his success" ("The Training of an English Gentleman in the Public Schools," *Nineteenth Century and After* 60 [September 1906]: 396–413, 401). While Welldon stressed the hierarchical nature of the teacher-student relationship, finding "obedience" the "first element in all noble character," he simultaneously indicated via his emphasis on empathy, love, and a relaxation of discipline that an equally important egalitarian impulse was also at work.

22. [Arthur Sidgwick], "Our Public Schools: Rugby," *New Quarterly Magazine* n.s. 2 (October 1879): 255–79, 266. As was often the case in such encomiums, Sidgwick, a schoolmaster, was a product of Temple's Rugby; one may read essays of this sort as (old) boys' tributes to their spiritual fathers.

23. [Everard Thurn], "Our Public Schools: Marlborough," *New Quarterly*

Magazine n.s. 3 (April 1880): 258–83, 280. The rhetoric of this article follows tradition: housemasters function "solely in the place of a parent"; "The constant presence among the boys of so many masters, free from private domestic ties, is the specially valuable and almost peculiar feature of Marlborough. . . . [their task is] no longer merely to drive a certain amount of letters into the heads of their boys, but to influence the whole lives of their boys during the school year. . . . [boys] regard masters no longer as enemies but as friends" (264, 266–67).

24. J. E. C. Welldon, "The Late Provost of Eton," *Cornhill Magazine* 3rd ser. 28 (February 1910): 202–9, 207. This profile closely conforms to Welldon's outline of the characteristics of the ideal academic, quoted above.

25. Pierre de Coubertin, "Are the Public Schools a Failure? A French View," *Fortnightly Review* n.s. 72 (1 December 1902): 979–86, 979, 980, 982. Newsome notes that Thring (headmaster of Uppingham from 1853 to 1887 and one of the most prominent Victorian educators) was primarily interested in forming character, to the point where he would preach sermons warning the boys against over-intellectualism, and took particular pride in offering pupils "decent surroundings" and "a sympathetic régime" (see *Godliness and Good Learning*, 220–22). Thring's combination of egalitarian encouragement, moral guidance, and pseudo-domestic comfort was especially appealing to Victorian educational critics.

26. [J. F. Boyes], "Schoolmasters," *Cornhill Magazine* 3 (June 1861): 696–707, 699, 704.

27. See Walter Houghton's classic *The Victorian Frame of Mind 1830–1870* (1957; New Haven: Yale UP, 1985), 201–2, for a discussion of Stephen's admiration of robust masculinity in English literati.

28. [Leslie Stephen], "Thoughts of an Outsider: The Public Schools Again," *Cornhill Magazine* 28 (November 1873): 605–15, 608, 615.

29. Not surprisingly, women were considerably more ready to gender education as a properly feminine activity. See, for instance, biographer Margaret Lonsdale's "Platform Women" (*Nineteenth Century* 15 [March 1884]: 409–15, 409, 410), which balances its injunction against women speaking in public with what amounts to a command for them to teach. Women are especially fitted for this task by virtue of their "great patience, power of entering into minute detail, and, above all, imagination, which enables us to put ourselves into the mental condition of our pupils"; in particular, "the instruction of her own children in religion is understood to be incumbent on every mother."

30. [Margaret Oliphant], "An Eton Master," *Blackwood's Edinburgh Magazine* 156 (November 1894): 693–99, 696.

31. [James Runciman?], "Corporal Punishment in Schools," *Macmillan's Magazine* 48 (October 1883): 481–84, 484.

32. Cott, "Notes toward an Interpretation of Antebellum Childrearing," 16.

33. Honey, *Tom Brown's Universe*, 205. Some writers, as we shall see shortly, embraced these "alternative values" as superior to those of the family; in general, however, when schools were presented positively they were depicted as entirely in harmony with family ideals. Of course, what actually took place in classroom and dormitory and on the athletic field is a separate issue altogether.

34. [Henry Lee-Warner], "A Few Last Words on Day-Schools and Boarding-Schools," *Macmillan's Magazine* 52 (May 1885): 64–67, 64, 65–66. A similar attitude appears in [C. Kegan Paul?], "Our Public Schools—Eton," *New Quarterly Magazine* 11, n.s. 1 (January 1879): 24–46. This writer damned Eton for its low academic standards and its toleration of flogging, fagging, athletics, and drunkenness; he found the ideal of the influential headmaster largely a fiction and fulminated that "to take a boy permanently away from his home, from the influence of his father, his mother, and his sisters, and to cast him into a society totally unlike anything which he will meet with in the world, where he will prematurely discover much of which he had better be ignorant, and remain ignorant of much which it is literally of vital importance that he should know, is not a natural method of education" (35).

35. "The Apple and the Ego of Woman," 381. Some commentators took a middle road, recommending that boys attend public schools as day scholars while continuing to live at home. Among these was Lee-Warner; see "House-Boarders and Day-Boys," *Contemporary Review* 46 (September 1884): 364–72.

36. De Fabeck, "The Making of Woman," 550.

37. Gathorne-Hardy, *The Old School Tie*, 45.

38. Lee-Warner, "House-Boarders and Day Boys," 365; Paul (?), "Our Public Schools—Eton," 35.

39. "Another Educator," "Immorality in Schools," *Shafts* 2 (October 1893): 147. See also J.M.D., "Women Teachers in Boys' Schools" (*Shafts* 4 [September 1896]: 111), who remarks that "we hear from one of the wisest and most respected of our public school masters that the grave faults of schoolboys are largely due to their separation from the influence of mothers and sisters. If such separation at the most excitable and the least reasonable period of life be fraught with much danger does it not seem very desirable to bridge the gap by other

valuable feminine association? . . . As all the world lies open to men it is not unfair to ask them to step out in large numbers from the profession in which women are by nature their superiors, and in the best interests of the children to let women step in."

40. [G. R. Gleig], "Military Education—Part II," *Blackwood's Edinburgh Magazine* 82 (November 1857): 575–92, 578.

41. Agnes Lambert, "Progress of 'Thrift among the Children,'" *Nineteenth Century* 22 (August 1887): 206–18, 211; see also Lambert's "Thrift among the Children" in *Nineteenth Century* 19 (April 1886): 539–60, or Anne Digby and Peter Searby's observation in *Children, School and Society in Nineteenth-Century England* of the influential nature of the views of James Kay-Shuttleworth, secretary of the new Education Department from 1839 to 1849, who was steadfast in his "harsh dismissal of the working-class family as vicious and improvident" and believed that it was up to the schools, as "a substitute family," to socialize children. This attitude toward the working classes will be treated more thoroughly in chapter 6.

42. "Elementary Education," *Westminster Review* 130 (December 1888): 664–73, 672. But as with the public schools, the ideal was "the milk of human kindness," "an Arnold" rather than "a Blimber" (the crammer in Dickens's *Dombey and Son*); of older boys the author wrote, "They want not a teacher so much as a friend; not instruction so much as converse, and the privilege of contact with persons whose refinement does not exclude sympathy" (673).

43. Quoted in Honey, *Tom Brown's Universe*, 55. Honey notes that in "regard[ing] it as a specific function of the school to propagate values divergent from those of the home," Woodard was "untypical" among headmasters (148), and indeed most headmasters consistently preached the ideals of the family. Writers for the periodical press, whose careers were less likely to depend on their maintaining amicable relationships with parents, could afford to take a more tendentious stance.

44. "Our Public Schools—Their Discipline and Instruction," 406. The idea that a boy should be trained solely for the public world, as far as possible from feminine domesticity—so that schools represented not an androgynous ideal but one of Spartan masculinity—seems to have gained force with the passage of time. In Noel Streatfeild's 1963 fictionalized autobiography, her grandmother gives the following explanation of boarding school to Streatfeild's younger sister in about 1907: "A boy . . . has to go out into the world; however sad it is for his Mummy, she knows that from the day he is born. That is why we send our little

boys away to boarding schools; they have to get used to living without Mummies and sisters" (*A Vicarage Family* [London: Fontana/Lions, 1979], 96).

45. [Henry Alford?], "Education and School," *Contemporary Review* 1 (January 1886): 80–95, 91, 94.

46. "A Grave Social Problem," 56.

47. "Our Public Schools: Harrow," *New Quarterly Magazine* 11, n.s. 1 (April 1879): 273–96, 282, 295; italics the essayist's. The quotation is from William Wordsworth's "Character of the Happy Warrior" (1807), a poem about ideal masculinity inspired by the death of Lord Nelson.

48. Austen Pember [Walter L. Bicknell], "Our Boys I: School-Boys' Parents," *National Review* 16 (January 1891): 582–93, 583, 584.

49. Bicknell, "The Religion of Our Boys," 739, 742.

50. Turner, *The Body and Society*, 97. Educator John Huntley Skrine, a disciple and biographer of Thring of Uppingham, hints at this problem in "The Romance of School" (*Contemporary Review* 73 [March 1898]: 430–38, 435): "[The] romance of home . . . has of late been singularly transferred to home's one-time antithesis, the school. Do the critics complain that the natural parent is being robbed of his boy by the professional parent, his master? . . . Has not the boy's love of the birthplace gone a straying, and settled on the threshold of his Alma Mater? Perhaps in truth neither parent nor birthplace is robbed at all: love 'spreads undivided,' or can be learnt abroad to be used at home." This rationalization, of course, might not always have convinced the jealous parent.

51. Honey, *Tom Brown's Universe*, 178.

52. A., "Is Schoolmastering a Learned Profession?" *Fraser's Magazine* n.s. 18 (October 1878): 414–22, 417; C. A. Vansittart Conybeare, "Is Schoolmastering a Learned Profession?" *Fraser's Magazine* n.s. 19 (January 1879): 79–87, 81. Conybeare does concede that for a headmaster "to insist on the boys being given over 'body and soul' by their parents into his keeping" even in the case of day scholars represents "a ridiculous if not a dangerous extreme" (82).

53. Lee-Warner, "House-Boarders and Day Boys," 364; "A Few Last Words on Day-Schools and Boarding-Schools," 67. The implication is that fathers, less important in the moral development of their children, can delegate their duties; it is not the father but the mother whose absence Lee-Warner regrets throughout the latter essay.

54. Sidgwick, "Our Public Schools: Rugby," 269.

55. Bicknell, "The Religion of Our Boys," 741.

56. William K. Hill, "The Responsibility of Parents for the General Fail-

ure of Modern Education," *Westminster Review* 148 (August 1897): 189–204, 194, 195, 197, 200. Hill was not alone in distrusting competitive examinations. An anonymous article on "The Education Act in the Counties" (*Edinburgh Review* 199 [April 1904]: 457–80, 459–60) decries them as well but notes of the situation in the 1870s, "Examinations were the one thing that [working-class] parents understood. Unable or unwilling to inquire into the scope and direction of their children's training, they welcomed an examination as the test of educational progress"; the Education Act of 1902, the writer hoped, would lead to informed and involved parents and reform the schools. An earlier example of this feeling is discussed in Kathy Triggs's biography of the moral novelist George MacDonald, which notes that he resigned his chair at Bedford College (one of his few paying jobs) when the school introduced external examinations: "Any form of competition was alien to MacDonald's concept of education," for men as well as for the women whom Bedford served. See *The Stars and the Stillness: A Portrait of George MacDonald* (Cambridge: Lutterworth, 1986), 77.

57. "B.A. (Oxon.)," "English Public Schools and Their Head-masters," *Westminster Review* 157 (May 1902): 552–63, 561.

58. While I concentrate in this chapter on male teachers and thus on the education of boys, it is important to note that commentary on girls' education reiterated the condemnations of fathers and the suggestion that women have a special aptitude for teaching. One example is provided by Elizabeth Eastlake's unsigned article "The Englishwoman at School" (*Quarterly Review* 146 [July 1878]: 40–69, 52, 54), which notes the frequency with which woman teachers are thwarted "by the intolerable apathy and silliness of the parents—this last 'noun plural' in most cases doing duty for one parent only," the father. Eastlake remarks approvingly on "the fair and upright judgment of the [School] Commissioners" in deeming the schoolmistress "to be by nature, and especially for girls, a better teacher than a man."

59. Quoted in [H. H. Lancaster], "A Liberal Education—Schools and Universities," *North British Review* 48 (June 1868): American ed. 155–80, 158 (emphasis Lancaster's).

60. Anne M. Boylan, "Evangelical Womanhood in the Nineteenth Century: The Role of Women in Sunday Schools," *Feminist Studies* 4 (October 1978): 62–80, 74. While Boylan's focus is on the United States, the same generalization may be made about Britain. Even such an early example as Spencer's "The Art of Education" (1854), as noted earlier, unites an expansion of Pestalozzian theory to a representation of the mother as the ideal educator.

61. K. Bathurst, "The Need for National Nurseries," *Nineteenth Century and After* 57 (May 1905): 818–27, 818, 827, 824. As Geraldine Hodgson wrote in "The Training of Teachers" (*Macmillan's Magazine* 89 [February 1904]: 253–60, 256), "those whom nature has decreed shall not be, training cannot make teachers"—but training can hone teacherly skills. That teachers are born, not made, was an argument more often used by women than by men. See, for example, Alford (?), "Education and School," which notes of teaching the stupid and the very young, "This knowledge and skill does not, as a rule, come by intuition. There are, indeed, instances where a man seems to possess the secret instinctively; but ordinarily it is an experience purchased, like every other experience, by time and practice and failure and perseverance" (87). It is perhaps no coincidence that even in Alford's day the task of teaching the very young (if not also the stupid) would frequently have gone to women.

62. The actual English figures are as follows: of 13,729 elementary teachers in 1870, 6,847 were female; of 94,943 in 1896, 68,396 were female. (The large increase in personnel overall reflects the impact of the 1870 Education Act, which raised the proportion of school-age children actually attending classes from 26 percent in 1871 to 46 percent a decade later; by 1911, after the 1902 act, the figure stood at 70 percent.) See Barry H. Bergen, "Only a Schoolmaster: Gender, Class, and the Effort to Professionalize Elementary Teaching in England, 1870–1910," *History of Education Quarterly* 22 (Spring 1982): 1–21, 12, 3. Feminist feeling about the importance and appropriateness of women's involvement in the schools is suggested by the frequency with which this topic is raised in journals such as *Shafts*.

Sally Mitchell argues of the flood of women into elementary classrooms that "the character of schoolteachers changed markedly when the profession was feminized. . . . Teaching became a job requiring cheerfulness and love of children, though as a man's profession it had needed intellect, system, order, and force of character" ("Girls' Culture: At Work," 255). As we have seen in the discourse on public schoolmasters, however, the "feminization" of the profession was occurring even in institutions that remained all-male.

63. George K. Behlmer, *Child Abuse and Moral Reform in England, 1870–1908* (Stanford: Stanford UP, 1982), 45.

64. Spencer, "The Moral Discipline of Children," 388.

65. [Charles John Evans], "The Two Tuppers," *Fraser's Magazine* 54 (October 1856): 484–86, 485.

66. Collins, "The Public Schools Report II," 229. In a later installment, "The Public Schools Report, Conclusion: Winchester and Shrewsbury" (*Blackwood's*

Edinburgh Magazine 96 [December 1864]: 696–718, 716), Collins suggested that "although the character of public-school life has very much softened of late years," in part because "There is very little flogging on the part of the master," still "there is not much need to fear that the modern schoolboy will degenerate into a milksop. . . . in spite of this march of peace principles, there is good reason to hope that the old 'pluck' is at the bottom still."

67. "An Old Boy," "Greenwich School Forty Years Ago," *Fraser's Magazine* n.s. 10 (August 1874): 246–53, 247, 252, 253. Against the inflated authority of school and headmaster, "good homes and kind parents" are of no avail: " 'He is my superior officer,' my father once said to my mother in answer to her remonstrance."

68. Sidgwick, "Our Public Schools: Rugby," 259, 261. He continued: "A good disciplinarian is not a man who punishes disorderly boys; he is a man in whose presence boys never think of being disorderly" (273).

69. Quoted in Runciman (?), "Corporal Punishment in Schools," 481.

70. Elmy, "The Individuality of Women," 509.

71. [Mrs. Christopher G. B. Corbett], "The Education of Children," *Macmillan's Magazine* 61 (January 1890): 186–92, 191, 187, 188.

72. Newsome, *Godliness and Good Learning*, 29. Or as Sidgwick wrote after summing up Arnold's secular reforms: "It was, however, on the religious side of education that he himself laid the greatest stress" ("Our Public Schools: Rugby," 259).

73. [W. J. Conybeare], "School Sermons," *Quarterly Review* 97 (September 1855): 335–50, 338. By 1865, an anonymous essayist on "Public School Education" in the Roman Catholic *Dublin Review* (n.s. 5 [July 1865]: 1–43, 35, 24–25), writing with no reference to Arnold, was castigating Eton for its perceived refusal of the "obligation to form and mould the man upon a higher type, and raise himself above his nature, and stamp a purer impress upon it"; among other failings, the public school provides a diet of entirely pagan authors for the impressionable young mind. Religious education, the article implies, is the supreme function of the public school. There is quite a difference between this stance and that of Samuel Butler, appointed headmaster of Shrewsbury in 1798; as Conybeare recounts, "when a parent on one occasion wrote to him complaining of the deterioration in a son's morals, he replied, 'My business is to teach him Greek, and not morality' " (338).

74. C. Kegan Paul, "Clergymen as Head-Masters," *Nineteenth Century* 14 (September 1883): 414–20, 420.

75. "Our Public Schools: Harrow," 293.

76. Arthur C. Benson, "Religious Education in Public Schools," *National Review* 47 (July 1906): 861–71. The son of an archbishop of Canterbury and formerly a student and housemaster at Eton, Benson became master of Magdalene College, Cambridge, in 1915. Eton's approach to religion had changed substantially from the carelessness denigrated by the 1865 *Dublin Review* writer; Benson notes that the students were exposed to lessons on the Old Testament and church history, to studying the New Testament in Greek, to religious tutorials and confirmation preparation, and to Sunday morning sermons (862).

77. For contemporary discussion of such questions, see, for example, [W. Lucas Collins], "The Education Difficulty," *Blackwood's Edinburgh Magazine* 107 (May 1870): 652–66; Henry Edward [Cardinal Manning], "Is the Education Act of 1870 a Just Law?" *Nineteenth Century* 12 (December 1882): 958–68; [H. H. Henson (?)], "The Educational Crisis," *Edinburgh Review* 180 (October 1894): 473–96; and John E. Gorst, "The Education Bill," *Nineteenth Century and After* 52 (October 1902): 576–90. While these articles differ in some of their conclusions, they share an assumption that working-class parents are often unable to bring up children aright.

78. Jenifer Hart, "Religion and Social Control in the Mid-Nineteenth Century," in A. P. Donajgrodzki, ed., *Social Control in Nineteenth Century Britain* (Totowa, N.J.: Rowman and Littlefield, 1977), 108–37; Hilton, *The Age of Atonement*, 282. As Barbara Welter notes in *Dimity Convictions: The American Woman in the Nineteenth Century* (Athens: Ohio UP, 1976, 87), "the idea of the Father-Mother God" and "the concept of the female Saviour" were also characteristic of religion in Victorian America, a circumstance that, as in Britain, "showed an appreciation for the values of femaleness."

79. "Womanhood and Religious Mis-education," 19; Mrs. A. Phillips, "Why Women Are Women," *Shafts* 1 (18 February 1893): 249; Nora Brownlow, "Libels on God," *Shafts* 1 (26 November 1892): 61.

80. John Shelton Reed, "'A Female Movement': The Feminization of Nineteenth-Century Anglo-Catholicism," *Anglican and Episcopal History* 57 (June 1988): 199–238, 238, 201.

81. Thomas Hughes, *Tom Brown's Schooldays* (1857; New York: Puffin, 1971), 288; Vance, *The Sinews of the Spirit*, 146; C. H. Spurgeon, quoted in John Springhall, "Building Character in the British Boy: The Attempt to Extend Christian Manliness to Working-Class Adolescents, 1880 to 1914," in Mangan and Walvin, *Manliness and Morality*, 52–74, 55. As Pamela J. Walker notes in "'I Live But Not Yet I for Christ Liveth in Me': Men and Masculinity

in the Salvation Army, 1865–90" (in Roper and Tosh, *Manful Assertions*, 92–112), the Salvation Army wrestled directly with the specter of effeminate piety, constructing a version of manliness whose virility depended, paradoxically, on its acceptance of feminine ideals. And for the American experience of late-century anxiety about Christ's androgyny, see Susan Curtis, "The Son of Man and God the Father: The Social Gospel and Victorian Masculinity," in Carnes and Griffen, *Meanings for Manhood*, 67–78.

82. [Frederick Oakeley], "The Creator and the Creature, or, The Wonders of Divine Love," *Dublin Review* 43 (September 1857): 235–56, 236. Faber's God, Oakeley noted, was slow to judge and quick to mercy (254).

83. Vance, *The Sinews of the Spirit*, 106 (and see also 55); Houghton, *The Victorian Frame of Mind*, 347 (which also references the Kingsley citations in this paragraph and the next).

84. "Clerical Celibacy," *Saturday Review* 27 (13 March 1869): 341–43, 342. Another example of this mindset is evident in the vignette in *Tom Brown's Schooldays* that shows Arnold surrounded by a group of his children, making a toy boat for a small son. It is clear to Tom and his cohorts (who have broken their curfew) that fatherhood is emblematic of mercy: "All looked so kindly, and homely, and comfortable, that the boys took heart in a moment" (Hughes, *Tom Brown's Schooldays*, 125).

85. [G. C. Swayne], "Colleges and Celibacy: A Dialogue," *Blackwood's Edinburgh Magazine* 83 (May 1858): 557–71, 568, 569.

86. J. E. C. Welldon, "The Children of the Clergy," *Nineteenth Century and After* 59 (February 1906): 230–38, 237, 232.

87. "The Religious Education of Children," *Westminster Review* n.s. 48 (October 1875): 374–90. As the public response to the Agar-Ellis case (discussed in chapter 4) suggests, the mother had supplanted the father as primary religious influence over the child—in part, as I argued in chapter 1, because the process of motherhood was itself seen as a physical manifestation of sanctity, one impossible even to those fathers ordained as ministers.

Chapter 6: Parenthood and the Motherland

The epigraph is by the anonymous author of "Women and the School Board Elections," *Shafts* 2 (November and December 1894): 349.

1. I take these phrases from the unnamed compiler of "Record of Events,"

Englishwoman's Review n.s. 9 (15 February 1878): 77–90, 84; "Democratic Tory," "A Key to Social Difficulties," *National Review* 4 (January 1885): 698–701; and Benjamin Waugh, "Street Children," *Contemporary Review* 53 (June 1888): 825–35, 826. There are, of course, many other occurrences. In each of the instances I cite, the usage was ironic—appropriately enough, given the ambivalence the Victorians felt toward paternity and paternalism alike.

2. Gertrude Himmelfarb, *Poverty and Compassion: The Moral Imagination of the Late Victorians* (New York: Knopf, 1991), 24, 31, 39.

3. Gillis, *For Better, for Worse*, 233, 245, 254. Similarly, David Levine notes in *Reproducing Families: The Political Economy of English Population History* (Cambridge: Cambridge UP, 1987, 175) that while at the beginning of the industrial era "men's labour might control as little as a quarter of the total [family] income, by the later decades of the nineteenth century the chief breadwinners generally brought home more than two-thirds of the cash," a shift that enforced what we now consider "traditional" sex roles. See also Wally Seccombe, "Patriarchy Stabilized: The Construction of the Male Breadwinner Wage Norm in Nineteenth-Century Britain" (*Social History* 11 [January 1986]: 53–76, 66), for a discussion of how strong working-class support for women's and children's employment gradually turned into "vigorous opposition."

4. Trevor Lummis, "The Historical Dimension of Fatherhood: A Case Study 1890–1914," in McKee and O'Brien, *The Father Figure*, 43–56, 53, 55.

5. Loane, "Husband and Wife among the Poor," 228, 229. Lummis cites also her 1910 publication *Neighbours and Friends*, in which she castigates philanthropists who "honestly believe that the one function performed by the father is to earn wages, and if these can be supplied from some other source they imagine that matters will go on very much as they did before—or even decidedly better" (quoted in "The Historical Dimension of Fatherhood," 44).

6. Frank J. Adkins, "Holidays for Children," *Westminster Review* 170 (November 1908): 574–81, 575.

7. Quoted in Himmelfarb, *Poverty and Compassion*, 131.

8. Himmelfarb, *Poverty and Compassion*, 122.

9. Disraeli's comment is quoted in Perkin, *Women and Marriage in Nineteenth-Century England*, 136; Churchill's in Springhall, *Coming of Age*, 46.

10. Jeffrey Weeks, *Sex, Politics and Society: The Regulation of Sexuality since 1800* (London: Longman, 1981), 57.

11. Octavia Hill, "Our Dealings with the Poor," *Nineteenth Century* 30 (August 1891): 161–70, 161. Similarly, reformer Helen Dendy Bosanquet argued in 1904 that the middle-class visitor acts as a surrogate parent who can

"make herself familiar with [a child's] home conditions, win the confidence of its parents, and ensure that the proper treatment, whatever it might be, was thoroughly carried out" ("Physical Degeneration and the Poverty Line," 74). The working-class family problem, she contended, is not economic but managerial: neither mother nor father knows how to raise children or run a home, skills that only middle-class women can teach them.

12. "Public Nurseries," *Fraser's Magazine* 42 (October 1850): 397–99, 397.

13. I share this stance with F. M. L. Thompson, who reminds us in *The Rise of Respectable Society* that "the content and aims of missionary efforts intended to save the working-class family" say more about "middle-class precepts and practices, and most of all perhaps about middle-class fears of the fragility of their own family ideals unless these were protected with constant vigilance by elaborate ramparts of morality, modesty, reticence, sexual segregation, parental discipline and authority, and male dominance" (89). I contend, however, that issues of authority and male dominance occasioned much ambivalence, both in middle-class beliefs about working-class life and in bourgeois self-examination.

14. "A Visit to the Hospital for Sick Children," *Fraser's* 49 (January 1854): 62–67, 63–64, 66.

15. [Lord] Cranbrook [Gathorne Gathorne-Hardy], "Hereditary Pauperism and Boarding-Out," *National Review* 2 (December 1883): 453–61, 454.

16. Charles Rolleston, "A National Danger," *Westminster Review* 164 (August 1905): 154–63, 156.

17. M. K. Inglis, "The State versus the Home: Should There Be a Central Government Department for Children?" *Fortnightly Review* n.s. 84 (1 October 1908): 643–58, 658.

18. "A Woman," "The Effects of Civilization upon Women," 34–35.

19. See Himmelfarb, *Poverty and Compassion*, especially 57–66; see also Sheila Jeffreys, " 'Free from All Uninvited Touch of Man': Women's Campaigns around Sexuality, 1880–1914," *Women's Studies International Forum* 5 (1982): 629–45, and *The Spinster and Her Enemies*, especially 68–79. The *Englishwoman's Review* reprinted the *Times* report on one notorious age-of-consent case, *Reg. v. Roadley*, in its column "Record of Events: Assaults on Children" (*Englishwoman's Review* n.s. 11 [15 June 1880]: 270–71); a similar case was that of John Sullivan, acquitted the following month of having assaulted a six-year-old since the child had consented to the encounter.

20. Mrs. [A.] Warner Snoad, "Hew Up the Root," *Shafts* 3 (September 1895): 79–80, 79.

21. See Jeffreys, *The Spinster and Her Enemies*, 77, 68.

22. A point that has also been made by Judith Lewis Herman, who writes in her 1981 study *Father-Daughter Incest* that the incestuous family represents "an exaggeration of patriarchal family norms, but not a departure from them" (quoted in Louise DeSalvo, *Virginia Woolf: The Impact of Childhood Sexual Abuse on Her Life and Work* [Boston: Beacon, 1989], 190). DeSalvo's study of Woolf suggests the powerlessness of middle-class girls, in particular, when faced with incestuous attacks: it was not girls like the Stephen daughters whom the SPCC was founded to protect.

23. F. M. Foster, "Women as Social Reformers," *National Review* 13 (April 1889): 220–25, 221.

24. Henry Iselin, "The Childhood of the Poor," *Macmillan's Magazine* n.s. 2 (April 1907): 470–80, 470, 472.

25. Pinchbeck and Hewitt, *Children in English Society*, 2:357–58; they further quote an 1871 letter in which Shaftesbury refused his support to a bill combating parental cruelty with the words, "The evils you state are enormous and indisputable, but they are of so private, internal and domestic a character as to be beyond the reach of legislation" (622). According to Jeffreys, this objection carried over even into the incest debate, where "the idea of the sanctity of the home and the desirability of domestic activities being safe from state intervention" blocked an assortment of bills between 1889 and 1908 (*The Spinster and Her Enemies*, 77).

26. In *Forgotten Children*, Linda A. Pollock cites 385 court cases dealing with child abuse between 1785 and 1860, noting that the majority of the defendants were found guilty. She persuasively contends that child-abuse laws such as those of 1889, 1894, and 1908 represent "part of a general response by the state to a national crisis"—not a sudden realization that child abuse was regrettable but a sense that it constituted a problem of which government needed to take note (92). Of course one must also bear in mind the widening scope of the problem and the expanded powers the 1889 act gave to the state vis-à-vis intervention in the family; for instance, many more than 385 court actions in seventy-five years would have resulted from the over ten thousand annual complaints the SPCC was looking into within a few years of its founding (cited in Thompson, *The Rise of Respectable Society*, 128).

27. Henry Edward [Manning] and Benjamin Waugh, "The Child of the English Savage," *Contemporary Review* 49 (May 1886): 687–700, 694.

28. Waugh, "Street Children," 835. Even the *Englishwoman's Review* was dubious about state intervention in childrearing, commenting of the Employ-

ment of Children Act in 1904, "It is strange that it does not seem to strike most people that the legal rights of parents as guardians of their children are in danger of being undermined by interfering legislation" ("Freedom of Labour Defence: The Employment of Children Act," *Englishwoman's Review* n.s. 35 [15 April 1904]: 104–8, 107). In 1906 the *Quarterly Review* remarked that "of all our traditions none has been more persistent than that which declares that an Englishman's home is his castle, and that a man has a right to do what he likes with his children. . . . The change that has come over the mind of the nation in recent years in its attitude towards children is one of the most striking recorded in our annals" ("The Cry of the Children," *Quarterly Review* 205 [July 1906]: 29–53, 30).

29. Behlmer, *Child Abuse and Moral Reform in England, 1870–1908*, 9. He notes that early domestic-violence legislation (the first such act passed in 1853) sought primarily to protect women—and one might add that Victorian novelists, too, were much readier to focus on problems in the marriage relation than on equivalent problems between parent and child.

30. See, for instance, Waugh's 1888 essay "Street Children," which demands that Parliament "reverse the antiquated and unjust practice of regarding the little vagrant as the law-breaker. The charge must, in future, be against the parent" and not against the "father's victim" (831). For Waugh, "this preeminent Moloch of 'parental right' " is the enemy against which he fights (827); predictably, the slave-driving and abusive parents he instances are mostly male.

31. Henry Dunckley, "Child-Labour II: The Half-Timers," *Contemporary Review* 59 (June 1891): 798–802, 799; Dunckley concluded with the hope that once compulsory free education took the place of employment, "the sacrifice exacted [might] tend to foster a worthier ideal of parental duty" (802). See also Cardinal Manning's companion to Dunckley's essay, "Child-Labour I: Minimum Age for Labour of Children" (*Contemporary Review* 59 [June 1891]: 794–97, 796), which remarks, "It is more than vain to talk about the claim of parents to profit by the wages of their children. Their children are not chattels, but human beings with rights of their own, which no parents for their own pleasures or uses may violate. And if parents fail to protect the rights of their children, the Commonwealth is bound to do so."

32. Waugh, "Street Children," 825; Edith F. Hogg, "School Children as Wage Earners," *Nineteenth Century* 42 (August 1897): 235–44, 242; John E. Gorst, "School Children as Wage-Earners," *Nineteenth Century* 46 (July 1899): 8–17, 9, 15.

33. See Behlmer, *Child Abuse and Moral Reform in England, 1870–1908*, 119, and Dewi, "Save the Children: A Plea," *Westminster Review* 160 (November 1903): 559–62, 560. Another Edwardian discussion of parental tyranny and insurance murder occurs in the unsigned article "The Cry of the Children," esp. 43, 51.

34. Himmelfarb, *Poverty and Compassion*, 73.

35. Jane Lewis, "The Working-Class Wife and State Intervention, 1870–1918," in Jane Lewis, ed., *Labour and Love: Women's Experience of Home and Family, 1850–1940* (New York: Basil Blackwell, 1986), 99–120, 107. Victorian writers on abuse typically (although not invariably) associated violence more with fathers than with mothers.

36. "Parental Rights," *All the Year Round* n.s. 4 (10 September 1870): 348–52, 351. Himmelfarb observes that the Charity Organisation Society objected on similar grounds to Barnardo's private children's homes, which appeared to them to "encourag[e] parents to abdicate responsibility for their children"; taking the usual tack of the ultra-interventionists, "Barnardo claimed that the parents had already abdicated that responsibility" by their abusive and/or neglectful conduct (*Poverty and Compassion*, 233).

37. Rolleston, "A National Danger," 159.

38. Thomas Holmes, "Youthful Offenders and Parental Responsibility," *Contemporary Review* 77 (June 1900): 845–54, 846. See also John E. Gorst, "Children's Rights," *National Review* 45 (June 1905): 705–15, 706–7, for the insight that the modern "aboli[tion]" of the home extends not only to institutionalizing orphans but to sending rich boys to public schools; in either case the child is "deprived of home influence at the most critical period of its life."

39. John Springhall's *Coming of Age* provides a useful overview of children and crime; see especially pages 158–77.

40. [W. R. Greg], "The Correction of Juvenile Offenders," *Edinburgh Review* 101 (April 1855): American ed. 197–213, 198, 199, 203, 204, 208.

41. [Caroline Cornwallis], "Young Criminals," *Westminster Review* 60 (July 1853): American ed. 72–87, 81, 79.

42. [R. J. Gainsford?], "Reformatory Schools," *Dublin Review* n.s. 3 (October 1864): 455–82, 461, 482. An exception to this model is provided by member of Parliament and future chancellor of the exchequer Stafford Northcote in an unsigned essay, "Reformatory Schools" (*Quarterly Review* 98 [December 1855]: 32–65, 42). He presents the ideal reform-school manager as combining the stereotypical virtues of motherhood with those of fatherhood: what is required

is a "peculiar union of qualities . . . sweetness of temper, depth of affection, patience, hopefulness, even playfulness of mind, combined with firmness, courage, good sense, keen insight into character, and power of inspiring respect and fear." Even so, the work is essentially domestic, a substitution of the reformatory "family system" for the "fearfully misused" authority of the "unnatural" parents. Essential to the successful master are "devotion of the heart" and "moral influence" (42, 39, 34, 41).

43. Elizabeth Surr, "The Child-Criminal," *Nineteenth Century* 9 (April 1881): 649–83, 655, 656, 658, 652, 653. Again the parents would be asked to pay toward maintaining their children, but the real problem is not the irresponsible father—Surr seems to have regarded fathers as dispensable in any case—but the "natural (or unnatural) mother."

44. Henrietta O. Barnett, "Special Police Courts for Children," *Cornhill Magazine* 3rd ser. 18 (June 1905): 735–45, 739, 745. In a later essay, "Babies of the State" (*Cornhill Magazine* 3rd ser. 27 [July 1909]: 89–100, 97), Barnett equated "the cruelty, the neglect, and the criminality of thousands of [working-class] parents" with the state's behavior in sending destitute infants to workhouses instead of putting them under the control of the more child-centered and woman-dominated Board of Education.

45. Henrietta O. Barnett, "The Home or the Barrack for the Children of the State," *Contemporary Review* 66 (August 1894): 243–58, 243.

46. Springhall, *Coming of Age*, 166.

47. Viviana A. Zelizer, *Pricing the Priceless Child: The Changing Social Value of Children* (New York: Basic Books, 1985), 185 and chapter 6. Zelizer's primary focus is on the United States, but a similar pattern is discernible in England.

48. Cornwallis, "Young Criminals," 82.

49. See, for instance, the unsigned article "Family Life for Pauper Children," *Englishwoman's Review* n.s. 13 (15 February 1882): 57–62, which comments on cottage schools in Surrey, and A. Shadwell, "Mrs. Close's Scheme for State Children," *National Review* 49 (August 1907): 933–43. While both find that men have a role in vocational education, they also present the matron as the center of the artificial family.

50. Barnett observed that when she joined the board of Forest Gate School, London, in 1878, order-obsessed administrators deprived the children of friendship, property, and even names. While ten years later toys, books, and mealtime conversation had been introduced, the pauper child was still deprived intellec-

tually, physically, and especially morally: "Parentless, relationless, firesideless, it is served, fed, tended, taught by officials who, however kindly, are themselves enjoying no home-life and, therefore, are unable to bring the simplest of natural joys within the reach of their charges" ("The Home or the Barrack for the Children of the State," 248). In Barnett's view, the more familial systems of fosterage, cottage homes, or small charitable institutions run by the middle class are far preferable; what the state must first and foremost do for destitute children is to "teach them to love" (258).

51. [Charles Lewes], "The Education of the Children of the State," *Edinburgh Review* 142 (July 1875): 89–110, 91, 93, 94, 95, 98, 99, 109. What Lewes is recommending is essentially a cottage school.

52. Maria Trench, "Girl-Children of the State," *Nineteenth Century* 13 (January 1883): 76–87, 85; Gathorne-Hardy, "Hereditary Pauperism and Boarding-Out," 456; Louisa Twining, "Fifty Years of Women's Work," *National Review* 9 (July 1887): 659–67, 662; (Miss) M. H. Mason, "Poor Law Children and the New Boarding-Out Order," *Nineteenth Century and After* 68 (November 1910): 841–55, 842.

53. "Help for the Children," *Englishwoman's Review* n.s. 11 (15 April 1880): 155–59, 156, 158, 158–59.

54. Isabella Tod, "Boarding Out Pauper Children," *Englishwoman's Review* n.s. 9 (14 September 1878): 400–404, 404. The *Review* regularly reported on children's institutions and fosterage, as on the numbers of women proposing themselves as Poor Law guardians, a number rarely great enough to satisfy the editors.

55. Henrietta L. Synnot, "Institutions and Their Inmates," *Contemporary Review* 26 (August 1875): 486–504, 502, 492, 495.

56. See "Record of Events: Boarding Out Association," *Englishwoman's Review* n.s. 19 (14 July 1888): 331–32, 331; Shadwell, "Mrs. Close's Scheme for State Children," 933.

57. W. Stanley Jevons, "Married Women in Factories," *Contemporary Review* 41 (January 1882): 37–53, 50, 44, 52. The Married Women (Maintenance in Case of Desertion) Act of 1886 allowed deserted wives to receive a public allowance of up to two pounds a week (less if they had funds of their own) without having to go to the workhouse.

58. "A Woman," "The Effects of Civilization upon Women," 35.

59. Quoted in Himmelfarb, *Poverty and Compassion*, 368.

60. H. G. Wells, "A Modern Utopia: A Sociological Holiday. Chapter the

Sixth: Women in a Modern Utopia," *Fortnightly Review* n.s. 77 (1 February 1905): 348–65, 359.

61. J. St. Loe Strachey, "The State and the Family," *National Review* 50 (December 1907): 637–50, 644, 650. Strachey was the editor of the Tory *Spectator* and an ideological foe of Wells's; for a description of some of their encounters, see Samuel Hynes, *The Edwardian Turn of Mind* (Princeton: Princeton UP, 1968), 198, 293–97.

62. Dwork, *War Is Good for Babies and Other Young Children*, 21. An example of such rhetoric is T. J. Macnamara's "Physical Condition of Working-Class Children," *Nineteenth Century and After* 56 (August 1904): 307–11, 311, which argues that it is "essential to our future prosperity as a nation to see that no child lacks warm clothing and comfortable housing," as well as adequate food.

63. H[ugh] Clarence Bourne, "Hungry Children," *Macmillan's Magazine* 65 (January 1892): 186–93, 187, 190. Likewise, Sir Charles A. Elliott warned in a 1909 discussion of the 1906 act that despite the state's new role in feeding children, the volunteer "influence of the teachers" must predominate over the work of mere "paid officials," or the assistance "will become more and more wooden and will lose much of the grace and spiritual beauty which it has till now possessed" ("State Feeding of School Children in London," *Nineteenth Century and After* 65 [May 1909]: 862–74, 869).

64. "Freedom of Labour Defence: The State Feeding of Children," *Englishwoman's Review* n.s. 36 (15 April 1905): 112–13, 112.

65. Mary A. Davies, "The Feeding of School Children and the Cookery Classes," *Contemporary Review* 87 (April 1905): 564–69.

66. Gorst, "Children's Rights," 706.

67. Jackson, "Housekeeping and National Well-Being," 298, 305.

68. Himmelfarb, *Poverty and Compassion*, 165.

Conclusion

1. Lynda Zwinger, *Daughters, Fathers, and the Novel: The Sentimental Romance of Heterosexuality* (Madison: U of Wisconsin P, 1991), 44–45.

2. Dianne F. Sadoff, *Monsters of Affection: Dickens, Eliot and Brontë on Fatherhood* (Baltimore: Johns Hopkins UP, 1982), 6. Sadoff's thrust is psychoanalytic rather than historical; thus while I agree with her premise that what she

describes as Freudian dramas of fatherhood are central to Victorian literature, I reach different conclusions about how these dramas are enacted.

A Note on Sources

1. The figure of fifty thousand comes from Christopher Kent's introduction to another useful reference for Victorian periodicals, *The Victorian and Edwardian Age, 1837–1913*, the third volume of Alvin Sullivan's *British Literary Magazines* (Westport, Conn.: Greenwood, 1984), xiii.

Works Cited

Primary Sources

A. "Is Schoolmastering a Learned Profession?" *Fraser's Magazine* n.s. 18 (October 1878): 414–22.

A.H. "Purity." *Shafts* 5 (September 1897): 250–55.

Ablett, John. "Co-Education." *Westminster Review* 153 (January 1900): 25–31.

[Adams, Reverend]. "Woman's Mission." *Westminster Review* 52 (January 1850): American ed. 181–96.

Adkins, Frank J. "Holidays for Children." *Westminster Review* 170 (November 1908): 574–81.

Adye, Frederic. "Old-Fashioned Children." *Macmillan's Magazine* 68 (August 1893): 286–92.

"The Agar Ellis Case in a New Aspect." *Englishwoman's Review* n.s. 14 (15 August 1883): 356–61.

[Alford, Henry?]. "Education and School." *Contemporary Review* 1 (January 1886): 80–95.

Allan, James Macgrigor. "On the Differences in the Minds of Men and Women." *Journal of the Anthropological Society* 7 (1869). Excerpted in *Women from Birth to Death: The Female Life Cycle in Britain 1830–1914.* Ed. Pat Jalland and John Hooper. Brighton: Harvester, 1986. 22–23, 33–35.

Allen, Grant. "The New Hedonism." *Fortnightly Review* n.s. 52 (1 March 1893): 377–92.

———. "Plain Words on the Woman Question." *Fortnightly Review* n.s. 46 (October 1889): 448–58. Rpt. *Popular Science Monthly* 36 (December 1889): 170–81.

Amos, Sarah M. "The Evolution of the Daughters." *Contemporary Review* 65 (April 1894): 515–20.

"The Apple and the Ego of Woman." *Westminster Review* 131 (April 1889): 374–82.

Arling, Nat. "What Is the Role of the 'New Woman'?" *Westminster Review* 150 (November 1898): 576–87.

Arnold, Arthur. "The Hon. Mrs. Norton and Married Women." *Fraser's Magazine* n.s. 17 (April 1878): 493–500.

Arthur, T. S. "Model Husbands." *Godey's Lady's Book* 50 (January–March 1855): 37–40, 110–12, 206–8.

B.A. (Oxon.) "English Public Schools and Their Head-masters." *Westminster Review* 157 (May 1902): 552–63.

Barclay, James W. "Malthusianism and the Declining Birth Rate." *Nineteenth Century and After* 59 (January 1906): 80–89.

Barnett, Henrietta O. "Babies of the State." *Cornhill Magazine* 3rd ser. 27 (July 1909): 89–100.

———. "The Home or the Barrack for the Children of the State." *Contemporary Review* 66 (August 1894): 243–58.

———. "Special Police Courts for Children." *Cornhill Magazine* 3rd ser. 18 (June 1905): 735–45.

Bathurst, K. "The Need for National Nurseries." *Nineteenth Century and After* 57 (May 1905): 818–27.

Baylee, J. Tyrrell. "Army Nursing Reform and Men Nurses." *Westminster Review* 155 (March 1901): 255–57.

[Beale, Dorothea]. "On the Education of Girls." *Fraser's Magazine* 74 (October 1866): 509–24.

Beale, Lionel S. *Our Morality and the Moral Question: Chiefly from the Medical Side.* London: J. & A. Churchill, 1887.

Becker, Lydia. "Is There Any Specific Distinction between Male and Female Intellect?" *Englishwoman's Review* 1 (July 1868): 483–91.

———. "The Political Disabilities of Women." *Westminster Review* n.s. 41 (1 January 1872): 50–70.

———. "A Reply." *Englishwoman's Review* 12 (July 1869): 245–47.

Bell, Jean H. "The Creed of Our Children." *Nineteenth Century and After* 68 (December 1910): 1076–81.

Benson, Arthur C. "Religious Education in Public Schools." *National Review* 47 (July 1906): 861–71.

[Bicknell, Walter L.]. "Our Boys I: School-Boys' Parents." *National Review* 16 (January 1891): 582–93.

———. "The Religion of Our Boys." *National Review* 13 (August 1889): 738–49.

"Biology and 'Woman's Rights.'" Rpt. in *Popular Science Monthly* 14 (December 1878): 201–13.

[Birrell, Augustine]. "Woman under the English Law." *Edinburgh Review* 184 (October 1896): 322–40.

Blake, Matilda M. "The Lady and the Law." *Westminster Review* 137 (April 1892): 364–70.

Bohun, Florence. "Back to the Home." *Englishwoman's Review* n.s. 41 (15 July 1910): 182–86.

Bosanquet, Helen Dendy. "Physical Degeneration and the Poverty Line." *Contemporary Review* 85 (January 1904): 65–75.

Boucherett, Jessie. "The Agar-Ellis Case." *Englishwoman's Review* n.s. 9 (14 December 1878): 537–48.

Bourne, H[ugh] Clarence. "Hungry Children." *Macmillan's Magazine* 65 (January 1892): 186–93.

[Boyd, A. K. H.]. "Concerning the Sorrows of Childhood." *Fraser's Magazine* 65 (March 1862): 304–17.

[Boyes, J. F.]. "Schoolmasters." *Cornhill Magazine* 3 (June 1861): 696–707.

Boyle, H. R. "Sexual Morality." *Westminster Review* 166 (September 1906): 334–40.

"Boy's Home-Training." *Blackwood's Edinburgh Magazine* 176 (August 1904): 244–54.

[Brabazon, Reginald], Earl of Meath. "Have We the 'Grit' of Our Forefathers?" *Nineteenth Century and After* 64 (September 1908): 421–29.

Bremner, Christina. "Woman in the Labour Market." *National Review* 11 (June 1888): 458–70.

Bright, Florence. "The True Inwardness of the Woman's Movement." *Fortnightly Review* n.s. 81 (1 April 1907): 733–39.

Brownlow, Nora. "Libels on God." *Shafts* 1 (26 November 1892): 61.

Buckle, Henry Thomas. "The Influence of Women on the Progress of Knowledge." *Fraser's Magazine* 57 (April 1858): 395–407.

Buckman, S. S. "Babies and Monkeys." *Nineteenth Century* 36 (November 1894): 727–43.

———. "The Speech of Children," *Nineteenth Century* 41 (May 1897): 793–807.

Burleigh, Celia. "The Rights of Children." *Victoria Magazine* 23 (June 1879): 106–22.

[Burrows, Montagu]. "Female Education." *Quarterly Review* 126 (April 1869): 448–79.

C.I.C. Letter to *Englishwoman's Review* 11 (April 1869): 223–24.

Caird, Mona. *The Morality of Marriage: And Other Essays on the Status and Destiny of Women.* London: George Redway, 1897.

——— . "The Morality of Marriage." *Fortnightly Review* n.s. 50 (1 March 1890): 310–30.

——— . "Phases of Human Development." *Westminster Review* 141 (January, February 1894): 37–51, 162–79. Rpt. *The Morality of Marriage*, 195–239.

——— . "Punishment for Crimes against Women and Children." *Westminster Review* 169 (May 1908): 550–53.

Cairnes, J. E. "Woman Suffrage—A Reply." *Macmillan's Magazine* 30 (September 1874): 377–88.

Cameron, Laura B. "How We Marry." *Westminster Review* 145 (June 1896): 690–94.

[Carlyon, Edward A.]. "People's Boys." *Macmillan's Magazine* 23 (March 1871): 432–35.

Carmen Sylva (Queen of Romania). "The Vocation of Woman." *National Review* 45 (June 1905): 611–24.

Case, Thomas. "Against Oxford Degrees for Women." *Fortnightly Review* n.s. 58 (1 July 1895): 89–100.

Cave-North, T. "Women's Place and Power." *Westminster Review* 170 (September 1908): 264–67.

Champness, E. I. "Heredity versus the Power of Thought." *Westminster Review* 168 (July 1907): 59–63.

——— . "Women and Purity." *Westminster Review* 166 (September 1906): 326–33.

Chapman, Elizabeth Rachel. "The Decline of Divorce." *Westminster Review* 133 (April 1890): 417–34.

——— . "Marriage Rejection and Marriage Reform." *Westminster Review* 130 (September 1888): 358–77.

[Chapman, John]. "Prostitution in Relation to the National Health." *Westminster Review* n.s. 36 (1 July 1869): 179–234.

"Chastity: Its Development and Maintenance." *Westminster Review* n.s. 58 (1 October 1880): 419–36.

[Cheney, R. H.]. "Public Schools." *Quarterly Review* 116 (July 1864): 176–211.

Chesterton, G. K. "The Modern Surrender of Women." *Dublin Review* 145 (July 1909): 128–37.

"Chivalry, Marriage, and Religion: A Woman's Protest." *National Review* 4 (January 1885): 669–82.

Clapperton, Jane Hume. "Miss Chapman's Marriage Reform: A Criticism." *Westminster Review* 130 (December 1888): 709–17.

"Clerical Celibacy." *Saturday Review* 27 (13 March 1869): 341–43.

[Cobb, Lyman]. "The Decay of the 'Family Affections.' " *Nation* (15 April 1869): 291–92.

[Cobbe, Frances Power]. "Celibacy v. Marriage." *Fraser's Magazine* 65 (February 1862): 228–35.

———. "Wife-Torture in England." *Contemporary Review* 32 (April 1878): 55–87.

Collins, Vere. "Education in Sex." *Westminster Review* 162 (July 1904): 100–105.

———. "The Marriage Contract in Its Relation to Social Progress." *Fortnightly Review* n.s. 77 (1 March 1905): 479–85.

[Collins, W. E. W.]. "The Preparatory School." *Blackwood's Edinburgh Magazine* 155 (March 1894): 380–94.

[Collins, W. Lucas]. "The Education Difficulty." *Blackwood's Edinburgh Magazine* 107 (May 1870): 652–66.

———. "The Public Schools Report: Eton," "The Public Schools Report II: Harrow and Rugby," and "The Public Schools Report, Conclusion: Winchester and Shrewsbury." *Blackwood's Edinburgh Magazine* 95, 96 (June, August, December 1864): 707–31, 219–40, 696–718.

Conybeare, C. A. Vansittart. "Is Schoolmastering a Learned Profession?" *Fraser's Magazine* n.s. 19 (January 1879): 79–87.

[Conybeare, W. J.]. "School Sermons." *Quarterly Review* 97 (September 1855): 335–50.

Cooper, Edward H. "The Punishment of Children." *Fortnightly Review* n.s. 73 (1 June 1903): 1060–67.

[Corbett, Mrs. Christopher G. B.]. "The Education of Children." *Macmillan's Magazine* 61 (January 1890): 186–92.

[Cornwallis, Caroline]. "Capabilities and Disabilities of Women." *Westminster Review* 67 (January 1857): American ed. 23–40.

———. "The Property of Married Women." *Westminster Review* 67 (October 1856): American ed. 181–97.

———. "Young Criminals." *Westminster Review* 60 (July 1853): American ed. 72–87.

"Correspondence." *Shafts* 1, 2 (18 February 1893, 15 February 1894): 253, 216.

Coubertin, Pierre de. "Are the Public Schools a Failure? A French View." *Fortnightly Review* n.s. 72 (1 December 1902): 979–86.

[Cowell, Herbert]. "Sex in Mind and Education: A Commentary." *Blackwood's* 115 (June 1874): 736–49.

Cox, John George. "The Changed Position of Married Women." *Dublin Review* 3rd ser. 9 (April 1883): 417–42.

Crackanthorpe, Montague. "Marriage, Divorce, and Eugenics." *Nineteenth Century and After* 68 (October 1910): 686–702.

———. "The Morality of Married Life." *Fortnightly Review* n.s. 12 (1 October 1872): 397–412.

———. "Population and Progress." *Fortnightly Review* n.s. 80 (1 December 1906): 1001–16.

[Craik, Dinah Mulock]. "About Money." *Contemporary Review* 50 (September 1886): 364–72.

———. "Concerning Men—by a Woman." *Cornhill Magazine* n.s. 9 (October 1887): 368–77.

———. "For Better for Worse." *Contemporary Review* 51 (April 1887): 570–76.

———. "A Woman's Thoughts about Women: Female Servants." *Chambers's Journal* 8 (1 August 1857): 68–71.

———. "A Woman's Thoughts about Women: Something to Do." *Chambers's Journal* 7 (2 May 1857): 273–75.

Creighton, Louise. "The Appeal against Female Suffrage: A Rejoinder." *Nineteenth Century* 26 (August 1889): 347–54.

"The Cry of the Children." *Quarterly Review* 205 (July 1906): 29–53.

Cusack, M[ary] F[rancis]. "Woman's Place in the Economy of Creation." *Fraser's Magazine* n.s. 9 (February 1874): 200–209.

"Custody of Children." *Justice of the Peace* 48 (14 June 1884): 369–71.

Darwin, Charles. "A Biographical Sketch of an Infant." *Mind* 2 (July 1877): 285–94.

Darwin, George. "On Beneficial Restrictions to Liberty of Marriage." *Contemporary Review* 22 (August 1873): 412–26.

Davies, Mary A. "The Feeding of School Children and the Cookery Classes." *Contemporary Review* 87 (April 1905): 564–69.

[Dawkins, W. Boyd]. "Darwin on the Descent of Man." *Edinburgh Review* 134 (July 1871): 195–235.

Dewi. "Save the Children: A Plea." *Westminster Review* 160 (November 1903): 559–62.

Dicey, A. V. "Woman Suffrage." *Quarterly Review* 210 (January 1909): 276–304.

"Doctors in Pettiloons." *Punch* 22 (1852): 208.

Dodd, Catherine. "A Study in School Children." *National Review* 32 (September 1898): 66–74.

"Domestic Economy Congress." *Englishwoman's Review* n.s. 9 (15 July 1878): 295–98.

Doughty, Frances Albert. "The Small Family and American Society." *Nineteenth Century and After* 44 (September 1903): 420–27.

[Dunbar, Charles]. "Answer to an Article Headed 'A Clerical View of Woman's Sphere.'" *Victoria Magazine* 18 (January 1872): 237–46.

Dunckley, Henry. "Child-Labour II: The Half-Timers." *Contemporary Review* 59 (June 1891): 798–802.

E.M.S. "Some Modern Ideas about Marriage." *Westminster Review* 143 (May 1895): 520–33.

Earle, Maria Theresa. "Mothers and Daughters." *National Review* 44 (December 1904): 673–84.

[Eastlake, Elizabeth]. "The Englishwoman at School." *Quarterly Review* 146 (July 1878): 40–69.

"The Education Act in the Counties." *Edinburgh Review* 199 (April 1904): 457–80.

Edwards, A. D. "Evolution, Economy, and the Child." *Westminster Review* 171 (January 1909): 78–85.

"The Effects of Civilization upon Women, by a Woman." *National Review* 9 (March 1887): 26–38.

"Elementary Education." *Westminster Review* 130 (December 1888): 664–73.

Eliot, Charles W. "The Part of the Man in the Family." *Ladies' Home Journal* (March 1908): 7.

Elliott, Sir Charles A. "State Feeding of School Children in London." *Nineteenth Century and After* 65 (May 1909): 862–74.

[Ellis, Havelock]. "The Changing Status of Women." *Westminster Review* 128 (October 1887): 818–28.

———. *Studies in the Psychology of Sex.* 1897–1910. New York: Random House, 1936.

———. "The Woman Question I: The Awakening of Women in Germany." *Fortnightly Review* n.s. 80 (2 July 1906): 123–34.

Elmy, Ben. "The Individuality of Woman: From a Masculine Point of View." *Westminster Review* 158 (November 1902): 506–14.

[Elmy, Elizabeth Wolstenholme]. "The Awakening of Woman." *Westminster Review* 152 (July 1899): 69–72.

———. "Practical Work for Women Workers: Bills before Parliament." *Shafts* 4 (June 1896): 69–71.

———. "The Summary Jurisdiction (Married Women) Act, 1895." *Shafts* 4 (February 1896): 7–8.

———. "Woman and the Law." *Westminster Review* 168 (October 1907): 394–97.

"Enforced Maternity." *Shafts* 1 (18 February 1893): 251–52.

"The Enfranchisement of Women." Rpt. *Victoria Magazine* 9 (October 1867): 561–65.

"The Englishwoman's Conversazione." *Englishwoman's Domestic Magazine* n.s. 10 (May 1871): 320.

"'Eppure Si Muove.'" *Englishwoman's Review* n.s. 3 (October 1872): 229–32.

"Espérance." "Woman's Place in Education." *Shafts* 1 (14 January 1893): 171.

[Evans, Charles John]. "The Two Tuppers." *Fraser's Magazine* 54 (October 1856): 484–86.

"Events of the Month." *Englishwoman's Review* n.s. 8 (15 March 1877): 119–44.

"Events of the Quarter: Paragraphs." *Englishwoman's Review* n.s. 3 (July 1872): 226–27.

Fabeck, L. Vansittart de. "The Making of Woman." *Westminster Review* 145 (May 1896): 544–51.

"Family Life for Pauper Children." *Englishwoman's Review* n.s. 13 (15 February 1882): 57–62.

[Farrar, F. W.]. "Hereditary Genius." *Fraser's Magazine* n.s. 2 (August 1870): 251–65.

"A Father's View of the Home." *The Independent* 61 (18 October 1906): 911–14.

Fawcett, Millicent Garrett. "The Electoral Disabilities of Women." *Fortnightly Review* n.s. 7 (1 May 1870): 622–32.

———. "The Emancipation of Women." *Fortnightly Review* n.s. 49 (1 November 1891): 673–85.

"Female Labour." *Fraser's Magazine* 61 (March 1860): 359–71.

Flowerdew, Herbert. "Suggestion of a Substitute for the Marriage Laws." *Westminster Review* 152 (September 1899): 293–300.

[Ford, Richard]. "Tom Brown's School-days; Rugby Reminiscences." *Quarterly Review* 102 (October 1857): 330–54.

"For the Sake of a Pure Life." *Shafts* 6 (September–October 1898): 173.

Foster, F. M. "Women as Social Reformers." *National Review* 13 (April 1889): 220–25.

"Freedom of Labour Defence: The Employment of Children Act." *Englishwoman's Review* n.s. 35 (15 April 1904): 104–8.

"Freedom of Labour Defence: The State Feeding of Children." *Englishwoman's Review* n.s. 36 (15 April 1905): 112–13.

[Gainsford, R. J.?]. "Reformatory Schools." *Dublin Review* n.s. 3 (October 1864): 455–82.

Galton, Francis. "Eugenics as a Factor in Religion." Rpt. in *Essays in Eugenics*. 1909. New York: Garland, 1985. 68–70.

———. "Hereditary Genius: The Judges of England between 1660 and 1865." *Macmillan's Magazine* 19 (March 1869): 424–31.

———. "Hereditary Talent and Character." *Macmillan's Magazine* 12 (June and August 1865): 157–66, 318–27.

———. "The History of Twins, as a Criterion of the Relative Powers of Nature and Nurture." *Fraser's Magazine* n.s. 12 (November 1875): 566–76.

Gathorne-Hardy, Gathorne, Lord Cranbrook. "Hereditary Pauperism and Boarding-Out." *National Review* 2 (December 1883): 453–61.

[Gay, Miss]. "The Legal Value of the Unrepresented." *Shafts* 1 (25 February 1893): 259–60.

Gilbreth, Frank B., Jr., and Ernestine Gilbreth Carey. *Cheaper by the Dozen*. 1949. New York: Bantam, 1963.

Gladstone, W. E. "The Question of Divorce." *North American Review* 149 (December 1889): 641–44.

[Gleig, G. R.]. "Military Education—Part II." *Blackwood's Edinburgh Magazine* 82 (November 1857): 575–92.

Gorst, John E. "Children's Rights." *National Review* 45 (June 1905): 705–15.

———. "The Education Bill." *Nineteenth Century and After* 52 (October 1902): 576–90.

———. "School Children as Wage-Earners." *Nineteenth Century* 46 (July 1899): 8–17.

Grand, Sarah [Frances Clarke McFall]. "The Modern Girl." *North American Review* 158 (June 1894): 706–14.

———. "The New Aspect of the Woman Question." *North American Review* 158 (March 1894): 270–76.

"A Grave Social Problem." *British Medical Journal* 1 (14 January 1882): 55–56.

"Greenwich School Forty Years Ago, by an Old Boy." *Fraser's Magazine* n.s. 10 (August 1874): 246–53.

[Greg, W. R.]. "The Correction of Juvenile Offenders." *Edinburgh Review* 101 (April 1855): American ed. 197–213.

————. "On the Failure of 'Natural Selection' in the Case of Man." *Fraser's Magazine* 78 [September 1868]: 353–62.

————. "Prostitution." *Westminster Review* 53 (June 1850): 448–506.

Grey, Maria G. "Men and Women." *Fortnightly Review* n.s. 26 (1 November 1879): 672–85.

————. "Men and Women: A Sequel." *Fortnightly Review* n.s. 29 (1 June 1881): 776–93.

Grove, Agnes. "'The Threatened Re-Subjection of Woman': A Reply to Lucas Malet." *Fortnightly Review* n.s. 78 (1 July 1905): 123–28.

Gwynn, Stephen. "The Modern Parent." *Cornhill Magazine* 3rd ser. 8 (May 1900): 662–78.

[Halliday, Andrew]. "Fathers." *All the Year Round* 14 (2 September 1865): 133–35.

————. "Mothers." *All the Year Round* 14 (9 September 1865): 157–59.

Hannigan, D. F. "The Legitimacy of Children." *Westminster Review* 133 (June 1890): 619–24.

[Harris], Susan, Countess of Malmesbury. "The Future of Marriage: A Reply." *Fortnightly Review* n.s. 50 (1 February 1892): 272–82.

Harrison, Frederic. "The Emancipation of Women." *Fortnightly Review* n.s. 49 (1 October 1891): 437–52.

Hartog, Marcus. "The Transmission of Acquired Characteristics." *Contemporary Review* 94 (September 1908): 307–17.

Hayllar, Florence. "The Superfluity of Women." *Westminster Review* 171 (February 1909): 171–81.

"Help for the Children." *Englishwoman's Review* n.s. 11 (15 April 1880): 155–59.

[Henson, H. H.?]. "The Educational Crisis." *Edinburgh Review* 180 (October 1894): 473–96.

"Heredity." *Shafts* 1 (21 January 1893): 186–87.

"Her Peculiar Sphere." Rpt. *Victoria Magazine* 18 (December 1871): 173–76.

Hewitt, Emma Churchman. "The 'New Woman' in Her Relation to the 'New Man.'" *Westminster Review* 147 (March 1897): 335–37.

[Higgins, M. J.]. "Eton College." *Edinburgh Review* 113 (April 1861): 387–426.

Hill, Octavia. "Our Dealings with the Poor." *Nineteenth Century* 30 (August 1891): 161–70.

Hill, William K. "The Responsibility of Parents for the General Failure of Modern Education." *Westminster Review* 148 (August 1897): 189–204.

Hodgson, Geraldine. "The Training of Teachers." *Macmillan's Magazine* 89 (February 1904): 253–60.

Hogg, Edith F. "School Children as Wage Earners." *Nineteenth Century* 42 (August 1897): 235–44.

Holmes, Thomas. "Youthful Offenders and Parental Responsibility." *Contemporary Review* 77 (June 1900): 845–54.

"Home Education." *Family Economist* 3 (1850): 127–29.

Hopkins, Ellice. "The Apocalypse of Evil." *Contemporary Review* 48 (September 1885): 332–42.

Houghton, Bernard. "Immorality and the Marriage Law." *Westminster Review* 168 (September 1907): 304–13.

Hughes, Thomas. *Tom Brown's Schooldays*. 1857. New York: Puffin, 1971.

Hutchinson, Woods. "Evolutionary Ethics of Marriage and Divorce." *Contemporary Review* 88 (September 1905): 397–410.

"Immorality in Schools, by Another Educator." *Shafts* 2 (October 1893): 147.

"The Influence of Parents on Women's Work." *Englishwoman's Review* n.s. 18 (April 1874): 90–96.

"Influential Lives: A Biographical Sketch [of] Elisa Lemonnier, Founder of the First Technical Schools for Women in France." *Shafts* 1 (26 November 1892): 50–52.

"Influential Lives: Miss Matilda Sharpe and Her Schools." *Shafts* 1 (3 November 1892): 3–4.

Inglis, M. K. "The State versus the Home: Should There Be a Central Government Department for Children?" *Fortnightly Review* n.s. 84 (1 October 1908): 643–58.

Iselin, Henry. "The Childhood of the Poor." *Macmillan's Magazine* n.s. 2 (April 1907): 470–80.

J.M.D. "Women Teachers in Boys' Schools." *Shafts* 4 (September 1896): 111.

Jackson, Clara. "Housekeeping and National Well-Being." *Nineteenth Century and After* 58 (August 1905): 298–305.

Jamieson, Herbert. "The Modern Woman." *Westminster Review* 152 (November 1899): 571–76.

Jeune, [Mary,] Lady. "A Rejoinder." *Saturday Review* 79 (8 June 1895): 753–54.

Jevons, W. Stanley. "Married Women in Factories." *Contemporary Review* 41 (January 1882): 37–53.

[Johns, B. G.]. "The Education of Women." *Edinburgh Review* 166 (July 1887): 89–114.

Johnston, Charles. "The World's Baby-Talk and the Expressiveness of Speech." *Fortnightly Review* n.s. 60 (1 October 1896): 494–505.

"The Judicial Separation of Mother and Child." *Westminster Review* n.s. 67 (April 1885): 430–59.

[Kaye, J. W.]. "The Employment of Women." *North British Review* 26 (February 1857): American ed. 157–82.

Kenealy, Arabella. "The Talent of Motherhood." *National Review* 16 (December 1890): 446–59.

"A Key to Social Difficulties, by a Democratic Tory." *National Review* 4 (January 1885): 698–701.

Kingsley, Charles. "Women and Politics." *Macmillan's Magazine* 20 (October 1869): 552–61.

"The Ladies of the Creation; or, How I Was Cured of Being a Strong-Minded Woman." *Punch* 23 (1852): n.p.

Lambert, Agnes. "Progress of 'Thrift among the Children.'" *Nineteenth Century* 22 (August 1887): 206–18.

———. "Thrift among the Children." *Nineteenth Century* 19 (April 1886): 539–60.

[Lancaster, H. H.]. "A Liberal Education—Schools and Universities." *North British Review* 48 (June 1868): American ed. 155–80.

Laski, H. J. "The Scope of Eugenics." *Westminster Review* 174 (July 1910): 25–34.

"The Law in Relation to Women." *Westminster Review* 128 (September 1887): 698–710.

"Lecture by the Rev. Ward Beecher on the Suffrage." *Englishwoman's Review* 3 (April 1867): 180–91.

[Lee-Warner, Henry]. "A Few Last Words on Day-Schools and Boarding-Schools." *Macmillan's Magazine* 52 (May 1885): 64–67.

———. "House-Boarders and Day-Boys." *Contemporary Review* 46 (September 1884): 364–72.

[Lewes, Charles]. "The Education of the Children of the State." *Edinburgh Review* 142 (July 1875): 89–110.

[Lewes, G. H.]. "Hereditary Influence, Animal and Human." *Westminster Review* 66 (July 1856): American ed. 75–90.

[Linton, E. Lynn]. "Apron-Strings." *Saturday Review* 27 (1 May 1869): 576–78.

———. "A Counter-Blast." *English Illustrated Magazine* 21 (October 1893): 85–89.

———. "The Future Supremacy of Women." *National Review* 8 (September 1886): 1–15.

———. "Gushing Men." *Saturday Review* 28 (4 September 1869): 315–16.

———. "The Modern Revolt." *Macmillan's Magazine* 23 (December 1870): 142–49.

———. *Modern Women and What Is Said of Them: A Reprint of a Series of Articles in the* Saturday Review. New York: J. S. Redfield, 1868.

———. "One of Our Legal Fictions." *Household Words* 9 (29 April 1854): 257–60.

———. "Our Civilisation." *Cornhill Magazine* 27 (June 1873): 671–78.

———. "The Philistine's Coming Triumph." *National Review* 26 (September 1895): 40–49.

———. "Viewy Folk." *Fortnightly Review* n.s. 59 (1 April 1896): 595–604, 602.

———. "The Wild Women: No. I, As Politicians." *Nineteenth Century* 30 (July 1891): 79–88.

———. "Womanliness." *Saturday Review* 30 (6 August 1870): 166–68.

Loane, M. "Husband and Wife among the Poor." *Contemporary Review* 87 (February 1905): 222–30.

Lonsdale, Margaret. "Platform Women." *Nineteenth Century* 15 (March 1884): 409–15.

"Love in a Cottage." *Saturday Review* 5 (23 January 1858): 85–87.

Low, Frances H. "The Parlour Woman or the Club Woman? A Reply to Miss Smedley." *Fortnightly Review* n.s. 83 (1 January 1908): 113–24.

Lowthime, M. "Concealment—A Cause of Impurity." *Shafts* 2 (15 September 1894): 328.

Lyttelton, Alfred. "Eton College: As a School." *English Illustrated Magazine* 14 (July 1890): 721–23.

Lyttelton, Edward. *The Causes and Prevention of Immorality in Schools.* London: privately printed for Rev. R. A. Bullen, 1887.

M.A.B. "Normal or Abnormal." *Englishwoman's Review* n.s. 20 (14 December 1889): 533–38.

M.A.E.L. "The Girl of the Future." *Victoria Magazine* 15 (September and October 1870): 440–57, 491–502.

M.C.J. "A Plea for the Little Ones." *Victoria Magazine* 12 (February 1869): 269–92.

MacKendrick, Alex. "Heredity and Environment as Factors in Social Development." *Westminster Review* 162 (August 1904): 180–87.

Macnamara, T. J. "Physical Condition of Working-Class Children." *Nineteenth Century and After* 56 (August 1904): 307–11.

[Maine, Henry Sumner]. "The Patriarchal Theory." *Quarterly Review* 162 (January 1886): 181–209.

[Manners, Janetta (Duchess of Rutland)]. "Employment of Women in the Public Service." *Quarterly Review* 151 (January 1881): 181–200.

"Manners and Morals, as Affected by Civilization." *Fraser's Magazine* 64 (September 1861): 307–16.

[Manning, Cardinal] Henry Edward. "Child-Labour I: Minimum Age for Labour of Children." *Contemporary Review* 59 (June 1891): 794–97.

———. "Is the Education Act of 1870 a Just Law?" *Nineteenth Century* 12 (December 1882): 958–68.

[Manning, Cardinal] Henry Edward, and Benjamin Waugh. "The Child of the English Savage." *Contemporary Review* 49 (May 1886): 687–700.

Marriott-Watson, H. B. "The American Woman: An Analysis." *Nineteenth Century and After* 56 (September 1904): 433–42.

[Marshall, Frederic]. "French Home Life II: Children." *Blackwood's Edinburgh Magazine* 110 (December 1871): 739–53.

Martineau, Harriet. Extract from *Household Education. The Family Economist* 3 (1850): 30.

———. "Middle-Class Education in England: Girls." *Cornhill Magazine* 10 (November 1864): 549–68.

Mason, (Miss) M. H. "Poor Law Children and the New Boarding-Out Order." *Nineteenth Century and After* 68 (November 1910): 841–55.

Maudsley, Henry. "Heredity in Health and Disease." *Fortnightly Review* n.s. 41 (1 May 1886): 648–59.

———. "Sex in Mind and in Education." *Fortnightly Review* n.s. 15 (1 April 1874): 466–83.

Maurice, Frederick. "National Health: A Soldier's Study." *Contemporary Review* 83 (January 1903): 41–56.

[Merivale, Herman]. "Galton on Hereditary Genius." *Edinburgh Review* 132 (July 1870): 100–125.

M'Ilquham, Harriett. "Marriage: A Just and Honourable Partnership." *Westminster Review* 157 (April 1902): 433–42.

———. "Some Necessary Marriage Reforms." *Westminster Review* 168 (October 1907): 398–403.

"Miss Becker on the Mental Characteristics of the Sexes." *The Lancet* no. 2349 (5 September 1868): 320–21.

Morgan-Browne, H. Review of *The Dangers of the Emancipation of Women*, by Adele Crepaz. *Shafts* 1 (10 December 1892): 89.

Mortimer, Geoffrey. "Enforced Maternity." *Shafts* 1 (14 January 1893): 167.

[Mozley, Anne]. "Clever Women." *Blackwood's Edinburgh Magazine* 104 (October 1868): 410–27.

[Munby, A. J.?]. "Primogeniture." *Fraser's Magazine* n.s. 2 (December 1870): 783–92.

Newman, F. W. "Marriage Laws." *Fraser's Magazine* 76 (August 1867): 169–89.

[Northcote, Stafford]. "Reformatory Schools." *Quarterly Review* 98 (December 1855): 32–65.

[Oakeley, Frederick]. "The Creator and the Creature, or, The Wonders of Divine Love." *Dublin Review* 43 (September 1857): 235–56.

[Oliphant, Margaret]. "The Condition of Women." *Blackwood's Edinburgh Magazine* 83 (February 1858): 139–54.

———. "An Eton Master." *Blackwood's Edinburgh Magazine* 156 (November 1894): 693–99.

———. "The Laws Concerning Women." *Blackwood's Edinburgh Magazine* 79 (April 1856): 379–87.

———. "Mill on the Subjection of Women." *Edinburgh Review* 130 (October 1869): American ed. 291–306.

"On Toleration: Part I" and "On Toleration: Part II." *Cornhill Magazine* 20 (August and September 1869): 246–56, 376–84.

"Our Modern Youth." *Fraser's Magazine* 68 (July 1863): 115–29.

"Our Public Schools, by a Public School Boy." *National Review* 56 (November 1910): 429–35.

"Our Public Schools: Harrow." *New Quarterly Magazine* 11, n.s. 1 (April 1879): 273–96.

"Our Public Schools—Their Discipline and Instruction." *Fraser's Magazine* 50 (October 1854): 401–13.

"Parental Authority in Matters of Religion." *Dublin Review* 3rd ser. 1 (January 1879): 208–23.

"Parental Rights." *All the Year Round* n.s. 4 (10 September 1870): 348–52.

[Patmore, Coventry]. "The Social Position of Woman." *North British Review* 14 (February 1851): American ed. 275–89.

Paul, C. Kegan. "Clergymen as Head-Masters." *Nineteenth Century* 14 (September 1883): 414–20.

[Paul, C. Kegan?]. "Our Public Schools—Eton." *New Quarterly Magazine* 11, n.s. 1 (January 1879): 24–46.

Payne, Annie M. "The Woman's Part in Politics." *National Review* 14 (November 1889): 401–18.

Pearce, I. D. "The Enfranchisement of Women." *Westminster Review* 168 (July 1907): 17–22.

Peck, Harry Thurston. "What a Father Can Do for His Daughter." *Cosmopolitan* 34 (February 1903): 460–64.

Petre, W[illiam J. P.]. "Large or Small Schools." *Dublin Review* n.s. 31 (July 1878): 98–105.

Pfeiffer, Emily. "The Suffrage for Women." *Contemporary Review* 47 (March 1885): 418–35.

Phillips, Mrs. A. "Why Women Are Women." *Shafts* 1 (18 February 1893): 249.

"Pioneer Club Records." *Shafts* 2 (15 June 1894, November–December 1894): 276, 346–47.

"Population and Progress." *Lancet* no. 4377 (20 July 1907): 170–71.

"The Probable Retrogression of Women." *Saturday Review* 32 (1 July 1871): 10–11.

"The Progress of Women." *Quarterly Review* 195 (January 1902): 201–20.

"The Property Earnings and Maintenance of Married Women." *Englishwoman's Review* 1 (October 1867): 263–75.

"Public and Private Schools." *Westminster Review* n.s. 44 (1 July 1873): 1–32.

"Public Nurseries." *Fraser's Magazine* 42 (October 1850): 397–99.

"Public Opinion on Questions Concerning Women." *Englishwoman's Review* 1 (July 1868): 503.

"Public Opinion on Questions Concerning Women: Women on School Boards." *Englishwoman's Review* n.s. 5 (January 1871): 14–16.

"Public School Education." *Dublin Review* n.s. 5 (July 1865): 1–43.

"Record of Events." *Englishwoman's Review* n.s. 9 (15 February 1878): 77–90.

"Record of Events: Assaults on Children." *Englishwoman's Review* n.s. 11 (15 June 1880): 270–71.

"Record of Events: Boarding Out Association." *Englishwoman's Review* n.s. 19 (14 July 1888): 331–32.

"Record of Events: Custody of Children." *Englishwoman's Review* n.s. 14 (15 December 1883): 552–63.

"Record of Events: The Infants Bill." *Englishwoman's Review* n.s. 17 (15 June 1886): 262–65.

"Record of Events: The Married Women's Property Bill." *Englishwoman's Review* 1 (October 1868): 12–26.

Reid, G. Archdall. "The Alleged Transmission of Acquired Characteristics." *Contemporary Review* 94 (October 1908): 399–412.

"The Religious Education of Children." *Westminster Review* n.s. 48 (October 1875): 374–90.

Review of *Sex Love*, by Edward Carpenter. *Shafts* 3 (October 1895): 97–99.

Review of *The Awakening of Women, or Woman's Part in Evolution*, by Frances Swiney. *Englishwoman's Review* n.s. 31 (17 April 1900): 130–32.

Review of *The Ethics of Love*, by W. W. H. Robinson. *Englishwoman's Review* n.s. 12 (15 December 1881): 563–64.

[Richmond], Effie Johnson. "Capacity in Men and Women." *Westminster Review* 153 (May 1900): 567–76.

———. "Marriage or Free Love." *Westminster Review* 152 (July 1899): 91–98.

Robinson, Louis. "The Child and the Savage: A Study of Primitive Man." *Blackwood's Edinburgh Magazine* 151 (April 1892): 568–72.

———. "Darwinism in the Nursery." *Nineteenth Century* 30 (November 1891): 831–42.

———. "The Meaning of a Baby's Footprint." *Nineteenth Century* 31 (May 1892): 795–806.

[Rogers, Henry]. "Marriage with a Deceased Wife's Sister." *Edinburgh Review* 97 (April 1853): American ed. 158–71.

Rolleston, Charles. "A National Danger." *Westminster Review* 164 (August 1905): 154–63.

Romanes, George J. "Mental Differences between Men and Women." *Nineteenth Century* 21 (May 1887): 654–72.

———. "Weismann's Theory of Heredity." *Contemporary Review* 57 (May 1890): 686–99.

[Runciman, James?]. "Corporal Punishment in Schools." *Macmillan's Magazine* 48 (October 1883): 481–84.

"Salary No Object." *Englishwoman's Review* n.s. 9 (15 January 1878): 1–7.

Saleeby, C. W. Lecture. Reported in *Eugenics Review* 1 (April 1909): 9.

———. "The Problems of Heredity." *Fortnightly Review* n.s. 78 (October 1905): 604–15.

———. "The Psychology of Parenthood." *Eugenics Review* 1 (April 1909): 37–46.

S'Arrac, William. Letter to "The Englishwoman's Conversazione." *Englishwoman's Domestic Magazine* n.s. 10 (April 1871): 256.

Schooling, William. "Marriage Institutions." *Westminster Review* 135 (April 1891): 385–95.

Shadwell, A. "Mrs. Close's Scheme for State Children." *National Review* 49 (August 1907): 933–43.

Sherwood, Mary Martha. *The History of the Fairchild Family; or, The Child's Manual: Being a Collection of Stories Calculated to Show the Importance and Effects of a Religious Education.* 14th ed. London: J. Hatcherd and Son, 1841.

[Shore, Louisa]. "The Emancipation of Women." *Westminster Review* n.s. 46 (1 July 1874): 137–74.

[Sibthorp, Margaret Shurmer]. "What the Editor Means." *Shafts* 2, 5, 6 (15 August 1894, January–February 1895, September 1897, November 1897, September–October 1898): 297–98, 365, 233–35, 297–303, 145–48.

[Sidgwick, Arthur]. "Our Public Schools: Rugby." *New Quarterly Magazine* n.s. 2 (October 1879): 255–79.

Singleton, Mary Montgomerie. "Two Moods of a Man: By a Woman." *Nineteenth Century* 31 (February 1892): 208–23.

Sitwell, Osbert. *Left Hand, Right Hand!*, vol. 1: *The Cruel Month: An Autobiography.* 1945. New York: Quartet, 1977.

[Skelton, John]. "People Who Are Not Respectable: A Lay Sermon." *Fraser's Magazine* 58 (December 1858): 719–29.

Skrine, John Huntley. "The Romance of School." *Contemporary Review* 73 (March 1898): 430–38.

Smith, Goldwin. "Conservatism and Female Suffrage." *National Review* 10 (February 1888): 735–52.

——— . "Female Suffrage." *Macmillan's Magazine* 30 (June 1874): 139–50.

——— . "Public Schools." *Edinburgh Review* 120 (July 1864): 147–88.

Snoad, Mrs. A. Warner. "Hew Up the Root." *Shafts* 3 (September 1895): 79–80.

——— . "A Plea for Justice." *Westminster Review* 138 (July 1892): 52–56.

"Speech of Mr. Shaw Lefevre, M.P., in the House of Commons." *Englishwoman's Review* 1 (July 1868): 504–14.

[Spencer, Herbert]. "The Art of Education." *North British Review* 21 (May 1854): 137–71.

——— . "The Moral Discipline of Children." *British Quarterly Review* 27 (1 April 1858): 383–413.

[Stead, W. T.]. "The Maiden Tribute of Modern Babylon." *Pall Mall Gazette* 42 (6, 7, 8, 10 July 1885): 1–6, 1–6, 1–5, 1–6.

[Stephen, Leslie]. "Thoughts of an Outsider: The Public Schools Again." *Cornhill Magazine* 28 (November 1873): 605–15.

[Stirling-Maxwell, William]. "The Law of Marriage and Divorce." *Fraser's Magazine* 52 (August 1855): 149–51.

Strachey, Amy. "Science and the Home." *National Review* 54 (October 1909): 282–89.

Strachey, J. St. Loe. "The State and the Family." *National Review* 50 (December 1907): 637–50.

Streatfeild, Noel. *A Vicarage Family.* 1963. London: Fontana/Lions, 1979.

Sully, James. "Baby Linguistics." *English Illustrated Magazine* 3 (November 1884): 110–18.

———. "Dollatry." *Contemporary Review* 75 (January 1899): 58–72.

———. "The Humorous Aspect of Childhood." *National Review* 27 (April 1896): 222–36.

———. "The New Study of Children." *Fortnightly Review* n.s. 58 (1 November 1895): 723–37.

Surr, Elizabeth. "The Child-Criminal." *Nineteenth Century* 9 (April 1881): 649–83.

"Suspicion and Caution." *Family Economist* 4 (1851): 82–87.

[Swayne, G. C.]. "Colleges and Celibacy: A Dialogue." *Blackwood's Edinburgh Magazine* 83 (May 1858): 557–71.

Swiney, Frances. "The Maternity of God: Part II." *Westminster Review* 165 (June 1906): 676–84.

———. "Women among the Nations: Part I." *Westminster Review* 164 (October 1905): 409–19.

Synnot, Henrietta L. "Institutions and Their Inmates." *Contemporary Review* 26 (August 1875): 486–504.

Tabor, Mary C. "The Rights of Children." *Contemporary Review* 54 (September 1888): 408–17.

Tayler, J. Lionel. "An Interrogatory Note on the Franchise of Women." *Westminster Review* 167 (April 1907): 456–58.

[Taylor, Harriet, and John Stuart Mill]. "Enfranchisement of Women." *Westminster Review* 55 (July 1851): American ed. 149–61.

[Taylor, Helen]. "The Ladies' Petition." *Westminster Review* 87 (January 1867): American ed. 29–36.

[Thackeray, W. M.]. "Roundabout Papers—No. II: On Two Children in Black." *Cornhill Magazine* 1 (March 1860): 380–84.

Thoresby, Frederick. "Woman and Woman's Suffrage." *Westminster Review* 166 (November 1906): 522–30.

[Thurn, Everard]. "Our Public Schools: Marlborough." *New Quarterly Magazine* n.s. 3 (April 1880): 258–83.

Tod, Isabella. "Boarding Out Pauper Children." *Englishwoman's Review* n.s. 9 (14 September 1878): 400–404.

Tozer, Basil. "Divorce versus Compulsory Celibacy." *Nineteenth Century and After* 65 (February 1909): 299–311.

Trench, Maria. "Girl-Children of the State." *Nineteenth Century* 13 (January 1883): 76–87.

Twining, Louisa. "Fifty Years of Women's Work." *National Review* 9 (July 1887): 659–67.

"The Two Guides of the Child." *Household Words* 1 (7 September 1850): 560–61.

Tylor, Edward B. "The Matriarchal Family System." *Nineteenth Century* 40 (July 1896): 81–96.

Untitled article from the *Saturday Review*. Rpt. *Victoria Magazine* 9 (July 1867): 258–62.

Van Nest, G. Willett. "Divorce in the United States." *Nineteenth Century and After* 61 (January 1907): 119–26.

"A Visit to the Hospital for Sick Children." *Fraser's* 49 (January 1854): 62–67.

Ward, C. Olivia Orde. "A School for Womanhood." *Englishwoman's Review* n.s. 41 (15 April 1910): 98–107.

[Warre-Cornish, F. W.]. "Old Eton and Modern Public Schools." *Edinburgh Review* 185 (April 1897): 355–81.

Waugh, Benjamin. "Street Children." *Contemporary Review* 53 (June 1888): 825–35.

Wedgwood, Julia. "'Male and Female Created He Them.'" *Contemporary Review* 56 (July 1889): 120–33.

———. "Social Reform in England." *Westminster Review* 87 (January 1867): American ed. 68–78.

Welldon, J. E. C. "The Children of the Clergy." *Nineteenth Century and After* 59 (February 1906): 230–38.

———. "The Late Provost of Eton." *Cornhill Magazine* 3rd ser. 28 (February 1910): 202–9.

———. "The Training of an English Gentleman in the Public Schools." *Nineteenth Century and After* 60 (September 1906): 396–413.

Wells, H. G. "A Modern Utopia: A Sociological Holiday. Chapter the Sixth:

Women in a Modern Utopia." *Fortnightly Review* n.s. 77 (1 February 1905): 348–65.

"What Cradle-Rockers Might Do," editorial addendum. *Shafts* 2 (March 1893): 9.

[Whyte-Melville, George]. "Strong-Minded Women." *Fraser's Magazine* 68 (November 1863): 667–78.

Williams, Llewellyn W. "The Punishment of Children." *Fortnightly Review* n.s. 74 (1 August 1903): 373–74.

Winch, W. H. "A Modern Basis for Educational Theory." *Mind* n.s. 18 (January 1909): 84–104.

"Womanhood and Religious Mis-education." *Shafts* 1 (12 November 1892): 19–20.

"Womanly and Womanish." Rpt. *Victoria Magazine* 12 (February 1869): 350–51.

"Woman's Mission." *Shafts* 7 (July–September 1899): 48–51.

"Women and Sanitary Knowledge." *Englishwoman's Review* n.s. 11 (15 October 1880): 441–45.

"Women and the School Board Elections." *Shafts* 2 (November–December 1894): 349.

"Women and the Suffrage, by a Peeress." *National Review* 8 (October 1886): 283–86.

Wright, Henry C. *Marriage and Parentage.* 1855. New York: Arno, 1974.

[Wrixon, H. J.]. "The Employment of Women." *Dublin Review* 52 (November 1862): 1–44.

Yates, Margarita. "Should Women Work for Their Living?" *Westminster Review* 174 (October 1910): 424–29.

Yonge, Charlotte M. *Womankind.* 2nd ed. New York: Macmillan and Co., 1882.

Secondary Sources

Anderson, Nancy Fix. *Woman against Women in Victorian England: A Life of Eliza Lynn Linton.* Bloomington: Indiana UP, 1987.

Ariès, Philippe. "The Family and the City in the Old World and the New." Tufte and Myerhoff 29–41.

Banks, J. A. *Prosperity and Parenthood: A Study of Family Planning among the Victorian Middle Classes.* London: Routledge, 1954.

———. *Victorian Values: Secularism and the Size of Families*. London: Routledge and Kegan Paul, 1981.

Banks, J. A., and Olive Banks. *Feminism and Family Planning in Victorian England*. Liverpool: Liverpool UP, 1964.

Banks, Olive. *Becoming a Feminist: The Social Origins of "First-Wave" Feminism*. Athens: U of Georgia P, 1987.

Behlmer, George K. *Child Abuse and Moral Reform in England, 1870–1908*. Stanford: Stanford UP, 1982.

Bergen, Barry H. "Only a Schoolmaster: Gender, Class, and the Effort to Professionalize Elementary Teaching in England, 1870–1910." *History of Education Quarterly* 22 (Spring 1982): 1–21.

Blake, Kathleen. *Love and the Woman Question in Victorian Literature: The Art of Self-Postponement*. Totowa, N.J.: Barnes and Noble, 1983.

Bland, Lucy. "Rational Sex or Spiritual Love? The Men and Women's Club of the 1880s." *Women's Studies International Forum* 13.1/2 (1990): 33–48.

Bloom-Feshbach, Jonathan. "Historical Perspectives on the Father's Role." *The Role of the Father in Child Development*. 2nd ed. Ed. Michael E. Lamb. New York: Wiley, 1981. 71–112.

Boylan, Anne M. "Evangelical Womanhood in the Nineteenth Century: The Role of Women in Sunday Schools." *Feminist Studies* 4 (October 1978): 62–80.

Branca, Patricia. *Silent Sisterhood: Middle Class Women in the Victorian Home*. Pittsburgh: Carnegie-Mellon UP, 1975.

Brandon, Ruth. *The New Women and the Old Men: Love, Sex and the Woman Question*. London: Secker and Warburg, 1990.

Bristow, Edward. *Vice and Vigilance: Purity Movements in Britain since 1700*. Totowa, N.J.: Rowman and Littlefield, 1977.

Brown, Carol. "Mothers, Fathers and Children: From Private to Public Patriarchy." *Women and Revolution: A Discussion of the Unhappy Marriage of Marxism and Feminism*. Ed. Lydia Sargent. Boston: South End, 1981. 239–67.

Burstyn, Joan N. *Victorian Education and the Ideal of Womanhood*. Totowa, N.J.: Barnes and Noble, 1980.

Caine, Barbara. "Feminism, Suffrage and the Nineteenth-Century English Women's Movement." *Women's Studies International Forum* 5.6 (1982): 537–50.

Calder, Jenni. *The Victorian Home*. London: Batsford, 1977.

Carnes, Mark C. "Middle-Class Men and the Solace of Fraternal Ritual." Carnes and Griffen 37–52.

Carnes, Mark C., and Clyde Griffen, eds. *Meanings for Manhood: Constructions of Masculinity in Victorian America*. Chicago: U of Chicago P, 1990.

Clarke, Norma. "Strenuous Idleness: Thomas Carlyle and the Man of Letters as Hero." Roper and Tosh 25–43.

Cleverley, John, and D. C. Phillips. *From Locke to Spock: Influential Models of the Child in Modern Western Thought*. Melbourne: Melbourne UP, 1976.

Contratto, Susan. "Mother: Social Sculptor and Trustee of the Faith." Lewin 226–55.

Cott, Nancy F. "Notes toward an Interpretation of Antebellum Childrearing." *Psychohistory Review* 6 (Spring 1978): 4–20.

Coward, Rosalind. *Patriarchal Precedents: Sexuality and Social Relations*. London: Routledge, 1983.

Curtis, Susan. "The Son of Man and God the Father: The Social Gospel and Victorian Masculinity." Carnes and Griffen 67–78.

Davenport-Hines, Richard. *Sex, Death and Punishment: Attitudes to Sex and Sexuality in Britain since the Renaissance*. London: Collins, 1990.

Davidoff, Leonore, and Catherine Hall. *Family Fortunes: Men and Women of the English Middle Class, 1780–1850*. Chicago: U of Chicago P, 1987.

Davin, Anna. "Imperialism and Motherhood." *History Workshop* 5 (Spring 1978): 9–65.

Degler, Carl. *At Odds: Women and the Family in America from the Revolution to the Present*. New York: Oxford UP, 1980.

Delamont, Sara. "The Domestic Ideology and Women's Education." *The Nineteenth-Century Woman: Her Cultural and Physical World*. Ed. Sara Delamont and Lorna Duffin. New York: Barnes and Noble, 1978. 164–87.

Demos, John. "The Changing Faces of Fatherhood: A New Exploration in American Family History." *Father and Child: Developmental and Clinical Perspectives*. Ed. Stanley H. Cath, Alan R. Gurwitz, and John Munder Ross. Boston: Little, Brown, 1982. 425–45.

———. "Images of the American Family, Then and Now." Tufte and Myerhoff 43–60.

DeSalvo, Louise. *Virginia Woolf: The Impact of Childhood Sexual Abuse on Her Life and Work*. Boston: Beacon, 1989.

Digby, Anne, and Peter Searby. *Children, School and Society in Nineteenth-Century England*. London: Macmillan, 1981.

Dubbert, Joe L. *A Man's Place: Masculinity in Transition*. Englewood Cliffs, N.J.: Prentice-Hall, 1979.

Dwork, Deborah. *War Is Good for Babies and Other Young Children: A History of the Infant and Child Welfare Movement in England 1898–1918.* New York: Tavistock, 1987.

Farrall, Lyndsay Andrew. *The Origins and Growth of the English Eugenics Movement 1865–1925.* New York: Garland, 1985.

Fee, Elizabeth. "The Sexual Politics of Victorian Social Anthropology." *Feminist Studies* 1 (Winter–Spring 1973): 23–39.

Gathorne-Hardy, Jonathan. *The Old School Tie: The Phenomenon of the English Public School.* New York: Viking, 1978.

Gillis, John R. *For Better, for Worse: British Marriages, 1600 to the Present.* New York: Oxford UP, 1985.

———. *Youth and History: Tradition and Change in European Age Relations 1770–Present.* New York: Academic, 1974.

Gilmour, Robin. *The Idea of the Gentleman in the Victorian Novel.* London: Allen and Unwin, 1981.

Gorham, Deborah. "The 'Maiden Tribute of Modern Babylon' Re-Examined: Child Prostitution and the Idea of Childhood in Late-Victorian England." *Victorian Studies* 21 (Spring 1978): 353–79.

Grossberg, Michael. "Who Gets the Child? Custody, Guardianship, and the Rise of a Judicial Patriarchy in Nineteenth-Century America." *Feminist Studies* 9 (Summer 1983): 235–60.

Hardyment, Christina. *Dream Babies: Child Care from Locke to Spock.* London: Cape, 1983.

Hare, E. H. "Masturbatory Insanity: The History of an Idea." *Journal of Mental Science* 108 (January 1962): 1–25.

Hart, Jenifer. "Religion and Social Control in the Mid-Nineteenth Century." *Social Control in Nineteenth Century Britain.* Ed. A. P. Donajgrodzki. Totowa, N.J.: Rowman and Littlefield, 1977. 108–37.

Hartman, Mary S. "Child-Abuse and Self-Abuse: Two Victorian Cases." *History of Childhood Quarterly* 2 (Fall 1974): 221–48.

Hilton, Boyd. *The Age of Atonement: The Influence of Evangelicalism on Social and Economic Thought, 1795–1865.* Oxford: Clarendon, 1988.

Himmelfarb, Gertrude. *Poverty and Compassion: The Moral Imagination of the Late Victorians.* New York: Knopf, 1991.

Holton, Sandra Stanley. "Free Love and Victorian Feminism: The Divers Matrimonials of Elizabeth Wolstenholme and Ben Elmy." *Victorian Studies* 37 (Winter 1994): 199–222.

Honey, J. R. de S. *Tom Brown's Universe: The Development of the English Public School in the Nineteenth Century.* New York: Quadrangle, 1977.

Horstman, Allen. *Victorian Divorce.* New York: St. Martin's, 1985.

Houghton, Walter. *The Victorian Frame of Mind 1830–1870.* 1957. New Haven: Yale UP, 1985.

Houghton, Walter, Esther Rhoads Houghton, and Jean Harris Slingerland, eds. *The Wellesley Index to Victorian Periodicals 1824–1900.* 5 vols. Toronto: U of Toronto P, 1966–89.

Hughes, John Starrett. "The Madness of Separate Spheres: Insanity and Masculinity in Victorian Alabama." Carnes and Griffen 53–66.

Hynes, Samuel. *The Edwardian Turn of Mind.* Princeton: Princeton UP, 1968.

Jackson, Margaret. "Sexual Liberation or Social Control? Some Aspects of the Relationship between Feminism and the Social Construction of Sexual Knowledge in the Early Twentieth Century." *Women's Studies International Forum* 6.1 (1983): 1–17.

Jalland, Pat, and John Hooper, eds. *Women from Birth to Death: The Female Life Cycle in Britain 1830–1914.* Brighton: Harvester, 1986.

Jeffrey, Kirk. "The Family as Utopian Retreat from the City: The Nineteenth-Century Contribution." *Soundings* 55 (Spring 1972): 21–41.

Jeffreys, Sheila. "'Free from All Uninvited Touch of Man': Women's Campaigns around Sexuality, 1880–1914." *Women's Studies International Forum* 5.6 (1982): 629–45.

———. *The Spinster and Her Enemies: Feminism and Sexuality 1880–1930.* London: Pandora, 1985.

Johansson, S. Ryan. "Centuries of Childhood/Centuries of Parenting: Philippe Ariès and the Modernization of Privileged Infancy." *Journal of Family History* 12 (October 1987): 343–65.

Kern, Stephen. "Explosive Intimacy: Psychodynamics of the Victorian Family." *History of Childhood Quarterly* 1 (Winter 1974): 437–61.

Kevles, Daniel J. *In the Name of Eugenics: Genetics and the Uses of Human Heredity.* New York: Knopf, 1985.

Kincaid, James. *Child-Loving: The Erotic Child and Victorian Culture.* New York: Routledge, 1992.

Lantz, Herman, Martin Schultz, and Mary O'Hara. "The Changing American Family from the Preindustrial to the Industrial Period: A Final Report." *American Sociological Review* 42 (June 1977): 406–21.

Leavy, Barbara Fass. "Fathering and *The British Mother's Magazine,* 1845–1864." *Victorian Periodicals Review* 13 (Spring/Summer 1980): 10–17.

316   Works Cited

Levine, David. *Reproducing Families: The Political Economy of English Population History.* Cambridge: Cambridge UP, 1987.

Lewin, Miriam, ed. *In the Shadow of the Past: Psychology Portrays the Sexes.* New York: Columbia UP, 1984.

———. "The Victorians, the Psychologists, and Psychic Birth Control." Lewin 39–76.

Lewis, Jane. *Women in England 1870–1950: Sexual Divisions and Social Change.* Bloomington: Indiana UP, 1984.

———. "The Working-Class Wife and State Intervention, 1870–1918." *Labour and Love: Women's Experience of Home and Family, 1850–1940.* Ed. Jane Lewis. New York: Basil Blackwell, 1986. 99–120.

Lewis, Judith Schneid. *In the Family Way: Childbearing in the British Aristocracy, 1760–1860.* New Brunswick: Rutgers UP, 1986.

Lewis, Peter M. "Mummy, Matron and the Maids: Feminine Presence and Absence in Male Institutions, 1934–63." Roper and Tosh 168–89.

Lowe, Nigel V. "The Legal Status of Fathers: Past and Present." McKee and O'Brien 26–42.

Lummis, Trevor. "The Historical Dimension of Fatherhood: A Case Study 1890–1914." McKee and O'Brien 43–56.

MacDonald, Robert H. "The Frightful Consequences of Onanism: Notes on the History of a Delusion." *Journal of the History of Ideas* 28 (July–September 1967): 423–31.

Mangan, J. A. "Social Darwinism and Upper-Class Education in Late Victorian and Edwardian England." Mangan and Walvin 135–59.

Mangan, J. A., and James Walvin, eds. *Manliness and Morality: Middle-Class Masculinity in Britain and America, 1800–1940.* Manchester: Manchester UP, 1987. 135–59.

Marks, Patricia. *Bicycles, Bangs, and Bloomers: The New Woman in the Popular Press.* Lexington: UP of Kentucky, 1990.

Marsh, Margaret. "Suburban Men and Masculine Domesticity, 1870–1915." *American Quarterly* 40 (June 1988): 165–86.

McKee, Lorna, and Margaret O'Brien, eds. *The Father Figure.* New York: Tavistock, 1982.

McLaren, Angus. *Birth Control in Nineteenth-Century England.* London: Croom Helm, 1978.

Mitchell, Sally. "Girls' Culture: At Work." Nelson and Vallone 243–58.

Mort, Frank. *Dangerous Sexualities: Medico-Moral Politics in England since 1830.* New York: Routledge and Kegan Paul, 1987.

Murray, Janet Horowitz, and Myra Stark. Introduction. *The Englishwoman's Review of Social and Industrial Questions* (facsimile ed.). New York: Garland, 1980. v–xxxi.

Nelson, Claudia. *Boys Will Be Girls: The Feminine Ethic and British Children's Fiction, 1857–1917.* Rutgers UP, 1991.

Nelson, Claudia, and Lynne Vallone, eds. *The Girl's Own: Cultural Histories of the Anglo-American Girl, 1830–1915.* Athens: U of Georgia P, 1994.

Nethercot, Arthur H. *The First Five Lives of Annie Besant.* Chicago: U of Chicago P, 1960.

Newsome, David. *Godliness and Good Learning: Four Studies on a Victorian Ideal.* London: Cassell, 1961.

Oppenlander, Ella Ann. *Dickens' All the Year Round: Descriptive Index and Contributor List.* Troy, N.Y.: Whitston, 1984.

Pascoe, Judith. "Stories for Young Housekeepers: T. S. Arthur and the Philadelphia Marketplace." Nelson and Vallone 34–51.

Pedersen, Joyce Senders. *The Reform of Girls' Secondary and Higher Education in Victorian England: A Study of Elites and Educational Change.* New York: Garland, 1987.

Perkin, Joan. *Women and Marriage in Nineteenth-Century England.* London: Routledge, 1989.

Pinchbeck, Ivy, and Margaret Hewitt. *Children in English Society*, vol. 2: *From the Eighteenth Century to the Children Act 1948.* London: Routledge and Kegan Paul, 1973.

Pivar, David J. *Purity Crusade: Sexual Morality and Social Control, 1868–1900.* Westport, Conn.: Greenwood, 1973.

Pleck, Joseph H. "American Fathering in Historical Perspective." *Changing Men: New Directions in Research on Men and Masculinity.* Ed. Michael S. Kimmel. Newbury Park: Sage, 1987. 83–97.

Pollock, Linda A. *Forgotten Children: Parent-Child Relations from 1500 to 1900.* Cambridge: Cambridge UP, 1983.

Poovey, Mary. " 'Scenes of an Indelicate Character': The Medical 'Treatment' of Victorian Women." *Representations* 14 (Spring 1986): 137–68.

———. *Uneven Developments: The Ideological Work of Gender in Mid-Victorian England.* Chicago: U of Chicago P, 1988.

Reed, John Shelton. " 'A Female Movement': The Feminization of Nineteenth-Century Anglo-Catholicism." *Anglican and Episcopal History* 57 (June 1988): 199–238.

Rendall, Jane. *The Origins of Modern Feminism: Women in Britain, France and the United States, 1780–1860.* Chicago: Lyceum, 1990.

Roberts, David. "The Paterfamilias of the Victorian Governing Classes." Wohl 59–81.

Roper, Michael, and John Tosh, eds. *Manful Assertions: Masculinities in Britain since 1800.* London: Routledge, 1991.

Rosenberg, Charles. "Sexuality, Class and Role in 19th-Century America." *American Quarterly* 25 (May 1973): 131–53.

Rotundo, E. Anthony. "Boy Culture: Middle-Class Boyhood in Nineteenth-Century America." Carnes and Griffen 15–36.

Sachs, Albie, and Joan Hoff Wilson. *Sexism and the Law: A Study of Male Beliefs and Legal Bias in Britain and the United States.* New York: Free Press, 1979.

Sadoff, Dianne F. *Monsters of Affection: Dickens, Eliot and Brontë on Fatherhood.* Baltimore: Johns Hopkins UP, 1982.

Savage, Gail. " 'The Wilful Communication of a Loathsome Disease': Marital Conflict and Venereal Disease in Victorian England." *Victorian Studies* 34 (Autumn 1990): 35–54.

Seccombe, Wally. "Patriarchy Stabilized: The Construction of the Male Breadwinner Wage Norm in Nineteenth-Century Britain." *Social History* 11 (January 1986): 53–76.

Sennett, Richard. *Families against the City: Middle Class Homes of Industrial Chicago 1872–1890.* Cambridge: Harvard UP, 1970.

Shanley, Mary Lyndon. *Feminism, Marriage, and the Law in Victorian England, 1850–1895.* Princeton: Princeton UP, 1989.

Shields, Stephanie A. " 'To Pet, Coddle, and "Do For" ': Caretaking and the Concept of Maternal Instinct." Lewin 256–73.

Shorter, Edward. *The Making of the Modern Family.* New York: Basic Books, 1975.

Showalter, Elaine. "Family Secrets and Domestic Subversion: Rebellion in the Novels of the 1860s." Wohl 101–16.

Smelser, Neil. "The Victorian Family." *Families in Britain.* Ed. R. M. Rapoport, M. P. Fogarty, and R. Rapoport. London: Routledge, 1982. 59–74.

Smith, F. Barry. "Sexuality in Britain, 1800–1900: Some Suggested Revisions." *A Widening Sphere: Changing Roles of Victorian Women.* Ed. Martha Vicinus. Bloomington: Indiana UP, 1977. 182–98.

Smith-Rosenberg, Carroll. *Disorderly Conduct: Visions of Gender in Victorian America.* New York: Knopf, 1985.

Soloway, Richard Allen. *Birth Control and the Population Question in England, 1877–1930*. Chapel Hill: U of North Carolina P, 1982.

Springhall, John. "Building Character in the British Boy: The Attempt to Extend Christian Manliness to Working-Class Adolescents, 1880 to 1914." Mangan and Walvin 52–74.

———. *Coming of Age: Adolescence in Britain 1860–1960*. Dublin: Gill and Macmillan, 1986.

Stearns, Carol Zisowitz, and Peter N. Stearns. *Anger: The Struggle for Emotional Control in America's History*. Chicago: U of Chicago P, 1986.

Stetson, Dorothy M. *A Woman's Issue: The Politics of Family Law Reform in Britain*. Westport, Conn.: Greenwood, 1982.

Strauss, Sylvia. *"Traitors to the Masculine Cause": The Men's Campaigns for Women's Rights*. Westport, Conn.: Greenwood, 1982.

Sullivan, Alvin, ed. *British Literary Magazines*, vol. 3: *The Victorian and Edwardian Age, 1837–1913*. Westport, Conn.: Greenwood, 1984.

Thompson, F. M. L. *The Rise of Respectable Society: A Social History of Victorian Britain 1830–1900*. Cambridge: Harvard UP, 1988.

Tosh, John. "Domesticity and Manliness in the Victorian Middle Class: The Family of Edward White Benson." Roper and Tosh 44–73.

Triggs, Kathy. *The Stars and the Stillness: A Portrait of George MacDonald*. Cambridge: Lutterworth, 1986.

Trudgill, Eric. *Madonnas and Magdalens: The Origins and Development of Victorian Sexual Attitudes*. London: Heinemann, 1976.

Tufte, Virginia, and Barbara Myerhoff, eds. *Changing Images of the Family*. New Haven: Yale UP, 1979.

Turner, Bryan S. *The Body and Society: Explorations in Social Theory*. New York: Blackwell, 1984.

Vance, Norman. *The Sinews of the Spirit: The Ideal of Christian Manliness in Victorian Literature and Religious Thought*. Cambridge: Cambridge UP, 1985.

Walker, Pamela J. "'I Live But Not Yet I for Christ Liveth in Me': Men and Masculinity in the Salvation Army, 1865–90." Roper and Tosh 92–112.

Weeks, Jeffrey. *Sex, Politics and Society: The Regulation of Sexuality since 1800*. London: Longman, 1981.

———. *Sexuality and Its Discontents: Meanings, Myths and Modern Sexualities*. Boston: Routledge, 1985.

Welter, Barbara. *Dimity Convictions: The American Woman in the Nineteenth Century*. Athens: Ohio UP, 1976.

Wishy, Bernard. *The Child and the Republic: The Dawn of Modern American Child Nurture*. Philadelphia: U of Pennsylvania P, 1968.

Wohl, Anthony S., ed. *The Victorian Family: Structure and Stresses*. New York: St. Martin's, 1978.

Zelizer, Viviana A. *Pricing the Priceless Child: The Changing Social Value of Children*. New York: Basic, 1985.

Zwinger, Lynda. *Daughters, Fathers, and the Novel: The Sentimental Romance of Heterosexuality*. Madison: U of Wisconsin P, 1991.

Index

128, 137, 141, 143, 146–47, 151, 174,
288 (n. 1); unimportance of, 29–30,
46, 54, 68, 75, 82, 86, 125, 189, 197,
204–5, 276 (n. 53); as complement to
motherhood, 42, 101, 128; and
education, 47, 51–52, 58, 67, 120–22,
158, 263 (n. 21); involved model of,
47–48, 52, 56, 61, 96, 102, 135, 149,
175; delinquent, 48, 69–70, 78, 84,
85, 112, 114–16, 118, 122–24, 126–
28, 132–33, 136, 157, 159, 179, 183,
185, 188, 195–96, 199–200, 202,
204; motherly, 57, 61–62, 64, 71,
201, 204; and altruism, 58–59, 80;
and heredity, 87, 204; and ministry,
167; working-class, 175–76, 179–82,
184, 192, 195, 200, 206. *See also*
Headmasters: as fathers; Judges:
absorption of paternal power by;
Masculinity; Reproduction: brevity of
male role in; State, as parent
Fathers: domestic invisibility of, 2, 37,
42, 44, 46, 53, 57, 210; authority of,
3, 5, 15, 65, 67, 71–72, 161, 199; and
loss of domestic power, 5, 14–15, 28,
43–44, 72, 136, 173, 181–82, 184,
197, 199, 205, 209; as moral
influence, 5, 27, 44–49, 58, 64, 122,
167, 168; and custody rights, 98, 109–
10, 112, 114–18, 120–22, 129, 131,
133, 205, 265 (n. 37); as scientists,
102–4. *See also* Men
Fawcett, Millicent Garrett, 18, 65, 97,
260 (n. 107)
Femininity: innate qualities of, 16, 28,
78, 132
Feminism, 23, 35, 86, 92; and attitudes
toward motherhood, 17, 20–21, 54, 81,
101, 116; and venereal disease, 84–85;
and marriage reform, 88, 99, 109,
111; and Annie Besant, 121, 249

(n. 20); and legal reform, 124, 126,
179, 203, 263 (n. 26); and employment
of women, 154, 160; and religion, 165;
and masculinity, 181; in U.S., 223
(n. 37)
Fenwick-Miller, Florence, 267 (n. 52)
Flowerdew, Herbert, 125, 262 (n. 14)
Ford, Richard, 145
Forest Gate School, 287 (n. 50)
Fortnightly Review, 92, 104, 213
Foster, Mrs. F. M., 181–82
Fowler, William, 261 (n. 9)
Fraser's Magazine, 64, 68, 145, 155, 177,
213
Frazer, James G., 99
Freud, Sigmund, 83, 258 (n. 88), 290
(n. 2)
Froebel, Friedrich, 32, 159, 162, 168

Galton, Francis, 87–89, 92–93
Gaskell, Elizabeth, 30, 113
Gathorne-Hardy, Gathorne (Lord
Cranbrook), 178, 193
Gay (*Shafts* contributor), 97
Geddes, Patrick, 21
Gilbert, William Schwenck, 136
Gilbreth, Frank B., 105
Giraud-Teulon, A., 96
Gladstone, William Ewart, 267 (n. 59)
Gleig, G. R., 154
Godey's Lady's Book, 231 (n. 18)
Gorst, John E., 183, 198, 280 (n. 77),
286 (n. 38)
Grand, Sarah (Frances Clarke McFall),
27, 243 (n. 89)
Greenwich School, 161
Greg, William Rathbone, 76, 79, 80,
187, 253 (n. 51)
Grey, Maria G., 228 (n. 2), 235 (n. 40)
Grove, Agnes, 22, 257 (n. 77)

114–15, 159, 205. *See also* Maternal instinct

Patmore, Coventry, 24, 27, 32

Paul, Charles Kegan, 163, 274 (n. 34)

Pearce, I. D., 26

Pearl, 246 (n. 5)

Pearson, Sir John, 120

Pearson, Karl, 20, 89

Penny Illustrated Newspaper, 85

Periodicals: and visions of parenting, 6, 106, 275 (n. 43); choice of in this work, 6, 211; contributors to, 7; readership of, 7; and social class, 7; and visions of women, 36; overview of major titles, 212–15. *See also under specific titles*

Pestalozzi, Johann, 159, 192

Petre, William, 149

Poor Law, 22, 33, 128, 174, 192, 194, 196, 265 (n. 39); 288 (n. 54)

Poor Law Act (1899), 191

Pope, Alexander, 5, 33

Pregnancy. *See* Reproduction

Prevention of Cruelty to and Protection of Children Act (1889), 128, 185, 190, 284 (n. 26)

Private sphere: moral superiority of, 16, 41, 58, 77, 92; father's alienation from, 41, 46–47, 53, 55, 59, 61, 68, 77, 99, 101, 119, 130, 136, 155, 157, 201–2, 204, 208. *See also* Domesticity; Family

Prostitution, 13, 18, 48, 76–79, 83–85, 110, 126, 179, 190, 250 (n. 22)

Provision of Meals Act (1906), 173

Public Schools Commission (1864), 142, 146–47, 159, 207, 208

Public sphere: as extension of private, 4, 18, 22–23, 41, 71; corruption of, 21, 26, 58, 59, 146, 148

Pugh, S. S., 166

Punch, 15, 55, 68, 211

Punishment of Incest Act (1908), 179

Quarterly Review, 15, 214, 285 (n. 28)

Quarterly Review of Science, 18

Racial degeneration, 32–33, 56, 80, 84–85, 91, 94, 179, 199, 206, 249 (n. 18)

Rape, 77, 97, 180, 263 (n. 26)

Reeve, Henry, 212

Reformatory Schools (Youthful Offenders) Act (1854), 185, 187–88

Reg. v. *Clarence* (1888), 268 (n. 60)

Reg. v. *Cochrane* (1840), 260 (n. 2)

Reg. v. *Jackson* (1891), 260 (n. 2)

Reg. v. *Roadley* (1880), 283 (n. 19)

Reg. v. *Sullivan* (1880), 283 (n. 19)

Reid, G. Archdall, 97, 256 (n. 68)

Religion: attacks on, 1; and fear of selfishness, 3; and domesticity, 3, 43–44, 46, 62, 99, 101, 166–68; and childhood, 72; and eugenics, 88; father's right to control, 119–21; and motherhood, 121; and public schools, 141, 163–64. *See also* Christianity

Reproduction: and pregnancy, 5, 25, 61, 76–77, 80, 95, 247 (n. 8); brevity of male role in, 18, 28, 76, 106, 204

Revolution, 230 (n. 10)

Rex v. *Delaval* (1763), 110

Richardson, Benjamin, 31

Richmond, Effie Johnson, 42, 99

Robinson, Louis, 104, 105

Rogers, Henry, 269 (n. 76)

Rolleston, Charles, 178, 186

Romanes, George J., 19, 26, 93

Rousseau, Jean-Jacques, 7–8, 33, 131

Routh, C. H. F., 249 (n. 21)

Royal Military Academy at Woolwich, 154

Rugby School, 142, 146, 150, 153, 161, 163

Saleeby, Caleb W., 89, 257 (n. 82)